Meech Lake: The Inside Story

From behind the closed doors of Meech Lake comes this insider's account of the negotiations that put Canada's future on the line. Patrick J. Monahan was there throughout the negotiations that began in the fall of 1986 and culminated in the week-long meeting of First Ministers in June 1990, after which the accord failed to be ratified. He tells a compelling story of deals and dealmakers, compromise and confrontation.

Many in English Canada believe that at Meech Lake the federal government sold out to the provinces, especially to Quebec, and that by conducting negotiations behind closed doors the government acted illegitimately. Not so, says Monahan. Far from being a sell-out, Meech represented a reasonable compromise between competing positions. Going back to the initial position put forward by the Bourassa government in 1986 he shows how that position was modified in the course of the negotiations. And closed doors, he argues, were essential in ensuring effective bargaining. There could have been no agreement without them.

Now, in the middle of 1991, Canada is once again negotiating its future existence. There are vital lessons to be learned from the Meech Lake round; Monahan articulates some of those lessons, and indicates how they ought to figure in the current process. Canadians, he argues, ignore them at their country's peril.

Patrick J. Monahan is Director of the York University Centre for Public Law and Public Policy.

MEECH LAKE:
THE INSIDE STORY

PATRICK J. MONAHAN

UNIVERSITY OF TORONTO PRESS

Toronto Buffalo London

© University of Toronto Press 1991
Toronto Buffalo London
Printed in Canada

ISBN 0-8020-5969-4 (cloth)
ISBN 0-8020-6896-0 (paper)

Printed on acid-free paper

Canadian Cataloguing in Publication Data

Monahan, Patrick
Meech Lake

Includes bibliographical references and index.
ISBN 0-8020-5969-4 (bound) ISBN 0-8020-6896-0 (pbk.)

1. Canada – Constitutional law – Amendments.
2. Canada – Politics and government – 1984–   .*
3. Federal-provincial relations – Canada – History.*
I. Title.

JL65.1991.M65 1991   342.71'03   C91-094579-9

Photographs by Bill McCarthy.
Reproduced by permission of the Prime Minister's Office.

This book has been published with assistance from the Canada Council
and the Ontario Arts Council under their block grant programs.

For Monica
and our sons
Brendan and Sean

Contents

FOREWORD by the Honourable Ian Scott, QC, former Attorney General of Ontario / ix

PREFACE / xiii

1. 23 June 1990: A Day of Reckoning? / 3

2. The Inheritance of 1982 / 14

3. The Genie Is Let Out of the Bottle / 38

4. The Making of the Meech Lake Accord / 63

5. A Marathon at Langevin / 101

6. Unravelling a Seamless Web / 137

7. Canada on a Collision Course / 170

8. This Dinner Has Seven Days / 198

9. Why Did Meech Lake Fail? / 238

10. The Way Ahead / 260

APPENDIXES

1. Constitutional Chronology 1985–1990 / 289

2. The Meech Lake Communiqué, 30 April 1987 / 294

3. The 1987 Constitutional Accord / 297

4. 1990 Constitutional Agreement (Final Communiqué, First Ministers' Meeting on the Constitution, 9 June 1990) / 306

A Note on Sources / 315

Notes / 317

Index / 335

Foreword

Canada has, for a generation, been in the grip of a curious constitutional malady unique among the nations of the world. The disease is potentially fatal, and, as I write, the prognosis is, at best, guarded. That this country, a federation 123 years old, whose origins can be traced back at least another century through earlier forms of political cooperation and union, is so afflicted seems extraordinary.

If the current constitutional malaise perplexes some of us at home, it strikes our friends abroad as incredible. Anyone who travels outside this country (or even crosses our border into the United States) quickly recognizes that Canada has a reputation for institutional and social stability. Canada is everywhere regarded as a land rich in resources and economic potential. Canada is universally thought to be blessed with a political system (by no means perfect but one that works as well as most others) designed to guarantee free debate and democratic choice. The established view abroad is that Canada is a country committed to religious, racial, and social pluralism. Our standard of living and mutual sense of social obligation are the envy of peoples across the world. In our most candid moments, we Canadians believe much of this to be true. Nevertheless, with so much to be grateful for and so much political, economic, and social achievement to build on, we seem stuck in a constitutional quagmire from which, for a generation at least, we have been unable to escape. This curious and troubling situation is made more dangerous by the fact that Canadians no longer seem able to talk to each other about the future in a language that everyone understands. There is no longer agreement on such fundamental questions as how we arrived at our present impasse, what our long history together may mean, or what, if anything, as Canadians we owe to one another. Almost every region and group asserts its alienation from the rest and not only advances different solutions to our problems but proposes a different identification of the problems that need fixing.

Historians and political scientists will no doubt long debate how Canadians came to this pass. A useful start has been made by Professor Charles Taylor of McGill University who, in a seminal paper entitled 'Shared and Divergent Values,'[1] argues convincingly that the Québécois and the rest of us do not share a simple vision about the objectives or purpose of local or national governments. But we have done much in the short term to exacerbate our difficulties. We have, for instance, escalated almost every political, social, or economic dispute to the level of constitutional adjudication. More often that not, national populations in other parts of the world see their constitutions as pacts designed to establish a *modus operandi* for governments, a framework within which the democratic play of political forces is permitted so that social-economic and other objectives can be debated and effected at a non-constitutional level.

As well, in the last generation, constitutional debate in Canada has taken on an additional and taxing dimension. Canadians increasingly demand to see the values of their national life incorporated in the very constitutional document itself. This expectation has no doubt been heightened by the increasingly aggressive individual-rights orientation that the Charter of Rights and Freedoms, with all its benefits, has established in the national mind, but it is none the less a new phenomenon for constitutional makers. It has always been difficult enough in Canada to agree on the framework of a system of governments; it will prove extraordinarily difficult if that system must reflect national values about which, in an increasingly pluralistic country, there is little agreement.

What is perhaps worse, the public constitutional debates in which we have been engaged have exhibited a lack of that century-old Canadian virtue: the ability and even the willingness to compromise. It is trite to say that this country was not only built but maintained through persistent and fundamental compromise. But compromise, which often means accepting one's second or third choice, now seems unacceptable to many of us. Indeed, the compromise is seen pejoratively as the kind of thing politicians do. The notion that politics in the best and highest sense is the art of the possible is widely derided.

And, at the end, many Canadians affect to see themselves bored by the challenge and the effort that will be necessary to sustain national unity in a country that is, in so many ways, blessed. Over the great national divide we hear: 'We must separate' or 'Let them go.' Many of us are afflicted with a kind of selfishness and meanness of spirit towards our fellow Canadians from different regions or different groups who may have aspirations different than our own. Each of us demands to be served first at the constitutional table, failing which we will prevent anybody else from being served at all.

These are among the reasons why I believe that Patrick Monahan's book about the Meech Lake Accord is important.

Monahan's credentials to trace the history of Meech and to help us draw lessons from it are unique. An able young professor of constitutional law at Osgoode Hall Law School, at York University, he joined my office just a year after I was appointed attorney general of Ontario in 1985. To prepare our government for the negotiations, Monahan helped assemble a team from the public and the private sectors that I believe to have been unrivalled in respect of constitutional knowledge and experience. He observed both the Meech and Langevin rounds from the perspective of the attorney general's office. In 1989, he was appointed constitutional policy consultant to the Honourable David Peterson, premier of Ontario, and participated in the ultimate stages of negotiations as a principal consultant to the premier and the government of Ontario.

I think that Professor Monahan's book will serve two significant public purposes. In the first place, it is a factual account of a critical series of events in the history of this nation. Monahan seeks to get behind the hype, the personalities, and the headlines in order to tell us what actually happened during the negotiations. He describes the context in which positions were taken and the pressures that the process and, indeed, the constitution itself imposed on the various players. He writes at first hand of the negotiations that led up to the signing of the accord in April 1987, the extended and more detailed negotiations at Langevin Block, and the meetings designed to rescue the accord at Ottawa in June 1990. Readers may discover a whole series of significant, previously little-known facts about the process and the way it played out. Monahan describes in detail the extent to which all participants to these negotiations had to make important compromises in order to reach an agreement. He clearly, and I believe correctly, connects the difficulties inherent in the Meech round with the results of constitutional negotiations in 1982. He describes the confused manner in which the week-long meeting at the Ottawa Union Station was actually conducted and the reasons why the meeting dragged on for seven days. Parenthetically, it will no doubt come as a surprise to many readers that the two main protagonists in a battle for the survival of a nation at that meeting were essentially isolated from each other during the final countdown. For the entire preceding six months, there was not even a single meeting between officials from Newfoundland and Quebec, at whose hands the debate was ultimately determined.

No doubt other participants will, in due course, provide their own accounts of what happened, and that is as it should be. But Professor Monahan has made a fine start. For my part, I believe his book is a complete and accurate account of how Meech was negotiated and the factors that led to its collapse.

The Meech Lake Accord is now as dead as the proverbial doornail. If Professor Monahan's book was simply a firsthand account of events designed as an initial contribution to the history of this period, its importance would be real but limited. The book, however, is, and obviously intends to be, much more than an account of what happened as seen from the inside. For Monahan attempts to describe the lessons that we might learn from this experience; the necessary limitations on constitutional negotiation, many of which are established by the constitution itself; and the essential framework of the process to which future negotiations to be successful will have to adjust. That is the great utility of his book in the summer of 1991. There will perhaps be many who will disagree profoundly with the conclusions that Monahan offers. But this disagreement is of secondary importance. What is important is that the work is the first step on the road to getting the facts right. If Canadians can agree on what happened and why it happened, then perhaps we can begin to come to terms with what the constitutional negotiations of this decade will mean for the future of the country. This book, then, is only superficially about events in the past. It is, I believe, part of the learning exercise that Canadians must go through if the country is to survive. I hope that it will be read by everyone who is concerned about the future of Canada because I think it will help to set us off in the right direction. It should be a useful analytical prologue for the important national work that lies ahead.

The Honourable Ian Scott, QC, MPP

Preface

In July 1986, I took a one-year leave of absence from Osgoode Hall Law School to serve as senior policy adviser in the Office of the attorney general of Ontario, Mr Ian Scott. The attorney general told me that the negotiations over Quebec's place in Confederation, which were then just beginning, would probably be concluded by the summer of 1987. I would then return to the halls of academe to reflect and write about the successful reintegration of Quebec into the Canadian constitutional fold.

Obviously, things did not turn out quite as expected. By the summer of 1987, the ratification process for Meech Lake was only just beginning and it seemed an inopportune time to leave the government. With the generous support of the dean of Osgoode Hall Law School, John McCamus, my leave of absence from the law school was extended. Months later, as 1988 grew to a close, the ratification of Meech seemed very much in doubt. Moreover, the issue was beginning to assume a much larger public profile and was consuming an increasing proportion of the time and energy of the premier, David Peterson. In early 1989, the premier asked me to join his staff as senior policy adviser with special responsibility for constitutional affairs. With the support of the new dean of Osgoode Hall, Jim MacPherson, I was able to accept the premier's very generous offer. I served directly under the premier throughout the final period of Meech's decline and fall, culminating in the very dramatic events of June 1990.

As an adviser to the attorney general and to the premier, I was a witness to history in the making. I was fortunate enough to have been able to attend the meeting at Meech Lake on 30 April 1987 as well as the nineteen-hour meeting at the Langevin Block on 2–3 June 1987. I also attended the week-long meeting of First Ministers in Ottawa in June 1990. In short, I was able to observe first-hand how the Meech process evolved from the very beginning right through to the end. I was able to trace how Meech Lake was put together and how and why it came apart.

When I left government in the fall of 1990, it seemed to me that I ought to try to record my recollections and observations about this turbulent and historic time in the life of the country. I was troubled by what I regarded as the extremely one-sided and misleading public perceptions about the Meech Lake Accord outside of the province of Quebec. Outside Quebec, it seemed that there was nothing good to be said for Meech Lake. The accord was painted as a massive 'sell-out' to Robert Bourassa that would have eroded charter rights and given away important federal powers to the provinces.

The conventional way of understanding Meech Lake is captured precisely by Andrew Cohen's account of Meech, *A Deal Undone: The Making and Breaking of the Meech Lake Accord*. Cohen portrays the Meech process as haphazard and unplanned, driven by the personal preferences and idiosyncrasies of the individual premiers and the prime minister. Reading Cohen's book, one almost gets the sense that the premiers were 'duped' into signing Meech Lake by a prime minister who succeeded in separating the premiers from their expert advisers. This interpretation of Meech is exemplified by Cohen's quotation from Manitoba attorney general Roland Penner: 'Mulroney just wrote to us and said " 'Come down to Meech Lake for a little chat,' said the spider to the fly." And so Penner and the rest of them did.'[1] According to Cohen, Meech Lake was ill-conceived and unnecessary, the product of incredible bungling and ineptitude on the part of the country's political leaders.

In this book I take direct issue with the conventional wisdom that has developed about the Meech Lake Accord. I argue that Meech Lake was a genuine compromise between competing positions. I claim it was a balanced and moderate set of proposals that would have made very little practical difference to the political life of the country. I argue that the critics of the accord consistently over-estimated its probable negative impact while entirely discounting any positive effects that would have resulted from it.

Thus my account of the negotiations that led to the signing of the accord is quite different from Andrew Cohen's. Cohen emphasizes the degree to which the accord was the product of the personal preferences and weaknesses of the prime minister and the individual premiers. In my view, this account pays insufficient attention to the context within which the political actors operated. I emphasize the degree to which the earlier constitutional settlement of 1982 coloured and constrained the political actors in the Meech Lake negotiations. I also argue that large parts of the accord had already been agreed to in the negotiations that took place prior to the meeting on 30 April 1987. This is not to deny that the political leaders played a decisive role in framing the terms of the actual agreement. But this role can be properly understood and evaluated only against the backdrop of the constraints, pressures, and larger political forces that shaped the negotiations and their final outcome.

I have no doubt that the thesis of this book will be regarded as controversial, particularly among those in English Canada who believe the Meech Lake Accord to be a total disaster. For the opponents of Meech Lake, a defence of the accord by a Meech Lake 'insider' will no doubt be dismissed as self-serving and even transparent. I expect that many readers of this book will be struck by the vigour with which I defend the Meech Lake Accord. I think it important, therefore, to offer a word of clarification at the outset about the precise nature of the argument that I intend to advance.

My argument is *not* that the Meech Lake Accord was a perfect document. There were many aspects of the accord that I regarded as problematic. The most obvious problem was the requirement of unanimous consent for future changes to the Senate. As I argue at great length in chapter 2, a requirement of unanimous consent is generally an extremely poor decision-rule for negotiating changes to a constitution. I should also make plain that I did not regard the flaws in the accord as trivial or unimportant. In fact, during the nineteen-hour marathon meeting held in the Langevin Block on 2–3 June 1987, I had serious doubts about whether the agreement ought to be signed at all. It seemed to me then that there was a serious case to be made for simply walking away from the agreement rather than accepting the accord with its existing deficiencies.

In the end, however, I was persuaded that David Peterson's decision to sign the accord on 3 June 1987 was demonstrably the right one. I believed it was right because politics is not the art of perfection, but rather the art of the possible. While I or anyone else could have gone away and designed a 'perfect constitution,' such perfection would have been of no practical value. What was needed was a document that might serve as the basis of a consensus involving all parts of the country. Any such consensus means that everyone has to give up something in order to achieve agreement.

The relevant question, therefore, is not whether the agreement was flawed or whether it required compromise on the part of the federal government or the other provinces. The critical question is whether the benefits inherent in the agreement outweighed its flaws. Were the compromises contained in the Meech Lake Accord so significant as to outweigh the clear benefit associated with the reintegration of Quebec into the Canadian constitution? Moreover, was there an alternative set of 'better' proposals that were achievable, given the political realities and constraints? After wrestling with these questions, I came to the view that the only answer that could be given to them was 'no.' It would have been easy to design a 'more perfect' accord. But this perfection would have been illusory, since it could not have served as the basis for a national consensus on the reintegration of Quebec within Confederation. In my view, the flaws in the accord, while far from trivial, were ultimately outweighed by the need to obtain Quebec's signature on the Canadian constitution.

A large part of the argument of the book is an attempt to situate the choices that were made by political leaders against the backdrop of the context in which they were made. An assumption of the book is that the choices of political leaders are often more constrained than popular accounts of their activities would lead one to believe. But while I try to situate the Meech Lake actors within a larger context, I do not argue that their choices were in any sense 'inevitable' or dictated by 'history.' Despite the important constraints that I describe, real choices and options did exist. Some of the choices that were made turned out to be right, but many others turned out to be wrong. My point is simply that the mistakes that were made were not the product of mere bungling or bad faith. Rather, the Meech process should be understood as an attempt to grapple with a complex and shifting set of political forces that eventually overwhelmed those who initiated the exercise.

Perhaps I might also offer a word of clarification about my argument regarding the process that was utilized in the Meech Lake negotiations. One of the main points I emphasize is that meaningful negotiations require some kind of 'closed-door' process. I argue that this is a kind of 'iron law' of political negotiations, applicable in a wide variety of settings, not simply in discussions over the Canadian constitution. In any situation where bargaining compromise is necessary, this compromise will be achieved only if political leaders are permitted an opportunity to meet privately. That does not mean, of course, that these negotiations must be conducted *entirely* behind closed doors. Indeed, it seems to me that one of the most significant mistakes made in the Meech process was not secrecy *per se* but the *degree* of secrecy that was employed. Any future round of negotiations must take account of the need to make the negotiations more accessible, while preserving the ability of political leaders to meet privately at various points in the process.

The argument that is advanced in this book is not simply of historical interest. With the demise of Meech Lake, Canada has been plunged once again into a divisive and life-threatening debate over its future. Much of the current debate will inevitably be taken up with an exploration of what happened in the Meech Lake round. The Meech Lake experience will be a constant reference point in the current debate, invoked in aid of or in opposition to various positions and arguments that are advanced. Given the importance of the Meech experience for the current debate, I believe it important that Canadians come to a more complete understanding of what actually happened during this period. Otherwise the important debate that we are now witnessing will be conducted on the basis of second-hand impressions that are inherently contested and unverifiable. Hence this book.

My greatest debt in writing this book is to Ian Scott and David Peterson. They provided me with the opportunity to participate in the negotiations that I describe. They also encouraged and assisted me in the writing of the manuscript, reviewing drafts of the chapters and offering suggestions for additions and changes. But my real debt to these two men lies in what they taught me about politics and about political leadership. It is a particular Canadian tendency to denigrate our politicians and to lament their apparently declining quality. But my experience of Ian Scott and David Peterson was of two leaders who combined a commitment to high principle tempered by the ability to fashion practical political compromise. I regard it as a very special honour to have had the opportunity to serve under each of them.

I am also grateful to a number of current and former government officials at both the federal and the provincial levels who agreed to be interviewed for this book. Norman Spector, former secretary to the cabinet for federal-provincial relations, and Roger Tasse, former deputy attorney general of Canada, were particularly helpful in reconstructing some of the events that are described in this book. My colleague at Osgoode Hall Peter Hogg very kindly reviewed a draft of the manuscript and made many helpful suggestions for its improvement.

One of my fondest memories of the Meech Lake experience will be of having been able to work closely with officials in the Ontario Public Service. During my four years at Queen's Park, I was struck by the professionalism, quality, and collegiality of those working in the Ontario government. It would be impossible to mention here everyone with whom I had the pleasure of working. I do want to make particular mention, however, of David Cameron, the former deputy minister of intergovernmental affairs. David taught me a great deal about the Canadian constitution, but he taught me even more about the values of civility, tolerance, and grace under pressure. I am very grateful to have had the opportunity to have worked alongside him.

This book would not have been possible without the assistance and encouragement of the current dean of Osgoode Hall Law School, Jim MacPherson. Jim smoothed my transition back to the law school following the election of 6 September 1990 and provided me with the opportunity to work intensively on the manuscript.

My wife, Monica, was and is a source of advice, encouragement, and support. Many times in the writing of this book it seemed to me that there were obstacles that prevented me from completing the task I had undertaken. Monica was able to show me how those obstacles were not really as large as I had at first supposed. Her quiet determination and dedication remain a constant source of inspiration that lights our road ahead.

P.J.M.
March 1991

The First Ministers confer during a break at the Meech Lake meeting.

At the Langevin meeting of 2 and 3 June 1987, discussion focused on objections raised by David Peterson and Howard Pawley. Here, Brian Mulroney discusses the draft agreement with the Ontario and Manitoba premiers.

30 April 1987: The Meech Lake meetings begin. *Left to right:* Oryssia Lennie (Director of Constitutional Affairs, Province of Alberta), Don Getty, Joe Ghiz, Howard Pawley, John Buchanan, David Peterson, Norman Spector (Secretary to the Cabinet for Federal/Provincial Relations), Brian Mulroney, Robert Bourassa, Richard Hatfield, Bill Vander Zalm, Grant Devine, and Brian Peckford.

The Ontario and Manitoba delegations meet to discuss strategy during a break in the Langevin meeting. David Peterson and Howard Pawley are seated at the table, on the right. Moving counter-clockwise around the table: Manitoba attorney general Roland Penner, Ontario attorney general Ian Scott, Patrick Monahan, Professor Peter Hogg, Ian McGilp, Richard Chaloner (deputy attorney general of Ontario, seated with his back to the camera), Vince Borg, Doug Kirkpatrick, Hershell Ezrin, Gary Posen (partially hidden from view).

3 June 1987, at 5.00 a.m. There is unanimous agreement on the text of the accord and the prime minister summons federal officials into the room as the agreement is signed by all First Ministers. *Left to right:* David Peterson, Frank Iacobucci (deputy attorney general of Canada), Norman Spector, Brian Mulroney, Bill Vander Zalm, Robert Bourassa, and Richard Hatfield.

Brian Mulroney and David Peterson discuss the possibilities of achieving a consensus during a break in the official proceedings at the First Ministers' meeting, June 1990.

Quebec premier Robert Bourassa ponders his position during the June 1990 meeting.

The First Ministers meet for six days in early June 1990 in an effort to salvage the accord. Here, New Brunswick premier Frank McKenna takes notes during the discusson.

Newfoundland premier Clyde Wells and Brian Mulroney discuss their differences in an effort to achieve unanimous agreement (June 1990).

MEECH LAKE: THE INSIDE STORY

1

23 June 1990: A Day of Reckoning?

For months, Canadians had been told to circle the date on their political calendars: 23 June 1990 was the day of reckoning – the date that the Meech Lake Accord had to be ratified by all provincial legislatures or else fall into constitutional oblivion. First political leaders, then increasing numbers of business groups, and finally the media all joined in a chorus warning that 23 June would likely prove to be the most fateful and important date of Canada's 123-year political life. Some claimed that failure to ratify Meech would lead to the breakup of the country. Others warned that resulting political instability would produce a run on the dollar, fuel the inflationary fires in the economy, and lead the Bank of Canada to further jack up already-exorbitant interest rates. The message was simple, blunt, and more than a little unnerving: ratify Meech – or else.

Similar dire predictions in the 1988 election campaign over the Free-Trade Agreement had swung public opinion in favour of the trade deal and permitted the Conservatives to capture a parliamentary majority. But the warnings of impending doom failed to move Canadians in June 1990. With the majority of Canadians entrenched firmly in the anti-Meech camp, the legislatures in both Manitoba and Newfoundland adjourned on 22 June without putting the accord to a formal vote.

The events of the weekend of 23 June seemed more comedic than catastrophic. Canadians were treated to a display of banana-republic ineptitude played out on national television throughout the day of 22 June. The script – too improbable to be believed had Canadians not seen it enacted on their television screens – consisted of missed or unanswered telephone calls, misunderstood messages, bruised egos, and wild charges of manipulation and broken promises. Then, on the appointed day of reckoning itself, the prime minister appeared on national television to confirm that the constitutional deal had died but that the Canadian patient was still alive. Appealing for calm, the prime minister told Canadians that the prophecies of doom that he and others had been proclaiming for some months were now to be revised in light of changing circumstances.

On the surface, at least, it seemed that the apocalyptic warnings of the previous months had been vastly overblown. When the Tokyo markets opened late on 24 June, the Canadian dollar stumbled briefly, then gained strength and began moving upward. Foreign investors increased their holdings of Canadian bonds. In a convention hall in Calgary, delegates to the Liberal leadership voted overwhelmingly for a candidate who had described Canada's constitutional crisis as akin to being stuck in a snowbank.

But the outward appearances of calm and continuity were deceiving: 23 June had indeed become a day of reckoning and of destiny, if only because Canadians themselves had come to regard it as such. Canadians had been told that the failure to ratify Meech would mean that their country would never be the same again. Thus 23 June was a constitutional line in the political sand: cross the line and say goodbye, forever, to the old and familiar ways of doing things. The fact that Canadians were so unmoved by those predictions – that they were so prepared and almost eager to cross over that line in the sand – demonstrated their profound dissatisfaction with the status quo and a deep hunger for something new. The act of crossing the line marked by 23 June 1990 was itself proof that Canada had entered a new political era, an era in which the only certainty would be change.

The abiding problem was that no one seemed able to agree on the direction that change should follow. Within the province of Quebec, the defeat of Meech was regarded as a rejection of the historic demands of the province and evidence that it was time to seek a new deal from the rest of the country. Premier Bourassa announced that Quebec would no longer negotiate with the other provinces as one among ten; its future relationship with the rest of the country would be worked out through bilateral discussions with the federal government alone. Bourassa also announced the creation of a special parliamentary commission to undertake a comprehensive review of Quebec's ties to the rest of the country. No one, not even the premier, would be able to predict with any precision the outcome of the commission's deliberations. But it was clear that the new Quebec agenda would go far beyond what had been negotiated at Meech Lake and embrace some form of limited or complete sovereignty for Quebeckers.

Elsewhere, however, there was little patience for another effort to deal with the 'Quebec question.' Unlike in the late 1970s, there was a widespread sense across English Canada that perhaps it was time to 'let them go,' coupled with the belief that a Canada without Quebec would be viable. At a minimum, there was an insistence that any future constitutional round must deal with the concerns of all regions and affected groups, rather than simply those of Quebec.

One point on which there was general agreement, however, was the need for fundamental political and constitutional change. Increasingly, voices were being raised in all parts of the country, arguing that the existing federal structure was outmoded and in need of reform. From coast to coast there was a growing sense that national political institutions were no longer capable of representing the diverse and conflicting interests found in this vast land. The growing popularity of regionally based parties – whether the Reform Party in the West or the Bloc Québécois in Quebec – was a manifestation of this desire for a 'new deal' in which the regions would be better represented in the political institutions that governed them. Our political institutions and the old-line parties seemed incapable of performing their historic, core function of fashioning compromises between competing interests and visions of the country. It was the ability of our institutions to achieve these compromises that had always permitted Canadians to remain under the same roof together. Now, the absence of the will and the institutions to make such compromises gave greater legitimacy and urgency to the voices arguing for fundamental reform.

The most troubling aspect of this predicament was the lack of an obvious or even likely way of bridging the differences between Canadians. The Meech Lake round had laid bare a conflict that had haunted but never overwhelmed Canadians. This conflict centred on competing visions of the 'true nature' of the country. One vision held that Canada was composed of two 'founding peoples' and that the province of Quebec had a special role to play as the homeland of one of those two peoples. The other vision maintained that all provinces and peoples were equal and that Quebec was a province essentially identical to the other nine.

Canada had survived in large part because it had never required the citizens of the country to declare firmly which of the two competing visions was the 'correct' one. Canada was all things to all people, a mirror in which the observer could glimpse his or her own reflection. All of that changed with the debate over the Meech Lake Accord. The accord in general, and the 'distinct society' clause in particular, became a lightning-rod for these competing symbolic ideas of the nature of Canada. For Quebeckers, the distinct-society clause became a symbol of belonging. By accepting the description of Quebec as a distinct society, the rest of the country would have signalled its acceptance of the idea of Quebec's particularity within Canada. But, to the opponents of the clause, 'distinct society' became synonymous with 'special status' and an abandonment of a deep conviction in favour of the equality of the provinces and of all Canadians.

The debate over Meech Lake thus brought to the surface these fundamentally contradictory ideas of the nature of the country. Having come into full public view, they could no longer be ignored or forgotten. Canadians now seem resigned to the need to arrive at some generally accepted common understanding of the nature of their country – or else to abandon once and for all the historic experiment commenced in 1867.

The prospects for achieving a consensus on a new constitutional arrangement are far from encouraging. The first obstacle is simply the fallout from the Meech Lake debate itself. The highly symbolic and emotional quality of the debate opened very deep wounds across the country and fed long-standing regional grievances. This heightened sense of grievance reduces the willingness of all parties to search for compromise and accommodation. The next round of constitutional discussions could easily descend into an unproductive and damaging exercise in settling old scores.

The debate is further complicated by the lack of any widely accepted and legitimate process for achieving consitutional change. The 1982 Constitution Act provides a role for governments and for legislatures but no formal role for popular participation in the process of constitutional amendment. This formula is premised on the legitimacy of political leaders debating and determining constitutional change, an approach that appears to represent a political anachronism in the Canada of the 1990s. One thing upon which everyone seems agreed is that the 'executive federalism' model of constitutional change is no longer viable. The problem is to find a credible and workable alternative. There have been few constructive or concrete suggestions as to what, if anything, should replace bargaining between First Ministers as a basis for amending the constitution. There is, instead, only an overwhelming cynicism about the motives of our political leaders and a rejection of their right to amend the constitution through a series of closed-door bargaining sessions.

The constitutional issue is complicated by a variety of other, nonconstitutional factors. The flow of trade in Canada is becoming increasingly north-south, rather than east-west, a trend that is exemplified by the Canadian-U.S. Trade Agreement. The primacy of north-south trade relationships means that the economic well-being of any one part of the country is no longer dependent on its other parts. Thus the commitment to regional sharing and redistribution of income along east-west lines is eroded. Also, the political will in favour of searching for creative compromises to the difficult political problems facing the country is reduced.

Internationally, one observes a movement towards the harmonization of economic policy in larger and larger trade blocs, coupled with a drive towards decentralization of community and political attachments. The trend towards economic harmonization reflects the globalization of world markets, a trend that diminishes the traditional sovereignty of the nation-state and its capacity to protect domestic consumers and producers from the grinding forces of international competition. In this context, nation-states, such as Canada, with no overriding cultural, linguistic, racial, or linguistic ties can expect their legitimacy and role to come into question. Moreover, this challenge comes at a particularly difficult time for Canada, since the fiscal incapacity of the federal government has already severely diminished its ability to play a positive and unifying national role.

So, it is certainly no overstatement to conclude that the Canada of 1991 is in significant trouble. Some years ago, it was common to hear Canadians quote with both pride and expectation Laurier's prediction that the twentieth century would belong to Canada. Now, we are facing a situation where there is a serious possibility that Canada as we know it will not even survive the century, much less lay claim to it.

Our ability to build a common future together will depend in large measure on whether we can come to terms with our recent past. The Meech Lake process was a severe shock to the Canadian political system, and we have not yet recovered from the trauma. In the aftermath of Meech, a whole host of misleading and simplistic explanations have been offered as to the causes of the accord's demise. As these misleading explanations multiply, they blind Canadians to the real nature of the choices we confront and reduce the prospects for reaching a new and genuine compromise. This book is premised on the belief that it is essential to have a clear understanding of where we have been if we are to have any hope of arriving at a common destination. My perspective is by no means an objective or unbiased one; as a participant in the negotiations leading to the Meech Lake Accord, I was a strong supporter of the accord and believed its ratification to be in the national interest. But, while this involvement colours my perspective, it also permits me to offer a number of insights about the accord that have not yet featured in the public debate surrounding it.

Thus far, the public debate over the Meech Lake Accord has centred in large part on the process and the personalities that led to its creation.

There seems unanimous agreement that the Meech Lake process was the product of misguided and élitist politicians, obsessed with secrecy, who simply bungled the attempt to bring Quebec back in to the constitution.[1] The criticisms of the process centre on the fact that the negotiations that produced the accord were conducted entirely behind closed doors, without any attempt at public consultation. Then, once the accord was drafted, it was treated as though it were carved in stone, with all the signatories insisting that not a single comma could be changed.

The criticisms of the contents of the accord – although less prominent than the attack on the process – also centre on the alleged bungling of the political leaders who drafted it. In essence, the attack on the contents of the accord is based on the claim that it does not represent a true compromise between competing viewpoints. The trouble with the Meech Lake Accord, according to its critics, is that the prime minister of Canada simply gave away the shop to Quebec, in particular, and to the provinces, in general. There was no attempt to force the provinces to compromise their claims or to grant concessions to the federal government, as had been the case in previous constitutional rounds. Instead, the prime minister simply acted as the 'head waiter' for the provinces, filling the orders of the premiers for more powers and jurisdiction. 'It would be difficult,' concluded former prime minister Pierre Trudeau, 'to imagine a more total bungle.'[2]

These popular criticisms of the Meech Lake Accord have become so deeply entrenched, particularly in English Canada, as to approach conventional wisdom. But, I will argue that these popular understandings are both misleading and dangerous – misleading because they fail to identify the real forces that shaped the Meech Lake Accord and that account for its failure, and dangerous because they foster the illusion that a mere change in political leadership is all that is necessary in order to overcome the challenges we face in the future.

This book is an attempt to counter the popular image of Meech as a 'total bungle.' There are two essential themes to my argument, the first relating to the process and the second relating to the substance of Meech Lake.

With respect to process, my argument will focus on the events of 1982 rather than 1987. I believe that the key to understanding the Meech Lake process lies in an analysis of the constitutional settlement of 1982, rather than of the shortcomings of political leadership in 1987. Two features of the 1982 constitutional settlement were key factors in shaping the Meech negotiations. The first was a new set of ground rules for constitutional change. The 1982 act established an extremely unwieldy and inflexible set of rules for constitutional change, making constitutional amendment extremely difficult and risky to achieve. The second significant feature of the 1982 constitutional settlement was the fact that it was enacted over the objections of the province of Quebec. The exclusion of Quebec in 1982 set in motion a political dynamic that was extremely difficult to control and had the potential to undermine the fabric of Canada.

My argument is that the secrecy and inflexibility exhibited in the Meech Lake round was largely a response to the political inheritance of 1982. That is not to praise or to justify politics based on 'élite accommodation.' It is merely to observe that, if the Meech process was faulty, it was so because of the conditions under which it was required to be negotiated, rather than because of a 'total bungle' perpetrated by politicians. The problem with the 'total bungle' thesis is that it mistakes effects for causes. It observes and describes political behaviour without attempting to identify the underlying causes of such behaviour. If we turn our minds to causes rather than to mere effects, it becomes apparent that the Meech process was a product of a set of contradictory and very powerful political forces originating in 1982. These pressures and constraints greatly limited the range of available options and induced political leaders to pursue a narrow and limited strategy. What is remarkable is not so much that this strategy failed but that it came so close to achieving success.

This insight is important because the constraints and pressures that shaped the now-discredited Meech process are still very much with us. These constitutional imperatives will exert a powerful influence on any future round of constitutional discussions. It thus becomes all the more essential that we begin now to come to an understanding of how they have operated if we are to have any prospect of avoiding a repetition of our past mistakes.

The other overriding theme of the book relates to the substance of the accord itself. Here, I will take issue with the 'prime minister as head waiter' thesis that has coloured the popular imagery surrounding the accord. Instead, I will argue that the Meech Lake Accord represented a genuine compromise between competing visions and interests. I will demonstrate that there was a long series of intensive negotiations in late 1986 and early 1987 in which the Quebec government modified its initial proposals. These modifications were designed to take account of the objections of the federal government and the other provinces to Quebec's original 'five conditions.' The result was that the Meech Lake Accord itself represented a balanced and carefully circumscribed set of proposals. Had they been enacted, they would not have had any revolutionary or major impact on the legal or constitutional affairs of the country.

I am not suggesting that the accord as drafted was perfect – far from it. A variety of provisions included in it represented significant flaws. The most obvious such flaw was the requirement that there be unanimous consent for future constitutional changes involving the Senate or the creation of new provinces. As I will make clear throughout this book, a requirement of unanimous consent is never a desirable decision-rule for constitutional amendments. The point is simply that flaws of this type in the accord were largely unavoidable. They were a direct result of the fact that Meech itself had to secure the unanimous consent of all provinces. This requirement was not simply dreamed up by the political leaders who sat down at Meech Lake in April 1987. Rather, it was a precondition to the negotiations, established by the constitutional settlement of 1982.

This book, then, is an attempt to provide a behind-the-scenes look at the pressures and the personalities that produced the Meech Lake Accord and the dramatic three-year struggle over its ratification. The story begins, not in 1987, but in November 1981. It was then that a number of fundamental political decisions were made that were to foreshadow both the process and the substance of the Meech Lake Accord. I will outline those political choices and identify the effects they had on the Meech Lake round.

The story then moves to the summer of 1986, when political leaders from across the country decided to commence a 'Quebec round.' I will outline the initial reaction to Quebec's 'five conditions' and the competing arguments that were raised as to the wisdom of commencing constitutional negotiations at that time. The constitutional issue was a 'genie in the bottle.' It was clearly understood that the bottle could be uncorked only at great risk to the country. It was because of the delicacy of the issues involved that it was agreed that there should be an informal series of closed-door negotiations designed to 'test the water' on Quebec's demands. Formal public negotiations would commence only when it was clear that success was assured. These 'informal negotiations' began with Quebec presenting other governments with a series of specific constitutional proposals in the fall of 1986. These constitutional proposals, which the Quebec government insisted be kept confidential, gave specific content to Quebec's 'five conditions.' But, there were a number of problems with these proposals. It was clear that significant changes would have to be made if they were to form the basis for an agreement among all governments. I will recount the intensive negotiations that took place among governments later in 1986 and in early 1987, which narrowed differences and set the table for the historic meeting of 30 April 1987.

When the eleven First Ministers emerged on the evening of 30 April to announce that unanimous agreement had been reached on Quebec's proposals, the rest of the county seemed genuinely taken aback by the achievement. But, to those close to the negotiations as they unfolded in early 1987, the success at Meech Lake came as no real surprise. By the middle of April, the ground had been carefully prepared, and the main elements of a consensus had emerged. Only two or three trouble spots remained when the prime minister and the premiers sat down at the table on the morning of 30 April 1987. Within hours, these remaining points of difficulty were resolved, and an agreement was in place.

But the meeting of 30 April was merely the beginning of the process rather than its conclusion. There was, first, the matter of translating the general principles agreed to at Meech Lake into a formal constitutional text. It was assumed that this matter was a relatively straightforward one, which could be handled by officials. First Ministers would meet simply to sign an agreed text reflecting the 30 April principles. But the reality was far different. The negotiations among officials turned difficult, with representatives of various provinces advancing rather different interpretations of what had been agreed to on 30 April. These private discussions among officials were conducted against the backdrop of a mounting public controversy over the accord, highlighted by former prime minister Pierre Trudeau's bitter polemic against the accord, published in late May. When the First Ministers reconvened on 2 June, there was the genuine prospect that they would be unable to reach agreement on the text of a formal constitutional amendment.

The marathon meeting of 2–3 June in the Langevin Block was in reality a second bargaining session in which the agreement of 30 April was significantly modified. There were only two items under discussion: the 'distinct society' clause and the so-called spending-power provision that limited the federal government's role in provincial shared-cost programs. On both of these items, the governments of Ontario and Manitoba secured significant concessions, changes to the original agreement that took account of the objections raised by Trudeau and others. Final agreement was not achieved until 5:00 a.m. on 3 June 1987, when Ontario's David Peterson indicated that he was satisfied with the changes that had been made.

The next three years tell the story of a rising tide of opposition to the agreement of June 1987. The political slogan of the opponents to the accord was based on the idea of a 'need to compromise.' What was required, it was said, was a 'compromise' between the advocates and the opponents of the Meech Lake Accord. The accord need only be amended, rather than totally scrapped, in order to be ratified. But, what this argument ignored was the fact that the compromises had already been made in the process leading up to the drafting of the accord. After June 1987, the political choice was as stark as it was simple: accept the accord as is, or reject it.

This stark reality was predictably unpalatable and therefore the subject of consistent denial and avoidance for close to three years. Not until early June 1990, with the three-year ratification period staring Canadians in the face, did the harsh realities of the situation intrude upon everyone's calculations. But old habits die hard. Even as the deadline approached, there was a lingering unwillingness truly to come to terms with the very limited political choice that had to be made.

If there is one overriding message to be derived from this book, it is that we must constantly resist the temptation to construct simplistic explanations for complex and dynamic political events. In keeping with this maxim, I will resist the impulse to attempt to identify a single 'cause' of the failure of Meech Lake. As my account will make plain, the accord did not expire from any single wound, but rather died a death of a thousand cuts. Yet, despite the complexity of the events that I will describe, it can be said that there was one particularly significant turning-point in the three-year struggle over the ratification of Meech – 18 December 1988. It was on that day that Robert Bourassa announced that Quebec had decided to override the Supreme Court's decision on the language of signs in Quebec. From that day forward, political support in the rest of the country for a 'Quebec round,' in general, and for the Meech Lake Accord, in particular, essentially evaporated. There was no longer any political rationale for an attempt to make amends for the 'wrong' suffered by Quebec in 1982. It was on that day that the idea of simply allowing the accord to die became a very real political option. The Meech Lake Accord may have died from a thousand cuts, but the wound suffered on 18 December 1988 was surely the deepest.

Understanding how and why Meech Lake failed is important for the simple reason that we are now facing a renewed round of constitutional discussions. This future constitutional round will be strongly shaped and influenced by Meech, just as Meech itself was, in many ways, a product of the 1982 constitutional negotiations. The net effect of the constitutional battles of the last three years is to limit even further our constitutional flexibility. Many doors that were once available have now been closed because of the Meech experience. In particular, the ability of governments and political leaders to amend the constitution behind closed doors has now been almost totally discredited. The problem is that no alternative process has yet been suggested that might have a fair prospect of actually achieving a constitutional amendment.

The final chapter of this book explores the lessons of Meech Lake for the future round of constitutional negotiations. In such an assessment, there is no room for false hopes, illusions, or miscalculations. Canada's constitutional future must be assessed in the light of some very hard and unpleasant political realities that simply cannot be avoided in the wake of the failure of Meech Lake. The main effect of these political realities, I will argue, is to limit dramatically the range of available options. While the range of theoretical possibilities is virtually limitless, the practical possibilities are fairly limited and can be identified in relatively precise terms.

The essential choice facing Canadians is between two quite stark alternatives. The first is a rebalancing of the roles of the federal and provincial governments in a manner that might accommodate the demands of the province of Quebec while retaining an important role for the national government. This rebalancing must be incremental and begin from the existing federal division of powers. Any attempt to start from scratch and comprehensively redraw the map of Canadian federalism is doomed to failure. The rebalancing of roles must also respect the principle of the equality of the provinces. Moreover, it can be achieved only within the constraints imposed by the current amending formula. The second alternative is the mirror image of the first, involving an attempt to jump outside of the existing constitutional arrangements entirely. This second option – involving radical constitutional change – would almost certainly mean the breakup of the country as we now know it. As I will explain, the most likely outcome of this second scenario would be a wholly independent Quebec with only the most vestigial political ties to the rest of the country.

This is a sobering conclusion, since such a new political arrangement could be achieved only at great cost, not only for Quebeckers but for Canadians in all parts of the country. But, if we are to resolve our current constitutional dilemma in a reasoned and constructive manner, it is essential that we face up in advance to the very hard realities that we confront. Our difficulties, while considerable, are by no means insurmountable. Yet, as we turn towards the future, we do so with the knowledge that, if we fail this time, we may not get another chance. This book represents an attempt to take a hard-headed look at where we have been and why, and in so doing to discover where we are going and how we might get there – all the while preserving the Canadian tradition of civility, accommodation, and honourable compromise.

2

The Inheritance of 1982

'You're asking me now if I consider [the 1981
constitutional agreement] a success? No, I
consider it an abject failure'
                            Prime Minister Pierre Trudeau,
                                    18 November 1981

As thousands of Canadians gathered on Parliament Hill on the morning
of 17 April 1982 to witness the Queen present Canada with its independence, the weather seemed a threatening omen of things to come. The
day had dawned sunny and warm. But, by mid-morning, with a crowd of
some 30,000 assembled to witness history in the making, the wind had
begun to blow and the skies had darkened. As the prime minister began to
speak of Canada acquiring its sovereignty from Britain, storm clouds
gathered over the Peace Tower, and the distant rumble of thunder
prompted the exposed spectators to grow restless. The prime minister
praised the new constitution as guaranteeing equal rights for both French-
and English-speaking Canadians across the country. As if in response, long
rolls of thunder could be heard, and flashes of lightning lit the morning
sky. Denouncing the refusal of the Quebec government to accept the new
constitution, Trudeau claimed that he, not Premier René Lévesque, was
defending the true interests of ordinary Quebeckers. 'By definition, the
silent majority does not make a lot of noise,' he opined; 'it is content to
make history.' A steady rain was now falling. The spectators fashioned
makeshift protection from green garbage bags, souvenir programmes, or
folded newspapers. By the time the Queen rose to speak a few moments
later, a downpour of rain and hail had drenched the crowd, and the storm
made it virtually impossible to hear a word the sovereign uttered.
    The inhospitable weather matched the mood of many in the country on
that day. Amid all the official pomp and ceremony, there was little evi-

dence of spontaneous joy or celebration at Canada's constitutional achievement. There was certainly a palpable sense of relief that the constitutional page had been turned and a truce declared in Canada's one-hundred-year constitutional wars. But many thoughtful Canadians wondered about the price that would eventually have to be paid for what was being signed into law under the dark Ottawa skies that April morning.

The trouble was obvious: Quebec had refused to sign the new constitution or to recognize its legitimacy. Shortly after the Queen began to speak on Parliament Hill, Premier René Lévesque was leading a crowd of some 15,000 Quebeckers through the streets of Montreal in protest. 'This horror of a constitution was made against us and behind our backs,' Lévesque shouted, as the crowd roared and waved a sea of fleurs-de-lis flags in approval. 'It is not ours,' he thundered.

Prime Minister Trudeau dismissed the protests emanating from Quebec as the puerile rantings of defeated nationalists. Lévesque had outflanked himself when, in April 1981, he had agreed to an amending formula without a special veto for Quebec. This concession, according to Trudeau, opened the door to the November 1981 constitutional agreement achieved without Quebec's participation. In any event, Trudeau believed that he, the federal prime minister whose party had won more than seventy of the seventy-five Quebec seats in the last election, had just as much right as René Lévesque to consent to the constitution on Quebec's behalf.

Others were not so sure. Within Quebec, it was a foregone conclusion that the refusal of the Quebec government to sign the constitution was a serious omission that had to be remedied. Claude Ryan, the leader of the Quebec Liberal party and a leader of the *non* forces in the referendum, observed that the constitution being proclaimed in April 1982 was simply unacceptable to Quebec in its present form. 'Until this deficiency has been corrected,' Ryan claimed, 'it will be a major source of difficulty for any provincial party worthy of its role.'[1] Most observers outside Quebec took a similar view. Quebec's non-participation could not simply be ignored or dismissed as the unauthorized antics of Quebec nationalists. Sooner or later there would have to be some attempt to secure the voluntary consent of the Quebec government to the 1982 constitutional changes. Such an attempt at reconciliation would be highly risky and fraught with difficulties, as Gordon Robertson, a former clerk of the privy council, predicted at the time. 'It would be optimistic in the extreme,' Robertson wrote, 'to think that we can avoid a new crisis on the question of separation in a very few years.'[2]

The problem was that the new constitution had been constructed in such a manner as to frustrate rather than to facilitate any such attempt at constitutional reconciliation. The new amending formula, which would govern all future changes to the constitution, was a study in constitutional constraint. Much of the commentary on the new amending formula had focused on the provisions permitting individual provinces to 'opt out' of constitutional changes. Of far greater significance were the rigidity and inflexibility that the formula imposed on all future efforts at constitutional reform. All future significant amendments would require the consent of at least seven and as many as ten, provinces. Moreover, each province would have to ratify the proposed amendment in the form of a legislative resolution. The net effect of this new amending formula, little appreciated at the time, was to stack the odds heavily against any major modifications in the constitution.

This, then, was Canada's unhappy inheritance from the constitutional bequest of 1982. The constitution had been patriated over the loud and angry objections of Quebec. The decision to proceed anyway made it mandatory that some future attempt be made to secure Quebec's consent. But the constitutional amending formula had been fashioned in such a way as to frustrate any future effort at accommodation. The authors of the 1982 act had proceeded on the basis that the constitution was a finished product, to which no changes were necessary. They had made no allowances for the possibility that significant changes would have to be made to accommodate the objections of the province of Quebec.

The political inheritance of 1982 made necessary the Meech Lake round of discussions, which began in 1986. But the 1982 act cast a long and haunting shadow over the Meech discussions, shaping the nature of the process that would be utilized and the outcome of the negotiations. The events of 1982 also go a very considerable distance in explaining the unhappy fate of the accord and the disarray that has emerged in its wake.

Because the 1982 act is so critical to an understanding of the Meech Lake round, it is appropriate to analyse the implications of the events of 1982 in some detail. I will begin by considering the significance of the exclusion of Quebec. I have claimed that Quebec's non-participation made it a foregone conclusion that an attempt at reconciliation would have to be undertaken at some point in the future. But this conclusion has never been conceded by former prime minister Pierre Trudeau, who has maintained, instead, that the idea that Quebec had to be 'brought back in' to the constitution was profoundly misguided. I will examine with some care the competing arguments on both sides of this important question.

I will also consider how the exclusion of Quebec would structure and constrain any future efforts at reconciliation. As I will explain, any attempt to 'bring Quebec back in' would be extremely risky and prone to failure. The issues in dispute would be highly symbolic, and attention would inevitably focus on questions of 'honour,' prestige, and political face-saving. These factors would diminish the room for manoeuvring, encourage inflexibility in negotiating positions, and limit the possibility of constructing compromises. The stakes in the negotiations would also be very high, with failure likely to produce significant political instability in Quebec. All of these factors would encourage the pursuit of a very narrow and focused strategy, centred on private and informal negotiations between officials and First Ministers behind closed doors.

The final set of constraints was supplied by the amending formula itself. I will set out in some detail how the inflexibility associated with it reinforced the tendencies towards private, informal discussions outlined above. I will also explain how the amending formula foreshadowed the substance of Meech itself and, in particular, the 'provinces' round' character of the accord. Finally, I will explain how certain elements of the amending formula played a key role in the eventual demise of the accord.

The events of 1982 provided the backdrop and the context for the Meech Lake negotiations. By highlighting the extent to which the 1982 constitutional settlement shaped and constricted the Meech process, we are returned to a more general principle, namely, that the actions of political leaders are always far more constrained than is suggested by popular accounts of their activities. The Meech Lake Accord, as with all political choices, must be situated in the context of the structural limitations and constraints that conditioned its development. That is not to suggest that the participants in the process were utterly powerless or rendered helpless in the face of external pressure. Nor should it be supposed that the political environment somehow predetermined the political choices that were made. Real choices and options did exist, despite the presence of the significant obstructions that I will describe. The point is simply that it is possible to come to a balanced assessment of these choices only if they are first situated within the context in which they were made.

Why a Quebec Round?

The 1982 constitution had been enacted without the consent or participation of the government of Quebec. However, the absence of Quebec's signature did not vitiate the formal legal validity of the constitution. As the Supreme Court of Canada made clear in its judgment handed down in

December 1982, the constitution had complete legal force in the province of Quebec, despite the objections of the Quebec government.[3]

Why, then, the need for a 'Quebec round'? To talk of the need to bring Quebec 'in to' the constitution was, surely, to entertain an absurdity. Quebec was already fully 'within' the Canadian constitution. Attempting to bring the province back in would be as futile as searching for the cure for a disease that did not exist.

That argument is essentially the one advanced by former prime minister Pierre Trudeau. Trudeau's basic claim is that the Quebec round was unnecessary because the constitution already had legal, moral, and political force in the province of Quebec. The legal validity of the constitution had been settled by the Supreme Court of Canada. As for its moral validity, Trudeau relied on the fact that the 1982 act had been overwhelmingly approved in Parliament by seventy-two of the seventy-five duly elected federal MPs from the province of Quebec. These elected MPs, according to Trudeau, had just as much right to represent the will of Quebeckers as did the separatist premier and government of Quebec. Moreover, it was appropriate to dispense with the consent of Mr Lévesque and his colleagues because they were separatists committed to the breakup of the country. The 1982 Quebec government would never have accepted any reasonable package of amendments designed to strengthen the Canadian federation as a whole. Finally, Trudeau claimed that the constitution had political validity within Quebec, pointing to the 'silent majority' that 'makes history rather than noise.' Ordinary Quebeckers, according to Trudeau, 'applauded the players and then, yawning, turned to other matters.'[5] There was no popular outcry over the exclusion of Quebec in 1982. It was only nationalists and intellectuals who claimed to have been humiliated, but these were 'snivellers' who should have simply been told to 'stop having tantrums like spoiled adolescents.'[6]

None of these arguments is particularly convincing. The first – that Quebec was legally bound by the constitution – is in itself no answer to the objections of Quebec. Formal legal validity is, of course, a necessary precondition to the existence of a constitutional order. But formal validity is an insufficient basis for an effective and functioning constitution, as political regimes around the world have been rediscovering recently. A constitution must enjoy political as well as legal legitimacy if it is to be viable. These matters are determined by the political process, not in courtrooms by lawyers and judges.

What assessment can be made of these larger political questions? Here, it is important to make a distinction between two quite separate political issues. The first is whether the federal government was justified in proceeding with its unilateral plan for patriation in 1982. The second is whether it was nevertheless necessary to reach an accommodation with the Quebec government at some later time.

The basic problem with Trudeau's argument is that he fails to recognize that these two questions are independent of each other and treats them as different versions of a single question. Trudeau's basic argument is that he was justified in proceeding with his unilateral package in 1982 because the Quebec government was led by separatists who would never have agreed to any form of renewed federalism. *Therefore*, Trudeau claims, there was no need to attempt to reach an accommodation with any future Quebec government.

It is evident that the second conclusion does not follow from the first. It is quite reasonable to observe, as Trudeau does, that the 1982 Quebec government was committed to independence and therefore would never have accepted any form of renewed federalism. But it does not follow that the federal government had no obligation *ever* to seek an accommodation with any future government of Quebec. Indeed, Trudeau's own argument leads to precisely the opposite conclusion. If the justification for proceeding in 1982 was the separatist leanings of the current crop of Quebec politicians, the removal of those politicians from office must alter the moral and political calculation. In the event that more moderate federalist politicians came to power in Quebec City, the government of Canada would necessarily come under an obligation to seek their acceptance of the 1982 constitution.

Such was particularly the case because of the circumstances preceding the patriation of the 1982 constitution. For two decades, successive Quebec governments had maintained that Canadian federalism must be renewed so as to grant greater autonomy to the province of Quebec. The province claimed that it needed additional powers because of its very special responsibilities as the only government in North America elected by a French-speaking majority. Quebec had also consistently argued for a greater provincial role in appointments to important federal institutions such as the Supreme Court of Canada and the Senate.[7]

There had never been agreement between Quebec and the federal government on these demands for greater autonomy. But, during the constitutional discussions of the late 1960s and 1970s, the federal government had recognized that some attempt ought to be made to accommodate the concerns of Quebec. At various constitutional conferences, the federal government had made a variety of proposals that would have granted greater autonomy to the Quebec government. To cite but one example, at the constitutional conference of September 1980, the federal government offered to recognize the 'distinctive character of Quebec society' in a preamble to the constitution.[8]

While none of these negotiations ever resulted in an agreement, the evidence is clear and incontestable: there was a recognition throughout the 1970s that Quebec's aspirations for greater autonomy and constitutional recognition were genuine and legitimate. It is, of course, true that the federal government was also putting forward proposals of its own, designed to strengthen the Canadian economic union or entrench individual rights. But, at the same time, there was never any doubt that any acceptable package would have to grant some of the traditional demands for greater autonomy advanced by the province of Quebec.

These failed negotiations provided the context for the referendum campaign of 1980, in which federal politicians had promised 'renewed federalism' in return for a *non* vote. Mr Trudeau was careful never to specify the precise content of any such renewal of federalism. His references to constitutional renewal consisted of vague references to the need for change and the willingness of Quebec MPs to 'lay our seats in the House on the line to have change.'[9] But, given the history and the context of the discussions of the previous decade, it was self-evident that any such renewal would have to include *some* attempt to accommodate Quebec's claims for greater autonomy. This conclusion was reinforced by the leading role of others on the *non* side who had committed themselves in this direction. Quebec Liberal leader Claude Ryan, for example, campaigned for a *non* vote on the basis of the 1980 'Beige Paper,' which had proposed a significant devolution of authority to the provincial government.

The difficulty stemmed from the fact that the 1982 constitutional settlement did not include any recognition of Quebec's traditional aspirations. The 1982 constitution explicitly recognized the multicultural character of the country as well as the rights of the aboriginal peoples of Canada, but made no mention of the distinctive character of Quebec. After years of Quebec's seeking to have its aspirations accommodated, culminating in the emotional referendum campaign of 1980, the terms of the new constitution essentially ignored Quebec's agenda for change.

That is not to suggest that the decision to proceed in the absence of the province of Quebec in 1981 cannot be justified. It may well be that the separatist commitment of the Quebec government of the time provided a moral justification for proceeding without their consent. But, the conclusion that the consent of Quebec's elected provincial representatives could be ignored forever is insupportable. At some point it would be necessary to make good on the promises and failed negotiations of the previous decade.

Purely pragmatic political considerations also figure in this argument. Trudeau claimed that his triumph had marginalized the nationalists and that the federation in its current form was 'set to last a thousand years.'[10] While it is true that Quebec nationalism was a dormant political force in the mid-1980s, Trudeau's confident predictions seemed unlikely to hold in the long term. No major provincial political party in Quebec supported the 1982 constitution in its current form. The Quebec Liberal party (QLP) voted with the Parti Québécois (PQ) in condemning the patriation package in 1982. When Robert Bourassa took over the QLP a year later, he reinforced this policy by putting forward five conditions for obtaining Quebec's signature on the constitution. It was clear that no Quebec government in the foreseeable future would accept the 1982 constitutional arrangements without some modifications. Had the rest of the country simply refused even to consider Bourassa's proposals, insisting that the 1982 constitution was fine in its existing form, the constitutional issue inevitably would have resurfaced in Quebec. If Canada had heeded Trudeau's advice to 'send the nationalists packing,' it would only have breathed new life into the very political forces that he sought to smother.

The only way to avoid this conundrum would have been for the federal government to appeal to the people of Quebec directly, through a referendum on the new constitutional package. Had Trudeau sought and obtained popular ratification of his constitutional proposals, any remaining objections of the government of the province would have been rendered superfluous. Trudeau himself undoubtedly understood this political reality quite clearly. At the constitutional conference in November 1981, he proposed to René Lévesque that their differences be settled by the people of Quebec directly, through a referendum. Lévesque immediately agreed to the referendum proposal, but other provincial governments were strenuously opposed. The idea of a referendum was quickly dropped, and there was no provision made for popular ratification of the agreement of 5 November 1981.

This decision represented a critical turning-point in Canada's constitutional evolution. Had there been a referendum on the 1982 constitutional proposals, it would have represented a definitive judgment on their fate. If the proposals were rejected, there would have been no basis for proceeding any farther; had they been ratified, any objections would have been rendered irrelevant. Conversely, the fact that a referendum was *not* held meant that the federal government lacked the moral and political authority simply to ignore the objections of the government of Quebec. At some point, there would have to be an accommodation made with the province over the 1982 constitutional amendments.

It is significant that, in the mid-1980s, prior to the meeting at Meech Lake, there was near unanimity across the country that the Quebec government's signature on the constitution was important. No one, not even Pierre Trudeau, was arguing at that time that the exclusion of Quebec could simply be ignored forever. The Macdonald Commission, in its comprehensive analysis of the future of the country, concluded that it was necessary to seek a 'renewed understanding between Quebec and the rest of Canada.'[11] The commission proceeded to advance a series of concrete proposals that might form the basis of this renewed understanding. At the same time, political leaders in all parts of the country, and from all political parties – including the prime minister and the leaders of the two major national opposition parties as well as the premiers of all the provinces – adopted a similar view. Even those who were later to become the most vigorous critics of the Meech Lake Accord initially supported the attempt to reconcile Quebec to the constitution. For example, the *Toronto Star* reacted to the proposals made by the Quebec minister of intergovernmental affairs, Gil Rémillard, at Mont Gabriel in May 1986 with the observation that the constitution lacked moral standing in the province of Quebec and that 'it behooves us to address Quebec's concerns.'[12] As the *Toronto Star* noted, to refuse to negotiate with Bourassa would simply "give ammunition to the separatists.' Other observers at the time were troubled by the fact that Quebec's absence from the constitutional table precluded progress on other important constitutional matters such as Senate reform and aboriginal rights. The significance of Quebec's absence was illustrated at the 1985 and 1987 First Ministers' conferences on aboriginal rights, in which it proved impossible to secure the necessary consent for a constitutional amendment.

The conclusion that flows from this analysis is that the constitutional package of 1982 was achieved with a price attached, namely the need to negotiate a subsequent accommodation with the government of Quebec. It may have been appropriate to dispense with the consent of Quebec in 1982, but this omission would have to be remedied sooner or later through negotiations designed to bring Quebec 'back in' to the constitution. As we shall see, any such set of negotiations would be fraught with difficulties.

Getting Quebec to Sign

Any negotiations designed to bring Quebec 'back in' to the constitution would necessarily be highly complex, with profound negative consequences in the event of failure. At the same time, the subject-matter of the negotiations would make the achievement of a negotiated settlement extremely difficult. In short, the decision to proceed without Quebec in 1982 was a fateful one with important consequences for the long-term unity of the country.

It is possible to identify in fairly precise terms the obstacles and the risks associated with a 'Quebec round' of constitutional negotiations.

1. *The decision to commence a Quebec round would constitute an implicit admission by the rest of Canada that Quebec had suffered a 'wrong' in 1982.*

Inevitably, credence would be lent to nationalist claims that Quebec had been 'excluded' in 1982. The idea of a Quebec round is premised on the idea that Quebec needed to be brought 'back in' to the Canadian constitution following the 1982 constitutional amendment. As such, it constitutes an admission by the official Canadian authorities that Quebec had a legitimate constitutional grievance against the rest of the country that had to be settled. It also lends legitimacy to the Quebec government's decision to boycott all constitutional negotiations, pending a resolution of Quebec's demands. In short, by commencing a Quebec round, Canada is forced to 'buy in' to the Quebec nationalist interpretation of the events of 1982. That is precisely why Pierre Trudeau was so bitter about the decision to negotiate with Quebec, arguing that it required political leaders to 'flail around on the one battlefield where the Péquistes have the advantage: that of the nationalist bidding war.'[13]

2. *A Quebec round would increase the stakes in the negotiations and, in particular, the negative fallout in the event of failure.*

Canadians had been discussing the constitution on a fairly continuous basis for about sixty years. These negotiations had never succeeded in securing unanimous agreement on the terms of a comprehensive package to patriate the constitution. But there had never been any significant risks associated with failure in these negotiations. The discussions over the constitution were primarily of interest to governments and professionals, with average Canadians exhibiting scant interest in the proceedings or their outcome.

The ground rules for a Quebec round of negotiations would be totally different. Here, failure could simply not be tolerated. These negotiations would be conducted against the backdrop of Quebec's exclusion from the 1982 constitutional agreement. Quebec now had a recognized and 'legitimate' grievance against the rest of the country. A failure to achieve an agreement would mean that the rest of the country had refused or failed to provide redress for that grievance. Thus a failure in the negotiations would inevitably call into question Quebec's status in confederation. It would reinforce nationalist voices in Quebec claiming that Quebec's special character could not be nourished within the confines of the larger Canadian union.

Here, then, is the first unique feature of the Quebec round: it was imperative that the negotiations produce an agreement; failure to do so would risk creating significant political instability within the province of Quebec. The negotiations would have to be conducted in such a manner as to maximize the possibilities of success.

3. *There were contradictory ideas of the purpose of the negotiations. Within Quebec, the negotiations were seen as a response to Quebec's constitutional grievances flowing out of the 1982 patriation. The negotiations would be highly symbolic, centred around restoring the 'honour' of the province.*

Within Quebec, the legitimate grievances of the province flowing from the 1982 patriation of the constitution provided the rationale for the negotiations. The negotiations themselves would be almost a kind of morality play, structured around the idea of restoring the 'honour' and 'dignity' of Quebec. Quebec would be portrayed as the innocent and helpless partner in the relationship, having been betrayed in the night of the 'long knives.' The rest of Canada was cast in the role of the wrongdoer, having conspired to exclude Quebec in 1982. The morality play would centre on the question of whether the wrongdoer was prepared to made amends for the damage that had been inflicted.

The centrality of the idea of 'honour' in the public debate within Quebec was reflected from the very beginning of the process. Prime minister Brian Mulroney, in his famous Sept-Iles speech of August 1984, framed the issue in terms of Quebec accepting the 1982 constitution with 'honour and enthusiasm.'[14] Quebec's minister of intergovernmental affairs, Gil Rémillard, announced Quebec's 'five conditions' in a speech entitled 'Nothing Less than Quebec's Dignity Is at Stake in Future Constitutional Discussions.'[15] In the main body of the speech, after enunciating the five conditions, Rémillard summarized his presentation by noting that 'what we are asking for is the respect of the dignity and pride of the people of Quebec and respect of the province's historic rights.' This emphasis on considerations of honour and dignity ran very deep throughout these discussions in the province of Quebec, exemplified by Premier Bourassa's declaration in early 1990 that Quebec refused to re-enter Confederation 'on our knees.'

This symbolism associated with the negotiations made the achievement of a negotiated settlement much more difficult. It is well known that symbolic questions are difficult to resolve through negotiations. Such questions are not readily quantifiable or subject to division and bargaining compromise. Instead, they tend to be intangible and assume an 'all or nothing' quality.[16] Moreover, conflict over symbolic questions tends to be intense and out of all proportion to their material significance.[17] Symbolic questions assume this importance and visibility because they connote issues of recognition, honour, and the distribution of social status in society. Individuals and groups will vigorously resist any attempts to reduce their own social status or to increase the social rank of other competing groups. Because symbolic questions focus on the very identity or relative self-worth of social groups, they tend to provoke bitter confrontation and an unwillingness to entertain compromise. Such was to prove particularly to be the case in the Meech Lake discussions.

4. *Within Quebec, it would be crucial that the negotiations be seen as providing a remedy for the 'grievance' of 1982. The Quebec government would have to be seen to be 'obtaining redress' for the wrong suffered in 1982.*

That 'wrong' was the whole rationale for the negotiations. Thus, for the negotiations to be successful, Quebec political leaders must be seen to have obtained appropriate redress. In these matters, perceptions would constitute reality. Whether the negotiations produced any tangible gains for Quebec was less important than whether they were *seen* as having produced this result.

At the same time, the Quebec government was extremely sensitive to the risks of failure in the negotiations. Thus, the Quebec government had to walk a fine line in formulating its conditions for agreement to the 1982 constitution. On the one hand, the demands had to be substantive. Quebec had to be seen to be obtaining something of significance in return for its signature on the constitution. On the other hand, the demands had to be 'do-able' – there had to be the prospect of actually reaching general agreement based on Quebec's agenda.

This dynamic was to reduce very significantly the bargaining flexibility of the Quebec government throughout the negotiations. When the Quebec government announced its list of demands in 1986, that list appeared to be short and manageable. The set of five conditions was far shorter than similar sets of demands issued by previous Quebec governments over the past twenty-five years. For example, the list did not contain any significant transfer of legislative jurisdiction from the federal government to the provinces. But in order to justify the limited nature of the list, and to fend off the inevitable criticisms from the nationalist forces in the province, Quebec had to describe the proposals as 'minimum conditions.' The proposals were openly and consistently described as a final as opposed to a negotiating position.

The framing of the Quebec proposals as 'minimum conditions' was a critical turning-point in the process. This approach effectively determined the bargaining strategy of the Quebec government, both during the negotiations leading up to the agreement and during the debate over its ratification. In terms of the former, it was imperative that Quebec be able to claim that all of its five 'minimum conditions' had been satisfied. Thus any concessions or compromises that the Quebec government made could not be publicly acknowledged. Any agreement that was signed would have to be seen, within Quebec, as satisfying the conditions that had been established by the province. Furthermore, in the event that an agreement was signed, there would be little or no scope for Quebec political leaders to agree to subsequent modifications. Any further concessions after the signing of an agreement would represent a fatal 'backing down' and nullify the symbolic purpose of the negotiations – the restoration of the 'dignity' of the province of Quebec. In fact, within Quebec it was seen as preferable for Quebec leaders to simply allow a negotiated agreement to lapse rather than to make concessions in the hope of obtaining ratification. While non-ratification of an agreement would give rise to serious negative consequences, the down sides associated with 'amending' the agreement were arguably even more serious.

5. *Perceptions within English Canada were precisely the opposite of those in Quebec. There was little support for the idea that Quebec had been 'wronged' in 1982. There was also strong support for the Charter of Rights and the principle of the equality of the provinces.*

For Canadians outside of Quebec, the failure of Quebec to sign the 1982 constitution was attributed to the presence of separatists at the helm of the Quebec government. Thus, any concessions made to Quebec in return for its signature on the constitution would likely be seen as compensation for a grievance that had no basis. While English-Canadian political leaders were preparing to commence a 'Quebec round,' there was little broad-based public support for the exercise. Beneath the apparent apathy of English Canadians towards the constitution, there were distinct limits to the extent to which concessions made in favour of Quebec would be tolerated.

The flexibility of English-Canadian political leaders was further limited by an emerging political ideology in favour of the 'equality of the provinces.' If the idea of 'special status' had been the rallying cry of Quebec nationalists, the idea of provincial equality had been an equally powerful organizing principle for the rest of the country. Pierre Trudeau had resisted Quebec's claim for 'particular status' on the basis that it violated the essence of the federal principle itself. The idea that provincial equality was 'inherent' in the idea of federalism had taken root in western Canada in the mid-1970s and had been reflected in the constitutional settlement of 1982. By the mid-1980s, it had begun to approach conventional wisdom in Canada outside of the province of Quebec. These two images of the country – particular or special status, on the one hand, and provincial equality on the other – were obviously contradictory. Within the context of a 'Quebec round' these contradictory images of the country would come face to face. Somehow, it would be necessary to pay homage to each of these competing ideals simultaneously. Quebec provincial leaders could no more afford to deny the idea of Quebec's distinct identity than English-Canadian leaders could afford to abandon the idea of provincial equality. Yet, it was not clear whether it was possible to square the circle represented by these competing constitutional ideas.

A final element that further limited the flexibility of English-Canadian political leaders was the changing demographic make-up of the country. Prior to the Second World War, the Canadian population had been dominated by persons of either British or French descent. Thus the central task of political institutions was to reconcile the competing claims of these two so-called charter groups in Canadian society. But, in the years following 1945, Canada had become increasingly multicultural and multiracial as the British and French make-up of the population declined dramatically. By 1981, 'other' – non-British and non-French – outnumbered the French component of the population. Now nearly one-third of the population is neither British nor French. By the first half of the twenty-first century, 'other' could be the single largest element of Canada's population.[18] At the same time, aboriginal peoples had become increasingly visible politically, and they, too, challenged the traditional image of Canada as being comprised of two 'founding peoples.'

These social and political developments had profound implications for any attempt to reintegrate Quebec into the Canadian constitution. A 'Quebec round' would inevitably be structured around the axis of French-English relations. But there were important elements of the Canadian population that had developed a political allergy to activity organized along French-English lines. As such, the symbolism associated with a 'Quebec round' would be just as great outside Quebec as it was within the province. Inevitably the stakes in the negotiations would be increased, making them all the more difficult to resolve.

Stepping back and reflecting for a moment on all of these various obstacles, one is struck by the magnitude of the difficulties and risks associated with a Quebec round. In fact, the road-blocks are so numerous and the risks of failure so high that one is tempted to ask why the exercise was ever commenced in the first place. Surely it was irresponsible to launch a political exercise with such limited chances of success and such incalculable consequences for the country in the event of failure? Yet, as I have argued, the events of 1981–2 had made such an undertaking necessary. The time for pondering the risks and the consequences was 1981, when the decision to proceed over the objections of Quebec had been taken.

The difficulties outlined thus far are, unfortunately, only part of the story. The other legacy of the events of 1982 was a new amending formula that would govern all future attempts to after the constitution. The net effect of this amending formula, as we shall see, was to reduce dramatically the likelihood of securing a constitutional amendment that would meet Quebec's demands. The 1982 amending formula was inflexible and unwieldy. It made it significantly more difficult to amend the constitution, a fact that was profoundly to affect the Meech Lake round of negotiations.

Three elements of the 1982 amending formula were to prove of enormous significance to our story. The first was the requirement of unanimous provincial consent for a number of important constitutional amendments; the second was the three-year time-limit for certain constitutional amendments; the third was the requirement that constitutional amendments be ratified by provincial legislatures. I will examine in turn each of these factors and their implications for the Meech Lake negotiations.

The Requirement of Unanimous Consent

One of the most important elements structuring any set of negotiations is the level of consent required in order to reach agreement. Prior to 1982, the precise level required for a constitutional amendment had been a matter of protracted political and legal debate. The 1982 act settled the controversy by providing that, for certain amendments, unanimous provincial consent was required.

This requirement proved significant in 1986 when Quebec announced its five 'conditions' for consenting to the 1982 constitution. Under the rules established by the 1982 Constitution Act, at least two of Quebec's 'five conditions' required the consent of all ten provinces and the federal Houses. Thus any constitutional settlement of Quebec's demands would require unanimous consent of all eleven governments and legislatures.[19]

A decision-rule requiring unanimity is bound to produce quite different bargaining behaviour than is a rule requiring some lesser degree of consent. A unanimity requirement, because it gives each party a veto, tends to encourage inflexibility and an unwillingness to compromise one's preferred or optimal bargaining position. A province that refuses to compromise can do so with the certainty that the other parties to the negotiation are powerless to override its objections. Some lesser requirement of consent, by contrast, introduces an element of uncertainty into the negotiations. Under this decision-rule, no single province or even group of provinces can hold to their original or preferred position without the fear that some other coalition will be formed that will override their objections. Each party to the negotiation faces the risk that the need for its consent will be dispensed with entirely, with the result that its concerns will not be reflected at all in the final bargain. This uncertainty acts as a powerful incentive for *all* the participants to compromise and to seek common ground, thereby increasing the likelihood of a negotiated settlement.

A requirement of unanimity makes it more difficult to reach agreement for a second, related reason. Because each party has a veto on the outcome, there is a strong temptation to attempt to link the subject-matter of the negotiations to other unrelated matters. Any party to the negotiations can attempt to extract concessions on these other, unrelated matters in return for agreement on the particular issues under negotiation. It is obvious that any attempt to introduce extraneous matters into the negotiations significantly reduces the likelihood of a successful outcome. It multiplies the issues that need to be resolved and makes it less likely that an acceptable set of trade-offs can be constructed.

The crucial effect of these different decision-rules on bargaining behaviour is dramatically illustrated by the 1981 round of constitutional negotiations. The distinctive feature of these negotiations was that they began on the footing that unanimous provincial consent was required, followed by a period when only 'substantial consent' was thought necessary. After September 1981, the Supreme Court had determined that some undefined level of provincial consent was required, and this requirement was conventional only, as opposed to strictly 'legal.'[20] By comparing the behaviour of governments in the first period with that following the

Supreme Court's decision , we can obtain an important illustration of the crucial impact that decision-rules have on bargaining behaviour. Significantly, the bargaining behaviour of the provinces varied dramatically, depending on which decision-rule governed the negotiations.

Prior to September 1981, when the provinces maintained that unanimous consent was necessary, the eight provinces opposed to the federal government's proposals maintained a common front of opposition. Each member of the 'gang of eight' adhered strictly to a common set of demands and refused to entertain any compromise in its position. The other thing to observe about this initial period was the sheer number of items on the table. Because each province had a veto, the agenda had a tendency to expand to include the preferred items of each of the negotiating parties. There were, at various points in the negotiations, twelve items on the table for discussion. It is hardly surprising that an agenda of this size proved unmanageable and that the parties were unable to reach agreement.

Consider how this behaviour changed after the Supreme Court determined that only 'substantial consent' of the provinces was required. Now, no single province could maintain its opposition without fear of being the subject of an 'end-run.' At the November 1981 First Ministers' conference, the common front of provinces opposing the federal government's proposals essentially dissolved. The catalyst for this dissolution was apparently the decision by Quebec premier René Lévesque to endorse Prime Minister Trudeau's call for a referendum. This action brought home to the other provinces the vulnerability of their own positions and intensified the search for an acceptable compromise. In this context of mutual vulnerability, the number of items under discussion was suddenly reduced; the only issues remaining on the table were the Charter of Rights and the amending formula. The paring of the agenda to its essentials permitted the outlines of a possible compromise to emerge. The federal government would accept the main elements of the provincially sponsored amending formula in return for a pared-down Charter of Rights.

One of the unfortunate features of the Meech Lake round was that the Supreme Court would be unable to repeat its performance of riding to the rescue at the eleventh hour. The amending formula had now been settled, and it would require unanimous consent of the provinces in order to achieve a constitutional amendment based on Quebec's demands. This requirement would pose two very significant problems for the negotiations. First, because each province had an absolute veto, it could hold to its original position without any danger of being overridden. Second, because each province's concerns would have to be satisfied in order to reach an agreement, there was a threat of agenda overload. The agenda would tend to expand continually in order to encompass the particular idiosyncrasies of each province.

There was an acute awareness of these difficulties as the First Ministers began constitutional negotiations in the summer of 1986. A number of strategic decisions made in 1986 were designed to overcome the tendencies associated with a requirement of obtaining unanimous consent. In essence, it was agreed that a two-pronged approach would be necessary. The first prong of the strategy was to agree in advance that the agenda would be limited to a discrete number of issues. The second prong was the principle that anything given to one province would be given to all. As we shall see in the next chapter, this strategy more or less 'worked,' in the sense that it enabled governments to overcome the obstacles posed by the requirement of obtaining unanimous consent. It was problematic in that it gave rise to a whole series of second-order issues, making it more difficult to sell the agreement to the public.

The Three-Year Time-Limit

The parties to the accord proceeded on the footing that the agreement was subject to a three-year ratification period.[21] Again, this premise can be contrasted to that of the 1981–2 round, in which there was no formal time-limit for the ratification by the federal Houses and the Parliament at Westminster.

The paradoxical effect of the three-year ratification period was that the maximum would tend to become the minimum. Because of the extended period available for ratification, a number of governments proceeded at a rather leisurely pace before seeking legislative ratification of the accord. By the end of 1987, nearly seven months after the accord had been signed, it had been ratified by only three provinces – Quebec, Alberta, and Saskatchewan. Contrast this with the experience in 1981: there was no time-limit for ratification, yet the period between intergovernmental agreement and ratification was less than five months.[22]

There is an inverse relationship between the length of time required for ratification and the likelihood that an amendment will become law. The first and most obvious reason is that the passage of time brings with it the possibility that governments might change. Given the inherently adversarial relationship between governments and opposition parties in a parliamentary system of government, opposition parties who come to power will not necessarily want to carry forward with the constitutional projects of their predecessors.

But the passage of time decreases the likelihood of an amendment being ratified for a second, less direct reason. In any political situation, delay tends to favour the opponents of a measure. Delay provides the political opposition with the opportunity to mobilize support and to focus attention on the political costs of any proposed measure. Indeed, many political battles are won or lost on process questions rather than on the substantive merits, with opponents concentrating their fire on issues of timing. It is commonplace to defeat a proposal through the simple expedient of forcing a delay in its consideration.

In the Meech Lake round, delay clearly worked against the ratification of the accord. Within months of the agreement, two governments who were not parties to it had been elected and had evinced doubts about proceeding with ratification. More important, a broadly based and well-organized opposition to the accord had developed among women's go-ups, native organizations, and other 'rights-seeking' groups. While the accord initially enjoyed significant public support, by the end of 1987 public support for it began to drop like a stone. Clearly, time was on the side of the opponents of the accord. As the deadline of 23 June 1990 approached, certain commentators suggested that the deadline was 'artificial' and should be extended to permit more time for public debate. But, given the inverse relationship between delay and the successful ratification of a measure, such further delay would have been futile, only further eroding public and governmental support and eliminating the slim chances of the accord becoming law. Thus there was no attempt to extend the deadline for ratification for the simple reason that such an extension would have decreased rather than increased the chances of the accord's success.

The Requirement of Legislative Ratification

The 1982 amendment procedure entrenched a requirement of ratification by all legislatures for certain constitutional amendments. This requirement represented a very significant change from 1981–2. Even though the Supreme Court of Canada had declared that the 'substantial consent' of the provinces was required for fundamental constitutional change, such consent was to come from governments as opposed to legislatures. The only legislative resolution in the 1981–2 round was that approved by the federal Senate and House of Commons.

There were three principal effects flowing out of the requirement of legislative ratification, all of them tending to make ratification more difficult. The first and most obvious effect was delay; with eleven legislative resolutions required, the time period between intergovernmental agreement and final ratification would be much longer. Given the inverse relationship between delay and the prospects for ratification outlined above, this longer time period represented a significant additional hurdle. The second, related effect of requiring legislative approval was to increase the opportunities for opponents of the accord to block ratification. Opponents of the accord could attempt to take advantage of the various mechanisms that opposition parties possess to block government measures within the individual legislative processes. This tactic was particularly significant in Manitoba with the government in a minority situation after 26 April 1988. The minority government position in the province meant that any modifications in the accord designed to permit its ratification had to receive the support of at least one of the opposition parties, in addition to the provincial government. Nor would the support of the party leaders necessarily guarantee ratification, as the experience in Manitoba in June 1990 illustrated. The opposition of a single member, Elijah Harper, resulted in the accord's never even coming to a vote prior to the 23 June deadline.

The third effect flowing out of the requirement of legislative approval was more indirect but was arguably the most important. No mechanism currently exists to coordinate the decisions or the deliberations of individual legislatures. Yet, the amending formula requires each legislature to enact precisely identical constitutional resolutions. This requirement of identical resolutions from eleven different legislatures presented a coordination problem of very considerable proportions. Each legislature would consider a constitutional resolution in isolation, without any framework for coordinating its individual deliberations with those taking place in other provinces or between governments. The absence of an effective 'feedback loop' meant that, if each legislature was permitted to enact amendments on its own, it would prove impossible to ensure that identical resolutions were enacted by all eleven legislatures, and the process would be rendered unworkable.

The only mechanism or forum that provided an opportunity for trade-offs to be made between competing provincial positions was negotiations among First Ministers. These negotiations are typically designed to reach agreement on a formal legal text embodying a proposed constitutional amendment. Any such legal text will necessarily reflect a series of trade-offs, with the final wording representing a delicate balance between the competing positions of the various parties.

What it is crucial to remember is that even a relatively minor change in that wording will upset that balance and eliminate the consensus that formed the basis of the agreement in the first place. Thus even apparently minor changes will require a reopening of negotiations designed to take account of those changes.

A concrete example from the Meech Lake discussions will illustrate the crucial impact of even minor changes in legal wording. The communiqué of 30 April 1987 included a stipulation that the federal government would provide compensation to a province that did not participate in a shared-cost program in an area of exclusive provincial jurisdiction if the province undertook an initiative that was compatible with 'national objectives.' There was a good deal of criticism of this provision between the Meech Lake meeting and the Langevin meeting in June 1987, with critics suggesting that there should be greater precision regarding the meaning of 'national objectives.' This matter was extensively debated during the Langevin meeting, with the governments of Ontario and Manitoba insisting that the 'national objectives' had to be defined by the Parliament of Canada, rather than by the provincial governments. There was some resistance to this argument from the province of Quebec, which had been maintaining publicly that the 'national objectives' did not necessarily refer to the particular objectives associated with the shared-cost program that was under consideration.

The result of these discussions was that the final legal text was clarified to specify that the shared-cost program was to be 'established by the Parliament of Canada'; this wording implicitly recognized that the objectives of the program would be defined by the Parliament of Canada rather than by the provinces. The English version of the final legal text also added the word 'the' prior to 'national objectives,' reflecting the view that the objectives must be linked to the particular shared-cost program rather than to some more generic conception of 'national objectives.'

This wording reflected a clear compromise between the desire to ensure that the federal government had the responsibility for defining the national objectives, countered by a desire to ensure flexibility for provincial governments in implementing those objectives. The clause had been clarified to a considerable degree, but further attempts to clarify it were considered and found unacceptable by the government of Quebec at the Langevin meeting.[23]

It is, of course, possible to denounce this relatively modest change in wording as trivial or insufficient to deal with the public concerns that had been expressed. The fact remains, however, that this modest change in wording, in conjunction with various other modifications agreed to at the Langevin meeting, permitted all governments to support the accord. If the text were to be modified, even slightly, then the compromise that constituted the basis of the agreement would also be altered, and the intergovernmental consensus would cease to exist.

This understanding of the significance of the final wording of the constitutional resolution helps to explain why it was so difficult to provide an opportunity for individual legislatures to consider amendments. Any amendments by individual legislatures, even apparently relatively minor ones, would alter the delicate balance between competing interests reflected in the legal text. Moreover, there is no mechanism for permitting the amendments proposed by individual legislatures to form the basis for a new series of trade-offs that might give rise to a new consensus. Each legislature considers amendments on its own, in isolation from the legislatures and governments in other provinces. There is no forum or process whereby the concerns or objections of individual legislatures might be traded off against one another. The result is that opening the process to amendments by individual legislatures leads to an inevitable unravelling of any agreement, as individual legislatures enacted amendments that met the particular concerns of their constituents, without addressing the concerns or perspectives of residents elsewhere. There was no 'feedback loop' to permit the concerns or objections of individual provinces to be coordinated with one another so as to enable the successful ratification of an amendment.

There is one obvious way in which this coordination problem could be overcome. Legislatures could be asked to approve a single constitutional resolution that had been agreed to by governments on a 'take it or leave it' basis with no opportunity to consider even apparently minor amendments. This approach would no doubt create a whole series of subsidiary problems. Despite the legal requirement of eleven separate legislative votes on the constitutional resolution, there would be no meaningful opportunity to consider amendments, no matter how minor or narrow they might appear to be. Even in a parliamentary system of government with executive control of the legislature, there is normally some scope for the legislature to modify proposals from the government. The absence of any such discretion in the consideration of a constitutional resolution would create an exceptional situation that seemed an affront to normal democratic principles and procedure. There would be an obvious and very public contradiction between the apparent and the real power of legislatures, a contradiction that would tend to undermine the credibility of the process.

Despite these shortcomings, there was no other obvious way to overcome the lack of a 'feedback loop' between legislatives and governments. The 1982 rules for legislative ratification had created a process without providing a mechanism to ensure that it could function effectively. The Constitution Act of 1982 had established a formal legal role for individual legislators. But no provision had been made to link legislative deliberations with the earlier discussions between governments, or with the deliberations of other legislatures. The only place where trade-offs between competing positions could be made was through discussions between First Ministers.

The absence of an effective 'feedback loop' linking individual legislatures with each other or with other governments represents a serious design defect in the 1982 constitutional rules. The means chosen to remedy the defect – essentially to deny any meaningful role for legislatures – was to have the unintended consequence of undermining public support for the process and the substance of Meech Lake. Thus this particular feature of the 1982 amending formula was to play a crucial role in the story of how and why the accord was to fail.

Conclusion: The Genie in the Bottle

The constitutional settlement of 1982 was hailed by its author as creating a constitutional equilibrium 'set to last a thousand years.'[24] Yet the analysis in this chapter suggests that there is little basis for accepting this extravagant prediction. Far from creating a constitutional equilibrium, the 1982 constitution set in motion a dynamic that had the potential to call into question the very survival of Canada itself.

On the one hand, the decision to proceed over the objections of Quebec made it necessary to pursue negotiations designed to secure the consent of the provincial government to the new arrangements. These discussions would be risky and prone to failure. The negotiations were risky because failure to conclude an agreement once the issue had been reopened could result in significant political instability within Quebec. But they were also prone to failure, given the highly symbolic nature of the negotiations and the contradictory 'collective memory' of the events of 1982 within Quebec as opposed to the rest of Canada. At the same time, the amending formula included in the 1982 constitutional settlement made it all the more difficult to bring the negotiations to a successful conclusion.

The obstacles and the risks associated with the negotiations made it necessary to proceed with extreme caution and deliberation. The constitution was a 'genie in the bottle.' Through design or happenstance, the genie had remained in the bottle in the years immediately following 1982. Everyone knew that the decision to release the genie was a fateful one, since, once freed, it might never be contained again. There was, in reality, only one plan that had even a fair chance of succeeding. By the summer of 1986, the general elements of this plan had begun to come into focus. The time was right, or so it seemed, to uncork the bottle and put the plan into operation.

3

The Genie Is Let Out of the Bottle

By the spring of 1982, Canadians had clearly grown weary of politicians talking about the constitution. The official signing ceremony on Parliament Hill that April morning in 1982 was as much a calling of a truce as it was a proclamation of a proud new constitutional order. The Queen's signature on the new constitution meant that Canadians would be spared further speeches on a subject that appeared to many to combine the incomprehensible with the arcane. For most Canadians, the cessation of constitutional hostilities came none too soon. Canada was in the midst of a deep recession, and adding more clauses to the constitution would do little to help meet the next mortgage payment. Interest rates were at historic levels, approaching 20 per cent. Ordinary Canadians had never evinced any great fascination with the constitution, but whatever minimal interest they might once have possessed had clearly evaporated in the face of grim economic times.

The premiers returned to their provincial capitals to find the voters restless and unhappy over the time and energy that had been expended on debating constitutional niceties. Saskatchewan's Allan Blakeney was to learn firsthand of the sour mood of the voters that spring. The prairie premier called an April election, hoping to capitalize on the favourable national publicity associated with his leading role in the constitutional wars. Blakeney and his attorney general, Roy Romanow, had been leading figures in fashioning the compromise that led to the agreement at the November 1981 First Ministers' conference. Blakeney had also been a key player in ensuring that a clause protecting aboriginal rights was reinserted into the constitutional package following the November meeting. The voters, it seemed, were not impressed. Blakeney was rudely dismissed from office, with his caucus reduced to a seven-member rump in the provincial legislature. Even his storied attorney general, Roy Romanow, was washed away by the Tory tidal wave, defeated at the hands of a twenty-two-year-old political neophyte who worked part-time in her father's Petro-Canada service station. In the other provincial capitals, the premiers and their advisers pondered the results in Saskatchewan and concluded that it would be best if voters' memories of the constitution were allowed to fade a little. There were no other elections called in Canada that spring.

Even in the province of Quebec, where debates over the constitution are something approaching a national sport, there was a palpable sense that it was time to get on with other business. There had been half-hearted discussions between Ottawa and Quebec City between November 1981 and April 1982 in an effort to see whether some accommodation could be reached over the new constitutional package. Jean Chrétien and Roger Tassé, his deputy attorney general, had put together a set of proposals designed to meet some of Quebec's objections. But Chrétien and Tassé ran up against a brick wall in Quebec City. Lévesque and his constitutional lieutenant, Claude Morin, felt profoundly betrayed by the constitutional deal put together in the middle of the night at the November meeting. They were in no mood to entertain proposals from the very perpetrators of the constitutional crime.

Beneath the rage and sense of exclusion, there was more than a little disarray in the ranks of the Parti Québécois. At the party's December convention, the delegates were whipped up into a paroxysm of rage over the treachery of Ottawa and the anglophone premiers. They even gave a standing ovation to Jacques Rose, who had been convicted for the kidnapping and murder of former Liberal cabinet minister Pierre Laporte in October 1970. The convention also endorsed a resolution that stated that the next election would be fought directly on a platform of independence, with a victory for the Parti Québécois (PQ) providing a mandate for a declaration of sovereignty. But René Lévesque told the delegates that he could not support the resolution and that he might have to resign as leader if it were not modified. The party retreated lamely from the bold rhetoric of the December conclave, rescinding the sovereignty motion at a subsequent meeting in February 1982. For the first time, Lévesque and his party seemed to have lost their political footing. It was no longer clear exactly what the party and its leader really stood for.

Lévesque tried one last gambit in the courts. Recourse to the courts had worked for the provinces in 1981; the Supreme Court of Canada had declared that provincial consent was required before the federal proposals could proceed to Britain. The 1981 Court judgment was a bold exercise in constitutional statecraft, with the Court's intervention providing the catalyst for the political compromise reached in November. But, by 1982, the courts were in no mood to overturn a set of amendments that had been endorsed by the federal government and nine of the ten provinces. Lévesque asked the Quebec Court of Appeal to declare that there was a basic constitutional principle requiring Quebec's consent before the constitution could be patriated. In early April, just days before the Queen was to arrive on Canadian soil for the formal constitutional signing ceremony, the Quebec judges gave their answer. Quebec's consent was not required, the Court said, and the new constitution had full legal force within the province of Quebec. The Quebec government appealed to the Supreme Court of Canada but the deal was, by then, a *fait accompli*. The Supreme Court decision in December 1982 displayed none of the bold rhetoric or reasoning of its earlier decision and unanimously dismissed the Quebec government's appeal.

The provinces and Ottawa regrouped and settled in for a waiting game. It was understood by everyone that some attempt would have to be made to end Quebec's isolation. But neither the timing nor the players were right for such a delicate salvage operation. A First Ministers' meeting on the economy in early 1983 ended in acrimony and bitterness, with the prime minister announcing that there were to be no more First Ministers' conferences until further notice. The only remaining activity on the intergovernmental front was a series of conferences to discuss aboriginal rights, which had been mandated under the 1982 constitution. But Quebec attended these meetings merely as an observer and refused to play an active role in the discussions. Quebec's non-participation meant that the passage of an aboriginal amendment would be extremely difficult. It would be necessary to have the support of seven of the other nine provinces before such a constitutional amendment could be entrenched in the constitution. In the end, nothing much turned on Quebec's absence from the bargaining table, as significant differences remained between the position of most governments and that advanced by the aboriginal peoples. The final aboriginal conference in March 1987 ended with the parties farther apart than even before on the issue of aboriginal self-government.[1]

In the meantime, the Quebec government continued its symbolic campaign of protest against the new constitution. In addition to its boycott of constitutional discussions, the Lévesque government passed an order-in-council exercising what it termed its 'historic right of veto' to block the constitutional amendment. Quebec also began routinely inserting in all legislation an 'override' clause, taking advantage of a provision inserted at the request of the western premiers in 1981. Under the override, the Quebec government could exempt its legislation from certain sections of the Charter of Rights. But these gestures were a mere side-show, a form of constitutional shadow-boxing. In essence, all was quiet on the constitutional front. Canadians and their political leaders needed time to recover from the exhausting constitutional confrontations of the early 1980s. Moreover, given the personal animus between Pierre Trudeau and René Lévesque, it was clear that it would be futile and counter-productive to attempt to end Quebec's self-imposed isolation while both men remained on the scene.

The Changing of the Guard

Pierre Trudeau was the first to leave politics, following his celebrated walk in the snow on 29 February 1984. Even with Trudeau's departure, the constitutional issue remained largely dormant. During the federal election campaign in the summer of 1984, media attention was preoccupied with Brian Mulroney's 'you had a choice' scolding of then prime minister John Turner during the televised leaders' debate. But while the constitutional issue was essentially ignored by the media, Brian Mulroney served notice during the campaign that a Progressive Conservative government intended to stake out new constitutional territory. In an important speech delivered at Sept-Iles, Quebec, on 6 August, Mulroney set out the philosophy that would guide his government in its relations with the provinces.

Mulroney dealt first with the Quebec question. He committed his government to attempting to secure the consent of the Quebec National Assembly to the new Canadian constitution 'with honour and enthusiasm.' But Mulroney was studiously vague on the terms of any such reconciliation and tentative in suggesting a possible timetable. The constitutional question must be approached with great caution, warned Mulroney, because there is a risk of making things much worse rather than better. Mulroney promised only that 'the necessary dialogue will open at an opportune moment' and that it would proceed 'within the framework of Canadian federalism, with the legitimate government elected by Quebec.' No clues were offered as to what sorts of proposals Mulroney might be prepared to propose or support, or even whether the 'dialogue' would take place within the normal four-year mandate of a government.

The remainder of the speech dealt with Mulroney's approach to federal-provincial relations more generally. Here Mulroney was more precise in defining the approach that would be followed by a Progressive Conservative government. Mulroney promised a much more decentralist, provincially oriented approach from his government. Criticizing previous Liberal governments for attempting to 'usurp provincial jurisdiction,' he promised that his government would be guided by the principle of 'respect for provincial authority.' He rejected the Liberals' policy of offering the provinces federal money only if the provinces satisfied certain conditions. By attaching these conditions, Mulroney argued, the federal government was in effect dictating provincial priorities and policies in areas of exclusive provincial jurisdiction.

This was the classic provincial argument against the federal 'spending power.' It had been advanced vigorously by various provinces over the years, notably Quebec and Ontario, but never fully accepted by the federal government. Now, the future prime minister was signalling that he was prepared to embrace the provincial point of view on this important issue. Mulroney's speech thus represented an important signal of the provincialist, decentralist philosophy that would structure his policy approach towards the provinces. Mulroney would seek to 'replace the bias of confrontation with the bias of agreement' by granting greater autonomy to the provinces. Thus, although he provided no details on how he would strike a deal with Quebec, the overall direction was clear and unmistakable. Mulroney would seek to reintegrate Quebec by accommodating the traditional claims of the province for greater autonomy within Canadian federalism.

The Progressive Conservative sweep on 4 September was regarded, at least within Quebec, as an opportunity to reopen the constitutional question. Both the Parti Québécois government and the Quebec Liberals, now once again under the leadership of Robert Bourassa, set out to define what would be required in order to obtain their consent to the 1982 constitution. There was considerable grumbling within the ranks of the Parti Québécois over René Lévesque's apparent willingness to consider a reconciliation. Lévesque had already convinced the party to drop its sovereignty plank for the next provincial election. Now he was preparing to negotiate a 'surrender' to the hated Canada Act of 1982. This conciliatory attitude was too much to stomach for many nationalists in the party, and seven cabinet ministers, including Jacques Parizeau, resigned in protest during the fall of 1984. Lévesque was undeterred. He met Mulroney in December, and the two leaders talked of reopening negotiations over Quebec's place in the constitution. Lévesque promised to publicly announce in the new year Quebec's specific proposals for consenting to the Canadian constitution.

The Quebec government's proposals were made public with considerable fanfare in May 1985. Speaking on province-wide television from the stately 'Salon Rouge' of the Quebec National Assembly, Lévesque said that Mulroney's promise of reconciliation with Quebec had 'stirred much hope here and elsewhere.'[2] He put forward a list of twenty-two major 'proposals' for changes to adapt the 1982 Canada Act to meet Quebec's requirements. The proposals contemplated sweeping constitutional change and represented a recapitulation of Quebec's demands for greater powers over the previous twenty-five years. The proposals fell into two parts. The first, which Lévesque termed a non-negotiable 'precondition,' was the constitutional recognition of the 'existence of a people of Quebec.' The second part, which Lévesque termed the 'conditions of an accord,' specified a series of sweeping changes to the Charter of Rights and to the federal-provincial division of powers. Quebec proposed that it be exempted from most of the Charter of Rights; that it be granted new powers in the areas of immigration, family law, labour law, and international affairs; that the federal 'spending power' be limited, and grants to individuals and institutions in the area of culture and education be submitted for approval by Quebec; that Quebec participate in the appointment of the three Quebec judges to the Supreme Court of Canada while assuming exclusive authority over appointments to the Quebec superior courts.

It was a long and daunting shopping list. Senior Quebec officials who briefed reporters on the proposals indicated that they represented a 'bargaining position' and that the province was prepared to compromise on many of the proposals.[3] But there was no indication where the room for compromise might be found. Reaction elsewhere was decidedly lukewarm. Most commentators within English Canada rejected the proposals as 'separatist mischief.'[4] The *Toronto Star* concluded that the proposals were 'little more than a blueprint for incremental separatism, advanced by a government that has lost its political raison d'être.'[5] The Toronto *Globe and Mail* agreed, observing that the PQ proposals 'deny the value and legitimacy of Canada in Quebec, deny Quebec as part of Canada.'[6] In the other provincial capitals, many observers even questioned whether the proposals were intended to be taken seriously. After all, the argument went, the Lévesque government was in the fifth year of its mandate and was low in the polls. It was apparent that a new constitutional impasse would raise the sagging political fortunes of the Parti Québécois. Was it possible that there was a hidden agenda behind these proposals, one prompted by electoral considerations? Then, on 20 June, barely a month after unveiling the proposals, Lévesque announced that he was resigning as premier. Lévesque's resignation seemed to place the whole constitutional question into a kind of suspended animation. With the Parti Québécois now preoccupied with a leadership contest, and an election looming within months, it was clear that the constitution would have to remain on the back burner for a while longer.

While the Parti Québécois was rethinking its constitutional position, the Quebec Liberal party was preparing its own shopping list of proposed changes to the 1982 constitution. The Quebec Liberal party position, unveiled on 3 March 1985, was much more modest than that proposed by the Parti Québécois. There were, nevertheless, some similarities between the positions of the two provincial parties. Like the Parti Québécois, the Liberals sought the constitutional recognition of Quebec as a 'distinct society'; while the Quebec Liberals made no reference to the 'people of Quebec,' they did envisage that that constitution would recognize Quebec as the 'homeland of the francophone element of Canada's duality.'[7] The Liberals also proposed a greater role for Quebec in the selection and settlement of immigrants to the province, a role in the appointment of the three Quebec judges to the Supreme Court of Canada, and limits on the federal spending power. These proposals had been advanced by numerous Quebec governments over the years and came as no surprise.

All of these proposals were stated in fairly general terms, with rather limited commentary. But, when the Liberal proposals turned to the question of the amending formula, they launched into a spirited attack on what they characterized as the ineptitude of the PQ government. According to the Liberals, the PQ was to blame for the absence of a Quebec veto over constitutional amendments in the 1982 constitution. Quebec had implicitly abandoned its 'historic right of veto' by agreeing to the amending formula proposed by the 'gang of eight' in April 1981. Under this formula, each province would have a right to 'opt out' of a proposed constitutional amendment, but no single province would have the right to block the amendment outright. In *Mastering Our Future*, the Liberals drove home the point that this amending formula implicitly recognized the principle that Quebec was simply a province like the others, with no distinctive claim to approve or block constitutional amendments. This concession, according to the Liberals, had opened the way for the very amending formula enshrined in the 1982 Canada Act. Under this formula, important amendments could be made to central institutions such as the Senate and the Supreme Court without the consent of the province of Quebec. Further, even though Quebec was permitted to 'opt out' of amendments transferring powers to the federal government, its right to compensation was limited to amendments dealing with language and culture. *Mastering Our Future* argued that it would be 'difficult to make up the ground which had been lost' and claimed that only a party that was 'authentically federalist' would have the credibility to carry off the enterprise.[8] Of course, *Mastering Our Future* nominated the Liberal Party of Quebec as the only possible candidate for this task. The Liberals proposed that Quebec be granted a right of veto over changes to federal institutions such as the Supreme Court and the Senate, coupled with an expanded right to compensation in cases of amendments transferring jurisdiction to the federal government.

The list was relatively short, and the rhetoric was modest and distinctly conciliatory. Yet it was not at all clear that *Mastering Our Future* represented a successful basis for reintegrating Quebec into the constitutional family. Some of the proposals appeared to pose no real difficulty. But at least two of the five conditions – the question of the Quebec veto and the limitation of the federal spending power – were far from straightforward. The demand for a special Quebec veto seemed to contradict the principle of the equality of the provinces, a principle that was virtually non-negotiable in other parts of the country. As for the idea of imposing limits on the federal spending power, this matter had been debated unsuccessfully for more than twenty years. Even taking into account Brian Mulroney's moderate statements on this issue in his August 1984 Sept-Iles speech, it was not clear that a successful formula could be discovered now.

While these questions remained, there was no doubt that the Quebec Liberal party's list of proposals was as modest as any proposed by a major Quebec political party since the 1960s. The unofficial reaction in federal government circles was distinctly positive. The prime minister was careful not to offer any public comment that might be construed as an attempt to interfere in the upcoming Quebec provincial election campaign. But, on 1 August, 1985, the federal government signalled its intentions by quietly hiring Gil Rémillard as a special constitutional adviser to the minister of justice. Rémillard was, at the time, a politically unknown constitutional expert at Laval. But he had played a key role in shaping the Liberal proposals in *Mastering Our Future*, and his views on the constitution were well known to professionals in the field. In accepting the appointment, Rémillard was reported as saying that he and the federal government 'agree on fundamental principles.'[9] Rémillard's appointment was important not simply because it signalled the policy leanings of the federal government on the Quebec question, but because it provided unmistakable evidence of the very close personal ties that were being developed between the Mulroney government and the Quebec Liberal party. Rémillard's appointment seemed to indicate a blurring of the lines between the Mulroney Conservatives and the Bourassa Liberals. One of the authors of the Quebec Liberal party position on the constitution was now advising the prime minister of Canada on how to react to these very proposals.

Professor Rémillard was to find himself unable to complete his one-year contract with the federal government. On 29 September, Pierre Marc Johnson replaced René Lévesque as PQ leader and premier. Within weeks, he had set 2 December as the date for the long-awaited Quebec provincial election. Rémillard resigned from his position in Ottawa in order to stand as a candidate for the Liberals. When Robert Bourassa led his party to a majority government on 2 December, he appointed Rémillard to the key post of minister of international relations and Canadian intergovernmental affairs. Professor Rémillard had once again effortlessly hopped back over the fence, assuming the task of presenting Quebec's brief to his former colleagues and employers in Ottawa. The federal government's restrictions on 'post employment' activity apparently did not cover Rémillard's unique career path.

Still, there was reason to celebrate the return of the Bourassa Liberals to the seat of power in Quebec City. Robert Bourassa was a pragmatist rather than an ideologue. His agenda was economic development, not nationalist sabre-rattling. As his new twenty-seven-member government was sworn in in the 'Salon Rouge' of the National Assembly on 12 December 1985, Bourassa gave clear signals as to where his priorities lay. The new government was to be market-oriented and would reduce the role of the state in the lives of ordinary Quebeckers. Copying a page from Ronald Reagan's political textbook, Bourassa created a new portfolio of 'deregulation' and appointed an anglophone, Herbert Marx, to the post. Marx was also the first English-speaking Quebecker appointed as provincial justice minister in the twentieth century. In an important symbolic move, Bourassa reinstalled the red Canadian flag alongside Quebec's blue fleur-de-lis in the National Assembly. The audience at a news conference following the swearing-in burst into prolonged applause when Bourassa acknowledged that the Canadian flag was back to stay in the Assembly.

Bourassa claimed that the economy was the number-one priority for his business-oriented government. But Bourassa reiterated his desire to reach an accommodation over the 1982 constitution. He spoke in positive terms of the possibility of a reconciliation, promising that Quebec would become 'within the Canadian federation a major and dynamic partner on whom the other members can count.'[10] Bourassa met with Brian Mulroney on the day after his swearing-in as premier and suggested that a new deal might be negotiated within the first two years of his mandate.

So, a number of important hurdles blocking a reconciliation with Quebec had been removed. In both Ottawa and Quebec City, high principle had given way to pragmatic politics. Pierre Trudeau, the uncompromising and cerebral intellectual, had been succeeded by Brian Mulroney, a conciliator who had promised to 'respect provincial jurisdiction.' René

Lévesque and his nationalist colleagues had been replaced by Robert Bourassa, who came to office with an economic, market-oriented agenda. Bourassa could not afford to ignore the nationalists in his province. But neither were they his primary audience. Bourassa wanted to resolve the constitutional question, not because he had any inherent interest in the subject, but simply so that he could get on to other, more fundamental challenges. At the same time, the Quebec question could not be resolved by Quebec City and Ottawa alone. Certain of Quebec's demands, such as the proposal to restore the Quebec veto, required a change to the amending formula in the constitution. This change would require the consent of all ten provinces before it could be implemented. What was the constitutional climate in the other provincial capitals at the end of 1985?

The signals from the other provincial capitals were somewhat mixed. The most positive indications were from Ontario, where David Peterson's Liberals had come to power in June 1985, ending forty-two years of unbroken Tory rule in the province. Peterson, like Mulroney and Bourassa, had no overriding constitutional ideology. But he came to office with a deep commitment to ending Quebec's constitutional isolation. Quebec's absence from the constitutional table had to be resolved, Peterson believed, so that Canada could get on with the challenges associated with globalization and international competitiveness. Peterson also understood that Ontario would necessarily play a central role in fashioning the terms of a reconciliation. One of his first decisions as premier was to establish a permanent Ontario office in Quebec City and to appoint Don Stevenson, a veteran deputy minister and Quebec watcher, to head up the office. Stevenson would act as the premier's eyes and ears in Quebec City, ensuring that the lines of communication between the two capitals were kept clear and static-free. In December 1985, just two days after the Quebec election, Peterson and Bourassa met at the Beaver Club in Montreal for dinner. The new Quebec premier had not even had time to meet with the prime minister of Canada, yet here he was dining with the premier of Ontario. This initial meeting between the two newly minted central Canadian premiers was symbolic of the close personal and political ties that both men regarded as a precondition to success in the forthcoming constitutional discussions.

Peterson instructed his attorney general, Ian Scott, to assemble a team of constitutional advisers to prepare Ontario's position for the coming round of constitutional talks. Scott, himself one of Canada's leading constitutional counsels, recruited Professor Peter Hogg, the foremost English-Canadian constitutional scholar, along with Toronto lawyer Ian McGilp, a partner in Scott's former law firm. Hogg and McGilp joined a seasoned team of civil servants led by Gary Posen, the deputy minister of intergovernmental affairs. The premier's instructions were brief and to the point: Quebec's isolation had to be ended, but on terms that did not compromise or tamper with any of the fundamentals of Canadian federalism.

So, the indications coming out of Queen's Park in late 1985 and early 1986 were entirely positive. But elsewhere, there were some unknown quantities. The four western premiers – Bill Vander Zalm, Don Getty, Grant Devine, and Howard Pawley – were all newcomers to the constitutional discussions. No one could predict with any certainty how they might react to an attempt to reopen the constitutional file. Alberta was a particular question mark, given the growing popularity of Senate reform in the province. A legislative committee had held hearings in early 1985 and taken up a proposal for a 'Triple-E' Senate – one that would have equal representation from all the provinces, exercise effective powers, and be elected. In May 1985, the Alberta legislature adopted the committee's recommendations and the Triple-E Senate became the official policy of the Alberta government. The emerging political support for Senate reform in the West had the potential to derail any attempt to reintegrate Quebec. The most obvious problem was the clear link between the Triple-E Senate proposal and a commitment to the equality of the provinces. The idea of a Triple-E Senate was directly in conflict with Quebec's claims to recognition as a province with special roles and responsibilities within Canadian confederation. It was difficult to see how Quebec could agree to equal representation as one among ten provinces in a reformed Senate. If the western provinces insisted on agreement to a Triple-E Senate as the price of acceptance of Quebec's constitutional proposals, unanimous agreement was likely to prove elusive, or even impossible.

In Atlantic Canada, three of the four premiers were hold-overs from the patriation round. Premiers Hatfield and Buchanan were known quantities. Neither premier had any particular constitutional agenda of his own and both could be expected to support any proposals acceptable to both Ottawa and Quebec City. Likewise with Joe Ghiz, the newcomer among the Maritime premiers. The Harvard-educated Ghiz was a keen student of federal-provincial relations but, as premier of Canada's smallest province, had neither the political nor the economic weight to play a decisive role in the negotiations. Among the premiers in Atlantic Canada, only Brian Peckford was regarded as a potential wild card. Peckford was a veteran of the constitutional battles of the early 1980s, where he had played an important role in the negotiations leading to the compromise agreement in November 1981. Further, Peckford had shown himself to be a skilful and persistent advocate for increased provincial powers whenever the constitution came up for discussion. It was feared that he, like Alberta's Getty or BC's Vander Zalm, might come forward with his own shopping list of demands before he would agree to Quebec's proposals. The result would be a constitutional bidding war that would effectively rule out the possibility of a unanimous agreement on Quebec's proposals.

Despite these question marks, the changing of the political guard in Canada between 1984 and 1986 had significantly increased the possibilities for ending Quebec's constitutional isolation. In Ottawa and the two central Canadian provinces, the constitutional ideologues who had fuelled the constitutional debates of the early 1980s had given way to pragmatic politicians who were schooled in the art of political compromise. For Brian Mulroney, Robert Bourassa, and David Peterson, the constitution was merely a means to an end rather than an end in itself. The constitutional question needed to be resolved because it represented a distraction from the task of building a stronger Canada able to compete successfully on the world stage. All three men believed that the resolution of the Quebec question was profoundly in the national interest. There was a time when the personal commitment of the prime minister of Canada and the premiers of Canada's two largest provinces to a project meant that the project was assured of success. But the ground rules in the Canada of the mid-1980s had changed. The personal commitment of Mulroney, Bourassa, and Peterson was certainly a prerequisite to the success of the exercise. The question was whether they could persuade their colleagues in the other provincial capitals, as well as Canadians in general, of the merits of their case.

The Game Plan Emerges

By early 1986, there were signs that the time to attempt to deal with the Quebec question might well be at hand. But there were still voices of caution, in Ottawa as well as the provinces, pointing out the obstacles that remained in the way of an agreement. Veterans of previous intergovernmental negotiations were acutely aware of the difficulties associated with achieving unanimous consent on the constitution. Moreover, it was evident that the risks of failure were very high and that it would be folly to commence negotiations unless there was some reasonable assurance in advance of a successful outcome. What was needed was a carefully developed strategy that took into account the many obstacles and proposed a method for overcoming them.

Brian Mulroney looked to Senator Lowell Murray and to Norman

Spector to formulate such a game plan. Murray had been appointed to the Senate in 1979 by Joe Clark and had voted against the patriation resolution in 1981 because of Quebec's opposition. Murray had a strong personal commitment to ending Quebec's isolation and possessed political credibility on the issue. He also enjoyed the total confidence of the prime minister, despite the fact that Murray was at one time regarded as a loyalist of former Tory prime minister Joe Clark. Norman Spector was handpicked by Mulroney in early 1986 for the important post of secretary to the cabinet for federal-provincial relations. Spector had worked in Ontario and British Columbia, where he had served as deputy minister in the office of Premier Bill Bennett. He had also been a key constitutional adviser to Bennett during the patriation round in 1981. Spector was seen as somewhat of a 'provinces man,' someone who was comfortable with the decentralist philosophy of Mulroney's August 1984 Sept-Iles speech. Spector was also a shrewd strategist and tactician, an intergovernmental veteran who would know what had to be done to seal a deal, a hard-headed practitioner of *realpolitik* who would not wilt in the face of pressure or adversity.

By the summer of 1986, Murray and Spector had formulated a strategy they believed could lead to success. There was an important, if unspoken, assumption underlying the federal strategy, namely, that the main objective was securing the unanimous agreement of the provincial governments for Quebec's proposals. This was a reasonable assumption, given the experience of previous constitutional negotiations. In nearly sixty years of discussions on the constitution, there had never been unanimous provincial consent on the issue of Quebec's place within the federation. It was assumed that unanimous provincial consent would prove just as elusive this time around. But it was also assumed that, if provincial consent could be obtained, everything else would simply fall into place and the Quebec question would be satisfactorily resolved. Of course, later events were to reveal that this assumption stood on extremely shaky ground.

The Murray–Spector strategy consisted of the following four elements.[11]

1. *Limit the agenda.* Murray and Spector were well aware of the problems posed by the requirement of obtaining unanimous consent. Because everyone had a veto, there was a temptation for everyone to present his own particular list of demands before agreeing to anything. There was also the danger that additional items would continually be added to the agenda as the negotiations proceeded, as various parties saw an opportunity to extract concessions on these other matters in return for agreement

on the constitution. The result would be to create a downward spiral leading nowhere. It was crucial, therefore, that there be some type of agreement in advance that the agenda would be limited to the specific concerns identified by Quebec. Such a prior agreement would act as a check on the inevitable temptation continually to expand the agenda. It represented an essential precondition to a successful outcome.

2. *Do not commence formal negotiations until success could be assured.* The federal government was acutely aware of the dangers associated with a failure in the negotiations. They were also aware of the lack of flexibility that Quebec political leaders in particular were facing. It was evident that a highly visible series of formal negotiations would limit this flexibility even more and increase the prospects of failure.[12] It was concluded that the chances of success could be maximized and the risks of failure reduced if a series of informal 'pre-negotiations' were conducted in advance. These informal talks would be distinguished from formal negotiations in the sense that they would be focused on general principles rather than formal legal texts. They would be carried on privately, with little or no publicity. The discussions would be also be conducted at the senior political level rather than between officials. Senator Murray and Norman Spector would be personally responsible for the dossier, and they would hold talks with similarly placed counterparts in the provinces. There would be no extensive involvement of the bureaucracy at either the federal or the provincial level.

This way of proceeding would maximize whatever flexibility the various parties might possess. It would avoid a premature focus on constitutional texts before it had been determined whether there was a consensus on the fundamentals. It would also permit the parties to draw back from commencing actual negotiations in the event that it became apparent that agreement was unlikely. By testing the water in this informal, low-profile manner, it was believed that the risks associated with a failure in the talks would be reduced. Since there would not have been any actual 'negotiations,' governments would not have to acknowledge that there had been a failure. It would simply be maintained that the time for commencing formal negotiations was not yet at hand. An informal and low-profile series of discussions, even if unsuccessful, were unlikely to inflame nationalist opinion in Quebec or arouse any particular reaction in the rest of the country.

3. *The principle of the equality of provinces had to be maintained. Thus Quebec's demands would be met by generalizing the proposals so as to include the other*

provinces. This was a key operating principle throughout the discussions. The equality of the provinces had become a bedrock principle, particularly in the West, in the late 1970s and early 1980s. It had been constitutionally entrenched in the amending formula of 1982, which refused to grant a veto to any individual province and treated all provinces as formal equals. It was assumed from the beginning that any attempt to treat Quebec in a manner that was significantly different from that accorded the other provinces would be unacceptable. The only way to accommodate Quebec was to craft its proposals so that they applied to all the provinces rather than to Quebec alone. By generalizing the proposals in this way, the principle of provincial equality could be maintained. This strategy also seemed to maximize the possibility of achieving unanimous agreement. Under this approach, all the provinces would gain something and no one would lose anything. Even if certain provinces were not entirely happy with various parts of the package, or wanted further concessions, they were still better off to agree than to walk away from the table empty-handed.

4. *The federal government would act as a broker between Quebec and the other provinces, waiting until the end of the process before advancing its own proposals.* Previous constitutional negotiations had tended to involve multilateral meetings between officials, followed by ministerial meetings, culminating in a meeting of First Ministers. The federal government, as chair of the proceedings, would take the lead role of preparing a 'rolling text' that was supposed to summarize the elements of any emerging consensus. But the task of preparing such a 'rolling text' was a tricky undertaking. While the 'rolling text' was notionally designed to reflect an emerging consensus, the reality was that no such consensus actually existed. The absence of consensus was reflected by the need to continue the negotiations. Thus the 'rolling text' would normally reflect the federal government's own preferred approach, as opposed to the approach favoured by the other parties around the table.[13] Such was particularly the case during the constitutional negotiations of the early 1980s, in which the federal government under Pierre Trudeau had a very well-defined constitutional agenda. Within such a setting, the federal government would become the focus and the target for the interventions and the proposals of other governments. It became a difficult task during these years to find compromises between the competing positions.

The strategy employed in the Quebec round was quite different. The province of Quebec, rather than the federal government, would be the protagonist. Quebec would have the responsibility for preparing proposals and texts and discussing them with the other provinces. The federal government would play a facilitative role, acting as an 'honest broker' between Quebec and the remaining provinces. This role would allow the federal officials to gain the trust of their provincial counterparts and to gain a real understanding of what the 'bottom lines' of the various provinces were. The federal government would then be in a position to bring forward its own proposals at the end of the process and to sell these proposals as a genuine compromise.

The advantage of this approach was that it seemed to hold out the real prospect of achieving agreement. It was a strategy designed on the traditional 'elite accommodation' model of Canadian federal politics.[14] Under this approach, the assumption is that political élites are more likely to share views and to be more amenable to compromise, more realistic, and more moderate than their followers. This is the classic 'consociational' view, in which hierarchical élites sharing common values maintain harmony by keeping the potentially more conflictual memberships apart. It is an approach that has been applied with considerable frequency, albeit with limited success, in segmented societies in such countries as Canada, Belgium, and Switzerland.[15]

But there were problems with the strategy, some of them understood at the time, others apparent only much later. The overriding concern at the time remained the possible negative fallout from failure in the negotiations. While the strategy of conducting informal 'pre-negotiations' seemed to respond to this concern, there was still a widespread fear that any failure would inevitably inflame nationalist passions in Quebec. But the greatest shortcoming of the strategy was one that was little understood at the time. The strategy was premised on the assumption that a unanimous agreement among governments was all that was necessary to resolve Quebec's isolation. There was little appreciation at the time of the enormous complications that the requirement of legislative ratification had introduced into the process. Further, there was little understanding that the approach that had been adopted to facilitate an intergovernmental agreement would hobble the ratification efforts. The secrecy surrounding the informal negotiations made it difficult to demonstrate that real trade-offs had been made by all the parties, including Quebec, in order to achieve an agreement. But the greatest problem with the strategy was its consciously élitist design. The secrecy provided a convenient and very potent target for attack by the opponents of the accord, who could point to its undemocratic origins as reason to be suspicious of its contents. Moreover, the federal government's role as 'honest broker' would give rise to invidious comparisons of Brian Mulroney with his predecessor. It would give credibility to the claim that 'no one spoke for Canada' during the negotiations.

With the benefit of hindsight, it can be seen now that these were fatal flaws in the strategy. It is said that the problem with most generals is that their battle plans are typically designed to win the previous war, rather than the battle that presents itself. This is as good a description as any of the problems attending the federal government's strategy entering the Meech Lake round. The game plan was designed for an era in which the only players were the federal government and the provinces. Interest groups and the public at large were cast in the role of mere spectators to a game played by political leaders. Much later, as the realization that this plan had been based on a profound miscalculation began to sink it, it was too late to turn back. The deck had been cut and the cards dealt. The hand appeared to be a losing one, but there was nothing to do but play it out and see for sure.

At the Starting Line

The strategy had been settled and the players were in place in Ottawa and Quebec City. Still, as the spring of 1986 began to hint at summer, the question remained: how to begin? Robert Bourassa was eager to get under way. He believed that the negotiations had to be concluded, one way or the other, within the first two years of his mandate. Now, nearly six months had passed, and nothing had been done. The clock was ticking, and his precious window of opportunity on the constitution was threatening to close. In early March, he had made an important gesture in announcing that Quebec would no longer automatically exempt its laws from the Canadian charter. 'We have absolutely nothing against the Charter of Rights in Quebec,' noted Gil Rémillard in making the announcement. 'On the contrary,' he asserted, 'we want Quebecers to have the same protection of their fundamental rights as other Canadians.'[16] Like the decision to restore the Canadian flag to pride of place in the National Assembly, this announcement was symbolic of the Bourassa government's willingness to regard Quebeckers as Canadians. It was a sign of good faith, a promise of a new era in Quebec-Canada relations. Yet, despite these positive overtures, no one seemed sure how, exactly, to begin. The prime minister, speaking in Toronto in mid-April, offered platitudes but few details or a concrete timetable. 'We will not rest,' intoned Mulroney, 'until we have created the right conditions for the kind of agreement which would enable Quebec to give its full approval to the Canadian Constitution, with honour and enthusiasm.'[17]

In early May, the Quebec government decided it could not afford to wait any longer. An academic conference on the Quebec issue had been planned for 9–11 May at Mont Gabriel, a ski resort north of Montreal. The conference would bring together officials from governments across the country, along with prominent scholars, business leaders, and journalists with an interest in the constitution. Gil Rémillard had been scheduled to speak on Saturday night, at the conclusion of the meeting. Shortly before the event, the academic organizers were informed of a change in plans: the minister would now like to speak on Friday afternoon, in what was billed as a major address setting out Quebec's position on the constitution.

Rémillard's speech lived up to its advance billing. The minister set out the formal policy that the Quebec government would be following in the upcoming constitutional talks. He began by expressing mild frustration over the lack of concrete progress that had been made to date. Rémillard stressed that it was not up to Quebec alone to act and that 'our federal partners must not sit back idly' waiting for Quebec to make the first move. Rémillard also complained that the decision to patriate the constitution in 1982 had been 'a pretext for substantially modifying the Canadian Constitution without taking Quebec's historic rights into account.' He cautioned that no Quebec government, regardless of its political tendencies, could sign the Constitution Act 1982 in its current form.

But, in the remainder of his address, Rémillard's tone was moderate and conciliatory. He praised certain elements of the 1982 constitution, making special mention of the Charter of Rights, which he described as 'a document which we, as Quebecers and Canadians, can be proud of.' The Charter of Rights was a positive development since it would gradually give Quebeckers 'a new outlook on the respect of human rights.' He explained that the new government had ceased the practice of automatically exempting its laws from the charter since 'we do not have the right to take Quebecers hostage for the purposes of constitutional talks.' Later, Rémillard stressed that the election of the Bourassa government was evidence of Quebeckers' sense of 'belonging to the Canadian federation.' The new government, Rémillard promised, would be 'faithful to our federalist commitment.'

These words, written and delivered just five short years ago, have already acquired a somewhat antique quality. One no longer hears such pledges of allegiance to Canada being uttered by prominent Quebeckers. Indeed, in the latter stages of the Meech Lake debate, Bourassa and Rémillard were often urged by their colleagues outside Quebec to provide greater evidence of their commitment to Canada. A common complaint was that

Bourassa and Rémillard never evinced any pride in being Canadian. It was probably too much to expect such expressions of fealty to Canada in the supercharged political atmosphere prevailing in the spring of 1990. But this makes the words of Rémillard at Mont Gabriel in May 1986 all the more wondrous and memorable. Here was a Quebec politician, less than five years after the 'betrayal' of November 1981, asking for Quebec to resume its role as a major partner in the Canadian federation.

Rémillard had made it clear that the problem with the 1982 act was not with the Charter of Rights. Rather, Quebec's objections were founded on a number of other aspects of the constitution, which Rémillard described as contradicting Quebec's 'historic rights.' Rémillard specified five changes that would have to be made in the Canadian constitution in order to make it acceptable to the Quebec government. First, a prerequisite to successful talks was the explicit recognition of Quebec's unique character as a distinct society. This explicit recognition was necessary, according to Rémillard, in order to assure Quebeckers that their unique identity would not in any way be jeopardized. It would also be necessary to guarantee Quebec increased powers in immigration, as well as participation in appointing judges to the Supreme Court of Canada. Rémillard reiterated the traditional Quebec complaint against the use of the federal spending power, describing it as a 'sword of Damocles hanging menacingly over all planned policies of social, cultural or economic development.' Rémillard proposed that federal spending in areas of exclusive provincial jurisdiction be made subject to provincial approval. Finally, he noted that the current amending formula permitted important constitutional amendments affecting Quebec's interests to be made despite Quebec's objections. He argued that Quebec must be granted a right of veto over amendments affecting Quebec's interests.

There was nothing terribly surprising in the list. It was essentially a restatement of the five proposals originally set out in *Mastering Our Future*. Any differences between the two sets of proposals appeared minor and fairly nuanced. The partisan rhetoric denouncing the ineptitude of the PQ government, so prominent in *Mastering Our Future*, had been excised from Rémillard's speech. *Mastering Our Future* had also specified that the recognition of Quebec's distinct character should be contained in a preamble to the constitution. Rémillard's speech was silent as to how the distinct identity of Quebec ought to be recognized, other than to state that such recognition must be 'explicit.' Most of those in the audience at Mont Gabriel were familiar with *Mastering Our Future* and simply assumed that any clause dealing with the distinct identity of Quebec would be placed in a preamble to the constitution.

These five proposals were described by Rémillard as 'stipulations' for supporting the 1982 constitution. This was not a mere 'negotiating position.' The suggestion, although implicit, was that all five of the conditions would have to be met before Quebec could agree to the 1982 constitution. At the same time, there appeared to be a considerable measure of ambiguity, and therefore flexibility, in the precise terms of each of the conditions. Rémillard spoke generally of the need for 'increased powers in matters of immigration' without specifying the precise content or scope of those powers. Quebec demanded the right to 'participate in appointing judges to the Supreme Court of Canada,' but it was not clear what was meant by 'participation.' There had to be a 'limitation of the federal spending power' but Rémillard did not tie himself to any particular proposal or formula. What was most encouraging about the five conditions, therefore, was their extreme generality. Rémillard had managed to present a short list of demands, while at the same time avoiding a discussion of specifics. Thus the Quebec government could approach the negotiations with a measure of flexibility while, at the same time, insisting, for purposes of public consumption, that they had established 'minimum conditions.'

The reaction to Rémillard's speech among the sixty intergovernmental professionals at Mont Gabriel was uniformly positive.[18] Rémillard was praised for having pared his list of conditions to the bare minimum. At the same time, it was recognized that the Quebec government could not be seen to backtrack in the negotiations. Agreement on three or four items would be insufficient. At the conclusion of the negotiations, Quebec must be able to point to a satisfactory resolution of every one of its five conditions. It was also absolutely essential that the discussions be limited to the five items identified by Rémillard. If other governments sought to air their own grievances, the conference participants noted, the agenda would expand uncontrollably, and it would be impossible to negotiate an agreement. It was also emphasized that great damage would be done if talks began and then failed. It was suggested that an informal series of discussions take place behind closed doors before moving the talks to a public phase.

As for the five specific conditions identified by Rémillard, the consensus was that the list was modest, restrained, and manageable. Three of the items on the list – distinct society, immigration, and Supreme Court appointments – attracted almost no comment. Everyone thought that these three items could be resolved with relatively little fuss. The two stumbling-blocks, or so it seemed to the participants at Mont Gabriel, would be the demand for a Quebec veto and a limitation on the federal spending power. The 'veto' issue was seen as the most explosive and

troublesome on the list. It was widely recognized that a special veto for
Quebec alone on constitutional amendments was simply not in the cards.
The only way to deal with this demand was to generalize it. Quebec could
be given a veto only if all the other provinces were granted a similar right.
The result would be an expansion of the list of items that required the
unanimous consent of the provinces. This change, it was thought by the
conference participants, was not a 'radical' one, since the constitution
already contained a list of items that could be amended only with unanimous consent. The virtue of the approach was that it did not single out
Quebec for special 'favours' and treated all provinces on a similar basis.

These conclusions, arrived at after two days of debate in the relaxed
atmosphere of a ski resort in the Laurentians, represented a distilled
version of the federal government's own strategy for the talks. Limit the
agenda. Begin with informal, behind-the-scenes discussions. Accommodate Quebec by generalizing its demands so as to include all provinces,
thereby maintaining the principle of the equality of the provinces. A
broad consensus on this strategic approach was emerging among the
governmental advisers across the country. The question was whether their
political masters, the premiers, could be persuaded of the merits of this
strategic direction. The basic question that the premiers wanted answered
was: why now? The country seemed at peace that late spring of 1986. The
constitutional wars of the early 1980s had begun to fade from the country's collective memory. Why awaken old ghosts that will only frighten the
house guests and spoil the party?

In a sense, however, Rémillard's speech had pre-empted any remaining
reluctance among the premiers. Rémillard's speech was widely reported
in both the English and the French media. Premier Bourassa served
notice that he intended to raise the issue with his fellow premiers when
they met in Edmonton in August. By 'going public' with the issue, the
Quebeckers forced their colleagues in the rest of the country to react.
Silence or prevarication would now be interpreted as an unwillingness to
meet Quebec's demands. Bourassa and Rémillard had essentially forced
the constitutional issue onto the public agenda. On 2 June, Mulroney and
the ten premiers gathered in Ottawa to discuss the progress in trade
negotiations with the United States. But, Bourassa took advantage of the
occasion to serve notice that Quebec intended to pursue the constitutional issue. Bourassa indicated that he wanted to send a team of officials
on a cross-country tour of the other provincial capitals in order to 'explain' Quebec's proposals. The Quebec tour would be done on a quiet,
private basis, designed to gain an informal reaction to the Mont Gabriel
speech. Bourassa reassured the doubters in the room that this new road

show did not mean that formal constitutional discussions had actually been commenced. The decision on whether to commence actual negotiations would be made later, by the First Ministers themselves, once the chances of success could be measured more precisely. Any objections? It was hard to think of any. A low-profile tour by Quebec officials seemed a reasonable idea and a cautious, low-risk way to proceed.

The Quebec team toured the provinces and Ottawa in June and July 1986. Diane Wilhelmy, Quebec's bright and elegant deputy minister for intergovernmental affairs, was accompanied by Professor André Tremblay from the Université de Montréal and Jean-Claude Rivest, a former member of the Quebec National Assembly and Bourassa's constitutional adviser. No politicians were involved on either side. At each stop on the tour, the Quebeckers did most of the talking. They would explain the proposals Rémillard had announced at Mont Gabriel and ask for comments. The questions were restrained and polite. Perhaps the visitors could clarify that last point? How about the first paragraph on page ten of the speech – what was meant there? But no one was going to raise any hard questions or reveal concerns with Quebec's proposals. It was too early for any of that. The idea was simply to listen and to begin to make an assessment of what constituted the real bottom lines on either side. To object at this stage would seem impolite and somehow beside the point.

The Quebeckers thought that things were going exceedingly well. No one seemed to have any fundamental problems with the proposals. Everywhere they went, the reception seemed to be positive. Some of the Quebeckers began to joke that they ought to put their presentation on a video and simply send it around to their counterparts. No one was rejecting the Quebec approach out of hand. Yet, clearly, the reactions from the officials were a little too good to be believable. Publicly, a number of the premiers had already begun to raise questions about Quebec's five proposals. Most of the reservations were centred on the demand for a Quebec veto. 'I think the veto is going to have to go by the board,' said Newfoundland's Brian Peckford in early July. 'Juridical equality means we're all equal around the table and that none has any special privileges.'[19] Saskatchewan's Grant Devine, Manitoba's Howard Pawley, and Nova Scotia's John Buchanan also publicly opposed a Quebec veto, as did cabinet ministers in Alberta and British Columbia. Even Ontario's David Peterson conceded that he expected 'trouble' on the veto issue and predicted that it would be difficult to settle. Peterson also identified the question of limitations on the federal spending power as the other key area of potential disagreement.

The Quebec issue was to be a prime focus for discussions when the premiers gathered in Edmonton in early August. The decision on whether to proceed or to simply close the file would have to be made at that time. The premiers would be looking to Bourassa for his frank assessment of whether the timing was right. Bourassa had a lot to lose and little to win by reopening the constitutional question. If Bourassa displayed the slightest hestitation or doubt, the whole thing had to be called off. But Bourassa was buoyant and positive when he briefed his colleagues in Edmonton. He reported on the positive reactions his officials had received in the various provincial capitals during their recent tour. He noted the reservations that a number of premiers had expressed about granting Quebec a special constitutional veto. Bourassa understood why this might pose difficulties, and he suggested an alternative. Why not simply change the amending formula so as to require the consent of seven provinces with 75 per cent of the population for most constitutional amendments?[20] This approach would not grant any formal privilege or status for Quebec. But it would have the effect of granting Quebec a veto, since the province represented over 25 per cent of the Canadian population.

Bourassa reiterated what he had told his colleagues in Ottawa in June. The five conditions were a minimum for Quebec. He must receive something on each of the five points or face a fire-storm in his home province. The other premiers would have to agree to restrict the agenda to the five points he had identified. Other matters, such as Senate reform or property rights, would have to be dealt with later. But, Bourassa reasoned that there would never be a time more propitious than the present for attempting to resolve the constitutional question. He warned that the longer the issue of Quebec's status in confederation remained unresolved, the more difficult it would become. He was prepared to be flexible and to take into account the political realities facing each of the other premiers around the table. But he was convinced that a deal was possible within a reasonably short time-frame.

The discussion of the issue was unexpectedly short and uneventful. Some of the other premiers noted that they had constitutional grievances of their own. But they all recognized, as Ontario's David Peterson emphasized in his intervention, that these other issues could be resolved only after Quebec was back at the table. Without the participation of Quebec, constitutional reform was a dead letter. In any event, what was the down side in simply agreeing to talk about something? The main political risks were being shouldered by Bourassa; he, not the anglophone premiers, was the one who would pay the price of failure. The others could simply walk away if the negotiations turned sour. And so the ten premiers agreed in Edmonton that discussions should proceed on Quebec's five proposals. It was understood that the discussions would remain bilateral and informal. Bourassa was still wary of attracting too much public attention to the talks in the event that they failed. Gil Rémillard would tour the country and meet privately with his ministerial counterparts, offering a more precise idea of exactly what terms Quebec was seeking from the other provinces.

The annual closing ritual at premiers' conferences is the issuance of a formal communiqué. These documents are always the subject of intense haggling among government officials, who typically meet late into the night in order to fight over wording and punctuation. But the communiqués have no binding effect on anyone. Once the haggling is concluded, the communiqués are issued and then forgotten. There are filing cabinets in government offices across the country bulging with these unread documents, their main function being to serve as ammunition for next year's exercise in communiqué-writing. But the communiqué issued at the conclusion of the premiers' conference in August 1986 proved an exception to the rule. Styled the 'Edmonton Declaration,' it symbolized a sort of starter's pistol announcing to the country that the Quebec round had commenced. It purported to define the subject-matter of the coming negotiations. The wording of the communiqué was uncharacteristically brief, although its meaning not entirely free of doubt. 'The premiers unanimously agreed their top constitutional priority is to embark immediately upon a federal-provincial process, using Quebec's five proposals as a basis of discussion, to bring about Quebec's full and active participation in the Canadian federation,' it read. 'There was a consensus among the premiers that then they will pursue further constitutional discussions on matters raised by some provinces, which will include, amongst other items, Senate reform, fisheries, property rights, etc.'

The main message was that the resolution of Quebec's status was the number-one item under discussion. Getty had made sure that Senate reform was mentioned, Peckford had gotten fisheries included, Hatfield and Vander Zalm had their reference to property rights. But the Quebec issue was the 'top constitutional priority.' It was to be addressed 'immediately.' Beyond this basic point, the communiqué lapsed into characteristic ambiguity. What, precisely, had been agreed? What was going to happen next? The communiqué did not elaborate. There was to be a 'federal-provincial process, using Quebec's proposals as a basis of discussion.' There were no clues as to what the nature of this process might be. Nor, apparently, was it even necessary to describe the content of 'Quebec's proposals.'

Some have described the Edmonton Declaration as a landmark in the evolution of the Meech Lake Accord. In retrospect, this description appears vastly overblown. In practical terms, the negotiations over Quebec's five conditions had already commenced in June with the cross-country tour by Quebec officials. All that was decided in Edmonton was that this process should continue. Nor was the decision to treat Quebec as the 'top constitutional priority' necessarily earth-shattering. The declaration was not binding on anyone. If the negotiations seemed to be nearing an agreement, there would be nothing to stop any province from adding items to the agenda. This is, in fact, precisely what happened. When the time for actually making decisions was at hand, the Edmonton Declaration would be just words written on paper.

There was still little enthusiasm around the table for constitutional negotiations in the summer of 1986. But those who had the least enthusiasm for the talks were also those who thought they would go nowhere. There seemed little reason to get into a lather over negotiations that were likely to fail. Bourassa was keen to begin. He believed that a deal was possible. The only reasonable thing to do was to go along, or so it seemed at the time. Looking back on the events of that fateful summer, it is tempting to conclude that the decision to reopen the constitution was a monumental blunder. 'Waiting would have had advantages,' concludes Andrew Cohen in his recent book on the accord.[21] That much is obvious. But as the history of the period begins to be written, it is worth remembering, if only in a footnote, that Robert Bourassa was right back in 1986 when he sensed the elements of a deal. Canadian politicians had been discussing the constitution for more than sixty years without an agreement. Bourassa correctly understood that, for the first time, a unique convergence of events had made an agreement possible. What was not foreseen, neither by Bourassa nor by anyone else around the table that day in Edmonton, was that, in Canada, in the late 1980s, an agreement between governments would no longer prove sufficient to amend the country's constitution.

4

The Making of the Meech Lake Accord

In August 1986, the premiers had agreed to undertake a 'federal-provincial process' based on Quebec's constitutional proposals. But the issue was regarded as so delicate and the risks of failure so significant that there was still hestitation over formally launching the process. Everyone had one eye cast back over his or her shoulder, contemplating the risks of failure, even as the exercise was just getting under way. Quebec's Robert Bourassa decided that it would be prudent to conduct one more round of pre-negotiations before going public with 'formal negotiations.' He instructed his intergovernmental affairs minister, Gil Rémillard, to tour the provincial capitals and offer his counterparts a more precise idea of exactly what Quebec wanted in return for its signature on the constitution. Rémillard's tour would take place in October and November, prior to the annual First Ministers' conference scheduled for Vancouver on 20 November. Then, when the First Ministers met in Vancouver, they could discuss the issue over a private lunch. Bourassa could get a frank and reliable assessment from his colleagues of the chances for success. Bourassa would return home, ponder the matter, and decide in December whether formally to launch constitutional negotiations. If Bourassa determined it was a go, the plan was to hold a series of federal-provincial meetings in early 1987 to hammer out the specifics of a deal. These discussions would be capped in June 1987 by a First Ministers' conference that would approve the settlement.

That was how matters stood in the fall of 1986. As Rémillard made preparations for his cross-country tour, the climate and mood of the country still seemed relatively positive. In Ottawa, the Mulroney government was mired in mid-term scandals and languishing below 30 per cent in the public-opinion polls. But the federal government had managed to avoid any major fights with the provinces during the first two years of its mandate. Mulroney had dismantled the much-reviled National Energy

Policy of the former government, signing energy accords with the Altantic provinces and with Alberta. Free-trade negotiations were under way with the United States, and there were rumblings of opposition from at least three provinces, including David Peterson's Liberal government in Ontario. But the trade negotiations were still in their early stages and it was not at all clear that they were going anywhere. The prime minister had held regular briefings with the premiers to keep them up-to-date on the progress in the trade negotiations. The discussions were civilized, and the mood positive. Everyone was still singing from the hymnbook of federal-provincial harmony and talking the language of national reconciliation.

The first cracks in the wall began to appear in October 1986. The federal cabinet awarded a lucrative contract to repair the CF-18 fighter plane to a Quebec company, even though a Winnipeg company had made a lower bid. Manitobans were outraged. The West had chafed under the bit for decades as successive Liberal governments in Ottawa displayed what was perceived as unwarranted favouritism towards Quebec. When Mulroney was elected in 1984 with strong representation from the western provinces, it was thought that the days of buying Quebec votes with the tax dollars of western taxpayers had finally been brought to an end. The Mulroney government's decision on the CF-18 contract seemed to symbolize the fact that those hopes were mere illusions. It was almost as if the old style of Canadian pork-barrel politics, in which the West always came out on the short end of the stick, was somehow inherent in the system. No matter whom you elected, westerners complained, the contracts and the political favours would always manage to end up in the same place – central Canada. The CF-18 decision fuelled a sense in the West that more fundamental political reforms – such as a Triple-E Senate – were necessary if they were ever to get their fair share of the fruits of confederation. The wounded premier of Manitoba, Howard Pawley, railed against the treachery of Mulroney and the Progressive Conservatives and led a delegation of local business and labour leaders to Ottawa to demand redress. Everyone knew that there was little that Pawley could do to reverse the decision. But, like a baseball manager who is victimized by an umpire's bad call, Pawley had to protest loudly and visibly, if only for the consumption of the audience back home. The meeting between Mulroney and Pawley went nowhere. The premier was sent home essentially empty-handed, although he did extract some vague promises that Manitoba would receive favourable consideration in the awarding of any future federal contracts.

The CF-18 incident was the first sign of the inclement weather that was still just over the horizon of federal-provincial relations. The mood in the

West had soured, and there was now bad blood between Mulroney and the premier of Manitoba. Still, there did not seem any cause for alarm. No one was talking or thinking about the constitution. The 'Edmonton Declaration,' announcing the beginning of a 'Quebec round,' had gone largely unnoticed. The quiet, behind-the-scenes work of Rémillard and his team of officials could continue uninterrupted, free of the glare of media attention or the need to explain what was going on.

Rémillard and his officials came with specific proposals as they toured the provinces in the fall of 1986. They had reduced the general conditions outlined in Rémillard's Mont Gabriel speech to the form of a draft constitutional amendment. The Quebeckers provided the other provinces with a seven-part proposal for a constitutional amendment dealing with their concerns. But the Quebeckers were paralysed with fear that their draft proposals might leak to the press. They warned their provincial counterparts that, in the event of a leak, the proposals would instantly become a final offer. The moment the proposals were publicly known, any modifications would be seen as a fatal 'backing down' in the face of pressure from the rest of the country.

In order to guard against the possibility of leaks, and thus to preserve their flexibility in the negotiations, the Quebeckers refused to leave any copies of their seven-part proposal with the other provinces. Indeed, they even resisted handing out any copies of the document during the meetings. Instead, the Quebec officials would orally dictate the terms of the proposed amendments to their provincial counterparts on the other side of the table. The other officials in the room would take down the dictation, compare notes, and have the proposals typed up afterwards. It was agreed that the typed versions would not be identified as having originated with Quebec. The proposals would be identified only as a 'working document' without any indication of its author. At some point in the process the Quebeckers even took to referring to the 'working document' by the code name 'Homer,' an apparent reference to the unknown identity of the Greek author. The suggestion was that the author of the 'working document' was equally mysterious. The Quebeckers thought that this rather circuitous way of proceeding gave them an exit line in the event that copies of the 'working document' fell into the hands of the press. The Quebeckers would be able to say with a straight face and a clear conscience that they had never seen the 'working document' before, and that it must have orignated elsewhere.

In presenting their proposals, Rémillard and his officials stressed that the title 'working document' was to be taken quite literally. Their document was an initial draft only and was in no sense intended to be regarded as a final position. The Quebeckers assured the other provinces that they were prepared to be flexible and to compromise on the proposals they were advancing. They encouraged frank and constructive criticism. All that was necessary was that Quebec obtain something of significance on each of the five major conditions Rémillard had outlined in his May speech.

The Quebeckers' apparent flexibility was fortunate, since the texts Rémillard advanced in the fall of 1986 contained a number of surprises. They were certainly based on the five conditions Rémillard had announced earlier. But, in a number of important respects, they went significantly beyond what had been outlined as the official Liberal party position in *Mastering Our Future* in 1985.

The first problem was with the proposal for recognition of Quebec as a 'distinct society.' In Rémillard's May 1986 speech, he had not indicated what form this recognition ought to take in the constitution. Most observers, however, had assumed that Rémillard envisaged the reference to the 'distinct society' being included in a preamble to the constitution. This had been the position adopted by the Quebec Liberal party in *Mastering Our Future* in 1985. But this assumption was proved wrong. Rémillard and his officials proposed that there be a reference to the 'specific character of Quebec as a distinct society' in the main body of the constitution. This proposal was important, since placing the reference to the 'distinct society' in the main body of the constitution would tend to give the concept greater legal weight. In addition, Quebec proposed that the constitution recognize the 'fundamental duality of the Canadian federation' and the fact that Quebec was the 'main homeland of Canadian francophones.' Quebec also wanted the constitution to recognize that the province of Quebec was vested with a 'special responsibility to protect and promote its specific character and Canadian duality.'[1]

When Rémillard met with Ian Scott, Ontario's attorney general, in Toronto, on 20 October 1986, Quebec's proposals on this point sparked an extended, morning-long debate on their possible scope and implications. Scott was particularly concerned about the implications of the clause referring to the 'special responsibility' of Quebec. Was this intended to expand the legislative jurisdiction of the province of Quebec? Scott asked. Would it lead to a situation where Quebec would have powers greater than those of the other provinces? Rémillard and his officials indicated that this was not the intention. They assured Scott that this clause did not involve any grant of new powers to Quebec. The point was simply to confirm that Quebec's existing powers could be used to promote

Quebec's distinctiveness. It was intended as a declaration of political principle, not a grant of 'special status' to Quebec.

Scott also questioned the proposal to include the reference to the distinct character of Quebec in the main body of the constitution rather than in a preamble. Scott pointed out that the 1985 Quebec Liberal party platform had specified that this reference would be included in a preamble only. Rémillard conceded this point, but indicated that they had been forced to rethink their position in response to pressure from the opposition Parti Québécois. It seemed that Pierre Marc Johnson, the former premier and now leader of the opposition in Quebec, had heaped scorn on Rémillard following his Mont Gabriel speech. Johnson had pointed out that the 1982 constitution contained interpretive clauses that referred to multiculturalism and to the aboriginal peoples of Canada. These other references were contained in the main body of the constitution. Why, Johnson had asked in the National Assembly, was Rémillard prepared to relegate the province of Quebec, one of the two 'founding peoples,' to the second-class status of the preamble? Rémillard had sputtered out some vague answer during Question Period but had subsequently begun to reconsider the government's position on the point.

Rémillard told Scott that Quebec's 'bottom line' on the point had shifted, and it was now absolutely necessary to have a reference to the distinct society of Quebec in the main body of the constitution. But Rémillard insisted that there was no problem with his proposal. He stressed that all he was asking for was a mere interpretation clause, which, Rémillard argued, does not grant any new powers. It is simply used by the courts to interpret the existing powers of a province. As such, it has a modest and narrowly defined impact on the constitution. Rémillard also indicated that Quebec had given some thought to advancing a more radical proposal, namely, the inclusion of a clause that simply affirmed that Quebec was a distinct society. Such a clause would not have been framed as an interpretation clause. As such, it would have had the potential to grant new legislative powers to Quebec. Rémillard told Scott that Quebec had decided that this would have been asking for too much and that they were content with a mere interpretation clause. But, he insisted, this interpretation clause must be in the main body of the constitution, not the preamble.[2]

Other parts of Quebec's proposals were equally surprising and potentially troublesome. On the issue of the amending formula, Rémillard's speech at Mont Gabriel had stated that the 'historic Quebec veto' had to be restored. This issue had proved to be a stumbling-block over the summer of 1986, with as many as six provinces indicating that they were opposed to a special constitutional veto for any one province. Bourassa had recognized the difficulties and the sensitivities on the issue when he met with the premiers in Edmonton in the summer. At that time, Bourassa had put forward a proposal that did not single out Quebec for any particular or special treatment. Under Bourassa's proposal, the general amending formula would be changed to require the support of seven provinces representing 75 per cent of the Canadian population, along with the federal government.[3] Quebec's population at the time was just over 25 per cent of the total Canadian population. In order to protect Quebec on a permanent basis, Quebec's population would be 'deemed' always to be more than 25 per cent. Under this '7 and 75' proposal, Ontario would also enjoy an outright veto, by virtue of its population. No other single province even approached 25 per cent of the population. Thus, under this formula, Quebec and Ontario alone would gain an outright constitutional veto.

This was the proposal Rémillard carried with him on his travels in the fall. It was evident that it was unlikely to prove acceptable to the other provinces. Because it gave Ontario and Quebec alone a veto, it seemed to contradict the principle of the equality of the provinces. The 'deeming' provision, under which Quebec would always be regarded as having 25 per cent of the population, was also a sticking-point. It seemed to smack of separate and privileged treatment for the province of Quebec, something that even Bourassa recognized was simply unacceptable to a majority of the provinces.

Rémillard's Mont Gabriel speech had also proposed limitations on the use of the 'federal spending power.' Rémillard had not indicated in the speech exactly what he had in mind in this regard. However, *Mastering Our Future* in 1985 had indicated that Quebec's primary concern was with so-called shared-cost programs. Under these programs, the federal government offers to share the cost of a joint program to be administered by the provinces in an area of exclusive provincial jurisdiction. *Mastering Our Future* had stated that any such programs should not be undertaken without provincial consent. However, the Quebec Liberal party policy in 1985 had deliberately omitted any attempt to impose limits on other forms of federal spending in areas of provincial jurisdiction. This was an important concession, because it would have meant that direct federal transfers to individuals and to institutions would have been unconstrained. The only limitation would have been on programs that were to be administered jointly with the provinces, such as medicare and post-secondary education.

The proposals put forward by Quebec officials in the fall of 1986 went significantly beyond the position stated in *Mastering Our Future*. Rémillard proposed to limit any and all forms of federal spending in areas of exclusive provincial jurisdiction.[4] Moreover, the limits Rémillard was proposing were entirely oriented to the interests of the provinces. They provided no recognition of the important national interest in developing shared-cost programs and of the important role that these programs had played in the past. In the case of new shared-cost programs, Quebec proposed that each province receive 'fair compensation' in the event that it decided not to participate in the program. But the significant point was that there would be no obligation on a province to undertake a program of its own with the money it might receive. So, if the federal government initiated a new child-care program, for example, any province might decide not to go along, receive compensation, and then spend the money on roads. As for existing shared-cost programs, such as medicare or post-secondary education, Quebec proposed that these might continue, but that any changes would have to be agreed to by the provinces. Quebec also proposed to limit the ability of the federal government to transfer money directly to individuals. Such payments would be permitted only if they were carried out under the terms of an agreement with the province. Further, Quebec's definition of what constituted a 'payment' was so broad that it might even have included 'tax expenditures,' or tax concessions to individuals. Thus, if the federal government wanted to initiate a child-care program by granting tax breaks to families or individuals, it would have to obtain the consent of the provinces before proceeding.

These proposals amounted to a sweeping limitation on the ability of the federal government to spend federal tax dollars. If accepted, they would have significantly diminished the capacity of the national government to establish and implement national policy. The power to tax is of limited value if it is not accompanied by the power to spend. At the 20 October meeting in Toronto, Scott questioned Rémillard about Quebec's apparent reversal of position from that outlined in *Mastering Our Future* in 1985. Rémillard conceded the shift, but defended it on the basis that previous constitutional discussions dating back to the 1960s had considered limits on all forms of federal spending. Rémillard thought it appropriate to broaden the scope of the current discussions to match those that had taken place earlier. What Rémillard neglected to mention was that there had never been serious discussion of a proposal as comprehensive and restrictive as the one he was advancing in the fall of 1986.

There were fewer surprises from Rémillard's proposals on immigration and the Supreme Court of Canada. Under the existing constitution, immigration is an area of joint federal-provincial responsibility, but federal laws take precedence over provincial laws. In 1978, the federal government had entered into an agreement with Quebec (known as the Cullen-Couture Agreement) that gave Quebec control over the total number of immigrants to be received in Quebec annually and the actual selection of those immigrants. However, the Cullen-Couture Agreement did not apply to family- and refugee-category immigrants and, by the late 1980s, these two classes represented a majority of all immigrants to Canada. Further, because of the paramountcy of federal laws in this field, the 1978 agreement was subject to unilateral amendment or abrogation by the Parliament of Canada. In *Mastering Our Future*, Quebec had made it clear that the Cullen-Couture Agreement had become obsolete, and that Quebec's powers in immigration had to be considerably expanded. Rémillard tabled proposals in the fall of 1986 that would have accomplished this objective.[5] Rémillard proposed first that the constitution be amended to give Quebec paramount authority over the number of immigrants to be admitted to the province and the selection of those immigrants. Under Rémillard's proposals, the federal government would retain exclusive jurisdiction over general criteria of admissibility to Canada as a whole, but Quebec would have the power to choose which immigrants might be admitted to the province, including refugees and family-class immigrants. Quebec also sought exclusive jurisdiction over settlement services, such as job training, that are provided to immigrants upon entry to Canada.

The potential implications of these proposals were considerably narrowed by the Charter of Rights, which guarantees freedom of movement to all permanent residents. Section 6 of the charter guarantees the right 'to move to and take up residence in any province' and 'to pursue the gaining of a livelihood in any province.' This right is not subject to the 'override' provision in section 33 of the charter. The result is that, once immigrants become permanent residents, they acquire the right to move to the province of their choice. Quebec's proposals would have given the province considerable control over which immigrants might come directly into the province from outside the country. But Quebec would not have gained the right to limit movement into or out of the province from other parts of Canada, except in cases where the courts found the limitation to be justified under section 1 of the charter. In general, Quebec's proposals on immigration seemed workable and a basis for broad agreement.

On the Supreme Court of Canada, Rémillard proposed to entrench constitutionally the requirement that three of the nine judges come from Quebec. He also proposed that the chief-justiceship alternate, on a seven-year term, between the Quebec and the English-Canadian incumbents.

Finally, he suggested that the three Quebec judges be chosen by agreement between the prime minister of Canada and the premier of Quebec. In the event that an agreement could not be reached, Rémillard proposed a 'tie-breaking' mechanism. The two attorneys general and the Chief Justice of Quebec would form a 'college' and would select the person to be appointed.[6]

The main difficulty with the proposal was with the tie-breaking mechanism. Under Rémillard's proposal, the final say in the appointment of a Supreme Court judge would have gone to the Chief Justice of Quebec, who would preside over the 'college.' But it is difficult to justify vesting the final responsibility for judicial appointments to other judges. Judges are unaccountable and unelected. It is not part of their traditional responsibility to determine who is entitled to sit as a judge. At the 20 October meeting in Toronto, Ian Scott maintained that judicial appointments were a profoundly political matter. Scott argued that it was appropriate that the political authorities make such decisions and assume responsiblity for them. Scott's view was that it would be necessary to preserve ultimate political responsibility for judicial appointments in any proposal designed to meet Quebec's desire for participation in the process.

As Rémillard shopped his proposals around the various provinces over the fall of 1986, the reception was polite but restrained. At each stop on the tour, Rémillard would be told that his proposals were not necessarily beyond the realm of possibility. But each province had problems with some aspects of what Rémillard was proposing. The most consistent objection was that the proposals granted powers to Quebec that were not available to the other provinces. Quebec wanted to expand its power over immigration but not that of the other provinces. Quebec's right to participate in the nomination of Supreme Court judges would be entrenched, with no mention of the other provinces. Even the proposed amending formula treated Quebec differently from the others, by 'deeming' Quebec to have 25 per cent of the Canadian population. All of these proposals violated the principle of the equality of the provinces. Rémillard was told that the principle of provincial equality was non-negotiable. The other provinces could never accept a package that granted special powers to Quebec alone, since that would be tantamount to 'special status.' If the proposals were to fly, they would have to be framed so as to treat all provinces equally.

The reaction to the idea of referring to Quebec's distinct society in the main body of the constitution was mixed. No one was ruling the idea out in principle. But there were concerns raised about the implications of the proposals, particularly the reference to the 'special responsibilities' of

Quebec to preserve and promote its distinct character. There were also concerns raised by some of the smaller provinces, particularly Manitoba and Newfoundland, about Quebec's proposals on the spending power. These provinces depended heavily on federal spending to sustain comparable levels of services for their local residents and were wary of the broad-ranging restrictions Quebec was proposing.

Senator Murray initiated his own tour of the provinces, in order to get a frank and independent sounding of the provincial reaction. Murray did not present any proposals of his own – that was to come later, much later. For now, Murray and his deputy, Norman Spector, were content to listen and take notes. Each province explained its particular difficulties with the proposals Rémillard had tabled. Murray and Spector agreed that Quebec's proposals would clearly have to be modified before they could form the basis of a consensus. The question was whether the proposals were so 'off the wall' as to be not worth discussing further. No one was prepared to say that further discussion would not be worthwhile. There were clearly problems with the proposals but, perhaps, with suitable modifications, they might be worked into some acceptable form. Murray and Spector were encouraged by the reaction and the willingness to talk further. They began to imagine that it might actually be possible to fashion a consensus around Quebec's proposals.

As the First Ministers gathered in Vancouver for their annual conference on the economy in late November, the main item on the agenda was trade. Canadian exports of softwood lumber to the United States were being threatened by protectionist forces south of the border. The main focus of the conference would be an attempt to arrive at a common Canadian position on the softwood-lumber issue.

The constitutional issue did not even make it to the official agenda of the conference. The premiers and the prime minister were scheduled to discuss progress in the constitutional talks over a working lunch on the first day of the conference. Bourassa hoped to sense sufficient support finally to launch a formal series of negotiations on Quebec's proposals. The informal negotiations had continued for nearly six months, with two separate cross-country tours by the Quebec officials to gauge reactions having now been completed. So far, no one was asking any hard questions. But Bourassa knew that the time to fish or cut bait was fast approaching.

The discussion in Vancouver was surprisingly brief and general. Bourassa seemed to have trouble getting his colleagues to focus on the substance of his proposals. The premiers were preoccupied with the softwood-lumber issue, with David Peterson rejecting a proposal advanced by the federal government and British Columbia designed to mollify the protectionist forces in the United States. The constitutional issue seemed fairly remote and academic. The premiers thought that some progress was being made, but they told Bourassa that they wanted more time to study his proposals. The general reaction was noncommittal. No one was prepared to reject the proposals out of hand. At the same time, the premiers couldn't assure Bourassa that formal negotiations would lead to a successful outcome.

The official conference communiqué was appropriately oblique in its reference to the Quebec constitutional issue. It stated that the premiers were satisfied with the 'important progress towards a better understanding' of Quebec's proposals that had been achieved since the premiers' meeting in Edmonton. It said the talks should continue and that the contacts should be 'intensified and expanded in order to evaluate more fully the chances of success in eventual formal negotiations.' When might these 'eventual formal negotiations' actually begin? No one seemed to know for sure. The point to remember was that the 'formal negotiations' remained somewhere off in the future. For now, all that had been scheduled were 'talks' designed to gain an understanding of Quebec's demands and to evaluate the chances for success in the 'formal negotiations.' Such was the story line that the prime minister and the premiers hoped to maintain for a while longer.

It was anyone's guess how long the story line would hold. In substance, the 'formal negotiations' had already been under way for six months. Calling them 'talks' was a convenient fiction that permitted Robert Bourassa to avoid having to reveal any of the details of the negotiations. Bourassa, haunted by the risks of failure, insisted that this distinction between the 'pre-negotiations' and the 'formal negotiations' be maintained at all costs. Bourassa believed that, by proceeding in this way, the risks of inflaming Quebec public opinion in the event the negotiations went nowhere could be contained. But everyone understood that there was a limit on how long this convenient fiction might be maintained with any credibility.

The federal Liberal party convention in Ottawa in November confirmed Bouassa's views about the extreme political sensitivity of the issues at stake. The main item on the convention agenda was whether to call for a review of the leadership of John Turner. While Turner was fighting, successfully, against the leadership review, the Quebec constitutional question was also featured on the agenda. The federal Liberals were trying to settle on a response to the 'five conditions' Gil Rémillard had announced in his Mont Gabriel speech. But the debate over the issue revealed very deep divisions within the Liberal Party of Canada over the status of Quebec and over the legacy of former prime minister Pierre Trudeau.

Earlier in the fall, the Quebec wing of the party had proposed a resolution calling for the recognition of Quebec's 'distinct character as the principal homeland of francophones in Canada.' The Quebec wing had also proposed a change to the amending formula that would have enabled Quebec to opt out of any constitutional changes transferring powers to Ottawa and to receive financial compensation. But Trudeau loyalists, such as Montreal MP Donald Johnston, objected vehemently to these proposals. Johnston claimed that the description of Quebec as the 'principal homeland of francophones' contradicted the philosophy of Trudeau and would open the door to the creation of a French-speaking 'ghetto' in Quebec. He also objected to the proposed change in the amending formula, arguing that the party was about to embrace the very proposal put forward by former premier René Lévesque in 1981, but rejected by Trudeau. A show-down between Trudeau loyalists such as Johnston and supporters of current Liberal leader John Turner seemed imminent and unavoidable.

At the last minute, however, compromise wording was suggested that seemed to mollify all factions in the party. The amended resolution still called for the 'distinct character' of Quebec to be acknowledged in the preamble to the constitution. But, instead of referring to Quebec as the 'principal homeland of francophones,' the amended resolution described Quebec as the 'principal, but not exclusive source of the French language and culture in Canada.' The wording changes were subtle, substituting 'source' for 'homeland' and making reference to the fact that the French language and culture also had a basis outside of the province of Quebec. These modifications satisfied the Trudeau loyalists, but still preserved the reference to the distinct character of the province of Quebec, a key demand of Quebec Liberals such as Raymond Garneau. The proposal on the amending formula was also modified, with the party abandoning the idea of expanding the right to opt out of constitutional amendments. Instead, the party proposed to return to the 1971 'Victoria' amending formula, under which both Quebec and Ontario were granted vetos over all constitutional amendments. This formula met the demand for a Quebec veto without contradicting the Trudeau legacy. Of course, it directly contradicted the principle of the equality of the provinces. A number of the provinces had already indicated publicly that they would never accept an amending formula drafted along these lines. But, to Quebec Liberals, that didn't really seem overly important. The crucial thing was to maintain a united front and to avoid a fight on the floor of the convention in Ottawa.

The compromise wording was worked out at a meeting of the Quebec wing of the party in early November and was endorsed by a large majority at the full party convention in Ottawa. Still, the struggle within the Quebec wing of the Liberal party revealed the very deep divisions and emotions that the Quebec issue could spark among Canadians. Words such as 'distinct character' and 'homeland' were highly symbolic and politically charged. The Quebec wing of the party had managed to paper over their disagreements and maintain a show of unity for the television cameras at the convention. But getting unanimous agreement on these proposals from the provincial premiers would be another matter entirely. It was evident that any public debate over the Quebec issue would immediately spark deep divisions both within Quebec and across the rest of the country. The Quebec issue was like a huge bear that had been in hibernation for the winter. You knew that the bear would have to wake from its sleep sooner or later. When it did, you were certain to have a hungry and irritable animal on your hands and it would be a good idea if you had remembered to bring along breakfast.

The question for Quebec and the federal government coming out of the Vancouver First Ministers' conference was whether to continue the discussions or to call a halt now and try to limit the damage. Murray met with Ontario's Ian Scott, Roland Penner of Manitoba, and Rémillard in early December to take stock of the situation and to assess the prospects for success. Murray reviewed with each provincial minister the reactions he had encountered in his tour of the provinces over the fall. It was clear that the three sticking-points were distinct society, spending power, and amending formula. But were there ways to accommodate the objections and yet still satisfy Quebec? Murray thought there might be. On distinct society, it was clear that the clause would have to be framed in such a way as to not grant any special legislative powers to the province of Quebec. It would have to be made plain that the recognition of Quebec's distinctiveness did not alter the present division of powers between the federal government and the provinces. The ghost of 'special status' would have to be clearly exorcised from any draft amendment. It would also be necessary, Murray believed, for the reference to Quebec's distinctiveness to be balanced by a reference to the pan-Canadian linguistic duality of the country as a whole. By balancing the reference to Quebec's distinct society in this way, it would counter the suggestion that Quebec was exclusively French while the rest of the country was exclusively English.

What about the question of including the reference to Quebec's distinctiveness in the main body of the constitution as opposed to the preamble? Murray canvassed his provincial counterparts for their reaction to Quebec's newly stated 'bottom line' on the question. Ontario's Ian Scott, at his 4 December meeting with Senator Murray, indicated that he had no difficulty in principle with including an interpretive provision in the main body of the constitution. The important question, Scott indicated, is not where you put the clause, but what it says. A poorly drafted clause would create just as much mischief in the preamble as it would in the main body of the constitution. Scott argued that the debate over where the clause is placed was really a red herring, a distraction from the more important question of the manner in which the clause was actually worded.

Murray was encouraged by Scott's positive reaction on the distinct-society clause. On spending power, Murray indicated that the federal government itself was unwilling to accept limits on all forms of federal spending in areas of provincial jurisdiction. Murray indicated that the federal government was willing to consider only limits on shared-cost programs, such as medicare and post-secondary education, which directly involve the provinces. Other federal programs not involving the provinces directly had to be left untouched. This, Murray suggested, was the position that the Quebec Liberal party itself had argued for in 1985. A more narrowly framed proposal along these lines might serve as the basis for a general agreement. Murray hoped that the smaller provinces, such as Manitoba and Newfoundland, would accept an amendment that was more narrowly framed than Rémillard's original proposals had been.

As for the amending formula, Murray recognized that it would be impossible to get agreement on any formula that treated Quebec differently from the other provinces. Rémillard's proposals in the fall would have given Quebec a veto over all constitutional changes by altering the general amending formula so as to require the consent of seven provinces with 75 per cent of the population. Rémillard had also proposed that Quebec would be 'deemed' to always have at least 25 per cent of the population. By virtue of this 'deeming' provision, Quebec would have acquired a permanent veto on all constitutional changes. Murray indicated that Rémillard's proposal was clearly not going to be acceptable. It changed the existing general amending formula and abolished the right to 'opt out,' a right that had been won by the provinces in 1982. They were unlikely to want to make this important concession now. The other problem with Rémillard's proposal was that Quebec alone was included within the 'deeming' provision.

Murray argued that Quebec's concerns could be dealt with by a more narrowly focused amendment. The senator said that the general amending formula should be left untouched, requiring the consent of only seven provinces with a total of 50 per cent of the population. However, the right to 'opt out' of an amendment and receive compensation should be extended to all amendments limiting provincial powers.[7] With respect to changes to national institutions, such as the Senate and the Supreme Court, opting out was a logical impossibility. The answer to the difficulty, Murray suggested, was to raise the threshold of consent required for these changes to a level above 75 per cent of the population.[8] Thus the 'deeming' provision would become unnecessary and yet Quebec would be given a veto over national institutions based on its proportion of the population.

Ontario's Scott shared Murray's assessment of the difficulties and where the possibilities for a broader consensus might be found. The tough question was whether Quebec was willing to make the necessary modifications in its proposals. When Murray met with Rémillard in December, he offered his frank assessment of the objections that had emerged through the initial round of talks. Rémillard indicated that he had been hearing the same objections and understood the compromises that would be necessary. Murray asked Rémillard whether Quebec wished to continue the process or preferred to call it off now. Rémillard indicated that Quebec was still not ready to agree to launch formal negotiations, but they believed that enough progress had been made to warrant continuing the informal discussions for at least a while longer.

Senator Murray and Norman Spector reported to the prime minister on two separate occasions, just before Christmas and again on 17 January 1987. Their report was upbeat and optimistic. They noted that Rémillard had run into some difficulties in the initial round of discussions. But, they told Mulroney, none of the objections of the other provinces appeared insurmountable. Furthermore, the Quebeckers seemed realistic about the prospects for success and understood that some compromises would have to be made in order to get an agreement. Murray and Spector concluded that the differences were being narrowed, and the areas of consensus were broadening. They saw the elements of a deal beginning to come together.

Mulroney, Murray, and Spector concluded that the informal discussions should be stepped up. The question was how to move the discussions ahead without attracting too much attention. Another tour by Gil Rémillard seemed unlikely to achieve any concrete results. The question was whether it was time to bring representatives from all the provinces together in the same room. Perhaps a low-key meeting between officials from all provinces should be held so that everyone could assess individually the consensus that seemed to be emerging. The idea seemed a sound one. Murray and Spector were given the go-ahead to convene a meeting with all the provinces. In late January, the federal government passed on the word that a meeting of deputy ministers from all governments would be held to assess jointly the progress to date and to identify possible areas of consensus. Deputy ministers from all the provinces gathered in Ottawa on 5 March 1987 for a two-day working session, chaired by Norman Spector.

Spector began by setting out the federal government's views as to where a possible consensus seemed to be emerging. He made it clear that the operating principle was that all provinces would be treated equally. There would be no special powers or 'special status' for Quebec. He argued that there was broad agreement in principle on the constitutional recognition of Quebec's distinct society. Quebec's distinct character would be balanced by a reference to the linguistic duality of the country as a whole. Spector also suggested that there was a consensus on entrenching the requirement of three Quebec judges on the Supreme Court, as well as on some form of provincial involvement in the appointment of Supreme Court judges. On immigration, there would seem to be no problem with entrenching a new Ottawa-Quebec agreement that would update the 1978 Cullen-Couture Agreement. It would also be possible for other provinces to negotiate similar arrangements with Ottawa on immigration.

The main areas of continuing controversy, according to Spector, were the amending formula and the limitation of the federal spending power. On the amending formula, Spector said the main problem was how to grant Quebec a veto over changes to national institutions and the creation of new provinces without violating the principle of the equality of provinces. The answer, he suggested, was to raise the level of consent required for such changes, but under a general formula that did not single out Quebec for any form of special treatment. On the spending power, Spector made it clear that the discussion had now narrowed to the issue of shared-cost programs involving the provinces. But, he said, questions remained as to the degree to which provincial opting-out from such programs should be permitted and the extent to which compensation should be paid by Ottawa.

Spector wanted to keep the discussion at the level of principles, so there were no formal texts on the table. But even with the discussion limited to generalities, there were a number of serious objections raised to Quebec's proposals. British Columbia officials objected to Spector's characterization of a supposed consensus on the distinct-society clause. They were not yet willing to concede the idea that there should be a clause in the main body of the constitution referring to the distinct identity of Quebec. The

BC officials were concerned that this amounted to some form of 'special status' for the province of Quebec. They warned that the principle of the equality of the provinces could not, and would not, be compromised by their premier. The Quebeckers, in the meantime, were arguing with Spector over his proposals on immigration, another supposed area of consensus. The Quebeckers were concerned that merely entrenching a new immigration agreement in the constitution would not give Quebec the additional powers it needed in this field.

At the end of the two days of talks, the prevailing view among the provincial representatives was that the negotiations were going nowhere. There was still no breakthrough, no consensus on Quebec's proposals. Even the items that Spector had said were the subject of broad agreement still needed more work. Provincial officials returned to their capitals to brief their premiers on the outcome of the two days of talks. The reports were far from optimistic. By all accounts, there had still not been enough progress to justify launching 'formal negotiations' on the constitutional question. Alberta premier Don Getty, after being briefed by his officials, told reporters that 'there will have to be additional groundwork done by ministers and their officials both, but it's not time for First Ministers at all.'[9] Getty said that informal contacts between the provinces and Ottawa should continue for some time before any 'formal negotiations' should begin.

Then Robert Bourassa dropped his own little bombshell on the negotiations. A First Ministers' conference on aboriginal rights had been scheduled for 26 and 27 March in Ottawa. Although Quebec had indicated that it would not actively participate in the conference, it had been hoped that Bourassa would at least attend. That hope was reinforced by his categorical rejection of the Parti Québécois practice of boycotting federal-provincial conferences prior to the 1985 Quebec election. Bourassa had denounced the Parti Québécois policy as 'a futile attitude, detrimental ... to Quebec's best interests,' and suggested that 'we must rise above simply defensive reactions, and reject the idea that Canada is nothing more than a fruit to be squeezed dry.'[10] But days after the officials' meeting ended on 6 March, Bourassa indicated that he would boycott the upcoming aboriginal rights conference as a protest against the lack of progress in resolving Quebec's demands. A Quebec representative would attend the conference, but only in the capacity of an observer.

Bourassa's announcement of his personal boycott of the aboriginal conference was a shock to the system. In Ottawa, the officials in the federal bureaucracy scrambled to make sense of what was happening. The federal officials had remained optimistic that an agreement could be reached, even after the open disagreement at the 5–6 March meeting. Norman Spector had listened to the objections around the table and observed later that none of the obstacles he had heard appeared insuperable. He assured the prime minister that that there were 'technical solutions' to all of the objections that had been raised. He also suggested that some of the objections that had been voiced around the table were a reflection of the very ingrained and personal views of certain provincial officials. Spector's assessment was that these objections did not necessarily reflect the views held by the premiers themselves. He still thought that the elements of consensus were there on all five of Quebec's conditions.

Still, the Bourassa boycott announcement indicated that the talks were in danger of going off the rails, and soon. It was clear that Bourassa's own officials had reported that the March meeting had gone badly. Some quick and decisive response would be necessary to see whether a deal could be put together. Up to this point, the prime minister had maintained a healthy distance from the talks, leaving the informal discussions entirely to Senator Murray and Norman Spector. Mulroney had also studiously avoided any detailed comments on Quebec's proposals, other than to suggest that they were a plausible starting-point for the negotiations. Now, the prime minister decided that the time had come to involve himself personally in the discussions, thereby risking his own fortunes on the outcome. On 17 March, he sent a telegram to the premiers, inviting them to the government's retreat at Meech Lake on 30 April to discuss progress in the talks. The Mulroney telegram attempted to play down the significance of the 30 April meeting, suggesting that the sole purpose of getting together was to 'take stock of the progress already made and consider next steps.' Mulroney stressed in the House of Commons that afternoon that the meeting would not be the beginning of 'formal negotiations' but simply a meeting designed to assess whether such 'formal negotiations' ought to commence.

Privately, however, federal officials informed their provincial counterparts that the 30 April meeting would be a decisive step in the process. The meeting would attempt to achieve a consensus on basic principles for each of Quebec's proposals. Such principles would have to be precise enough that they could serve as instructions to officials so that the drafting process could begin. A positive outcome would be reflected in a communiqué setting out the general principles on which the consensus was based and announcing the agreement to launch formal negotiations. A multilateral meeting of officials would then be convened to begin the process of developing precise constitutional texts. But if the 30 April meeting failed to achieve consensus, the whole process would be immediately called to a halt.

Publicly, the prime minister attempted to downplay the significance of the 30 April meeting. Yet, it was self-evident that the decision to convene the premiers had changed dramatically the nature of the exercise and raised the stakes enormously. The previous nine months of quiet diplomacy and behind-the-scenes discussions had been carried on almost unnoticed. But Mulroney's decision to gather the premiers on the shores of Meech Lake meant that those days were over. The media, who swarm to First Ministers' meetings like bees to honey, would be out in full force at Meech Lake. They would dissect every aspect of the proceedings, devouring any hint of conflict or controversy between the premiers. The inevitable hunt for winners and losers, and for villains and heroes, would consume media accounts of the meeting. A failure to achieve agreement would be characterized as an 'impasse' or a 'deadlock' over Quebec's proposals. It was understood that, in the event of failure, Premier Bourassa would be obliged to hold a press conference on the spot and announce Quebec's response. At a minimum, it was expected that Bourassa would have to adopt a more nationalist and isolationist policy if the meeting failed to achieve agreement.

The prospects for success were difficult to predict with any certainty. Federal officials were upbeat and told their counterparts in the provinces that a deal was possible. But there were bad vibrations coming out of Alberta. Premier Don Getty's reaction to the prime minister's invitation to Meech Lake was hard-edged and combative. Getty reiterated his earlier stance that Alberta would not tolerate any proposal that would give special status under the constitution to Quebec. 'We wish to make very clear that there can be no special status for any province,' he told a news conference in Edmonton within minutes of receiving the prime minister's invitation. 'It is our fundamental position that Canada must be made up of ten provinces with equal status in all respects. There cannot be provinces with special status. There cannot be A and B provinces . . . This is not a bargainable position.'[11]

Getty was particularly critical of the federal New Democratic Party, which had agreed to a new policy on Quebec just the previous weekend in Montreal. The NDP's national convention had endorsed a resolution that proposed that the preamble to the constitution recognize Quebec as unique, being the one province with a French-speaking majority. The NDP resolution, presented to the convention by party leader Ed Broadbent, proposed that Quebec have a veto on constitutional changes to federal institutions such as the Supreme Court and the Senate. The NDP also wanted Quebec to be able to opt out of constitutional changes transferring provincial powers to the federal government and to receive financial compensation. Premier Getty condemned the NDP resolution in categorical terms, saying that it proposed to grant powers to Quebec that were not available to the other provinces. 'Just to get a vote, they're prepared to sell off the position of the other provinces,' Getty said. 'I think that's a disgraceful position, dictated out of Toronto or Ontario, I suppose. It is not something the people of Alberta would ever support.'[12]

Getty's strong language did not sound like the sentiments of a man preparing to make an accommodation with Quebec. The phone lines between the intergovernmental spies across the country began burning up, trying to get a fix on where Getty was heading. The sense was that Getty was coming under increasing pressure to get 'something' on Senate reform in return for his signature on an agreement with Quebec. Of course, the 'Edmonton Declaration' of the previous August had indicated that Senate reform would be dealt with only *after* Quebec's conditions had been resolved. But nine months is a long time in politics. The pressure for Senate reform in the West was growing. The fledgling Reform party was in the process of being founded, and a major plank on its platform was Senate reform.

The Albertans recognized that it would be unrealistic to expect there to be a comprehensive agreement on a fully reformed Senate immediately. But they began talking about obtaining some form of 'incentive' that would guarantee that the Senate would actually be reformed in the long run. It was not yet clear what form this 'incentive' might take. One suggestion that began circulating in March was an immediate moratorium on all future appointments to the Senate, pending meaningful Senate reform. The clear message coming out of Edmonton was that Getty was preparing to back away from the Edmonton Declaration and demand something on Senate reform at Meech Lake. At a party convention in the first week in April, Getty pledged to bring up Senate reform when the premiers met at Meech Lake. Getty told the party delegates that Senate reform must be on the agenda at the same time as any discussions about Quebec's constitutional aspirations. He claimed that his only leverage on the Senate issue was to link it to negotiations with Quebec, and he committed himself to making the linkage.

In Ottawa, federal officials recognized that the prime minister would have to play a leading and active role if an agreement was to emerge on 30 April. Mulroney spoke to each of the premiers by phone, and promised that he would commit to paper the details of concrete federal proposals on each of Quebec's five conditions. The federal proposals would set out where a consensus on each of Quebec's conditions might be achieved. These proposals would be sent to the premiers in advance of the Meech Lake meeting. Then, on 30 April, all eleven First Ministers would be in a position to come to a collective judgment as to whether a deal was possible.

First, however, there was the matter of the aboriginal rights conference on 26 and 27 March. This was the final First Ministers' conference on aboriginal matters required under the 1982 constitution. At the previous conference in 1985, the governments and the aboriginal organizations around the table had been very close to reaching agreement on the terms of a constitutional amendment. Three of the four national aboriginal organizations and at least five provinces had supported an approach that would have entrenched the general principle of aboriginal self-government in the constitution. The principle would then have been defined more precisely through agreements negotiated between governments and the aboriginal peoples. In the period since the 1985 conference, a series of ministerial-level meetings had been held with the aboriginal organizations in an attempt to narrow the differences and secure an amendment. All that was necessary was to secure the agreement of seven provinces representing 50 per cent of the population, so the Quebec boycott of the process was not necessarily fatal.

But over the two years of ministerial meetings, the differences around the table seemed to widen rather than narrow. By the time prime minister Mulroney called the conference to order in the Ottawa Conference Centre on 26 March 1987, the aboriginal organizations had hardened their position considerably. Now, none of the four national organizations was willing to accept the approach that had been discussed in 1985. They rejected the idea that the principle of aboriginal self-government should be made subject to the negotiation of subsequent agreements. Instead, they wanted a 'free-standing' right to self-government, one that would be directly enforceable in court, entrenched in the constitution. Only the government of Manitoba and, possibly, Nova Scotia indicated a willingness to accept this 'free-standing' right to self-government. The conference ended in failure. At the closing ceremonies, Georges Erasmus, national chief of the Assembly of First Nations, complained bitterly of the lack of 'political will' to deal with the native issue. Erasmus contrasted the constitutional negotiations over the native issue with the parallel talks that were continuing on Quebec's five conditions. Erasmus predicted that Quebec's demands would be successfully accommodated, simply because there was the political will to achieve an accommodation. He suggested that an agreement on Quebec's demands would be further evidence of the double standard that applied to native issues in Canada.

Erasmus's prediction of success at Meech Lake was the exception to the rule in early April 1987. Most public commentary on the upcoming Meech Lake meeting suggested that little was likely to happen. The conventional wisdom was that there was virtually no chance of securing an agreement. The one place where this pessimism did not prevail was in the prime minister's office in Ottawa. Mulroney and Senator Murray had drafted two separate letters to the premiers, reviewing the progress in the negotiations and suggesting where a consensus might be found on 30 April.

Mulroney's six-page letter to the premiers, dated 10 April 1987, set out the general approach he proposed to advance at the Meech Lake meeting. Mulroney indicated that his letter was intended to identify the main areas of consensus as well as the principal outstanding issues that would need to be addressed on 30 April. Mulroney also promised that Senator Murray would be providing a detailed federal proposal on each of the outstanding areas of disagreement prior to 30 April. Mulroney noted that the task of bringing Quebec back into the fold was a Canadian priority, since Quebec's absence from the constitutional process 'jeopardizes the capacity of Canada to adapt its constitutional and institutional framework to meet new challenges.' Mulroney also suggested that Quebec's isolation would become the more difficult to resolve the longer it was allowed to persist. Mulroney argued that the time was ripe to heal the wounds of the recent past, and that to leave the matter unresolved would mean it might have to be addressed 'in more difficult circumstances and less tranquil times.' The key issue, Mulroney wrote, was how to strike a balance between two competing principles. The first principle was the equality of the provinces; the second, the role of Quebec in protecting and enhancing the distinctiveness that the province brings to Canada.

The prime minister proceeded to identify the areas where there was 'broad agreement in principle.' Mulroney claimed that there was general consensus on constitutional recognition of Quebec's distinct society and of Canada's two major linguistic communities. Mulroney referred to the existence of French-speaking Canada, centred – but not exclusively so – in Quebec, and of English-speaking Canada, concentrated in the rest of the country, but present also in Quebec. This language, which prefigured the terms of Meech itself, was obviously a conscious attempt to track the Liberal party's resolution of the previous November. The prime minister also thought there was broad consensus on Quebec's demand for increased powers in the field of immigration and, in particular, the constitutional entrenchment of the Cullen-Couture immigration agreement. Mulroney made it clear that other provinces would be permitted to negotiate similar immigration agreements of their own. Mulroney also stated that there was consensus on the entrenchment of the requirement that at least three judges on the Supreme Court be from the Quebec bar.

The prime minister also identified the principal outstanding areas where consensus had not yet been achieved. The two problem areas remained the amending formula and the limitation of the federal spending power. On the amending formula, Mulroney made it clear that a special veto for Quebec was obviously a non-starter. The discussion should therefore focus around providing a full right to opt out of any constitutional amendment and to receive reasonable compensation. In cases where opting out was not possible, involving changes to federal institutions such as the Senate and the Supreme Court, Mulroney suggested that they would have to raise the threshold of agreement from the current level set out in section 42 of the constitution. But Mulroney did not suggest precisely what he had in mind as a solution to the problem.

In reference to the other problem area, the spending power, Mulroney indicated that it would be particularly important 'not to hobble the ability of the federal government to pursue positive economic and social measures and not threaten existing social and economic programs.' Mulroney indicated that two aspects of the issue would have to be examined: the circumstances in which provinces might opt out of national shared-cost programs and the extent to which they should receive compensation in cases where they had opted out. Once again, however, Mulroney did not suggest answers to the issues he had raised. Mulroney concluded by stating that he hoped to 'establish the basis for a successful resolution of this issue' at the 30 April meeting. If this were accomplished, he noted, it could lead to 'early and definitive action by Parliament and the legislative assemblies so that Canadians might turn their attention to other important constitutional questions.'

Mulroney's letter was followed five days later by a six-page letter from Senator Lowell Murray, setting out detailed federal proposals on each of the outstanding issues. Murray's letter was a key stage in the evolution of the Meech Lake Accord. The proposals Murray advanced on three of the five Quebec conditions – distinct society, immigration, and the Supreme Court – were to be adopted essentially unchanged at Meech Lake. His proposals on the other two of Quebec's conditions – amending formula and spending power – were modified, but not radically, by the First Ministers at Meech. In effect, Murray's 15 April letter is the first rough draft of the Meech Lake Accord itself. It merits close attention; by comparing Murray's language with the language of the accord, it is possible to identify the thinking and the concerns that went into the drafting of the agreement.

What Murray's letter also indicates is that the popular accounts of the accord, which have characterized the process as slipshod or haphazard, are simply factually incorrect. The First Ministers did not conceive the accord by scribbling on the corners of napkins as they ate lunch on the second floor of Willson House. Nor did they arrive at Willson House without a clear idea of what to expect. The concrete proposals that the federal government intended to put on the table had been circulated in advance and analysed by the First Ministers and their advisers. Each First Minister had had an opportunity to be briefed on any possible difficulties or objections that might be raised in relation to the federal proposals. When the eleven leaders emerged from Willson House on the evening of 30 April with a unanimous agreement, their consensus reflected very closely the language proposed by Senator Murray in his 15 April letter.

On distinct society, Murray proposed that there be a recognition of the 'distinctive nature of Quebec society as the principal though not exclusive centre of French-speaking Canadians,' and that 'a fundamental characteristic of the Canadian federation is the existence of French-speaking Canada, centred in but not limited to Quebec, and English-speaking Canada, concentrated in the rest of the country but also present in Quebec.' Murray also proposed a constitutional 'stipulation' that the Quebec National Assembly have a responsibility to preserve and promote its distinct identity, and that Parliament and the provincial legislatures have a responsibility to preserve and promote the two major linguistic communities.[13] Murray noted that this recognition would be in the form of a interpretation clause that would not alter the present distribution of powers between the federal and provincial governments.

On the Supreme Court of Canada, Murray proposed to entrench the requirement of at least three Quebec judges on the Supreme Court. He also proposed that, where a vacancy occurred on the Court, the federal government would appoint a person from a list of candidates submitted by the province from whose bar it was proposed to make an appointment. On the issue of immigration, Murray proposed that the constitution require the government of Canada to negotiate an immigration agreement appropriate to the needs of a province that so requests. Any such agreement would then be entrenched in the constitution. Murray also noted that any agreement would have to recognize the federal government's power to set national standards and objectives for immigration. Murray suggested that the first such agreement to be negotiated would be with the province of Quebec. This agreement would replace the Cullen-Couture Agreement of 1978 and would guarantee that, within the annual total established by the federal government for all of Canada, Quebec would receive a number of immigrants proportionate to its share of the population of Canada, with a right to exceed that figure by 5 per cent.

The Murray proposals on these three issues are incorporated, virtually unchanged, in the Meech Lake Accord itself. Murray's claim that a consensus had already emerged on these three issues is confirmed by the events of 30 April. When the First Ministers gathered at Meech Lake, they ratified an agreement on these issues that had been substantially worked out in advance.

The two remaining issues are more difficult, as Murray acknowledges in his letter. On the amending formula, Murray proposes to extend the right to receive compensation for a province 'opting out' of an amendment affecting its powers. The difficult remaining question is how to preserve a Quebec veto for changes to national institutions such as the Senate and Supreme Court without offending the principle of the equality of the provinces. Murray proposes that the level of consent for changes to these institutions be raised to seven provinces representing at least 80 per cent of the population. This stipulation would guarantee Quebec and Ontario vetoes over changes to these institutions, without making any special rule applicable to the province of Quebec.

Murray describes the issue of spending power as a 'difficult area,' noting that 'there is substantial concern that the ability of the federal government to pursue positive economic and social measures not be hobbled, and that existing programs not be threatened.' Murray proposes that any new shared-cost program in an area of exclusive provincial jurisdiction would have to be approved by at least seven provinces representing 50 per cent of the population. Murray also proposes that any province that 'opts out' of a shared-cost program dealing with 'education or other cultural institutions' would be entitled to reasonable compensation if the province established its own program consistent with national standards, 'it being understood that national standards are not to include regulations as to the administration of the program.'

Murray also proposed to entrench a second round of constitutional conferences. There would be a requirement to convene a constitutional conference in each of the succeeding five years, with the agenda to include: the functions and role of the Senate; the powers of the Senate; the method of selection of senators; the distribution of Senate seats; and fisheries and property rights.

Each of Murray's proposals on these points was changed, in some cases quite substantially, at the Meech Lake meeting. But the proposals contained in Murray's letter established the framework and the parameters for the discussion on 30 April. Further, it is important to pay careful attention to the precise nature of the changes made at Meech Lake. These changes represented a set of key compromises that made a unanimous agreement possible. Without these key compromises, it is certain that the meeting would have ended in failure, and the process would have come to an immediate halt.

Within days of dispatch of Murray's letter, the contents had been leaked to the press. Jeffrey Simpson's column in the *Globe and Mail* on 17 April contained an accurate summary of Murray's proposals to the premiers. Within a week, the leaks were so widespread and confusing that federal officials began holding 'off-the-record' briefings to clarify the details of what had been proposed in the supposedly confidential correspondence.[14] The publicity associated with the proposals forced the premiers to begin reacting publicly to what Ottawa had offered. The reaction from Quebec and Ontario was positive. Robert Bourassa indicated that he was 'modestly confident' about the chances for success at the Meech Lake meeting and indicated that the federal proposals represented clear progress in breaking up the constitutional log jam.[15] Bourassa also argued that Canada would be the main loser if the Meech Lake meeting failed to resolve Quebec's constitutional grievances. The free-trade talks with Washington made it important for Canada to be sure of its own identity. Bourassa suggested that 'Canada needs Quebec to reinforce its originality.' Ontario premier David Peterson was also supportive, indicating that he found the proposals realistic and an 'excellent basis for discussion.'[16] Peterson also argued that failure to achieve a consensus now would mean that Quebec would not enter the constitutional fold for many more years – if at all.

But the reaction from most of the other provinces was more negative. Most of the criticism centred on the federal proposals for the amending formula. A total of six provinces – the four western provinces along with Newfoundland and Nova Scotia – indicated publicly that Ottawa's proposal was unacceptable because it granted a veto for Ontario and Quebec alone. Saskatchewan premier Grant Devine summarized the view from these six provinces on the issue: 'If you want a veto, give us all a veto.'[17] At least two provinces, Newfoundland and Manitoba, also objected to the federal proposals on the spending power. Finally, Alberta premier Don Getty reiterated his earlier pledge to raise the issue of Senate reform at the Meech Lake meeting.

Federal officials had expected there to be some negative reaction to their proposals on the amending formula and the spending power. But the wild card was Senate reform. Getty had now publicly committed himself to raising the issue, which meant he could not afford to return to Alberta empty-handed. The question was what it would take to satisfy him. Murray and Spector flew out to Medicine Hat on 21 April to meet with Alberta intergovernmental affairs minister Jim Horsman and his officials. Their mission was to determine what proposals Alberta was likely to put on the table at Meech Lake. The Albertans were reluctant to lay their cards on the table in advance of the meeting. They confirmed, however, that Getty was likely to demand some form of guarantee of future Senate reform in return for agreement to Quebec's conditions. The guarantee would likely take the form of an immediate change in the way senators were appointed, as a kind of 'down-payment' on comprehensive reform of the Upper Chamber.

When Murray and Spector returned to Ottawa, they recognized that Getty might well scuttle the talks with his demands on the Senate. From the very beginning, their strategy had been premised on the assumption that the agenda had to be limited to the five items identified by Quebec. The moment the agenda was opened up, the whole exercise threatened to become unmanageable as each province brought forward its own series of constitutional demands. External affairs minister Joe Clark was dispatched to Alberta to warn Getty to honour his promise to deal with Quebec's constitutional demands as a priority matter.[18] Speaking at a PC policy conference in Camrose on 25 April Clark questioned whether the so-called Triple-E Senate, which was quickly gathering political steam in Alberta, was even workable. He argued that the Triple-E Senate could lead to a situation of deadlock between the House of Commons and the Senate. Mentioning Premier Getty by name six times in his fifteen-minute address, Clark argued that Quebec had to be brought back in to the constitutional fold before the difficult question of Senate reform could be resolved. At the same time, Clark indicated that the federal government was not proposing to grant any special or unique privileges to the province of Quebec. Anything offered to Quebec would be offered to the other provinces, Clark promised. Deputy prime minister Don Mazankowski was in the audience, and he told reporters that Clark's speech was 'setting the record straight about the process that was agreed to' by the premiers in Edmonton the previous August.[19]

In the meantime, Ontario premier David Peterson dispatched his attorney general, Ian Scott, to Quebec City for a last-minute consultation with Gil Rémillard. Scott was then to travel to Ottawa for a private dinner with

Senator Murray and Norman Spector to brief the federal team about the mood in Quebec City. Scott flew to Quebec City on 27 April for lunch with Rémillard and his senior officials. Scott had expected a fairly positive reaction from the Quebeckers to the federal proposals, given the favourable comments reported from Robert Bourassa. But Rémillard was cautious and began criticizing certain aspects of Senator Murray's 15 April letter. Rémillard was particularly concerned about Murray's proposals on the spending power. Rémillard said the proposed right to opt out of shared-cost programs was too narrow. Murray's letter had referred to a right to opt out of a shared-cost program in the areas of education and cultural matters. Rémillard said this restriction was unacceptable and that the right to opt out should extend to any shared-cost program in provincial jurisdiction. Further, Rémillard did not like the fact that an 'opted-out' province would have to meet federal standards in order to qualify for compensation. He objected to the use of the word 'standards,' arguing that the language should be loosened to permit greater flexibility in the design of the provincial program.

As Scott flew to Ottawa that evening for his dinner with Murray and Spector, he was discouraged by the reaction from the Quebeckers. Scott knew that a number of the provinces, including Manitoba and Newfoundland, thought the federal government had already gone too far in permitting provinces to opt out of federal programs. Now Quebec was arguing that the right to opt out did not go far enough. Scott briefed Murray and Spector over dinner in Ottawa. Scott reported that the Quebeckers were not satisfied with the federal proposals on the spending power. He speculated whether the gap between Quebec's position and that of Manitoba and Newfoundland might well be too great to be bridged. But Murray and Spector were upbeat about the prospects for success. Murray told Scott that the prime minister had talked to all the premiers over the weekend and that the elements of a general consensus were clearly present. Murray discounted Rémillard's negative comments, claiming that the federal proposals were very close to what the Quebec Liberal party had proposed in *Mastering Our Future*. The question for Quebec, Murray argued, was whether they were willing to say yes to their own proposals.

The discussion turned to the question of the amending formula and, in particular, how to secure a veto for Quebec without offending the principle of the equality of the provinces. Murray and Spector indicated that the federal proposal contained in Murray's letter of 15 April was clearly not going to fly. Six provinces had indicated that they were unwilling to accept a formula that gave a veto to Ontario and Quebec alone. The only way to square the circle, in Murray and Spector's opinion, was to give a veto to all provinces over changes to national institutions. This approach would achieve the initial goal – a veto to Quebec – but ensure that all provinces were treated equally. The problem was how this proposal would affect Don Getty and his campaign for Senate reform. Under the revised federal proposal Mulroney would table at the meeting, Senate reform would be made more difficult. Instead of requiring the support of seven provinces, unanimous consent would be required, giving further impetus to Don Getty's pledge that he had to obtain something meaningful on Senate reform now, rather than wait for a second round in which agreement would prove more elusive. The question was what was it going to take to satisfy Getty.

The answer to this question was to come two days later on the eve of the gathering of First Ministers. By late on Wednesday, 29 April, most of the premiers and their advisers had gathered in Ottawa and were preparing for the meeting. Word began circulating of a new Alberta proposal on appointments to the Senate. Alberta would ask that the provinces be granted the immediate right to directly appoint half of all the senators, pending full reform of the Upper Chamber. This was Getty's down-payment. If the provinces had the right to appoint senators directly, the federal government would have an important incentive to move fast on Senate reform. The longer the Senate remained in its current form, the larger the number of provincial government appointees in the Upper Chamber. Of course, the Senate would retain its full legal powers to block legislation from the Commons. Thus, with the passage of time, the government would gradually become subject to the influence and control of appointees of the provinces. Getty saw his proposal as a way to sharpen the interest in Senate reform in Ottawa officialdom. The fact that the provinces would also be granted an important new source of patronage in the meantime certainly did nothing to diminish the attractiveness of the proposal.

The meeting on 30 April was to begin late in the morning. Ontario's David Peterson gathered his advisers for a final briefing at his Ottawa hotel before heading across the river to Meech Lake. The focus of discussion was the Getty proposal for appointments to the Senate. Many of Peterson's advisers were uncomfortable with Getty's proposal. It would strip Ottawa of the ability to control the Upper Chamber and undermine the principle of responsible government. But there was an obvious counter-proposal that seemed more workable. The federal government had already proposed to appoint Supreme Court judges from lists of candidates submitted by the provinces. Why not apply the same idea to the Senate? This would give Getty and the other provinces a role in Senate appointments, while leaving the final say to Ottawa. Peterson's advisers reported that the 'appointment from lists' idea had already been circulating among many of the delegations and would likely be raised by the federal government as a response to Getty's proposal. Getty and Peterson spoke by telephone, and Getty seemed receptive to the idea.

The long-awaited Meech Lake meeting itself got under way shortly after eleven o'clock on the second floor of Willson House. The premiers were alone in the room except for Norman Spector and Oryssia Lennie, Alberta's senior constitutional adviser, who were to serve as note-takers. The remaining provincial advisers remained on the first floor, while the federal delegation was closeted above the premiers on the third floor. The physical arrangements maximized the authority and influence of the federal officials. The federal delegation would work away on drafts throughout the day without having to discuss them with or explain them to their provincial counterparts. The provincial officials would have to rely on their premier to keep them abreast of what was happening on the second floor. But the information coming out of the room to the provincial advisers downstairs would be incomplete and fragmentary. Only the federal officials would have a complete understanding of what drafts were on the table and what possible modifications were being considered. At such meetings, the most scarce and prized commodity is reliable information. The federal advisers had effectively cornered the market, thereby increasing their leverage and bargaining power.

The federal strategy was to begin with the items that seemed least contentious, working their way down finally to the two items that promised to be most controversial – spending power and the amending formula. The first item up for discussion was the Supreme Court. The federal proposal was to entrench the Supreme Court of Canada in the constitution along with the requirement that there be three judges from Quebec on the Court. Senator Murray's 15 April letter indicated that the federal government was prepared to appoint all future judges to the Court from lists provided by the provinces. The prime minister had been told that this item would provoke relatively little controversy, since provincial reaction to the federal proposal had been uniformly positive. But Mulroney was in for a surprise. The idea of appointments from lists was generally accepted. But BC's Bill Vander Zalm wanted to know why Quebec alone was guaranteed a number of seats on the Court. What about British Columbia? Why shouldn't it be guaranteed a quota of Supreme Court judges? Vander Zalm wondered. In raising this issue, Vander Zalm was voicing a traditional British Columbia concern. The established practice was to appoint two judges from the four western provinces. But no single western province was guaranteed that it would have a judge on the Court. The two 'western' spots would generally rotate among the four western provinces. British Columbia had long argued against this practice, claiming that it ought to be guaranteed one of the two western seats on the Supreme Court.

Vander Zalm's intervention sparked a long discussion of the idea of guaranteeing specific regions or provinces representation on the Supreme Court. Why should Quebec alone be singled out in this way? If Quebec was to have specific representation on the Court, why not the other provinces? Richard Hatfield, who had been at the Victoria constitutional conference in 1971, recalled that then BC premier W.A.C. Bennett had sought a BC seat on the Court. But Bennett had been rebuffed in the 1971 Victoria Charter. The Victoria Charter guaranteed seats to Quebec only, with no specific provision made for representation from the other provinces. Nova Scotia's John Buchanan thought this was reasonable since it reflected Quebec's distinctive civil-law legal system. The use of the civil law in Quebec had been constitutionally protected and recognized since the Quebec Act of 1774. The Supreme Court Act dating back to 1875, had always made special provision for Quebec representation on the Supreme Court. The federal proposal was essentially to entrench constitutionally the status quo. After more than an hour of heated discussion, all the premiers were prepared to accept the federal proposal and the specific guarantee of three Quebec seats. Even so, the discussion revealed the extreme sensitivity to the idea of singling out Quebec for any special treatment. The guarantee of specific judges for Quebec had been legally required under the Supreme Court Act for 112 years, but the suggestion that this established legal requirement might be put into the constitution caused a number of the premiers to squirm. Any deviation from provincial equality, even one based on long-standing legal tradition, was obviously going to be a hard sell.

The discussion moved on to immigration. There were few problems here. All provinces were to be treated on an equal footing. The federal government agreed that it would negotiate an immigration agreement with Quebec that would update the 1978 Cullen-Couture Agreement. But it would be open to any province to negotiate a similar agreement and to have it entrenched in the constitution. Everyone around the table thought the proposal in Senator Murray's letter was a good idea.

On to the distinct-society clause. This clause was later to become the focus of opposition to the accord and the lightning-rod for arguments that Quebec had obtained some form of 'special status.' But there was little controversy about the idea at Meech Lake. The prime minister explained that the federal proposal was to entrench an interpretation clause, something that would guide the courts in their interpretation of the constitution. The federal government wanted the courts to take into account Quebec's status as a distinct society in interpreting the constitution. Courts would also have to recognize that the province of Quebec had a role in promoting the distinctive character of Quebec society. But Mulroney stressed that the reference to Quebec's distinct character would be balanced by the requirement that the courts also take into account the linguistic duality of the country as a whole. This linguistic duality would be recognized as a 'fundamental characteristic' of Canada and would make particular reference to the English-speaking minority in the province of Quebec. Mulroney also indicated that the interpretation clause would not change the division of powers between the federal government and the provinces; it would be used by the courts to interpret and apply powers that governments already possessed under the constitution.

No one had any trouble with the idea. David Peterson spoke eloquently of the importance of this symbolic recognition of Quebec's place in Canada. The constitution had to signal publicly to Quebeckers that they were understood and accepted by the rest of the country. The rest of the premiers were not particularly enthusiastic, but no one had any objections. There was general agreement to the principles that Murray had proposed in his 15 April letter.

By mid-afternoon, there had been a consensus on three of Quebec's five conditions. But now the meeting had come to the crucial sticking-points – the issues that had been publicly identified as problems by a number of the premiers. The prime minister opened the discussion on the amending formula by indicating that he understood that a number of the premiers were unhappy with the proposal in Senator Murray's letter. Mulroney's preferred position was as stated in Murray's letter – require the consent of only seven provinces representing 80 per cent of the population for changes to national institutions. But, Mulroney said, he understood that others around the table were unwilling to accept a situation where Ontario and Quebec alone were entitled to exercise a veto over issues such as Senate reform. The prime minister said that he was prepared to give everyone a veto if that was what it would take in order to guarantee a veto for Quebec.

Immediately a discussion of the substance of Senate reform broke out. Alberta's Getty said that, if Senate reform were to be made subject to a unanimity requirement, it would be essential that there be some guarantee that reform would actually take place. He proposed that the provinces be granted the immediate right to half of all future Senate appointments. Mulroney balked at the idea. Newfoundland's Brian Peckford then suggested a compromise. The idea of appointing Supreme Court judges from lists supplied by the provinces had already been accepted. If it was good enough for the Supreme Court, why not for the Senate as well? Peckford asked. Future Senate appointments would be made by the federal government from lists supplied by the provinces until comprehensive reform were achieved. Getty liked the idea. But Vander Zalm was still uncertain. He was reluctant to subject Senate reform to a unanimity requirement without a more tangible guarantee of reform.

The discussion turned to the constitutional entrenchment of a second round of negotiations. Senator Murray's letter had proposed a requirement of constitutional conferences in each of the next five years. Senate reform would be the first item on the agenda for these conferences. But the premiers understood from personal experience that a time-limited obligation to hold constitutional conferences was no guarantee of a successful outcome. A total of four First Ministers' conferences on aboriginal rights had been held from 1983 to 1987. The premiers around the table at Meech Lake had themselves participated in the final conference, which had ended in failure just one month earlier. The constitutional obligation to convene a conference on aboriginal rights had died with the March 1987 meeting, and there was no indication when a subsequent conference might be convened. So Vander Zalm was wary of any guarantee to discuss Senate reform for five years only, fearing a repeat of the failure in the aboriginal process. The idea of entrenching a requirement to discuss Senate reform beyond the five years proposed in the Murray letter then emerged. Why not entrench the requirement to continue meeting annually until comprehensive reform was actually achieved? The requirement of annual conferences would assure the proponents of Senate reform that the issue would remain constantly on the national agenda. Sooner or later, meaningful Senate reform would be achieved.

Vander Zalm liked the idea of annual conferences on Senate reform, and most of the others around the table were willing to go along. The exception was Newfoundland's Brian Peckford. Observing the success of Getty and Vander Zalm on Senate reform, he decided to press his claims on the fishery. Senator Murray's letter had proposed that the issue of 'fisheries' should be included on the agenda of the five conferences to follow in the second round. Peckford argued that the reference to 'fisheries' was too vague and general. He wanted the agenda to indicate specifically that jurisdiction over the fisheries was to be discussed at the future conferences. Peckford had long argued that his province ought to be granted greater authority over the fishery. But Peckford's intervention provoked an argument from the other Maritime premiers, who objected that Ottawa should not cede any jurisdiction to the provinces in this area. They specifically refused to accept any wording that would indicate that jurisdiction over the fishery would be included on the second-round agenda. Compromise wording was suggested, to the effect that 'fisheries roles and responsibilities' would be included on the permanent agenda of future constitutional conferences. This wording was acceptable to Nova Scotia's John Buchanan and New Brunswick's Richard Hatfield on the basis that 'roles and responsibilities' did not include the issue of 'jurisdiction' over the fishery. Peckford, however, would be able to claim that he had won a promise of a greater 'role and responsibility' for his province in relation to the fishery.

Everyone seemed willing to live with this set of compromises on the amending formula. Quebec would get a veto over changes to national institutions, but so would all the other provinces. Thus the principle of the equality of the provinces would be maintained. Getty and Vander Zalm had to agree to subject Senate reform to unanimity, but they had won an immediate role for their provinces in Senate appointments as well as the guarantee of annual constitutional conferences until comprehensive reform was achieved. Brian Peckford had won a concession through the reference to 'fisheries roles and responsibilities' on the permanent agenda of future constitutional conferences. As for the prime minister, he had secured unanimous provincial agreement on the amending formula, while still retaining the ultimate authority for Senate appointments. It did not seem too high a price to pay for achieving consensus on Quebec's proposals.

The only other difficulty was the question of limits on the federal spending power. Senator Murray had proposed that new shared-cost programs in areas of exclusive provincial jurisdiction require the approval of seven provinces representing 50 per cent of the population. Further, Murray had offered provinces the right to 'opt out' of the program with compensation if the province undertook its own program that was 'consistent with the national standards of the shared-cost program.' Manitoba's Howard Pawley and Newfoundland's Brian Peckford had already expressed misgivings about this proposal in advance of the meeting. They had argued that the proposed restrictions on the ability of the federal government to introduce new shared-cost programs were too tightly drawn. They were particularly troubled by the requirement that any new program had, first, to receive the approval of seven provinces before it could be introduced. Quebec's Robert Bourassa, in contrast, approached the issue from precisely the opposite direction. He was unwilling to accept the requirement that the province establish its own program consistent with 'national standards' in order to receive compensation for opting out.

As the discussion unfolded at Meech Lake, the elements of a possible compromise began to emerge. Manitoba's Howard Pawley argued that there should be no restriction on the federal government's ability to initiate a new shared-cost program. The federal government should be able to initiate the program without any requirement to obtain provincial consent. Pawley suggested dropping the requirement of obtaining provincial consent prior to launching a shared-cost program. Bourassa indicated that he might be willing to go along, in return for a broadened right to receive compensation for 'opting out.' Bourassa argued that a province should not have to necessarily meet national 'standards' in order to qualify for federal compensation. He suggested substituting the words 'national objectives' for 'national standards.' Bourassa also wanted the province to be entitled to compensation if it agreed to undertake 'an initiative or program that is compatible with' national objectives.

Bourassa's wording would have signficantly loosened the requirements provinces would have to satisfy in order to qualify for compensation. But the overall effect of the Pawley/Bourassa compromise wording was to inject additional flexibility in the design of future cost-shared programs. The federal government would retain the right to design and to introduce the programs. No province would be able to prevent the federal government from undertaking a program in provincial jurisdiction. But the provinces would enjoy a high degree of flexibility in adapting or modifying the program to meet provincial needs. Because neither level of government would be able simply to dictate terms to the other, the conditions for successful bargaining over the establishment of future programs would have been established.

Pawley and Peckford liked the compromise proposal on spending power. So did Bourassa. Everyone else indicated that they were in favour. Suddenly, all the pieces in the constitutional puzzle had magically fallen into place. It was hard to believe, but it appeared that the eleven First Ministers had actually come to a consensus on Quebec's proposals.

The meeting was seven hours old. It was now shortly after six o'clock in the evening. The First Ministers agreed to break for dinner, consult with their advisers downstairs, and reconvene for a final discussion shortly after eight o'clock. The premiers appeared downstairs, bearing copies of the draft agreement for perusal by their respective delegations. Various provincial officials had suspected that something was up and that considerable progress was being made. The mere fact that the First Ministers had continued meeting until the early evening was a positive sign. But few had suspected their political masters would emerge from the room with a draft agreement in principle. Each 'principle' was printed on a separate sheet of paper. The six pieces of paper were circulated within and among the provincial delegations.

The traditional protocol at these types of meetings dictates that each province caucuses separately and does not share its views with colleagues from other provinces. But, in the early evening of 30 April 1987, this traditional way of proceeding went out the window. The invisible lines between delegations disappeared. It was almost as if the representatives from the ten provinces had become part of a single delegation working on a collective enterprise. The analysis of the advisers was that the draft principles contained no great surprises. The draft agreement clearly tracked the proposals in Murray's letter of 15 April. Premiers briefed their advisers on the nature of the changes that had been agreed to and the reasons for them. The consensus was that the draft agreement was a reasonable and fair compromise of the various interests at stake in the negotiations.

The premiers reconvened upstairs with the prime minister shortly after eight o'clock. Downstairs, the fifty provincial advisers sat around in rattan chairs in a state of mild shock. It was almost as if a tornado had swept through the first floor of Willson House, leaving four dozen dazed sur-vivors in its wake. Most of the veterans of these gatherings had come to Meech Lake with relatively low expectations. They had been through countless years of these kinds of meetings and conferences, all of which seemed to end the same way – inconclusively. Now, it appeared that they had stumbled upon a meeting that would represent a turning-point in the history of the country. The boredom of the early afternoon, replaced by growing curiosity as the afternoon wore on, now gave way to growing excitement. In one of the back rooms, a small television set blared out the play-by-play of an NHL play-off game. But few were interested in hockey that night. Most of the advisers wandered around the various rooms on the first floor of Willson House in a kind of stunned amazement at what was happening. Someone joked that the whole thing had to be a charade, a kind of colossal April Fool's joke staged thirty days late at the expense of lowly bureaucrats. Any moment now the crazed director of the proceed-ings would appear, tell everyone he had only been joking, and order them to go home. Everyone would come back tomorrow for the real meeting. But, of course, the unbelievable really was coming true. There was no charade. Just before ten o'clock the word was passed downstairs: the deal was done. The prime minister and premiers had come to unanimous agreement on Quebec's acceptance of the 1982 constitution.

The officials crowded upstairs to congratulate the premiers and their colleagues from across the country. Canadian bureaucrats are not normally prone to public displays of emotion. But that night, more than a few tears were shed as officials went around the room, shaking hands and embracing each other. It was a historic moment for Canada and, seemingly, a magic time to be a Canadian. What made it so incredible was the apparent ease of the achievement. After decades of deadlock, Canadians seemed to have suddenly discovered an untapped capacity to put aside regional differences and focus on the things they had in common.

The representatives of the media were assembled in the meeting room on the second floor of Willson House for the official announcement of the agreement. Even a few of the reporters began shaking hands with nearby officials and declaring what a great day it was for Canada. As the premiers stood smiling before their respective provincial flags, the prime minister entered the room. The ten premiers began applauding Mulroney as he shook the hands of each provincial leader in turn. The prime minister sat at a small table in front of the premiers and told the horde of reporters that the agreement in principle 'completes a very important dimension of Canada's nationhood.' 'It is a fundamental change,' Mulroney intoned. 'It represents the adherence of Quebec to the Constitution ... what you have now is a whole country as opposed to part of a country.' Mulroney indicated that the agreement in principle would be handed over to officials who would begin the task of translating it into formal legal language. There would be a subsequent meeting of First Ministers 'within weeks' in order to sign off on the legal text. The formal resolution would then be sent to the ten legislatures and the federal Parliament for ratification before the end of the year.

As the official proceedings broke up, each premier faced a media scrum on the grounds outside the building. Most of the premiers were given an easy time of it by reporters. The tough questioning would come later. Tonight there was a sense of euphoria, even among the media, and the main order of business seemed to be allocating the credit for the achievement. Quebec's Robert Bourassa was the only premier to face any hard questions. A huge scrum of reporters, mostly from Quebec, wanted to know what he had won in return for Quebec's signature on the constitution. The focus of the questioning was on the Quebec veto, with reporters wanting to know why Bourassa had failed to get a veto for Quebec over all future constitutional amendments. Bourassa agreed that he had obtained a veto only over changes to national institutions. But, he argued, this 'veto concession' could easily be sold to the people of Quebec on the basis that Quebec could 'opt out' of any other amendments that affected its powers. 'We have the power to say no when [a proposal] goes against the interest of Quebec, so we got what we were asking for,' Bourassa told a crush of reporters, with Gil Rémillard standing directly behind him. Bourassa argued that Quebec had made 'spectacular gains' in the agreement and that 'if common sense has the smallest place possible in our province, then I think we will get very strong support.' Bourassa singled out Brian Mulroney and Ontario's David Peterson for particular praise, suggesting that they had played key roles in forging the unanimous agreement on Quebec's demands. Bourassa promised public hearings in the Quebec National Assembly before any subsequent meeting to approve the formal legal text.

There were few dissenters to be found anywhere as Canadians woke up the next morning to the news of the agreement. Everyone with an opinion on the subject seemed to think the agreement a good thing for the country. Even those who would later dedicate their energies to killing the constitutional deal joined in the initial chorus of support. Consider the opinion of constitutional expert Eugene Forsey, subsequently a leading critic of the accord and an adviser to Newfoundland premier Clyde Wells at the June 1990 constitutional meeting. In the initial euphoria surrounding the announcement of the deal, he pronounced himself in favour of what had been negotiated. Forsey said that, while he was 'not wildly enthusiastic about some of the things that are proposed ... if we want to get results and get Quebec and the other provinces alike satisfied, we have to pay a certain price.' 'And on the whole,' Forsey concluded, 'it looks to me as if the price that would be paid is not an unreasonable one.'[20]

It was clear that there were formidable obstacles remaining before the constitutional deal could be finally put to bed. The drafting of a formal text had to be completed and the amendment had to be ratified in each of the legislatures. Constitutional deals had unravelled before, most recently in 1971 when Robert Bourassa had agreed to a proposed amendment at the Victoria Conference but changed his mind a few days later. This time, however, everyone expected the deal to go through. 'I think it's a go,' Senator Murray proudly told reporters on the morning after the Meech Lake gathering. 'I won't break out the champagne until the royal proclamation, but I think it's a go.'[21]

5

A Marathon at Langevin

As the premiers began returning home in the early morning hours of 1 May 1987, everyone knew that the initial euphoria of the Meech Lake meeting had to come to an end sometime. But most expected a kind of 'constitutional honeymoon' to linger for at least a little while across the country. A unanimous agreement among the prime minister and the ten provincial premiers doesn't come along every day. Everyone assumed that they would be able to bask in the achievement for a few weeks before the inevitable criticisms and doubts began to emerge.

The honeymoon was to be considerably shorter than anticipated. On 1 May, the day after the agreement was negotiated, Brian Mulroney appeared in the House of Commons and received praise from all sides of the House for his historic achievement. But, even in the midst of congratulating the prime minister for winning the unanimous agreement, the opposition parties began voicing doubts and concerns about the deal. Opposition leader John Turner congratulated the prime minister for his efforts, but later asked about the impact of the agreement on future new national programs such as child care. 'Does this mean that in future a national child-care program is impossible?' Turner asked. 'What about a guaranteed annual income? Would medicare have been possible under this agreement?' NDP leader Ed Broadbent was generally supportive, but he, too, raised concerns about the proposed limits on Ottawa's power to launch shared-cost programs. 'There is a crucial necessity of ensuring that the power and the authority of the central Government is fully adequate ... to initiate ... ways that can make our country even better,' Broadbent argued. He cited a national child-care program as an example.

In the first few days following the announcement of the agreement, the debate among English-speaking Canadians centred on the questions raised by Turner and Broadbent in the House of Commons. The major concern expressed about the agreement centred on the limitation on the federal spending power. Critics argued that the proposed limitation on the power to spend federal money would effectively preclude any new national shared-cost programs. Former Liberal justice minister Jean Chrétien told a reporter that 'Trudeau's not going to like this deal' because it gave too much power to the provinces.[1] Trudeau himself maintained a Sphinx-like silence on the new accord in the first week of May, and not even his closest associates seemed to have any idea of his reaction to the deal. But even with Trudeau staying above the fray, the pressures for modifications in the agreement began to build among English Canadians. On Tuesday, 5 May, Howard Pawley began to voice second thoughts about the agreement he had signed just five days earlier. Pawley's reservations were focused on the spending-power provision. The Manitoba premier thought he might have to seek changes to ensure that provinces had to meet federal 'standards' rather than federal 'objectives' in order to receive federal compensation. 'We have to be quite satisfied about the federal spending power,' Pawley said. 'That is most important to us, to the smaller provinces.' A provincial program should have to meet a list of specific national criteria, rather than merely some general objectives, Pawley argued. 'It might require some additional legal wording in order to ensure that there's no misunderstanding of the intent,' the premier concluded.[2]

Pawley's attempt to link his proposed amendments to the 'intent' of the Meech Lake agreement was surprising to those who had been at the meeting and understood what had been agreed to. The wording in Senator Murray's 15 April letter had proposed the use of the term 'national standards' in relation to the spending power. But this wording was specifically changed to 'national objectives' at the Meech Lake meeting at the insistence of Premier Bourassa, who objected to the term 'national standards.' Thus for Pawley to claim that the 'intent' of the agreement was to require provinces to meet 'national standards' was simply factually incorrect. Pawley was evidently developing second thoughts about what he had signed at Meech. Under the pretext of seeking a 'clarification,' he was effectively trying to renegotiate the terms of the deal.

While Pawley was musing about the need to amend the accord, the Quebec government appeared to be developing second thoughts of its own, but from the opposite direction. The initial impression in Quebec was that Premier Bourassa had swept the boards on all fronts, obtaining satisfaction on all five of Quebec's conditions. Pierre Marc Johnson's denunciation of the accord as the 'Meech Lake monster' the day after the agreement was announced had seemingly fallen on deaf ears. But on

Friday, 8 May, Leon Dion, a respected Quebec political scientist and constitutional expert, published an analysis of the accord in the Montreal daily *Le Devoir*. Dion's article was generally supportive of the accord, congratulating Bourassa for achieving an agreement that exceeded his expectations. But Dion raised concerns about the 'distinct society' clause, suggesting that it could actually be interpreted as having diminished Quebec's authority to promote the French language. Dion pointed to the fact that the accord described the English-speaking minority in Quebec as a 'fundamental characteristic of Canada.' This wording left it open to the courts to interpret Quebec's distinctiveness as including the presence on its territory of a highly organized English community with its own media and educational, cultural, and economic institutions. Dion suggested that an amendment to the clause was necessary to make it clear that this was not the intention. The amendment ought to make it clear that Quebec's distinctiveness was derived from its French-speaking character, and that the Quebec government had a right to promote French throughout the province.

That very afternoon, Gil Rémillard appeared before the Quebec National Assembly commission examining the Meech Lake Accord. Rémillard was questioned about the Dion article and the possibility that the distinct-society clause might actually have weakened Quebec's ability to promote the French language. Rémillard, who had earlier boasted of the 'significant gains' Quebec had achieved under the clause, now seemed to reverse course. He suggested that the National Assembly should 'study seriously' the amendment proposed by Dion. 'Speaking objectively,' Rémillard continued, 'here is a respected observer, extremely competent on politics both in Quebec and Canada, who is proposing an amendment. I hope that the Opposition will accept that Mr Dion appear as a witness at the parliamentary commission ... that he should come and explain his amendment to us and it will be our duty as parliamentarians to study it as objectively as possible.'[3] Rémillard's praise for Dion and his injunction to 'study seriously' the proposed amendment were clear evidence that the Quebec government had begun to rethink its position on the distinct-society clause. Perhaps the unimaginable had occurred. Perhaps Quebec had entered into negotiations designed to bolster its powers under the constitution but had unwittingly emerged with a deal that achieved the opposite result. What Rémillard did not tell the parliamentary commission was that the Quebec government was so concerned about this possibility that it had commissioned a series of independent legal opinions on the point. The opinions had not yet been delivered. But when these opinions did arrive a little later in the month, their conclusions were to send shock waves through the ranks of the Quebec constitutional delegation.

Rémillard's comments had come during a preliminary meeting of the parliamentary commission examining the accord. The commission's formal public hearings commenced the following Tuesday, 12 May. The focus of testimony at the hearings was twofold. The concern over the distinct-society clause was the first focus of attention. Experts were concerned over the fact that English Canada was described as 'a fundamental characteristic of Canada,' and was specifically referred to as existing within the province of Quebec. The fear was that this wording would limit the ability of the Quebec government to promote unilingual French policies. Leon Dion appeared before the commission and repeated his argument that the distinct-society clause meant 'absolutely nothing' if it were not amended to make it clear that Quebec had full authority to promote its predominantly French character.

The other focus of debate was the 'spending power' clause. Critics of the clause argued that it had the perverse effect of strengthening rather than limiting the federal power to spend in provincial jurisdiction. The critics relied on the fact that this was the interpretation that was being given to the clause by prominent political leaders outside Quebec. The comments of Ontario attorney general Ian Scott on this clause were referred to repeatedly. Scott had been pressed in the Ontario Legislature by critics who had argued that the clause represented an unacceptable weakening of federal authority to initiate shared-cost programs. Scott had argued that, far from weakening federal power, the clause actually strengthened federal authority. Scott pointed out that, under the Meech Lake Accord, the right of the federal government to spend in areas of exclusive provincial jurisdiction was being formally recognized in the constitution. Scott's comments had the effect of temporarily quelling the discontent in Ontario. But his argument about the strengthening of federal power was immediately seized upon in Quebec as evidence that the province had lost rather than gained under the accord.

Viewed from one perspective, Scott's comments were entirely innocuous. He was simply pointing out the obvious. Under the terms of the accord, the federal government had the right to initiate shared-cost programs, but this right was subject to certain conditions. Yet Quebec's Gil Rémillard seemed thrown on the defensive by this reading of the spending-power clause. Rather than downplaying Scott's comments, he rose to the bait and denied that the clause was intended to strengthen federal power. The clear intention, he suggested, was to give the provinces a free hand in opting out of national programs. He maintained, in fact, that Premier Bourassa had been instrumental in securing changes to the wording at Meech Lake, substituting 'national objectives' for 'national standards.' The effect of this wording, Rémillard claimed, was that the province could opt out of a program and receive compensation, as long as it met objectives of a 'general nature.' Rémillard went so far as to argue that the 'objectives' did not necessarily have to be tied to the specific shared-cost program being launched by Ottawa. Rémillard gave the example of a federal program to build sidewalks across Canada. He suggested that the province could opt out of the program, receive cash from Ottawa, and use the money to build a bridge. 'That's the spirit of Meech Lake,' Rémillard argued. 'The words are "national objectives", not "criteria", "norms", or "standards."'[4] Rémillard and Quebec premier Robert Bourassa said that the interpretation that was being put on this clause by Ian Scott and others contradicted what was agreed to at Meech Lake. They indicated that they were drafting 'new wording' that would clarify their understanding of the clause.

Ian Scott's comments had been used within Quebec to undermine Bourassa's and Rémillard's claims about the accord. Now the Quebeckers' comments were turned back onto Scott as evidence that Scott's own understanding of the spending clause was faulty. The spending-power clause had been portrayed outside of Quebec as a total abdication of federal authority to undertake new shared-cost programs. Rémillard's argument that the province could get money for sidewalks and spend it to build a bridge only heightened this perception. Ian Scott was forced to publicly reject Rémillard's interpretation of the clause. Scott said it was his understanding that a province receiving compensation under this clause had to spend the money in the same area as the national program. It was incorrect, Scott argued, to suppose that the province could receive money for one purpose and spend it on another.[5] But Scott's rebuttal only fuelled the controversy over the clause by highlighting the differing interpretations of its intent. If this were the 'real meaning,' Scott was told in the legislature, then the clause should be amended to say so. Surely it was inappropriate to propose a constitutional amendment unless there was a common understanding of its intent.

What was happening here? Just weeks before, there had been unanimous agreement on Quebec's five conditions. Now, it had almost begun to appear as though the agreement had been a fabrication. There were apparently very wide differences over the meaning of a key clause in the accord. In fact, however, the differences in interpretation were far more subtle and modest than the press reports might indicate. Ian

Scott's comments, for example, merely stated what was axiomatic in the spending-power clause itself: the clause recognized the fact that it was legitimate for the federal government to spend money in areas of exclusive provincial jurisdiction. But the federal government had always exercised this power to spend. There was no net accretion in federal authority, no 'new' power to intervene in provincial jurisdiction. Yet, Scott's relatively innocuous comments were seized upon by the Quebec media and waved in the face of Quebec government officials as evidence of their failure to secure real gains for Quebec. In turn, Quebeckers were put on the defensive and forced to advance their own, apparently extreme interpretations of the meaning of the clause. These broader interpretations were then seized upon by the media outside of Quebec and waved in the face of English-Canadian political leaders.

It is worth noting that the comments of Gil Rémillard on the spending-power clause were far more innocuous than media reports tended to suggest. Close attention to what Rémillard actually said reveals that he was not suggesting that Quebec could receive money for one purpose and then spend it for a different purpose. In fact, Rémillard's main point was simply that the province had a measure of discretion in deciding how to design its own program to meet national objectives. Yet the actual words themselves somehow became less important than the perceptions they created. The whole process had a tendency to feed on itself, fuelled by the media interest in identifying the 'winners' and the 'losers' from the deal. Of course, the assumption within the Quebec media was that the Quebec government was the 'loser,' whereas the rest of Canada was the 'winner.' Every public statement or commentary that might tend to confirm this interpretation was highlighted, and interpretations that might contradict it were downplayed or ignored. In the rest of Canada, the assumptions were the mirror image of those prevailing in Quebec: every comment that might tend to show that Quebec 'won' and the rest of Canada 'lost' became the central preoccupation.

Thus, mere weeks after the agreement at Meech Lake, there were very powerful centrifugal pressures threatening its survival. The pressures for changes on both sides were building inexorably. The Quebec government had now publicly indicated that it was preparing amendments to clarify its interpretation of the clauses dealing with the distinct society and spending power. In Ontario and Manitoba, the pressure to advance amendments that directly contradicted Quebec's position was just as great. So far, the agreement had not yet collapsed under the pressure. But there was real reason to suppose that the differences that were emerging might eventually become so wide as to become unbridgeable.

In the midst of this verbal jousting over the accord, civil servants in Ottawa had been at work attempting to translate the agreement in principle into a formal legal text. By 14 May, the first draft of the legal text had been sent to the provinces for their analysis. A meeting of federal-provincial officials was scheduled for Wednesday, 20 May, in Ottawa, to review the text. The meeting was originally billed as a technical exercise – a meeting to dot the i's and cross the t's. But it quickly threatened to turn into a continuation of the public squabbling over the distinct-society and spending-power clauses. Officials from Quebec indicated that they would be proposing wording that clarified their interpretation of these two clauses. Quebec indicated that the distinct-society clause should be clarified to indicate that Quebec was predominantly French-speaking. They were at pains to counter the possibility that the reference to English-speaking Canada would diminish their authority in language matters. The Quebeckers also wanted the spending-power clause spelled out to indicate that the powers of Parliament were in no way extended or strengthened.

But Quebec's proposals ran into rather heavy weather from the other provincial officials around the table. The other provinces argued that Quebec was trying to reopen the deal and negotiate more favourable terms. At the same time, Manitoba and Ontario indicated that they might be proposing amendments of their own on these two contentious clauses. These amendments, like those from Quebec, were styled as mere 'clarifications' of what had already been agreed to at Meech Lake. But they were clearly at odds with Quebec's proposals. Ontario and Manitoba wanted to clarify that the distinct-society clause did not suggest that Quebec was a French-only society. Ontario and Manitoba also wanted it made plain that the 'Rémillard' interpretation of the spending-power clause was specifically ruled out. The clause would have to specify that, when a province received compensation under this clause, it had to spend the money in the same area as the national program.

Everyone was talking the language of 'clarification.' No one admitted that these new proposals might amount to substantive changes in the agreement. In fact, however, the distinction between a mere 'clarification' and a 'change' had become essentially meaningless by this point. Any additional words, whatever their purpose, would be seen as substantive changes by the media and the larger public. Further, any additional words would inevitably be subjected to minute scrutiny in order to declare a winner and a loser in the constitutional battle. The task of 'clarifying' the agreement was shaping up as an extremely delicate task. The flexibility of the various participants was quickly disappearing, and the pressure to emerge with concessions from the 'other side' was growing on a daily basis. Some people began to wonder whether there would not be a repeat of the 1971 Victoria agreement, which had fallen apart after Robert Bourassa changed his mind and refused to proceed.

Norman Spector, who was chairing the meeting of officials, repeatedly reminded his provincial counterparts that they should not turn the proceedings into a negotiating session. Their mandate, Spector argued, was technical, not political. They should focus on the areas where there was general agreement and leave the contentious issues to their political masters. Bearing in mind this injunction, some progress was made on the issues of immigration, Supreme Court appointments, and the amending formula. Everyone seemed generally satisfied with the text that had been circulated by Ottawa on these points. But there were quite serious disagreements on the spending power and distinct society, disagreements that went to the heart of what had been agreed to at Meech Lake. After a day-long meeting, it was agreed that at least one more meeting of officials would be held prior to calling the First Ministers to Ottawa. The hope was that the differences might be narrowed and a final text prepared for the signature of the First Ministers. A second draft of the formal legal text would be drafted by federal officials, circulated to the provinces, and discussed at a meeting on Friday, 29 May.

When the accord was signed at Meech Lake, the expectation was that the follow-up meeting of First Ministers would be held in public at the Conference Centre in Ottawa. But these plans were predicated on the assumption that officials would have previously agreed on the wording of a legal text. The First Ministers would gather to formally sign an agreed legal text. Now, with the failure of the officials at the 20 May meeting to achieve a consensus, plans began to change. Reports out of Ottawa indicated that the premiers and the prime minister might meet in private in order to hammer out an agreement on the legal text. Only if success were assured would the prime minister open a televised meeting with the premiers in the Conference Centre. Quebec's Robert Bourassa gave credence to these reports when he suggested that 'details' surrounding the meeting to approve the legal text had not yet been settled. 'The method, the place, whether it would be public or private,' Bourassa said. 'I haven't given my agreement on any of that.'[6]

Bourassa indicated that the chief stumbling-block to a final agreement was the manner in which the article on spending power would be drawn up. But Bourassa insisted that his interpretation of the clause had been specifically accepted by the other First Ministers at Meech Lake. He reiterated his view that the words 'national objectives' were specifically included in the agreement in place of 'national standards,' the wording originally proposed by Senator Murray. He described the dispute over the spending clause as purely 'technical' since 'we all agree on the substance of the agreement but it's not easy to put that in a text.'[7] Bourassa also indicated that he was studying legal opinions on the meaning of the distinct-society clause. He did not reveal, however, the content or conclusions of those opinions, other than to indicate that he was considering asking for a 'clarification' of the distinct-society clause.

Elsewhere in the country, the Meech storm clouds continued to darken. Manitoba's Howard Pawley responded to Bourassa's comments by stating that 'our position is certainly at variance from the position that Premier Bourassa has enunciated over the weekend in Quebec.'[8] Pawley suggested that the wording of the spending-power clause should perhaps be tightened by substituting the word 'criteria' for 'national objectives.' In Ottawa, federal officials were quoted as saying that it would be 'quite dangerous' for Robert Bourassa to try to reopen the Meech Lake deal.[9] The federal officials suggested that the moment Bourassa asked for any changes, a number of other premiers would seek changes of their own, and the whole deal would unravel.

In the midst of this growing division over the accord, Pierre Trudeau broke his silence in dramatic fashion. Just days earlier, media reports had indicated that the former prime minister had decided not to speak out on the accord.[10] This made his front-page articles in the *Toronto Star* and in Montreal's *La Presse* on 27 May all the more sensational. Trudeau condemned the accord as a 'total bungle' that would lead to disaster for the country if it were ratified. Trudeau's attack on the accord and its authors was savage, his language heavily laced with sarcasm and outright contempt. Brian Mulroney was a 'sly fox' for having forced Bourassa to 'take up his responsibilities on the world stage'; Quebec's current political leaders were 'flaunting their political stupidity' by rushing to the rescue of nationalists in Quebec, who were 'perpetual losers'; the accord would render the Canadian state 'totally impotent,' destined to be 'governed by eunuchs.'

The sheer violence of Trudeau's language tended to distract the reader from the substance of his argument. This was perhaps no accident. Stripping away the *ad hominem* attacks and insults, it was apparent that surprisingly little of the article (only about one-quarter) even mentioned the contents of the accord itself. Moreover, the single passage in Trudeau's article that actually discusses the accord contains no real argument. Instead, it is made up of a series of conclusory statements, speculations, or assertions of fact, none of which reveal any serious or balanced objections to the substance of the accord.

Trudeau points to the accord's reference to Quebec as a 'distinct society' and to the fact that the Quebec government's role to promote this distinctiveness is affirmed. 'It is easy to predict,' Trudeau writes, 'what future awaits anglophones living in Quebec and what treatment will continue to be accorded francophones living in provinces where they are fewer in number than Canadians of Ukrainian or German origin.' Trudeau's statement is more enigmatic than enlightening. He hints at some dark and horrible future awaiting anglophones within the province of Quebec. 'It is easy to predict,' he says, as though predictions are somehow self-evidently valid and incontestable. But what of the fact that the accord also refers to the presence of English Canadians within Quebec as a 'fundamental characteristic of Canada'? And what of the fact that the province of Quebec has already assumed the role of 'promoting' the rights of the French language and culture in Quebec? In this sense, the accord's reference to the role of the Quebec government in promoting the province's distinct character merely contemplates a continuation of existing policies. Is Trudeau suggesting that this long-established role for the Quebec government is somehow illegitimate and ought to be abandoned? Unfortunately for the reader, he offers no enlightenment on these points, but instead moves on to attack other aspects of the accord.

Trudeau writes that the accord is a victory for those who never wanted a charter of rights entrenched in the constitution. This is so, he argues, because of the reference to the role of the Quebec government to promote the distinct identity of Quebec. 'It follows,' he says, 'that the courts will have to interpret the Charter in a way that does not interfere with Quebec's "distinct society" as defined by Quebec laws.' But, the reader wants to know, why does this necessarily follow? All that the clause in question seems to say is that the courts shall interpret the charter in a manner sensitive to the distinct character of Quebec society. There does not seem to be anything radical in this proposition. Indeed, to interpret the charter in any other way would be to launch a judicial attack on a whole generation of Quebec law designed to promote the French language and culture. In any case, the charter itself already contains a clause that states that it shall be interpreted in a manner consistent with the 'preservation and enhancement of multiculturalism.' These words do not seem far off the 'preservation and promotion of distinct identity.' Trudeau himself agreed to the multiculturalism clause in 1982. If it is acceptable to instruct courts to take into account the 'enhancement of multiculturalism' in interpreting the charter, what can be wrong with also asking them to consider the distinct identity of Quebec?

Trudeau's analysis of the other provisions of the accord is equally one-sided and selective. The provision permitting the provinces to submit lists of names for Supreme Court appointments, will 'transfer supreme judicial power to the provinces.' Trudeau conveniently avoids comment on the fact that the ultimate power of appointment remains in the hands of the federal government. The provision permitting provinces to 'opt out' of national shared-cost programs will 'enable the provinces to finish off the balkanization of languages and cultures with the balkanization of social services.' But there is no mention of the fact that 'social services' is a long-standing field of exclusive provincial jurisdiction and that programs in this area differ widely from one province to another. And why not? Why shouldn't provincial programs be shaped to reflect the needs and desires of the local taxpayers? What is the virtue in requiring a program in Sherbrooke, Quebec, to be identical to one in Kamloops, British Columbia? There is no attempt to provide answers to these pertinent questions. The use of the word 'balkanization' is the key to the whole 'argument,' since it evokes images of disintegration and of a threat to something distinctively Canadian. It permits Trudeau to avoid mentioning the fact that existing social programs in Canada are already administered by the provinces with wide variation from one province to another.

Trudeau concludes by suggesting that the whole idea of negotiating with Quebec in the first place was a colossal error. The nationalists should have been sent packing and told to 'stop having tantrums like spoiled adolescents.' The Quebec problem was a non-issue, until it was created by Bourassa and Mulroney, who chose to flail around on the battlefield of the nationalist bidding war, espousing the virtues of 'moderate' nationalism. Trudeau's argument is that the exclusion of Quebec in 1982 should simply have been ignored, even by Premier Bourassa, thus guaranteeing that the federation would 'last a thousand years.' What Trudeau fails to explain is why no Quebec premier in the last thirty years has been able to get elected on the type of platform he proposes. A precondition for success in Quebec politics since the 1960s has been the acceptance of some form of national-ism, whether moderate or radical. No conceivable government in Quebec could have simply accepted the Constitution Act of 1982 without demand-ing some sort of modifications. Trudeau's argument ignores the realities of contemporary Quebec politics.

Trudeau's article was the constitutional equivalent of blitz warfare. He fired on everyone and everything in sight and took no prisoners. There was not even one redeeming feature of this 'total bungle' perpetrated at

Meech Lake. Trudeau followed up his newspaper polemic with two days of television appearances. These were well suited to the Trudeau style, permitting him to denounce his opponents in broad-brush and categorical terms. No one bothered to request details or to ask difficult questions. Television isn't a very useful medium for carrying on a dry discussion of constitutional texts. Viewers across the country saw the former prime minister, an acknowledged constitutional expert, telling them that the Meech Lake Accord was a form of national suicide. Could they afford to ignore the warning? What if he were right? Maybe this Meech Lake thing wasn't such a great idea after all!

The premiers scrambled to assure everyone that they were unmoved by the Trudeau broadside. The western premiers, meeting in Humboldt, Saskatchewan, reaffirmed their support for the accord. Ontario premier David Peterson said that Trudeau's caustic denunciation of the accord would probably stiffen the premiers' resolve to sign it. At the same time, there were indications that the Trudeau attack had thrown the defenders of the accord on the defensive. Manitoba premier Howard Pawley had been musing for some weeks about the possibility that the wording of the spending-power clause should be clarified. Now, in the wake of the Trudeau polemic, Pawley stated definitively that changes were necessary before he would agree to sign it.[11] In Ontario, Premier David Peterson faced questioning in the legislature from opposition leader Larry Grossman, brandishing a copy of Trudeau's article. Peterson promised that there would be full public hearings on the accord before it was ratified in Ontario. He also spoke for the first time of the three-year ratification period for the accord, promising that there would be ample time for a committee of MPPs to tour the province and receive public submissions.[12]

The federal government's response came in the form of a front-page article in the Toronto *Globe and Mail* and Montreal's *Le Devoir* by Senator Lowell Murray. Titled 'Trudeau one who bungled,' the article pointed out that virtually all the elements of the Meech Lake Accord had been proposed by governments headed by Pierre Trudeau. Trudeau himself had proposed in 1980 to recognize the 'distinctive character' of Quebec society in the constitution, as well as the fact that the French community has its 'focus and centre of gravity in Quebec.' Trudeau's government had signed an immigration agreement with Quebec in 1978 that was based on the same principles as the immigration provisions in the Meech Lake Accord. Trudeau had offered to subject the use of the federal spending power to provincial approval back in 1969. Murray had clearly delved deeply into the files in Ottawa in order to rebut the stinging Trudeau attack. The senator argued that, in light of Trudeau's past proposals on the constitution, his present criticisms of the accord were inexplicable. Trudeau was like a general 'who longs for war during peacetime.' Murray claimed that it is necessary to know how to build a lasting peace with Quebec and that 'the quiet strength of those who foster peace is no less necessary for a country than the panache of the warriors.'

Senator Murray's closely argued rebuttal of Trudeau's attack did little to blunt the impact of the former prime minister's polemic. Trudeau's article was important less for what it said than for what it symbolized. Trudeau had labelled the accord a sell-out to Quebec and to the provinces generally. He had conjured up the image of Mulroney as head waiter to the premiers. 'No one spoke for Canada' was the main message of his critique. Murray's response – that Trudeau himself had made similar offers in the past – did little to counter this negative image of the prime minister and of the accord itself. The fatal problem for Murray was that he was unable to identify anything that the federal government actually gained under the agreement. Murray did point out that the federal government had obtained the agreement of the province of Quebec to the 1982 constitution. But to most English-speaking Canadians, that did not represent any real advantage or concession from Quebec. For most Canadians, Quebec was already 'in' the constitution. To argue that a whole series of concessions was necessary in order to obtain Quebec's signature seemed to Canadians outside of Quebec to be an absurdity. The rest of the country was being asked to pay a second time for something it thought it already possessed.

Trudeau's powerful imagery of the accord as a 'sell-out' to Quebec nationalists would stick to the document like flypaper during the next three years. As will be apparent in later chapters, this negative imagery was to play a key role in the growing public sentiment that developed against the accord. In this sense, the Trudeau intervention was an important contributing factor to the eventual demise of the Meech Lake Accord. But Trudeau's intervention was a key moment in the Meech Lake story for a second, quite different reason. When Trudeau unleashed his broadside, governments were in the midst of negotiations aimed at reducing the general principles agreed to at Meech Lake into a formal legal text. By the third week in May, those governmental negotiations were in serious trouble and seemed to be heading for failure. The effect of Trudeau's attack was to sharpen the resolve of governments to put aside their differences and to reach agreement on the terms of a legal text. In fact, had Trudeau not intervened in the manner he did, it is quite possible that the agreement in principle signed at Meech Lake would have dissolved before it could be translated into a legal text. Thus the immediate effect of Trudeau's article was to save the accord from a premature death.

The idea that Trudeau's intervention might actually have kept the accord alive – at least in the short term – may seem paradoxical, particularly given his vociferous condemnation of the accord. But it is important to recall the contradictory political pressures building around the accord in the days leading up to the publication of Trudeau's article on 27 May. By late May, the Meech Lake Accord was in serious trouble. Two key clauses in the accord – the 'distinct society' clause and the 'spending power' clause – were coming under sustained attack. Premier Bourassa had committed himself to seeking amendments to these two clauses designed to strengthen Quebec's gains; they were unlikely to prove acceptable to the other premiers around the table. At the same time, pressures within the rest of the country were building for amendments in the opposite direction. Howard Pawley, in particular, had voiced public misgivings about the spending-power provision.

What was happening was that a number of premiers were considering opening up the accord and pressing for amendments. The problem was that there seemed to be almost no flexibility on either side that would have permitted such amendments to be acceptable in all parts of the country. Amendments favouring the province of Quebec were politically unacceptable outside of Quebec; amendments that limited Quebec's gains under the accord were equally unacceptable within the province of Quebec. It was a classic 'zero-sum' bargaining situation in which a gain to one party would be perceived as a loss to another. The danger was that, the moment the accord was opened up, it would collapse under the contradictory political demands that would be pressed by the different parties around the bargaining table.

Thus, by late May 1987, there was a powerful political dynamic at work undermining the integrity of the accord. Trudeau's article had the immediate, short-term effect of reversing this political dynamic and of reinvigorating the accord. It did so in two quite distinct ways. First, the effect of Trudeau's article was to restore a measure of political flexibility and bargaining room to the negotiations. This newly found flexibility grew out of the fact that Trudeau's attack relieved the nationalist pressure on Premier Robert Bourassa. Quebec nationalists had been arguing that Bourassa had failed to achieve enough meaningful gains in the agreement. Now, along comes Pierre Trudeau claiming that the Quebec premier had picked the pocket of the prime minister of Canada. The unintended effect was to bolster Bourassa's credibility and undermine the arguments of the nationalists and give Bourassa much-needed flexibility going into the meeting of First Ministers over the terms of the legal text. Prior to Trudeau's intervention, the pressure was on Bourassa to emerge from the second meeting with amendments designed to strengthen or at least consolidate Quebec's gains under the accord. Bourassa was in the impossible position of having to emerge with some additional concessions that could be used to blunt the nationalist criticism of the accord. The position was impossible in the sense that the other premiers were unwilling to grant any such concessions, as subsequent events were to demonstrate. But Trudeau's broadside effectively spiked the guns of the nationalists. The pressure on Bourassa was relieved, making it possible for him to go into the second meeting without the imperative of achieving additional concessions. In fact, after Trudeau's attack on the accord, it was even possible for Bourassa himself to offer some small concessions on the distinct-society and spending-power clauses. These concessions played a key role in the Langevin meeting of 2–3 June. Certain key concessions by Bourassa enabled the other premiers to sign on to the legal text and maintained the political unanimity in favour of the accord.

Trudeau's article had the effect of salvaging the accord in a second, separate way. Prior to Trudeau's intervention, a number of the other premiers did not perceive themselves to have much at stake in the discussions. These other premiers had agreed to participate in the negotiations over Quebec's demands, but they did not believe that their own political interests were directly implicated. This political calculation changed appreciably after Trudeau's attack on the accord and its authors. After 27 May, all eleven First Ministers perceived themselves as having an important stake in seeing the agreement survive. This change in perception was a direct result of the vicious personal character of Trudeau's assault. Trudeau had described the eleven First Ministers as power mad, opportunistic, stupid, and selfish. According to Trudeau's account, it seemed that Canada's political leaders possessed absolutely no redeeming qualities. No one likes to be labelled in this fashion, particularly if the attack comes from a former politician who is, in effect, saying that he could have gotten it right if only *he* had been there. It was necessary to somehow prove Trudeau wrong, to demonstrate that Meech Lake was not the 'total bungle' Trudeau had described. But there was really only one way to achieve this result: to agree on the terms of a constitutional amendment and to ratify it in each of their legislatures. To back away from the accord in the wake of Trudeau's attack would have seemed an implicit admission of guilt. It would have given the impression that Trudeau had caught the premiers red-handed, their fingers in the country's cookie jar, and that only his slap on the wrist had saved Canadians from disaster.

Thus, Trudeau's attack had the unintended effect of providing the country's leaders with an incentive to put aside their differences and agree on a legal text. There was an unspoken but quite powerful understanding that, if the agreement collapsed, it would be taken as proof of the validity of Trudeau's critique. On a very personal level, all eleven First Ministers now had a quite powerful stake in the success of the enterprise.

It was clear that agreement on the terms of a legal text was far from a foregone conclusion. By the last week in May, it had been agreed that the eleven First Ministers would assemble in Ottawa at 11:00 a.m. on 2 June in order to consider the legal text. The idea was for the prime minister and the premiers to meet privately over lunch, it was hoped to resolve all outstanding differences, and then go before the television cameras in the Conference Centre for the official signing ceremony. A final meeting of the officials was scheduled for the previous Friday, 29 May, in order to see whether the differences could be ironed out in advance of the First Ministers' meeting. There was still some faint hope that a consensus might be reached among the officials and a single, agreed text of the amendment prepared for First Ministers.

The officials' meeting of 29 May, far from fashioning a consensus, indicated that the agreement was in real danger of collapsing. The discussion around the table became so heated that it became necessary to carry on late into the evening, and then to reconvene on Saturday morning. By the end of the two days of meetings, the differences on the two key items of contention – distinct society and the spending power – were as wide as ever.

On the distinct-society issue, Quebec officials were insisting that the clause be amended to specify that the French language was a 'fundamental characteristic' of Quebec's distinctiveness. They also sought an amendment stating that the province of Quebec had the constitutional role of promoting the French language. Other provinces rejected these references to the French language, arguing that they altered the meaning of what was agreed to at Meech Lake. In addition, Manitoba and Ontario officials suggested that the accord be amended to specify that the division of powers between the federal and provincial governments was not affected by the distinct-society clause. Manitoba and Ontario also proposed an amendment stating that charter rights as well as the rights of aboriginal peoples were not affected by the distinct-society clause. Quebec officials were objecting to these amendments, arguing that they would effectively strip the distinct-society clause of all meaning.

On the issue of spending power, Quebec was seeking an amendment stating that the clause did not extend federal power. This amendment was generally acceptable to the other governments around the table. But Quebec was resisting amendments proposed by Manitoba and Ontario that would have stated that the federal government alone had the right to set the 'national objectives' of shared-cost programs. Quebec suggested that the national objectives had to be established jointly by both orders of government. Manitoba and Ontario also wanted it stated that provinces had to meet the national objectives associated with the particular shared-cost program under consideration in order to receive federal compensation. The province could not receive money for one purpose and spend it on another. The point of this amendment was to counter the suggestion made by Quebec's Gil Rémillard that Quebec could get money intended to be used for sidewalks and use it to build a bridge. Again, these proposals were running into resistance from the Quebeckers, who saw them as an attempt to amend what had been agreed to at Meech Lake.

After two days of argument, it became apparent that the officials were simply unable to resolve these differences. What was really happening was that both sides were attempting to reopen the two key sections of the accord, matters that could be definitively resolved only by the First Ministers themselves, not by officials. It was agreed that the most useful way of proceeding would be to prepare a text containing all the various suggestions for amendments and to put that text in front of the First Ministers for their consideration. The areas of disagreement could be identified by the use of square brackets, with the bracketed sections indicating clauses that remained in dispute. It would be up to the First Ministers themselves to determine whether the areas of disagreement could be bridged in some fashion.

Federal officials worked late into the evening on Saturday, 30 May, preparing the text with the proposed amendments. Just before midnight, the final version of the text was drafted, including the various proposals for amendments highlighted in square brackets. The twelve-page text was circulated around the provincial capitals on Sunday, 31 May. Then, the unexpected happened. Up until this point, the various texts and proposals on the table had remained confidential. But the 30 May text somehow found its way into the hands of Pierre Marc Johnson, the Parti Québécois leader and former premier of Quebec. On Monday afternoon, in the National Assembly, Johnson rose during Question Period to ask Bourassa whether the document accurately represented the current state of the negotiations over Quebec's demands. Johnson said that the text demonstrated that provinces such as Manitoba were attempting to limit the importance of the recognition of Quebec as a distinct society. Johnson was particularly concerned about proposed amendments that stated that the distinct-society clause would be subordinate to the Charter of Rights.

Bourassa appeared momentarily shaken as Johnson flourished the twelve-page confidential negotiating document. But Bourassa recovered quickly, suggesting that the text that Johnson had obtained was only one of several 'working documents' that were being studied. He refused to comment on the specifics of the document, retreating to generalities about his commitment to defend the 'superior interests' of Quebec. The Quebec premier claimed that Quebec's five conditions for signing the constitution had been met at Meech Lake and all that remained was to agree on the legal formulation. Bourassa said that he remained confident that a deal would be signed by the federal government and all the provinces.

While the Quebec premier repeated his customary protestations of optimism in Question Period, later in the day he sounded a note of caution about the upcoming meeting. Bourassa met with his cabinet for two and a half hours on the afternoon of 1 June to plan Quebec's bargaining strategy for the Ottawa meeting the next day. Emerging from Cabinet, the Quebec premier began talking about the need to obtain 'guarantees' for Quebec's cultural security in the formal text of the accord. Bourassa indicated that he was particularly concerned about how the courts might interpret the distinct-society clause. 'The Quebec government simply wants to assure itself . . . that Quebec's cultural security can in no way be affected by an eventual interpretation of the new constitutional dispositions before the courts.'[13] But Bourassa refused to be more specific about what he meant by the need to obtain 'guarantees' for Quebec's cultural security. The other premiers and the rest of the country would have to wait until the next day in Ottawa to get a more precise idea of what the Quebec premier had in mind.

The furore in Quebec City over the leak of the legal text, as well as Bourassa's vague comments about the need to obtain some type of new 'guarantees,' was a clear signal that the 2 June meeting would prove long and difficult. A meeting that was originally expected to be little more than a formality had now assumed much larger proportions. The 2 June meeting would be a full-scale bargaining session, in which the debate over the two key clauses of distinct society and spending power would have to be refought from the beginning. Moreover, the atmosphere had changed dramatically in the thirty-three days since the gathering at Meech Lake. On 30 April, at Meech Lake, the atmosphere had been informal and friendly, with all involved sharing the sense that they were working together as part of a common enterprise. Each premier had been accompanied by a small delegation of only five or six officials, not all of whom were even lawyers. The participants and the atmosphere for the 2 June meeting, Meech Lake II, were quite different. For Meech Lake II, each premier would bring along a full delegation of ten or twelve officials, top-heavy with lawyers and constitutional experts. Attitudes had hardened over the thirty-three days between Meech Lake I and Meech Lake II, most notably because of the unsuccessful meetings of officials held in late May. These discussions had been increasingly heated and acrimonious. The mood around the negotiating table had become more formal and combative. No one harboured any illusions about being part of a collective or joint enterprise. Instead, there was the sense that the divisions around the table were growing more pronounced and that people were in the process of choosing up sides. All of a sudden, everyone became conscious of the sound of people digging in their heels.

Opposition to the accord in the country at large was also beginning to mobilize by the beginning of June. Pierre Trudeau's 27 May article condemning the accord galvanized the opponents of Meech and encouraged them to come forward with their concerns. The Canadian Ethnocultural Council, a coalition of thirty-five ethnic organizations, announced itself dissatisfied with the accord and indicated that amendments were necessary to ensure that the interests of multicultural communities were protected. Joe Volpe, a prominent Toronto-area Liberal, published a front-page article in the 1 June edition of the Italian community newspaper *Il Corriere Canadese* in which he called for a full public debate on the accord. Volpe echoed the objections of the Ethnocultural Council and argued that Ontario premier David Peterson should not sign anything until there had been an opportunity for greater community input.

The Assembly of First Nations and other native groups had also condemned the accord, arguing that it 'reeks of racism' because it excluded their participation and the protection of their rights. The Canadian Council for Social Development, a coalition of social groups, had raised questions about the spending-power provision in the accord. The social groups were concerned that giving the provinces the right to opt out of future national shared-cost programs could jeopardize the creation of new programs like day care.

On the whole, however, the dissidents were disorganized and scattered. There was not yet any broad-based or well-organized opposition to Meech

Lake. In fact, a poll published by the *Toronto Star* on 1 June, the eve of the meeting of First Ministers, found that Canadians generally were supportive of the accord.[14] The *Star* poll did find that Canadians were fairly evenly divided on the provision recognizing Quebec as a distinct society. But all the other parts of the accord were supported by Canadians by a wide margin. The accord had not yet set off any alarm bells for ordinary Canadians.

The prime minister had moved the starting time of the meeting up one hour, to 10:00 a.m., in recognition of the fact that there were serious differences that would have to be resolved by the First Ministers. The meeting was to take place in a large conference room on the fourth floor of the Langevin Block, a government office building on Wellington Street, across the street from Parliament Hill. As the premiers made their way into the building on the morning of 2 June, they were greeted by the usual media scrum searching for clues as to what was to transpire behind closed doors. Nearby, a small group of demonstrators from the Parti Indépendantiste chanted 'Le Québec aux Québécois' and 'La constitution, c'est un torchon.' Gilles Rheame, the leader of the demonstrators, confronted Robert Bourassa and Gil Rémillard on their way into the meeting. Rheame told the Quebec leaders that they would bitterly regret it if they signed the constitution. 'You can't please everyone,' Rémillard responded. 'It's not an accord for indépendantistes or sovereignistes, it's an accord for people who believe in federalism, and in Quebec as a distinct society.'[15]

Bourassa said he was confident that the First Ministers would reach an agreement. The premier was scheduled to appear with financier David Rockefeller at a charity dinner in New York that evening to help raise funds for a Montreal museum. The premier said he expected to be able to keep his engagement. Most of the other premiers also sounded upbeat as they talked to reporters on their way into the Langevin Block. Alberta's Don Getty told reporters: 'we're here to sign it; we're not here to break it apart.' Newfoundland's Brian Peckford said the main task was to translate the general principles that had been accepted at Meech Lake into a legal text. He scorned the criticisms of former prime minister Pierre Trudeau, maintaining that Trudeau's sharp personal attack 'will ensure that there will be an agreement.'

But Manitoba's Howard Pawley and Ontario's David Peterson sounded much more cautious about the prospects for success and warned that the meeting could be a long one. Pawley confirmed that he would be proposing amendments on the two key clauses of spending power and distinct society. Pawley said that he was not issuing any ultimatums to the other premiers, but that he expected some 'give and take' on his proposals. David Peterson also raised publicly for the first time his concerns about the distinct-society and spending-power clauses. Peterson said he was 'disturbed' about some of the comments he had heard since Meech Lake on the issue of spending power. He argued that provinces had to conform to national objectives and that money received from Ottawa for a specific program should not be diverted for other purposes. Peterson said he had been content with the wording of the spending-power clause but some refinement now seemed necessary because some premiers were holding to different interpretations. 'I was clear coming out of Meech Lake,' Peterson told reporters. 'Others appear not to be so clear.'[16]

The prime minister called the meeting to order shortly after ten o'clock, and the premiers took their seats around the large conference-room table in room 414. As at Meech Lake, the only officials in the room with the First Ministers were Norman Spector, the top federal negotiator on the file, and Oryssia Lennie, Alberta's director of constitutional affairs. There were close to one hundred other assorted advisers from the provinces and the federal government crammed into meeting rooms and small offices nearby, waiting to be summoned for advice or encouragement.

Mulroney opened the meeting by reviewing the public and press reaction to the Meech Lake agreement. The prime minister noted the favourable reviews that Meech had received from newspaper editorials in the *Globe and Mail* and the *Montreal Gazette*. Mulroney categorically rejected the criticisms that had been made of the accord, focusing in particular on the polemic by Pierre Trudeau of the week before. Trudeau was not only wrong in substance, Mulroney claimed, but his motives were also suspect. Mulroney reviewed each of Trudeau's criticisms in detail, arguing that the former prime minister had offered a totally one-sided and shallow analysis of the accord. The prime minister pointed out that most of what was contained in the Meech Lake Accord had been offered by Trudeau himself at various points in his own tenure as prime minister. Mulroney concluded that Trudeau had written more out of petty jealousy than out of genuine concern over the accord. Others around the table who were veterans of the Trudeau era joined in the criticism of the former prime minister, with Newfoundland's Brian Peckford and Nova Scotia's John Buchanan recalling the poisonous atmosphere that had surrounded federal-provincial relations during that period. The fact that the meeting began in this fashion was certainly no accident. The eleven First Ministers around the table had been badly stung by the personal attack of the former prime minister. Trudeau's attack gave them something in common – a strong desire to prove the former prime minister wrong.

The discussion moved on to the substance of Meech Lake. Mulroney indicated that officials from all governments had already agreed on the provisions dealing with the Supreme Court, immigration, and the amending formula. No one had any objections or concerns on these items. That meant, according to Mulroney, that there were really only two matters to be resolved – distinct society and spending power. Everyone agreed that the discussion would be limited to these two items.

The first item up for discussion was the spending-power provision. Both Pawley and Peterson pressed their case for amendments. The Manitoba and Ontario premiers argued that it was necessary to state clearly that the federal Parliament had the authority to define national objectives. It was also necessary, they argued, that provinces establish programs that met the specific objectives set down by Parliament before they could get funding. Bourassa was balking at these suggestions. He was getting support in his resistance from British Columbia's Bill Vander Zalm and Alberta's Don Getty. The two western premiers asked what business it was of the federal Parliament to tell the provinces how to administer programs in areas of provincial jursidiction. They disputed Pawley and Peterson's interpretation of the 'intent' of what had been agreed to at Meech Lake.

It was clear that there were fairly sharp divisions on the spending-power provision. After an initial discussion around the table, Mulroney suggested that they break for lunch and reconvene in the afternoon to deal with the other issue in dispute – the distinct-society clause. The premiers dined on a cold buffet of fiddleheads, salmon, and cold cuts, and took the opportunity to consult with their advisers in the adjoining rooms. Shortly before 2:00 p.m. the prime minister called the meeting back to order and opened discussion on the distinct-society clause.

Quebec premier Robert Bourassa's comments in the National Assembly a day earlier had sparked some concern in the other provincial capitals. Bourassa had spoken vaguely of the need to obtain some type of 'guarantee' to protect Quebec's cultural security. Bourassa clearly was worried about something. But what did he have in mind? Now, as the discussion turned to the distinct-society clause, the Quebec premier revealed what had been up to that point a closely guarded secret.

Bourassa told his fellow premiers that he had commissioned a series of legal opinions from constitutional experts in Quebec on the meaning of the distinct-society clause. Bourassa said that these opinions had been solicited with great care. The experts were Quebec's most respected constitutionalists. One of them was even a former Supreme Court of

Canada judge from Quebec who had since retired and returned to private law practice in Quebec. Bourassa did not name the judge in question but it was clear from the description that it had to be Yves Pratte, a Trudeau appointee who had retired after only a few years on the Court in the late 1970s. Bourassa's point was simply that these opinions had not come from just anybody and that they had to be taken seriously. Bourassa indicated that the constitutional experts had been asked to consider the impact of the distinct-society clause on Quebec's authority to legislate in the area of language and culture. They were to consider in particular the arguments raised by Professor Leon Dion to the effect that the distinct-society clause might actually be interpreted in a way that would diminish Quebec's authority to promote the French language throughout Quebec.

The opinions had come back and the answers were not to Bourassa's liking. It seemed that the majority of the experts, including the former Supreme Court judge, was of the view that Quebec's authority over language might actually be diminished under the terms of the distinct-society clause. The basis of this conclusion was the reference in the clause to the presence of English Canada in Quebec as a 'fundamental characteristic of Canada.' The fact that the English community was described in this manner had the potential to limit the authority of the Quebec government to restrict the use of the English language. In fact, the opinions came to the conclusion that Quebec might be worse off if the distinct-society clause were enacted than if the constitution were simply left in its current form.

A particular area of concern identified by the legal opinions was the 'French only' sign requirements in Quebec's Bill 101. These requirements were at the time the subject of a challenge under the Charter of Rights. The Quebec Court of Appeal had found the French-only provisions to be contrary to the charter, and the Quebec government had appealed that decision to the Supreme Court of Canada. But the legal opinions emphasized that, even if Quebec lost before the Supreme Court of Canada, it could choose to maintain the legislation through invoking the 'override' provision in the charter. Under the 'override,' or 'notwithstanding clause, the Quebec Legislature could simply declare that the signs legislation was to be applied, notwithstanding the fact that it violated the charter. The override provision was a sort of 'safety valve' that gave the legislature rather than the courts the final say on the balance between individual rights and collective interests.

Bourassa's legal opinions emphasized that, under the existing 1982 constitution, Quebec had an absolute discretion in deciding whether to invoke the override. The use of the override was not itself subject to judicial review or supervision. But the legal experts believed that this situation might change if the distinct-society clause were enacted. The distinct society clause made explicit reference to the English-speaking community in Quebec and stated that the constitution, including the Charter of Rights, had to be interpreted consistent with the fact that this community was a fundamental characteristic of Canada. This reference to the English community, the experts thought, could lead the courts to impose restrictions on Quebec's use of the override clause. The courts might conclude that Quebec could not use the override provision in the charter so as to restrict the use of the English language in Quebec. In effect, the courts might interpret the distinct-society clause as *taking away* from Quebec the right to impose French-only signs. The result would be that, under the distinct-society clause, bilingual signs would be required in the province of Quebec.

Bourassa was clearly very concerned about this possibility. He did not want to lose the right to invoke the override in the event that he lost the 'signs' case at the Supreme Court. It was evident that he was reconsidering his earlier pledge, made during the 1985 election campaign in Quebec, to allow bilingual signs in the province. Of course, events some eighteen months later, in December 1988, would confirm the extent to which Bourassa was preparing to shift course on this issue. For the moment, the Quebec premier insisted that all he wanted was to keep his options open.

Bourassa argued that the distinct-society clause would have to be amended to make it clear that Quebec could use the 'override' provision in the charter in the event of an unfavourable ruling by the Supreme Court of Canada. He put forward a suggestion that struck the others around the table as unusual and almost byzantine. Bourassa proposed that the distinct-society clause be amended to include a second 'override' provision, modelled on the existing one in section 33 of the charter. This second 'override' would state that the distinct-society clause did not limit the right of the Quebec government to invoke section 33 of the Charter of Rights.

This proposal was what Bourassa had been referring to in the National Assembly when he had spoken of the need for a 'guarantee' of cultural security. In effect, what Bourassa was afraid of was the possibility that the courts would interpret the distinct-society clause as limiting the use of the override clause in the Charter of Rights. Bourassa wanted a 'fail-safe' mechanism built into the distinct-society clause so that he would not be bound by such a court ruling.

Bourassa's proposal for a second override was clearly a non-starter. The other premiers around the table were already smarting from Trudeau's criticism to the effect that they had sold out the English-speaking community in Quebec. They were clearly not going to grant any additional powers to Bourassa that might reinforce this negative impression about the intent of Meech Lake. At the same time, there was something strangely comforting in the Quebec premier's deep concern over the implications of the distinct-society clause. Bourassa's legal opinions seemed to confirm that the distinct-society clause was carefully crafted and reasonably balanced. It was not a 'sell-out' to Quebec nationalists seeking to promote a unilingual Quebec, as Trudeau and others had alleged. In fact, the clause was so well balanced that it might actually strengthen the position of the English-speaking minority in Quebec.

Bourassa's attempt to obtain amendments to protect Quebec's 'cultural security' met with a cool reception. The discussion became complicated by the fact that others around the table, most notably Ontario's David Peterson and Manitoba's Howard Pawley, put forward amendments of their own to the clause. Peterson and Pawley argued that there had to be protections for charter rights and for aboriginal Canadians and multicultural groups written into the clause. They also objected to the use of the terms 'English Canada' and 'French Canada' in the original Meech Lake wording. Peterson and Pawley suggested that this wording promoted an image of 'two Canadas,' an image that had been roundly condemned by Pierre Trudeau in his 27 May article. While Peterson and Pawley did not explicitly say so, it was evident that Trudeau's criticism on this score had hit home.

It was now approaching the dinner hour. Some small progress had been made on the distinct-society clause. There seemed general agreement on the idea of deleting the reference to 'English Canada' and 'French Canada.' The clause would be amended so as to refer to 'English-speaking Canadians' and 'French-speaking Canadians.' But apart from this relatively minor and cosmetic change, there was no agreement on any of the other proposals that had been put forward for amendments. There was a growing sense of dismay and restlessness among the premiers and their advisers. The deal seemed to be slipping away as the meeting dragged on. Mulroney proposed that they break for dinner, consult their advisers, and reconvene in the evening. Dinner arrived at 6:30 – a choice of veal or scallops sent over from the National Arts Centre kitchen across the street.

The First Ministers were back at the conference table by 7:15, but the pace had slowed and progress was being measured in inches. There was no sign of a consensus on either of the two key items in dispute. The discussion wandered back and forth between the issues of distinct society and spending power. David Peterson, in an effort to break the log jam on the distinct-society clause, instructed his delegation to meet separately with the Quebec officials and see whether there was the possibility of an Ontario-Quebec consensus. Peterson indicated that if he and Bourassa could arrive at a common position on distinct society, Mulroney and the others would go along. He was confident that if this issue could be put to bed, the rest of the deal would quickly fall into place.

The Ontario delegation, led by Attorney General Ian Scott, sought out Jean Samson and André Tremblay, two of the key Quebec legal advisers, to see whether there was any common ground on the distinct-society issue. The Ontario delegation proposed to Samson and Tremblay that it should be possible to draft an amendment that provided Quebec with 'cultural security' while, at the same time, meeting Ontario's concerns about the clause. Ontario proposed that the distinct-society clause be amended to provide that Quebec's powers were not 'altered' by the clause. The effect of this amendment would be to preserve the status quo. Quebec's powers would not be enlarged or diminished by the distinct-society clause. Thus Quebec would receive the comfort it sought that it would not lose any of its existing powers. But the proposed amendment would also make it clear that Quebec would not gain any new powers under the clause. Thus greater assurances for the protection of minority rights in the province would be provided, even though there would be no explicit mention of the Charter of Rights.

Around midnight, the Quebec officials indicated that they were prepared to take this compromise proposal forward to their political masters for consideration. But when Gil Rémillard was informed of the discussions, he was totally unreceptive to the proposal. He liked the idea of an amendment stating that Quebec would not have its powers diminished under the distinct-society clause. But he was unwilling to accept an amendment stating that Quebec did not gain any additional powers. Peterson was told that the effort to find a Quebec-Ontario consensus had failed, and there was still no agreement on the distinct-society clause.

By midnight, some progress had been made on the spending-power provision. Over the course of the evening, Bourassa had agreed to some subtle wording changes that had the effect of clarifying the clause in the direction sought by both Peterson and Pawley. Bourassa was prepared to agree to the clarification that national shared-cost programs would be 'established by the Government of Canada.' This wording was important because it meant that the Government of Canada, rather than the provinces, would have the responsibility for defining the 'national objectives' of the program. Bourassa also agreed to wording that stated that the province must 'carry on' a program in order to qualify for federal funding. This wording was important because it made it clear that the province must undertake a program on a continuing or permanent basis in order to qualify for funding. Finally, Bourassa was prepared to accept the inclusion of the single word 'the' in front of 'national objectives' in the English version of the final text. This change was significant because it reinforced the argument of Peterson and Pawley that the province had to meet the objectives associated with the particular shared-cost program, not some objectives defined more generally.

The amended version of the clause still included a reference to 'national objectives.' Some critics of Meech Lake had argued that this wording should be changed to bind the province to 'national standards,' a more precise term, in order to qualify for federal funding. Howard Pawley had indicated in the period between Meech Lake and Langevin that he preferred the word 'standards' over 'objectives.' But despite Pawley's musings on this issue, there was no serious discussion of an amendment along these lines at the Langevin meeting. There had been a deliberate choice at the Meech Lake meeting to use the words 'national objectives.' There was little enthusiasm around the table for revisiting an issue that had been debated and agreed upon at Meech Lake. Howard Pawley raised the point for discussion but, in the absence of any support from the other premiers, was unprepared to press his position with any vigour. The focus of the discussion was on the limited package of amendments designed to clarify certain ambiguities in the clause.

The meeting had now dragged on into the early hours of the morning. The elements of a consensus on the spending-power clause seemed to be in place. The remaining problem was still the distinct-society clause. Did the clause grant Quebec any additional powers? Would it threaten the rights of the English-speaking minority in Quebec? The debate on the issue seemed at an impasse. What was emerging was the possibility of a split between Peterson and Bourassa on the issue. This was a nightmare scenario, a result that David Peterson had sought to avoid from the very beginning. The object of the exercise was to heal the breach between Quebec and the rest of the country, not to open a new one.

In an effort to resolve the impasse, the First Ministers called three senior constitutional experts into the room at about 12:30 in the morning to provide their independent interpretation of the distinct-society clause. The three officials were Frank Iacobucci, the deputy attorney general of Canada; Roger Tassé, Iacobucci's predecessor and one of the chief architects of the Charter of Rights; and Professor Peter Hogg, a member of the Ontario delegation and the author of the leading Canadian text on the constitution. Two other senior advisers from the Quebec delegation, Jean

Samson and André Tremblay, were also in the room, seated behind Bourassa. They were there to provide the Quebec premier with their analysis of the comments of the three invited experts. Iacobucci, Tassé, and Hogg were given only a few minutes' advance warning before being summoned into the room. They were not told the reason for the invitation, nor were they given any opportunity to consult with one another.

After Iacobucci, Tassé, and Hogg were ushered into the conference room, the prime minister told them that the First Ministers were having difficulties with the meaning of the distinct-society clause. Mulroney said that he had been getting a lot of questions about the clause over the past fourteen hours. The main question was the extent to which it would diminish the rights of the English-speaking minority in Quebec. Mulroney asked the three experts to provide their opinions on the extent to which minority rights would be affected.

Iacobucci spoke first, followed by Tassé, and then Hogg. Although they had not consulted with one another, the answers they gave to Mulroney's question were broadly similar. They each indicated that the distinct-society clause would be used in interpreting the extent to which the Quebec government could place limits on individual rights. The clause would permit the government to argue that it was appropriate to limit individual rights, including the right to use English, in order to promote the predominantly French-speaking character of the province. But, they noted, this did not imply that the right to use English would necessarily be diminished, since the clause also referred to the existence of the English-speaking community as a fundamental characteristic of Canada. The three experts suggested that the clause would probably have relatively little impact on the manner in which the courts would interpret the charter. The courts had already indicated that it was legitimate for Quebec to undertake measures to promote the French language in the province. Thus the distinct-society clause would in effect merely confirm the direction that the courts had already adopted in their interpretation of the charter.

The advice of the three constitutional experts calmed many of the fears being voiced around the table. But Ontario's attorney general, Ian Scott, still had some qualms about the possible scope and implications of the distinct-society clause. He continued to press David Peterson to obtain additional wording that would guarantee the rights of the English minority in Quebec. Scott wanted an amendment that would specify that the clause did not extend Quebec's legislative powers. Peterson indicated that Bourassa was unwilling to accept such a broad limitation on the distinct-society clause. The most that Bourassa would accept was a provision stating that aboriginal rights and the multicultural character of the country were not affected. Bourassa was also apparently prepared to agree to a statement that the powers of the federal Parliament were not diminished by the distinct-society clause. This wording was important because it was an attempt to achieve indirectly what Scott wanted to state directly. If the powers of the federal Parliament could not be diminished, the implication was that the powers of the Quebec National Assembly could not be enlarged. The only way for the Quebec Assembly to gain new powers would be at the expense of the federal Parliament. But Bourassa was not prepared to accept a direct statement to the effect that Quebec's powers were not enlarged under the distinct-society clause. He wanted to preserve a measure of ambiguity in the manner in which the clause was drafted.

By three o'clock in the morning, the arguments had gone back and forth numerous times without any prospect of a final resolution. Finally, Peterson suggested that Ian Scott be invited into the room to make his case to the First Ministers personally. Mulroney and Bourassa agreed, and shortly after 3:00 a.m., Scott and a small number of Ontario legal advisers were summoned into the conference room. Iacobucci and Tassé were also present, seated behind the prime minister and Norman Spector, ready to provide their commentary on whatever arguments Scott might offer.

Scott provided the First Ministers with an impromptu account of his concerns about the possible scope of the distinct-society clause. Scott indicated that he was particularly concerned about a section in the clause that referred to the 'role' of the government of Quebec to promote the distinct identity of Quebec. Scott suggested that the use of the word 'role' was ambiguous and that it might be construed by the courts so as to confer additional powers on the province of Quebec. He argued that this interpretation would prejudice the position of the English-speaking minority in the province. He suggested that the clause should be amended to rule out this possibility.

Peter Hogg had accompanied Scott into the room as part of the small Ontario legal delegation. He was provided the opportunity to address the First Ministers for a second time that morning. Hogg supported Scott's proposal for an amendment to the distinct-society clause. When questioned by Quebec premier Robert Bourassa about the necessity for the amendment, Hogg suggested that it would certainly clarify any doubts about the meaning of the clause. Frank Iacobucci and Roger Tassé then weighed into the debate. The federal officials did not take direct issue with Scott or Hogg. They simply maintained that the amendment being proposed was unnecessary. They did not have any substantive objection to the amendment Scott was proposing. They simply regarded it as being superfluous.

Bourassa then spoke, indicating that he was opposed to the amendment Scott was suggesting. The Quebec premier said that he had already made a number of concessions in the wording of the distinct-society clause. He argued that these concessions would be politically costly to him when he returned to the province of Quebec. Bourassa pointed in particular to the amendment stating that the powers of the federal Parliament were not diminished by the distinct-society clause. Bourassa said that, by implication, this amendment conceded the very issue Scott was raising. The effect of this amendment would be to prevent Quebec from gaining any new powers under the distinct society clause. Bourassa said this was as far as he was prepared to go. The amendment proposed by Scott was simply asking too much.

Scott retired from the room, and the First Ministers took a final break to consider their positions. The Ontario delegation had commandeered a small suite of offices down the hall from the meeting room. It was now around four o'clock in the morning. Peterson told his delegation that the negotiations had essentially concluded, and the time had come to make a decision. There were no more compromises forthcoming from Bourassa. The question was whether to accept the package that was on the table or to turn it down and walk away. Peterson revealed that the fate of the accord rested on his shoulders alone. The other First Ministers had all more or less indicated that they were willing to accept the deal. The question for Ontario was whether to sign on, or else be the one responsible for scuttling the accord.

The arguments pro and con were canvassed. On the one hand, Peterson had not succeeded in obtaining all of the amendments he had attempted to secure. On the other, Bourassa had made a series of important concessions on both the distinct-society and spending-power clauses. The implications of Ontario being the one responsible for scuttling the accord featured prominently in the argument in favour of Peterson signing. The concern was that if David Peterson, the premier of Canada's largest province, was the one to walk away from the table, the result would be a dramatic negative impact on public opinion in the province of Quebec. Within Quebec, Ontario was seen as the leader of English-speaking Canada. The actions of an Ontario premier always carried greater symbolic and substantive significance than those of the other provinces. Some argued that it was absolutely essential that Peterson not be the one responsible for cratering the talks. Peterson was told that there were already reports circulating among the Quebec media assembled on the sidewalk outside that Ontario was to blame for the fact that the talks had dragged on into the middle of the night. If he walked out now, there would be a fire-storm in Quebec directed at his province, and at him personally. It would be said that Peterson had reneged on the agreement he had accepted at Meech Lake and betrayed his friend Robert Bourassa and, through him, all Quebeckers.

Peterson listened to the advice quietly. He did not argue or comment on what was being said, leaving it to his advisers to put forward arguments on either side of the issue. He thanked the delegation for their advice and returned to the conference room at the end of the hall without indicating what his final decision would be. At 4:45 a.m. the prime minister called the meeting to order in room 414 for the final time. He asked each premier in turn whether or not there was a deal. He began with Bourassa, then worked his way clockwise around the table. First Bourassa, then Hatfield, Vander Zalm, Devine, and Peckford – all indicated in turn they were prepared to agree to the package. Mulroney then worked his way back up the other side of the table. Getty, Ghiz, Buchanan said they were in. Howard Pawley said he was prepared to sign, although he indicated that he intended to hold public hearings on the proposals back in Manitoba.

Nine votes in favour. That left Peterson as the final arbiter. Meech Lake would live or die according to his signal. The Ontario premier reviewed his concerns about the accord and rehearsed the arguments on either side. He noted that Bourassa had agreed to a number of amendments and that he understood that no further compromises would be forthcoming. He indicated that he still had reservations about the wording of the distinct-society clause. He said that it would be necessary to hold public hearings on the resolution when he returned to Toronto. But, in the end, Peterson said that his remaining concerns were not so significant that he would be justified in walking away from the table. Peterson said that he, too, was prepared to sign. The tenth and final piece fell into the puzzle. The Meech Lake Accord had survived a nineteen-hour marathon, battered and bruised, but still in one piece.

Mulroney, a man with considerable experience in such matters, knew it would be unwise to let anyone out of the room without first getting signatures on a piece of paper. There would be an official signing ceremony later that day in front of the television cameras in the Conference Centre. But the prime minister insisted that they all sign the formal legal text on the spot. The signing ceremony under the lights at the Conference

Centre would be a mere formality. Federal officials were ushered into the room with copies of the final version of the legal text. Each First Minister initialled the document, and the deal was official.

The prime minister was the first to emerge from the Langevin Block and inform the media that a unanimous agreement had been signed. It was nearly dawn – just past 5:30 a.m. – as Mulroney told reporters that the new deal was 'a very strong statement of national unity, of bringing Canada much more closely together.' But there was none of the euphoria or sense of accomplishment that had surrounded the announcement of the agreement at Meech Lake. The prime minister seemed almost to be anticipating some resistance to the accord when he stated that, since 'the document is composed by human beings, it is, of course, far from perfect.'[17] Mulroney promised that there would be public hearings before the accord was ratified by Parliament.

Ontario premier David Peterson also sounded a cautionary note as he emerged on the sidewalk on Elgin Street. He indicated that a legislative committee would hold public hearings in Ontario after the federal hearings were concluded. Peterson promised that, if the public demanded amendments to the legal text, the deal could be changed and the First Ministers would be summoned together again to approve a new deal. 'If there are mistakes made or something that should be changed that's obvious, then it can be changed,' Peterson told reporters.[18] Manitoba premier Howard Pawley said he was satisfied with the changes that had been negotiated in the marathon session and promised to recommend the ratification of the accord to his legislature. 'I believe we have achieved a balance in the wording we have agreed to today,' claimed Pawley. But he also promised that there would be public hearings in Manitoba before any move to ratify the agreement.

Quebec premier Robert Bourassa uttered his customary and obligatory statements about the 'substantial gains' Quebec had won in the all-night bargaining session. Bourassa claimed that the Quebec government had won a 'safeguard clause' that protected the powers of the National Assembly over language issues. Bourassa was referring to an amendment to the distinct-society clause that stated that nothing in the clause diminished the powers of the National Assembly to legislate in language matters. What Bourassa did not mention was that, in order to obtain this 'safeguard,' he had to accept a similar clause protecting the rights of the federal Parliament over language. The practical result of the amendment, in short, was to diminish the significance and scope of the distinct-society clause. The amended version of the clause made it clear that it would not alter the division of powers between the federal and provincial governments. This reworked clause, in fact, represented an important concession from Bourassa. The amended version of the clause contradicted some of the more extreme statements that had been made in Quebec about the 'new powers' the province was likely to gain under the accord.

Before continuing with the Meech Lake story, it is important to take a moment to assess the significance of the Meech Lake/Langevin experience in the spring of 1987. The events in April, May, and June 1987 were obviously a critical point in the whole exercise. It was during this period that the accord was negotiated and the terms of the three-year ratification debate were fixed. What conclusions emerge from these events? What do the events of this period tell us about the three-year debate that was to follow? What conclusions can we draw about constitution-making in general in this country?

I will have more to offer on this subject later in this book. For now, I simply want to identify three preliminary conclusions that emerge from the story thus far.

1. The first conclusion is that the momentum had already begun to turn away from the proponents of Meech Lake and in favour of its opponents by June 1987. The agreement had very nearly fallen apart during the all-night bargaining session. Both Peterson and Pawley had demanded and won significant concessions from Bourassa in return for their continued support. But, despite these concessions, there was considerable doubt until the very end of the meeting whether or not there would be a unanimous agreement. Moreover, Peterson, Pawley, and Mulroney were talking about the need for public hearings and further public debate on the accord as they emerged from the all-night session. Although they had committed themselves to passing the constitutional resolution 'as soon as possible,' the reality was that the process was going to take some months, and possibly even years. Hearings would have to be held in Ottawa, followed by hearings in Ontario and Manitoba. Who could say when the process might be brought to an end? What was little appreciated at the time was the extent to which this delay would favour the opponents of the accord. The point is simply that, even by 3 June 1987, the momentum had changed and the obstacles on the road to ratification were far greater than anyone appreciated.

Why had the agreement held together rather than collapsing under the pressure of an all-night bargaining session? There are at least two obvious reasons. The first was the fact that there had been a unanimous agreement in principle at Meech Lake just thirty-three days earlier. This previous agreement made it far more difficult to walk away from the table at Langevin. Putting the matter another way, if there had not been a previous unanimous agreement involving all the parties at the table, it is unlikely that the Langevin meeting would have resulted in agreement on a legal text. The second explanation for the result at Langevin was the Trudeau article of 27 May. Trudeau's strong personal attack had given each of the premiers an important stake in ensuring that the meeting resulted in a signed agreement.

2. A second conclusion flowing from the Langevin meeting has to do with the process utilized. The Meech process, in which political leaders meet behind closed doors in order to agree on an constitutional amendment, has now become totally discredited. Canadians seem to want their constitutional discussions to be conducted in the open, with full public participation. What the Langevin meeting demonstrates, however, is that *some* form of private discussion is absolutely essential if a unanimous agreement is to reached. A unanimous agreement involves trade-offs and compromise. It requires the parties to the negotiations to be willing to take risks, to remain flexible, and to make concessions. This type of behaviour will simply not occur in a public setting. Within a public setting, the paramount consideration will be one of political prestige. Any compromises or trade-offs that might be made will be too obvious, particularly to those whose interests might be affected. Thus compromises will be extremely difficult to offer, since any such offer will involve significant political costs. With risk-taking and flexibility discouraged, it will be virtually impossible for the negotiations to result in agreement. If the negotiations are entirely in public, the result will be entirely predictable: rather than conduct real negotiations, the parties will simply adhere to fixed, pre-established positions.

The remarkable thing about this principle is that it applies generally. Whenever negotiations require the making of concessions, these concessions will typically not be made in public. It does not matter what the subject-matter is or who the parties might be. Whether the bargaining involves a treaty between sovereign nations, negotiations between political parties in a parliamentary setting, or litigants in a court case, the identical characteristic is exhibited. The parties to the negotiations will reach agreement only if they are provided the opportunity to meet in private. The Meech Lake and Langevin meetings confirm this general principle. It can be stated quite categorically that the concessions necessary to reach agreement would simply not have been forthcoming in a public setting. It follows that future constitutional negotiations will also have to be conducted in private, at least in part, if the intention is to arrive at an agreement.

3. A third conclusion flowing from the Meech Lake/Langevin experience relates to the difficulty in conducting a public debate on the issues involved. It was already apparent that it was almost impossible to conduct a national public debate on the Meech Lake Accord. The problem was the quite different political environment in Quebec from that in the rest of the country. Within Quebec, the only relevant question was whether the Meech Lake Accord granted new powers to Quebec. In order to sell the accord in Quebec, it was absolutely necessary to claim that Quebec had gained new or special powers. But the moment these claims were made within Quebec, they would provoke a negative response in the rest of Canada where the ground rules were precisely the opposite. Outside of Quebec, it was absolutely necessary to deny that Quebec gained any new or special powers. Of course, the moment such denials were issued, they would rebound into Quebec politics and undermine support within Quebec for Meech Lake.

The dynamic involved was nicely illustrated by the exchange between Quebec's Gil Rémillard and Ontario's Ian Scott in May 1987. Rémillard, in seeking to sell the agreement to Quebeckers, claimed that it granted substantial new powers to Quebec. Scott, by contrast, was busy telling his constituents that the agreement maintained the status quo and might even involve a small addition to the powers of the federal government. Rémillard's comments immediately caused a furore in Ontario, while Scott's comments provoked headlines in Quebec. Each was forced to contradict the other, which fuelled the debate and promoted the sense that the authors of the document didn't know what they had signed.

One criticism that is often made of Meech Lake, even by those who supported the agreement, is that political leaders failed to 'sell' the agreement to the public. It is sometimes suggested that, if political leaders had attempted to conduct a real national debate on the subject, the fight for its ratification might have been different. It is quite true that political leaders, particularly the prime minister, were not very forthcoming about the agreement. Mulroney tended to restrict his comments to the level of generalities, talking over and over about the need to bring Quebec 'back in' to the constitution. But the explanation for Mulroney's reticence is quite obvious. No matter what he might say about the agreement, it would be turned against him. A claim that the agreement did not grant new powers to Quebec might sell well in Thunder Bay but it would be disastrous in Quebec City. Alternatively, a claim by Mulroney that the agreement granted Quebec new powers would satiate nationalist appetites in Sherbrooke but would inflame passions in Moose Jaw or Cornerbrook. The only way to avoid this whipsaw effect was to remain silent. Thus, Mulroney studiously avoided any comment on the issue of the extent to which the agreement involved a grant of new powers to Quebec.

This political dynamic was already at work in June 1987, and it would continue to exert a powerful hold on the debate over the next three years. It should also be noted that this dynamic played a crucial role in undermining public support for the accord. It was extremely difficult to offer any public response to critics of the accord, because any response that might be made would backfire. Political leaders thus tended to abandon the field of public debate to the critics of the accord. Not only did this tactic reinforce the sense that the critics of Meech outnumbered its supporters, it also led to claims that there was some kind of 'conspiracy of silence' among supporters of Meech Lake. Within such an atmosphere, the prospects for ratification of the agreement were far from certain, despite the show of unanimity on the morning of 3 June 1987.

6

Unravelling a Seamless Web

'The Accord is a seamless web and an integrated
whole.'

Senator Lowell Murray, testifying
before the Special Joint Committee
on the Meech Lake Accord,
4 August 1987

On 3 June 1987, the prime minister and a number of the premiers had promised meaningful public hearings on the agreement that had been hammered out during the all-night Langevin bargaining session. The clear implication was that the agreement was not carved in stone and that proposals for future changes would be seriously entertained. But these promises of public input were misleading. It was clear to most of those who had participated at the Langevin meeting that any attempt to change the accord would cause it to unravel. The simple problem was that changing the agreement required someone to give up something. Someone would be cast in the role of 'winner,' someone else in the role of 'loser.' Given the highly symbolic character of the issues involved, none of the signatories to the agreement was in a political position to make any such concessions. If the agreement were modified so as to reduce the gains Quebec had achieved, Quebec's Premier Bourassa would be exposed to the nationalist critique that he had 'caved in' to demands from English Canada. But a change designed to increase Quebec's gains under the agreement was an obvious non-starter in the rest of the country. Outside of Quebec, the most telling critique of the agreement was that it granted too much power to the provinces in general, and to Quebec in particular. The prime minister and the premiers could not seriously entertain any proposals designed to enhance the gains Quebec had already achieved.

Coming out of the Langevin meeting, Robert Bourassa was acutely aware of the fact that he could not be seen to be making concessions to the rest of the country. He was also astute enough to understand that he could not hope to extract any further concessions from any of the other premiers or from the federal government. In effect, the only way for the accord to succeed was to have it ratified in its current form. There was thus no advantage for Bourassa in delaying the ratification of the accord. The Quebec premier understood that any delay in ratification would only provide nationalist forces in his province with an opportunity to mobilize opposition to the accord. In turn, pressure would mount to obtain modifications in the accord, modifications that Bourassa realized would be impossible to obtain from the other premiers. Bourassa came to the conclusion that the most prudent course was to ratify the accord as quickly as possible, and to hope that the other provinces and the federal government would follow suit.

Bourassa introduced the resolution into the Quebec National Assembly immediately upon returning to Quebec City from the Ottawa meeting. He argued that public hearings on the resolution were unnecessary, since there had already been hearings during May on the Meech Lake Accord. His plan was to bring the resolution to a vote prior to the Assembly's rising for the summer on 23 June. The opposition Parti Québécois denounced both the process and the terms of the agreement itself, arguing that further public hearings were necessary. PQ leader Pierre Marc Johnson argued that the Langevin agreement represented a 'step backward' from the original agreement signed at Meech Lake. Johnson was particularly opposed to changes that had been made in the distinct-society clause, which he argued made the clause essentially meaningless. But Bourassa ignored the objections and used his legislative majority to force the resolution through the Assembly on 23 June.

Bourassa's quick action to ratify the accord was a clear signal to the other governments across the country. Meech Lake would have to be ratified 'as is' or not at all. Quebec would ask for nothing more, but would accept nothing less. Such had been Bourassa's message during the all-night Langevin meeting. His quick action to ratify the accord reinforced and underlined the message. Bourassa's hope was that other governments would follow his lead and move to ratify the accord quickly.

Even by the end of June 1987, however, it was clear that there was little chance of ratification proceeding on a fast track. The federal government had promised public hearings on the accord, and it was expected that these hearings would not conclude until sometime in the fall. Both Ontario and Manitoba had committed themselves to public hearings after the conclusion of the federal hearings. Thus ratification in those provinces was unlikely to occur until sometime in 1988. Moreover, Ontario premier David Peterson was in a minority position in the Ontario Legislature, and an election was widely expected sometime before the end of the year. Meech Lake might become an issue in the election campaign, with Peterson facing pressure to modify his support for the accord. This was a particular concern in Quebec City, where there were vivid memories of the heated debates with Peterson and his advisers during the all-night Langevin meeting. In fact, Quebec media accounts immediately following Langevin had painted Peterson as the villain of the piece, arguing that he had led the opposition to Quebec's distinct-society clause and caused the meeting to drag on for nineteen hours. Peterson had downplayed the Quebec media reports, arguing that the story of his role had been 'blown out of proportion'.[1] But the doubts about Peterson's commitment to the deal lingered for some time in the corridors of Quebec City.

There was also uncertainty in New Brunswick, where Premier Richard Hatfield's five-year mandate was due to expire in September. The legislature had risen for the summer in June without having considered the constitutional resolution. It was thus clear that the constitutional issue would not be dealt with until sometime after the provincial election. Liberal leader Frank McKenna, who was leading in the public-opinion polls, had already expressed reservations about the accord and called for public hearings. McKenna had also served notice that he did not feel bound by the agreement signed by Richard Hatfield on behalf of the province. 'All our options ... remain open,' McKenna had indicated in early June, noting that there was a full three years to consider the ratification of the agreement.

Still, public support for the Meech Lake Accord remained relatively high. A number of opinion polls released over the month of June showed that Canadians favoured the Meech/Langevin agreement by a 2-to-1 margin.[2] But this level of support was deceptive. The same opinion polls indicated that a clear majority of Canadians knew little or nothing about what was in the agreement. It was evident that the relatively high approval rating was 'soft' and subject to change. Canadians were generally supportive of the agreement, but they knew little about it. In this context, public opinion could easily shift in the opposite direction if respected political figures or interest groups began expressing reservations about the accord.

The federal government moved to begin the public hearings on the accord as quickly as possible. A special joint committee of the House of Commons and Senate was struck in July and began sitting the first week of August. The first witness before the committee was Senator Lowell

Murray, who explained the official government position on the accord. What was most significant about Murray's testimony was the position he took on the issue of amendments to the accord. Murray effectively ruled out the possibility of changing the accord, arguing that it was 'a seamless web, the product of compromise and conciliation.' The senator argued that the federal government was prepared to change only what he termed 'egregious drafting errors.' Even in the case of an 'egregious error,' which Murray did not define, he stipulated that a change would be possible only if all other governments agreed. Any change would have to meet what Murray termed the 'test of unanimity' in order to be acceptable. Murray proposed that any flaws in the agreement be dealt with in a 'second round' of negotiations, following the ratification of the accord. He urged the committee to indicate areas of the accord that might be improved in this 'second round.'

Murray's hard-line position on amendments was like waving a red flag in front of the opponents of the accord. Parliamentary committees are normally given some latitude in proposing amendments to government bills. But the government was attempting to adopt a different standard in the case of the constitutional resolution. That not even a comma or subclause could be altered, except in the case of an unspecified 'egregious error,' enraged both the members of the opposition and the growing number of critics of the accord, who pointed out that a constitutional amendment was a permanent change and thus ought to be subject to greater rather than lesser scrutiny. Liberal MP André Ouellet complained that the government was holding the hearings as a kind of publicity stunt, designed to 'publicize the Accord and not to change it.' 'Our position is the reverse,' Ouellet added, 'that the hearings should lead to some changes.'[3]

Lowell Murray's attempt to rule out the possibility of changes had precisely the opposite effect. His description of the accord as a 'seamless web' became a lightning-rod for criticism of the accord and fuelled opposition to it. Witness after witness before the committee fastened on Murray's 'egregious error' comments, complaining angrily that the whole committee proceedings were meaningless and little more than a sham. Murray's comments had the unintended effect of fanning the flames of opposition to the accord and of providing a focus of attack for the accord's critics. When the hearings began, opposition to the constitutional proposal had been fragmented and disorganized. But, over the five weeks of hearings, the issue of the 'process' began to emerge as a common reference point for opponents of the accord. The 'process' critique was not limited to the parliamentary hearings themselves. Critics began to question the manner in which the accord had been negotiated in the first place. A recurring objection was that the accord had been negotiated entirely behind closed doors, with no opportunity for meaningful public input. This tact made it all the more essential, the critics maintained, that there be a willingness to consider suggestions for changes at the committee stage.

The other key issue that emerged over the five weeks of hearings was the concern expressed by women's groups. Women's organizations had been largely silent on the accord during the period between Meech Lake and the Langevin meeting on 3 June. But during the all-night session at Langevin, the First Ministers had added a clause to the accord specifically protecting the rights of aboriginal peoples and multicultural groups. The amendment written in at Langevin stated that the distinct-society clause could not affect multicultural or aboriginal rights. The result was that women's organizations were alerted to the possibility that the distinct-society clause might be used to diminish equality rights under the charter. During the committee hearings in August, a least half a dozen national women's organizations came forward to demand specific protection for equality rights. The argument of the women's organizations was that the specific reference to aboriginal and multicultural rights gave rise to the implication that equality rights were negatively affected.

Two prominent Toronto constitutional lawyers, Mary Eberts and John Laskin, drafted a lengthy legal opinion, setting out the reasons supporting their demand for an amendment protecting equality rights. The opinion was tabled before the committee by the Ad Hoc Committee of Canadian Women on the Constitution on the second-last day of the committee's hearings. Mary Eberts testified before the committee, arguing that 'you cannot say that there is no risk of harm to women's equality rights.' Eberts attempted to argue that women across the country, and not just in Quebec, might be adversely affected by the accord. But her argument was based on a complicated hypothetical example involving affirmative-action programs designed to bring more women into the civil service. Eberts argued that, under the distinct-society clause, such affirmative-action programs might be eliminated in favour of programs that were 'language oriented.' But the complicated and hypothetical nature of the Eberts argument tended to reduce its political impact. There was no clear or compelling example that could be used to drive home the Ad Hoc Committee's objections to the accord.

One of the ironies in the debate over the impact of the distinct-society clause on women's rights was the position taken by certain prominent women's groups in the province of Quebec. On the very day that Mary

Eberts was appearing before the parliamentary committee to voice her concerns, a prominent Quebec women's organization appeared to contradict Eberts's claims about the distinct-society clause. Francine McKenzie, head of the Quebec Council on the Status of Women, told the parliamentary committee that the distinct-society clause would not affect women's equality rights under the charter.[4] McKenzie stated that arguments raised by women's groups outside the province of Quebec were 'maternalistic' and assumed unreasonably that Quebec had a bias against women. The Quebec Council stated in its brief that it 'believes that we can have trust in our institutions and in the women's associations still alive and well in Quebec.'

The division between women's organizations within and outside of the province of Quebec was seized on by the federal government in its defence of the distinct-society clause. Senator Lowell Murray appeared before the parliamentary committee on 2 September as its final witness. Flanked by Norman Spector and by Frank Iacobucci, the deputy attorney general of Canada, Senator Murray rejected all the criticisms that had been levelled against the accord during the month-long public hearings. Murray denied that the accord would threaten equality rights under the charter, arguing that he would personally vote against the accord if he thought it threatened to take away rights from anyone. The senator also rejected the criticisms of former prime minister Pierre Trudeau. Trudeau had appeared before the committee in the final week of August to repeat his view that the accord created 'two Canadas,' one French, the other English. But Senator Murray argued that this possibility existed only in Trudeau's 'own mind,' since the accord specifically referred to the existence of the English-speaking community in the province of Quebec. The senator concluded his four-and-a-half-hour presentation by calling on the committee to recommend that the accord be ratified unamended. Murray argued that to make any changes in the accord would cause the delicate series of compromises contained in it to unravel.

The committee ultimately heeded the senator's call to recommend in favour of ratification of the accord unchanged. But the committee's report, tabled in the House of Commons on 21 September, had some surprisingly harsh criticism for a number of provisions in the accord. The committee was critical of a provision that permitted the provinces to nominate judges to the Supreme Court but denied the same right to the two territories. The committee described this omission as 'anomalous' and said that 'we have not heard any reasonable justification for it.' The report was also sympathetic to the concerns of the two territories that the accord would make it impossible for them to ever acquire provincial status. The committee said that the requirement of obtaining unanimous provincial consent in order to create new provinces would 'impose artificial and unnecessary constraints on the natural evolution and development of the northern third of the land mass of our country.'

The committee rejected as unfounded the fears of women's groups that the accord would jeopardize the Charter of Rights. But the report accepted the criticisms that had been raised of the Meech Lake process. It denounced the absence of any public input into the drafting of the accord and stated that there should be an opportunity for public comment prior to any meeting of First Ministers.

Despite identifying these substantial shortcomings, the Conservative and New Democrat MPs on the committee recommended that the accord be ratified unamended. New Democrat Pauline Jewett declared: 'we are going to support the accord despite these shocking anomalies.'[5] The majority accepted Senator Murray's argument that to reopen the accord would cause it to unravel. They were prepared to overlook what they regarded as 'shocking anomalies' in the interests of securing Quebec's signature on the constitution. The committee argued that the flaws in the accord could be dealt with at the annual constitutional conferences provided for in the accord. Even the Liberals, who wrote a separate minority report proposing a series of eight amendments, conceded that they would vote to ratify the accord if their amendments were defeated.

The prime minister claimed vindication from the committee's report and promised swift action to bring the accord to a vote in the House of Commons. In one sense, the government's position had been vindicated: the committee had recommended the adoption of the accord without any changes. But the reality was that the committee's report represented a significant set-back for the government. Senator Lowell Murray had attempted to persuade the committee that there were no major flaws in the accord and that the criticisms of its substance and process ought to be rejected. He had clearly failed in his efforts. The committee had bluntly criticized certain features of the accord and denounced the closed-door negotiations that had produced it. The pointed criticisms advanced by the committee gave added credibility to the opponents of the accord and bolstered the legitimacy of their claims that the accord ought to be amended. Moreover, the parade of witnesses at the hearings opposed to the accord created the clear impression that the accord was massively unpopular among ordinary Canadians. The principal supporters of the accord appeared to be academics and constitutional experts, whose language and discourse had no purchase with ordinary Canadians. The opponents of the accord, by contrast, appeared to be broad-based coalitions of women's organizations, multicultural groups, nurses, day-care advocates, and aboriginal people. The contrast between the supporters and the critics could not have been more stark and politically devastating for the pro-Meech forces.

In getting the accord through the parliamentary committee in a single piece, the government had cleared one hurdle on the road to ratification. But it was apparent that the political momentum was shifting inexorably in favour of the opponents of the accord. The hearings had brought to light the 'weak link' in the government's position on the accord – the demand that the accord had to be approved without any changes. The government was forced into the position of admitting that certain criticisms of the accord might well be valid, but that these objections could only be dealt with in a 'second round' of negotiations following ratification. The 'no changes' line was a catalyst for opposition to Meech Lake. Ordinary Canadians may have had little understanding of the contents of the accord, but they could understand and identify a 'political fix' when they saw one. The 'undemocratic Meech process' became the rallying cry for the opponents of the accord, arousing suspicions among English Canadians that the government was trying to 'ram through' constitutional changes without appropriate consultation. On its own, the undemocratic Meech process might not have been enough to seal the fate of the accord. But combined with a number of other factors, it contributed very powerfully to the political momentum working against the ratification of Meech Lake.

In 1982, constitutional changes had simply required a resolution passed by the Parliament of Canada, followed by a statute approved in Great Britain. Had this procedure been in place in 1987, the outcome of the Meech Lake debate would probably have been quite different. But, in 1987, constitutional change was governed by a new amending formula that required the passage of constitutional resolutions in all the provinces in order to entrench completely the Meech Lake Accord in the constitution. Thus the accord had to survive eleven different legislative encounters without any changes in order to become law.

This was a tall order, as the Meech ratification process was to illustrate in dramatic fashion. The first problem presented by the new rules for constitutional change was simply that they required a good deal more time to operate. The passage of eleven constitutional resolutions takes a lot longer than the passage of a single resolution. Time is a crucial variable in any political context. The longer the time required to approve a measure, the less likely it is that the measure will, in fact, be approved.

The passage of time is important for two reasons. First, it provides a political opposition with the opportunity to mobilize support. Second, and more significantly, the passage of time makes it more likely that some subsequent political event will occur that will undermine support for a proposal. This subsequent political event could take any one of a variety of forms. Perhaps a government that had supported a constitutional proposal will be turned out of office. Perhaps a subsequent political controversy will put a new, less favourable light on an earlier constitutional proposal. Perhaps a government that had supported a constitutional proposal in the past will reconsider its position in light of subsequent politicial developments. In the Meech Lake debate, all of these various factors were to come into play at different points in the process.

The other difficulty with the requirement of obtaining resolutions from eleven legislatures was the fact that each resolution had to be in precisely identical form. If any one legislature made modifications in the proposal, all other legislatures would have to make precisely the same modifications. Yet, there was no way of coordinating the deliberations of the various legislatures. The practical result was that individual legislatures would be asked to approve the constitutional resolution on a 'take it or leave it' basis. They would be asked to vote on a constitutional proposal, but would be denied any opportunity to change the proposal. The controversy surrounding Senator Murray's 'egregious error' comments had already highlighted how politically unpopular this position could be. The refusal to entertain changes to the agreement would, over time, call into question the legitimacy of the whole constitutional-reform process.

The 'bottom line' conclusion? In essence, the longer it took to ratify Meech, the less likely it would ever receive the required approval from all ten provincial legislatures. When the accord was being negotiated, there was some hope that it might be ratified in time for a royal visit from the Queen planned for October 1987. This original plan had become completely obsolete by the fall of 1987. It was clear by the fall that the ratification process would take longer, far longer, than had earlier been anticipated. The two key events in the fall of 1987 were the provincial elections in Ontario and New Brunswick. In Ontario, there was widespread opposition to the accord, particularly among women's groups and multicultural organizations based in Toronto. But the Meech Lake issue barely surfaced in the election campaign. The dominant issue was the free-trade negotiations with the United States. David Peterson was returned with an overwhelming majority and promised to carry forward with plans to hold public hearings on the accord in early 1988. The accord emerged relatively unscathed from the electoral contest in Ontario.

The outcome in New Brunswick was quite different. There, Liberal leader Frank McKenna had been raising concerns about the accord since it had been signed in June. In late August, he had appeared before the parliamentary committee in Ottawa to express his reservations. McKenna had a long list of proposed changes to the accord. He argued that the accord failed to adequately protect the rights of women, aboriginal peoples, and linguistic minorities in all provinces. He was concerned about the proposed limits on the federal spending power, as well as the provincial role in nominations to the Supreme Court of Canada. McKenna opposed the reference to 'fisheries' on the permanent agenda of constitutional conferences mandated under the accord. McKenna told the people of New Brunswick that he would regard a victory in the 13 October provincial election as a vote for changes to the accord. He promised that, if elected, he would 'go in and negotiate the best deal possible.'

McKenna's stunning 58 to 0 shut-out on 13 October was hailed by the opponents of Meech as the key to upsetting the constitutional agreement. McKenna called his election victory a 'broad mandate' to reject, or negotiate changes to, the accord.[6] But close examination of McKenna's comments indicated a subtle ambiguity in his position. While McKenna clearly was committed to seeking changes in the agreement, he appeared to leave open the question of what might happen if the other governments refused to agree to his proposed amendments. McKenna did not definitively commit himself to rejecting the accord if the changes he sought could not be achieved.

McKenna's strategy over the next two and a half years was to maintain and to cultivate this fundamental ambiguity in his position. McKenna seemed to believe that his bargaining leverage was increased if he refused to reveal his final position. The other element of McKenna's strategy was to delay the date upon which he would be forced to take a definitive position on the accord. From the moment he was elected, McKenna stressed that there was a full three years to consider the proposed constitutional resolution. There was no need to rush into a hasty or ill-considered decision on the accord. McKenna committed himself to holding public hearings on the accord before bringing the matter to a vote in the New Brunswick Legislature. Those hearings were not scheduled to take place until the fall of 1988. It would thus be sometime in 1989, at the very earliest, before the Meech issue would be resolved one way or the other in New Brunswick. Before then, there would likely be a federal election as well as a number of other provincial elections. McKenna's theory was that time was on his side, and that sooner or later the other governments who were supporting Meech would have to come to him.

But the McKenna strategy made sense only on the assumption that it was, in fact, possible to negotiate changes to the accord. If this assumption was false, then the McKenna strategy would have two effects, neither of them in the long-term interests of the country. First, his approach of delaying the final moment of decision would decrease the chances of the accord's ever being ratified. Rather than an improved or modified accord, the result would be no constitutional amendment at all. Second, McKenna's approach would increase the stakes associated with the failure of the accord. By keeping the issue on the public agenda for a prolonged period of time, the significance and symbolism of the accord were bound to increase. Thus, if and when the accord did fail, the implications for the country would be far greater than if the issue had been resolved in a more expeditious manner.

As the eleven First Ministers gathered for their annual conference on the economy in Toronto, on 26 November 1987, the main focus of public attention was the Canadian–U.S. trade agreement. But a side-bar to the main proceedings was the Meech Lake controversy and, in particular, McKenna's opposition to the constitutional amendment. In his opening statement at the conference, the New Brunswick premier fuelled specula-tion that he would oppose the accord in its present form. McKenna argued in favour of a strong central government and warned against a 'loose coalition of ten provinces.' These remarks were interpreted by reporters as a veiled criticism of the Meech Lake Accord, although McKenna did not refer to the accord by name. But McKenna was careful not to commit himself to outright opposition to the accord. Privately, he told the other First Ministers that he did not want to scuttle Meech, but merely to 'improve' it. He began talking about adding to Meech Lake without subtracting anything from the accord. McKenna promised to send a team of New Brunswick officials on a tour of the provinces early in the new year to explain his concerns and the changes he was proposing.

Bourassa said little about the accord or about McKenna's objections to it. He indicated that he would be willing to discuss McKenna's objections after Meech Lake was ratified. McKenna's concerns could be listed as part of the agenda for the 'second round' of negotiations. But Bourassa in-sisted that Meech be ratified first, unamended. Only then would Bourassa be willing to entertain a discussion of McKenna's concerns.

What was not clearly appreciated at the time, and is apparent only with the benefit of hindsight, was that there was a fundamental confusion developing around the table. The supporters of Meech Lake, such as Quebec and the federal government, were confused about McKenna's intentions. At the same time, McKenna himself was badly mistaken about Robert Bourassa's real 'bottom line' on the Meech Lake Accord.

McKenna seemed to believe that Bourassa possessed a measure of flexibility and would eventually be willing to consider amendments to the accord. This belief was encouraged to a certain extent by Bourassa's vague comments about the possibility of a hypothetical 'second round' of negotiations. McKenna and his advisers discounted Bourassa's comments about the necessity of approving Meech unamended. They simply refused to believe that Bourassa could remain intransigent in the face of the growing opposition to Meech Lake across the country. McKenna and his advisers began talking about a 'companion resolution' that would be passed at the same time as the Meech Lake Accord. Under this approach, two resolutions would be approved simultaneously. The first resolution would be the Meech Lake Accord itself. The second would be a package of amendments to the accord. In this way, the New Brunswickers thought, both Bourassa and McKenna would achieve their stated objectives. Bourassa would achieve his objective of ratifying Meech, but McKenna would achieve his objective of securing amendments to Meech through the device of the companion resolution.

The problem with the approach was obvious. The 'companion resolution' was a transparent attempt to do indirectly what Bourassa had said he could not do directly. Bourassa had ruled out from the very beginning any substantive amendments to Meech Lake. If this was his real 'bottom line' position, as opposed to a mere bargaining ploy, then there was simply no way he could ever agree to a companion resolution of the type McKenna was proposing. But McKenna clearly believed otherwise. His whole strategy throughout the next two years was premised on the belief that, sooner or later, Bourassa would accept amendments to Meech Lake in the form of a 'companion resolution.' It was not until the very end of the process that it became crystal clear to McKenna and the other opponents of Meech that Bourassa had not been bluffing.

Bourassa was a hard bargainer, but he was a model of consistency. He had insisted at the Langevin meeting in June 1987 that it would be 'Meech Lake or nothing.' He continued to adopt that position until the very end of the process three years later. But Bourassa was as confused about McKenna's position as McKenna was about Bourassa's. Bourassa seemed to be under the impression that McKenna's opposition to Meech Lake was some elaborate form of posturing. The assumption was that McKenna would eventually fold his cards and concede once he understood that Bourassa was not bluffing. This assumption was bolstered by the ambiguity in McKenna's position – by his refusal to state definitively that he would reject Meech if it were not amended. And so, Bourassa, like McKenna, thought that time was on his side. McKenna was new to the realities of power, Bourassa and his advisers reasoned. Give him time to get his bearings and to understand the real nature of the choice he would have to make. Eventually McKenna would come to his senses and realize that the stakes were too high to gamble with the future of the country – or so Bourassa thought in the late fall of 1987.

This fundamental confusion about the real 'bottom lines' of the various parties was to dog the Meech process until the very end. Each party assumed that the other was bluffing and that it was only a matter of time before they modified their position. The mistaken assumptions about the real intentions of the parties induced everyone to delay the final moment of decision. Everyone was prepared to bide his time, expecting the others to reveal their 'true' position. This collective bubble of confusion persisted until the evening of 7 June 1990. At that moment, Robert Bourassa stuck a very large pin in the bubble by issuing a press release stating that he was not willing to discuss changes to the distinct-society clause. For the first time, everyone understood the real choices that had to be made. Unfortunately for the country, by then the debate had escalated to the point where the future of Canada seemed to be directly at risk. The tragedy was that, by this point, it no longer seemed to matter what the First Ministers decided. A set of political forces had been set in motion that threatened the future of the country and seemed beyond the ability of anyone to control.

At the First Ministers' conference in November 1987, Frank McKenna suggested sending his officials on a tour of the provinces to outline his concerns. The other provinces agreed to undertake these discussions in the hope that some form of consensus could be found. But while the New Brunswickers began their cross-Canada tour, the Meech Lake Accord was running into problems in Manitoba. The flashpoint was not Meech Lake itself, but the Canadian – U.S. Trade Agreement. The premiers had been called to Ottawa on 17 December for a briefing on the proposed trade agreement. The agreement had been negotiated in October and the official signing by U.S. president Ronald Reagan and Prime Minister Mulroney had been scheduled for 2 January 1988. At the 17 December meeting, Ontario, Manitoba, and Prince Edward Island indicated that they were opposed to the agreement. The three provinces called on Mulroney to delay the official signing until there could be further public consultation. Mulroney refused, indicating that he intended to push ahead with the signing ceremony as scheduled, despite the objections of the three provinces.

An irate Howard Pawley returned to Manitoba and announced that he was withdrawing his support for the Meech Lake Accord. Pawley said he was angry with Mulroney's decision to push ahead with the trade agreement. As a result, he told reporters, he had decided that he 'will not promote or push for Meech Lake.'[7] Pawley justified his decision by claiming that Mulroney's position on the trade agreement had undone the conciliatory atmosphere between Ottawa and the provinces that had prevailed during the Meech negotiations. 'I believe that much of the good will and nation-building that took place in the writing of the Meech Lake accord are being undercut by the trade agreement,' Pawley claimed.[8] Pawley denied that he was using the Meech Lake issue as a bargaining chip in the trade negotiations. But he stated that he would not be introducing the accord into the Manitoba Legislature until the free-trade issue had been resolved. He also indicated that he was contemplating permitting a 'free vote' on the accord, in which members of the legislature would be released from party discipline to vote as they wish.

Despite Pawley's protestations, it was obvious that he was linking the trade issue with Meech Lake. Of course, the temptation to make such linkages is always present in a situation where unanimous consent is required for a measure. Pawley was exercising his veto power over the Meech Lake Accord as a means to influence the evolution of the trade issue. The immediate result was a further delay in the Meech ratification process. It was apparent that the debate over Meech Lake would extend, at a minimum, well into 1989.

In rethinking his support for the accord, Pawley was also attempting to respond to the massive unpopularity of the accord within Manitoba. The memory of the CF-18 débâcle in the fall of 1986 was still fresh in the minds of Manitobans. There was widespread opposition to the new constitutional deal, which was thought to threaten charter rights and grant 'special status' to the province of Quebec. Over the winter of 1987–8, a total of sixty municipalities in Manitoba passed resolutions condemning the accord. The Manitoba premier had received a letter from seventy-five prominent NDP provincial party members asking him to reopen the accord. At the Manitoba NDP convention in the first week in March, the delegates debated a motion to repudiate the Meech Lake Accord. If the resolution had been passed, it would have become the official policy of the provincial party and signalled the end of the accord in Manitoba. Pawley appealed to the delegates not to take a definitive position on Meech Lake at that time. He promised that there would be public hearings in Manitoba, and the opportunity to consider amendments to the accord. The convention eventually passed a resolution calling for 'meaningful' public hearings that could result in amendment or rejection of the accord. Pawley had avoided outright repudiation of the accord by his party. But it was clear that the sentiment against Meech Lake ran very deep in Manitoba.

Two days later, on 8 March 1988, Pawley's government was defeated in the legislature on a vote of non-confidence over the provincial budget. Pawley called an election for 26 April and resigned as party leader. On 30 March, midway in the campaign, Gary Doer was selected as NDP party leader. Meech Lake was not a dominant issue in the six-week campaign. The focus of attention was on automobile insurance rates and a proposed 18 per cent rate high by Autopac, the provincial insurance monopoly. The Conservatives under Gary Filmon entered the campaign with a commanding lead in the public-opinion polls. But the star of the campaign, and the big winner, was provincial Liberal leader Sharon Carstairs. She took her party from the political wilderness in Manitoba to twenty seats and status as the official opposition in the legislature. In the process she denied Gary Filmon a majority government and reduced Gary Doer and the NDP to third-party status with only twelve seats.

Carstairs was the only one of three Manitoba leaders to make Meech Lake an issue in the campaign. The Liberal leader was dead opposed to the accord and had vowed to kill it if she were elected as premier. The previous summer, she had travelled to Ottawa to offer moral support to her friend Frank McKenna when he had testified before the parliamentary committee. At the time she had been unnoticed, the lone Liberal member in the Manitoba Legislature. Now, some eight months later, she was the leader of the official opposition with the power to block or delay the passage of Meech Lake in Manitoba. As the poll results came in on 26 April, Carstairs proclaimed that 'Meech Lake is dead.' She promised to exercise her new-found muscle in the Manitoba Legislature to block any attempt by Filmon's minority government to push the accord through. Her comments provoked a flurry of negative comment from officials in Ottawa, who suggested that Carstair's Meech obituary was the rash statement of a politician new to power. Later in the week, Carstairs seemed to backtrack slightly, suggesting that 'when I say dead, I mean dead in its present form.'[9] Carstairs indicated that, like Frank McKenna in New Brunswick, she intended to campaign for changes to the accord, not outright rejection. She was confident that the accord could be amended, referring to the fact that refinements were made to the agreement at the

Langevin meeting of 2–3 June 1987. 'If Meech Lake Two was better than Meech Lake One, then why not Meech Lake Three?', she queried.

Newly elected premier Gary Filmon had been cautious in his public statements on the accord. During the election campaign, he had avoided comment on Meech Lake, other than to promise that the public hearings in Manitoba would be meaningful and not a mere rubber-stamp for the accord. Filmon had promised to listen to the concerns about Meech and to seek amendments if he became convinced that the accord was fundamentally flawed. Following the election on 26 April, Filmon maintained this discreet and noncommittal posture on Meech. He indicated that Meech Lake was not a priority and that 'it may well be that Meech Lake doesn't come into the agenda for quite some time.'[10] He had little more to say about the constitution over the spring and summer, concentrating on domestic provincial issues as he attempted to get his bearings as premier.

It was now a year since the accord had been signed at Meech Lake, and it was clearly in very serious trouble. By 30 April 1988, Meech had been ratified by the federal House of Commons and by three provinces – Quebec, Saskatchewan, and Alberta. But two of the eleven signatories of the original accord were no longer in office. There was now at least one government committed to seeking changes to the accord. A second government was noncommittal on the accord, but was in a minority position in a province where the accord was extremely unpopular.

Moreover, public support for the accord was beginning to erode fairly substantially. In June 1987, days after the all-night meeting at the Langevin Block, 56 per cent of Canadians had indicated that they thought the accord was a good thing for the country. Only 18 per cent had been opposed. Now, by April 1988, a Gallup poll indicated that only 28 per cent of Canadians thought the accord was a good thing for the country.[11] Opposition to the accord had remained fairly constant – according to Gallup, 25 per cent were opposed to Meech Lake. The big change was a massive upswing in those who were undecided about the accord. Fully 47 per cent of those polled by Gallup indicated that they were unsure of whether the accord would benefit the country. The year-long debate over Meech Lake had obviously taken a significant toll, causing large numbers of Canadians to pause and to rethink their initial support for the agreement. But the concern had not yet hardened into outright opposition. Canadians had suspended judgment, waiting to observe the arguments and the actions of the players, before reaching a final conclusion on the merits of Meech Lake.

While the situation was obviously deteriorating in the spring of 1988, there was no reason to believe that the accord was doomed to failure. Plans for ratification were proceeding in five other provinces – Prince Edward Island, Nova Scotia, Ontario, British Columbia, and Newfoundland. By early July 1988, the accord had been ratified by a total of eight provinces. The House of Commons had rejected changes proposed by the Senate and ratified the accord for a second time on 22 June. This left only the two hold-outs, New Brunswick and Manitoba, blocking the final approval of the accord. Neither of the hold-outs had firmly committed itself to rejecting the accord. The strategy of the pro-Meech provinces remained the same as it had been since the previous fall. Promise the hold-outs that their concerns would be addressed during a 'second round' of negotiations and, on that basis, persuade them to ratify the accord unamended.

The most worrying problem was that there seemed no way to force the issue to a quick resolution. Both New Brunswick and Manitoba continued to insist that they were in no rush to proceed and that the ratification process could extend until June 1990. Both provinces were committed to holding public hearings, but these hearings had not even been commenced. There were not even any serious negotiations under way between governments designed to narrow the differences. Everyone was playing a waiting game, uncertain how to proceed.

There were periodic reports in the press of 'secret negotiations' under way that might lead to a 'deal' between Quebec and the hold-out provinces.[12] But these press reports were based on little more than conjecture or idle gossip and were essentially unfounded. Various meetings were scheduled from time to time, either involving First Ministers themselves or their officials. But nothing of any substance would develop at these meetings. Instead, the participants would simply present their different points of view and agree to disagree.

The meeting between Robert Bourassa and Frank McKenna in Fredericton on 17 March 1988, was typical of these exchanges. Bourassa flew to the New Brunswick capital to sign a $650 million Quebec hydro-supply contract. But the main subject of discussion at the private seventy-five-minute meeting between the two leaders was the Meech Lake Accord. McKenna presented the Quebec premier with a list of substantial changes he wanted made to accord. He wanted, among other things, an amendment stating that the federal government had a duty to 'promote' as well as 'preserve' Canada's bilingual character. He wanted clearer language establishing that limitations on federal spending power would not deprive have-not provinces of federal shared-cost programs. He wanted Bourassa to agree 'in principle' to an elected and an equal Senate. What was significant about McKenna's list of changes was that he wanted to reopen the two most sensitive clauses of the accord – the distinct-society and the spending-power clauses. These were the very clauses that had been debated and refined at the all-night meeting at Langevin in June 1987. He also wanted Bourassa to agree in advance to an 'equal' Senate, in which Quebec would have its existing representation reduced to the level of the other provinces.

It was clear that these proposals were simply non-starters. There was absolutely no way that Quebec would be prepared to make such substantial concessions in return for Meech Lake. McKenna's required concessions went to the very heart of the accord. If Bourassa agreed to these changes, he would be vilified by the nationalist forces in the province of Quebec. Moreover, if Bourassa gave McKenna what he was seeking, he would expose himself to facing additional demands from Manitoba in return for its support of the accord. And if New Brunswick and Manitoba obtained changes, what about the other provinces that had been supporters of the accord? There would be a clear incentive for provinces such as British Columbia or Alberta, where the accord was increasingly unpopular, to break ranks and demand concessions of their own.

Bourassa did not tell McKenna that his ideas were totally unacceptable. He indicated that he would be willing to sign a 'political accord' in which he would agree to discuss McKenna's concerns during a second round of negotiations. But McKenna would have to ratify Meech before those discussions could begin. If the accord were reopened now, it would simply unravel.

At the press conference following their meeting, the two leaders wore smiles and exchanged pleasantries, but it was clear that little real progress had been made. McKenna told reporters that 'very clearly, we have a sharp difference of opinion ... a fundamental difference of opinion.'[13] In his strongest statement to date on the issue, McKenna indicated that changes had to be made to the accord in order for it to be ratified in New Brunswick. McKenna rejected the argument that a crisis would ensue if the accord were not ratified in its current form. McKenna's adamant position on this point in March 1988 was ironic, given the metamorphosis he was to undergo later. By June 1990, McKenna would be one of the main proponents of the view that dire consequences would befall the country in the event that Meech was not ratified. The country was 'sleepwalking into a crisis,' McKenna told Canadians in the spring of 1990. Ironically, it was McKenna's own insistence on changes back in the spring of 1988 which had contributed to the very crisis he was so earnestly lamenting two years later.

Over the summer and fall of 1988, the reality was that Meech Lake had entered a holding pattern. As Frank McKenna had indicated at his 17 March news conference, there were 'fundamental differences of opinion' about the accord. But, while the battle lines had been drawn, there was no process or even an agreed timetable for resolving differences over the accord. Frank McKenna and Sharon Carstairs continued to insist that substantial changes had to be made in the accord. Gary Filmon maintained that the accord was not an issue in Manitoba and would be dealt with at a later date. Robert Bourassa and Brian Mulroney called on the hold-outs to ratify the accord first and discuss their concerns in a second round of negotiations. Everyone had his or her script down pat. First Ministers would meet from time to time, repeat their established lines, and retreat back home to watch and wait for a while longer.

The federal government tried periodically to apply pressure to McKenna and Filmon to move the issue along towards some kind of resolution. From time to time, the prime minister would speak darkly of the untold consequences that would befall the country if the accord were not ratified. But these warnings appeared to fall on largely deaf ears. Brian Mulroney had no real leverage to force the issue to a head. The only legally relevant deadline was 23 June 1990. McKenna in particular continued to insist that there was no way he was going to be rushed into a quick decision. The New Brunswick premier had scheduled public hearings on the accord for the fall of 1988, and the hearings actually commenced on 29 September. But, three days later, on 1 October, the prime minister called a federal election for 21 November 1988. McKenna announced that the Meech Lake hearings would be suspended during the election campaign and not resume until sometime in 1989. It was back to a waiting game for the Meech Lake Accord.

The turning-point for Meech was to come in mid-December 1988. Up until that point, ratification remained a live possibility. There was still a reasonable basis to assume that McKenna and Filmon could be persuaded to ratify the accord and to have any outstanding concerns dealt with during a second round of negotiations. But the events of December 1988 changed those calculations entirely and dealt a determining and fatal blow to the prospects for the accord.

The critical events in the Meech Lake story unfolded over five days in December. On 15 December 1988, the Supreme Court of Canada released its long-awaited decision in the 'Quebec signs' case. Quebec had passed legislation in 1977 that prohibited the use of any language other than French on commercial signs in the province. In the early 1980s, following the enactment of the Charter of Rights, a number of individuals and corporations in Quebec had challenged the constitutional validity of the 'French only' signs requirement. The argument was that the prohibition on languages other than French was a violation of the guarantee of freedom of expression, protected not only by the Canadian charter but by Quebec's own Charter of Rights. The challenge had been successful in the lower courts, with the Quebec Court of Appeal ruling that the law was unconstitutional in late 1986. The Quebec government had appealed to the Supreme Court of Canada. On 15 December, the Court gave Quebec its answer: the signs law was unconstitutional. Quebec could require the use of French on commercial signs, and even stipulate that French must occupy a position of 'marked predominance.' But, the Court ruled unanimously, it could not ban outright the use of languages other than French on commercial signs in the province.

Bourassa had had a good deal of time to ponder his response to the Court's judgment. In 1985, the Quebec Liberal party platform had promised to permit the use of bilingual signs. But following his election, Bourassa decided to await the outcome of the pending court action before making any changes in the law. When the Quebec Court of Appeal had ruled against the law in December 1986, Bourassa once again decided to postpone a decision until after the Supreme Court of Canada could rule on the appeal.

Publicly, the Quebec premier gave no indication that he was reconsidering his campaign pledge in favour of bilingual signs. But those who had participated in the Langevin meeting on 3 June 1987 had reason to believe that Bourassa was indeed preparing to shift his ground and maintain the ban on bilingual signs. At the Langevin meeting, Bourassa had been particularly troubled about the possibility that his powers over language might be reduced by the distinct-society clause. He and his officials had specifically referred to the example of the signs law. They argued forcefully that it was absolutely essential that Quebec not lose the right to use the 'override' – the notwithstanding clause – in the event that they lost the signs case at the Supreme Court of Canada. The Quebeckers did not directly state that they intended to use the notwithstanding clause to override an unfavourable court ruling, but that was the clear implication of their preoccupation with preserving an absolute right to invoke the notwithstanding clause.

Over the fall of 1988, with the Supreme Court's judgment pending, there were growing fears about Bourassa's possible reaction. Manitoba's Gary Filmon and Ontario's David Peterson, in particular, warned Bourassa that the use of the notwithstanding clause would be fatal to the prospects for the Meech Lake Accord. Just a week before the court handed down its judgment, Manitoba's attorney general, Jim McCrae, met with Quebec's Gil Rémillard in Quebec City to warn about the consequences that would ensue if Quebec ignored the Supreme Court of Canada's decision. McCrae told Rémillard that the use of the notwithstanding clause would make it 'very difficult' for Manitoba to continue supporting Meech Lake. Quebec might save its signs legislation, but it would kill Meech in the process.

Over the fall of 1988, as everyone awaited the Supreme Court's decision, Bourassa and his officials seemed to have already made up their minds on how they would respond. In private conversations with officials from other provinces, the Quebeckers hinted strongly that they had settled on an 'inside-outside' solution to the signs issue. Under this approach, bilingual signs would be permitted inside stores but French would continue to be required on all external signs. The only real question was whether they would be required to invoke the notwithstanding clause in order to get to this preferred 'solution.'

The court ruling was handed down on a Thursday. Bourassa announced that he would consult with his cabinet, caucus, and party and announce a new policy on Sunday, 18 December. In the meantime, and entirely by accident, there was action on the Meech front in Manitoba. For months, Gary Filmon had been pondering when and how to deal with the Meech Lake Accord. In the Manitoba Throne Speech in July, he had promised that the accord would be introduced for debate during the current session of the legislature. He had decided to bring the accord into the legislature just before Christmas and to begin public hearings in 1989.

In early December, Filmon and his advisers fussed over numerous drafts of his speech introducing the resolution. The issue was a sensitive one in Manitoba, and Filmon knew he would have to be extremely careful. There was a strong and growing anti-Meech sentiment in Manitoba, led by aboriginal groups and women's organizations. Filmon would try to walk a fine line, supporting the accord, while at the same time recognizing the legitimate concerns of those opposed to it. The speech went through numerous refinements, with Jim Eldridge and Don Leitch, two of Filmon's senior constitutional advisers, working fourteen-hour days in an effort to settle on an agreed text. The final draft was taken to the Manitoba Conservative caucus, which was particularly concerned that Filmon recognize the need for changes in the accord.

Filmon's speech in the Manitoba Legislature on 16 December was a carefully balanced attempt to support Meech while promising to address the concerns of the critics of the accord. Filmon began his speech by arguing that the accord would have to be approved or else the process of constitutional change would be set back a generation. If Meech is rejected, Filmon told the legislature, 'realistically we will face a wait of eight or ten years before the process on constitutional renewal can begin again.' Filmon peppered his speech with quotations from former Manitoba premier Howard Pawley and federal NDP leader Ed Broadbent, designed to show that many of the concerns that had been raised about the accord were overblown or unsubstantiated. A direct amendment to the accord would kill it, Filmon argued, since the other First Ministers were simply not prepared to consider amendments to the agreement at this late stage.

But, while Meech Lake was a 'necessary first step,' Filmon suggested that there were significant flaws in the accord. He indicated that some of the concerns that had been expressed by the opposition parties in Manitoba were shared by 'all of us in this House and many others across Manitoba.' Filmon said the basic flaw in the accord was that it was too narrow and that it 'does not go far enough in charting the next steps in constitutional renewal.' Filmon's answer to this deficiency was a 'companion resolution' that would set out the concerns of Manitobans and would be passed at the same time as Meech Lake. Filmon was vague as to what this companion resolution might contain, but he indicated that it might include constitutional guarantees for aboriginal people or stronger guarantees of women's rights and private-property rights. He proposed that the other First Ministers might sign 'letters of intent' indicating that Manitoba's concerns would be dealt with in future rounds of constitutional discussions. These 'letters of intent' would provide the province with assurances that the flaws in the accord would be corrected following its ratification.

Filmon's speech could be read in either of two ways. On the one hand, he was continuing to call for the ratification of Meech Lake. On the other, he was recognizing the need for changes and the necessity of obtaining some kind of assurances that those changes would be addressed. 'Manitoba's Filmon makes plea to save Meech' was the headline in the anti-Meech *Toronto Star*, while the pro-Meech *Globe and Mail* reported that 'Filmon voices doubt on Meech Lake agreement.'[14] Sharon Carstairs dismissed Filmon's call for a companion resolution as mere window-dressing, arguing that it represented nothing more than a 'wish list' for future constitutional change. Carstairs insisted that what was needed was a direct amendment to Meech Lake itself. But NDP leader Gary Doer welcomed Filmon's speech as an olive branch extended to the opposition. Doer had recently announced that he and his party would push for amendments to the accord. He saw Filmon's speech as a positive sign. 'I think he moved slightly. It's a symbolic change. It's important,' Doer concluded.

Filmon was still on board the Meech Lake boat, but it clearly would not take very much to induce him to jump overboard. Robert Bourassa's reaction to the Supreme Court of Canada's 'signs' decision was evidently going to be very significant in terms of maintaining Filmon's support. Meech was already extremely unpopular in Manitoba. If Bourassa acted to override the Supreme Court's decision, that would represent the little push that would drive Filmon over into the anti-Meech camp.

Robert Bourassa was well aware of the high stakes riding on his decision. He had been warned numerous times over the fall that the use of the notwithstanding clause to override the Supreme Court would prove fatal to the prospects for Meech Lake. But Bourassa had already settled on the broad outlines of his new policy – the 'inside-outside' solution. The only remaining question was whether this policy was permissible under the Supreme Court's reasoning in the 'signs' case or whether it would be necessary to invoke the notwithstanding clause. On Friday night, Bourassa discussed the new policy with the members of his caucus. On Saturday, 17 December, Bourassa convened an emergency four-hour session of the Quebec Liberal party's general council, a group of 450 top organizers, cabinet ministers, and rank-and-file members. He presented the outlines of his new policy, under which French-only signs would be permitted on the exterior of stores, while other languages could be used inside stores provided that French was in a position of 'marked predominance.' Bourassa told the general council that he would prefer not to use the notwithstanding clause to override the charter, but he would use the override if legal experts told him that the new law could be open to court challenge. The general council approved the new 'inside-outside' policy. The majority of the council also urged him to use the notwithstanding clause to protect the new policy from subsequent challenges in the courts.

Sunday, 18 December, was Bourassa's day of decision. The premier had called a press conference for 5:00 p.m. to announce his new signs policy. Earlier in the day, 18,000 people had converged on the Paul Sauvé Arena in a rally that appeared to breathe new life into Quebec's independence movement. The massive rally was the largest in the province since the 1980 referendum on Quebec independence, with 12,000 supporters crammed inside the arena and an additional 6,000 outside in the bitter cold. The rally featured artists, writers, labour leaders, students, and politicians, including PQ leader Jacques Parizeau. The crowd erupted into a thunderous call for independence as Parizeau branded Bourassa a sell-out and condemned his 'inside-outside' signs plan. The crowd chanted nationalist slogans, calling on Premier Bourassa not to tamper with the French-language guarantees of Bill 101 and urging him not to erode further the 'French face' of Quebec. The rally was told that Quebec should not 'give an inch' on language policy and that even to permit bilingual signs inside stores would grant a large opening to the 'pro-bilingualism propaganda machine.'[15] A group of students burned the Canadian flag to emphasize their opposition to bilingualism in the province. The parade of about thirty pro-independence speakers at the three-and-a-half hour rally called on Bourassa to use the notwithstanding clause in order to reinstate fully the provisions of Bill 101 that had been struck down by the Court.

Bourassa spent Sunday in meetings with his caucus and cabinet. In the morning, he met Liberal MNA's from predominantly English-speaking ridings, including four cabinet ministers – Richard French, Clifford Lincoln, Herbert Marx, and John Ciaccia. The English faction in the party understood the direction that Bourassa was likely to take. They presented their own last-minute compromise, a proposal to invoke the notwithstanding clause for a one-year period only, with an understanding that bilingual signs would be allowed after that. But this last-minute compromise presented Bourassa with the worst of both worlds – he would be denounced by Quebec nationalists for caving in to pressure from the bilingualism 'propaganda machine,' while at the same time facing condemnation for invoking the override in the first place. Bourassa told the English faction of his caucus that he was going ahead with the inside-outside plan and that he had decided to invoke the notwithstanding clause. He argued that this policy was a compromise and he urged the English members to remain in the caucus. At noon, Bourassa told his cabinet of the decision, followed by a meeting with the full Liberal caucus in the early afternoon.

When Bourassa announced his decision at his 5:00 p.m. press conference, he attempted to paint his proposals as a compromise solution. Bourassa conceded that he was asking the anglophone community to make an 'enormous concession' in agreeing to a ban on the use of English on exterior signs. But, Bourassa argued, he was loosening the rules in Bill 101 so as to permit the use of English signs inside stores. He also noted that the new law would not prohibit an anglophone shopkeeper, 'who already must give prominent display to French inside his store, from using his own language when dealing with his customers.'[16] Yet, even the Parti Québécois, in drafting Bill 101 in 1977, had never contemplated extending the reach of the law so as to restrict the language of communication between shopkeepers and their customers. To argue that the law was a 'compromise' because it failed to include such a Draconian measure was surely a red herring.

Bourassa was clearly sensitive to the fact that his use of the notwithstanding clause would fuel anti-Meech sentiment. But the Quebec premier's remarks at his press conference served only to further undermine the legitimacy of the accord. The premier suggested that invoking the notwithstanding clause was necessary because Meech Lake had not been ratified. He hinted that, if the accord were ratified, and Quebec gained extra powers to protect its language and culture, it might be possible to repeal the notwithstanding clause. Bourassa lashed out at the opponents of Meech Lake, arguing that some of these opponents would attempt to use his decision on signs in order to kill Meech Lake. This tactic would be a mistake, Bourassa warned, his voice rising in anger, since it would destroy the 'unique chance to solve a question that has been there since the beginning of the century.' He hoped that 'common sense would prevail' and that Quebec's 'justified and rational' proposals on the language of signs would be accepted by the rest of the country.

Bourassa's argument was that Meech Lake and the language-of-signs issue were two entirely separate questions. Therefore, he maintained, his decision on the signs question should not be used to undermine Meech Lake. But Bourassa himself had contradicted his own argument. He had explicitly drawn a connection between the use of the notwithstanding clause and Meech Lake. Bourassa had suggested that it might not have been necessary to invoke the notwithstanding clause had Meech Lake already been in force. The clear implication of Bourassa's remarks was that Meech Lake would permit Quebec to impose French-only signs without even having to resort to the notwithstanding clause. Although Bourassa did not say so explicitly, the real purpose of Meech Lake was to permit Quebec to maintain its 'French-only' public face and character. The critics of Meech Lake had argued for eighteen months that the hidden agenda underlying the accord was the denial of the rights of the anglophone minority in Quebec. Now, Bourassa had seemingly confirmed that this, indeed, was the hidden agenda, the 'real meaning' of the Meech Lake Accord.

Bourassa's statements at this 18 December press conference were to haunt the proponents of Meech Lake throughout the remaining debate over its ratification. How could anyone credibly argue that the accord did not undermine charter rights when the Quebec premier had implied that this was precisely the purpose and intent of the accord? Bourassa played right into the hands of the opponents of the accord by confirming their worst fears about its effects on the anglophone minority in Quebec. What is even more incredible is that Bourassa knew perfectly well that his claims about the effect of Meech Lake were profoundly exaggerated. The Meech Lake Accord explicitly referred to the anglophone minority in Quebec as a 'fundamental characteristic of Canada.' At the Langevin meeting in June 1987, Bourassa had expressed fears that the 'distinct society' clause might actually reduce Quebec's powers to promote the French language. Bourassa knew full well that it was outlandish to imply that Meech Lake would somehow represent a substitute for the notwithstanding clause in the constitution. In fact, when confronted by Ontario attorney general Ian Scott in the final morning hours of the Langevin meeting, Bourassa had explicitly denied that the intention of the distinct-society clause was to undermine the charter in Quebec. Now, pressured by nationalists in Quebec, he was reversing his course and making entirely unsubstantiated statements about the 'new powers' that Quebec would gain under the accord. Unfortunately for Bourassa, there were those who would make it their business to remember these boasts about the effects of Meech Lake. The same statements would be turned on Bourassa when he sought later to claim that the Meech Lake Accord was a 'reasonable compromise' and that the opponents of Meech Lake were seeking a 'compromise on a compromise.'

In Manitoba, Premier Gary Filmon sat watching Bourassa's news conference on television. Filmon and Bourassa had spoken on the telephone twice over the weekend. On Saturday, Bourassa had called Filmon to tell him that he was considering using the notwithstanding clause. Filmon told Bourassa that doing so would cause serious problems for Meech Lake in Manitoba, and he urged Bourassa to reconsider. On Sunday, Bourassa called to inform Filmon of his decision to use the notwithstanding clause. Filmon warned that such an action might cause him to re-evaluate his continued support for Meech Lake. But Filmon had not yet made up his mind how he would react to Bourassa's announcement. Now, once the Quebec premier had announced his decision, it became clear that only one response was possible in Manitoba. Filmon would pull the Meech Lake resolution out of the Manitoba Legislature and suspend consideration of the issue.

In order to withdraw the resolution from the legislature, Filmon would need the support of the opposition leaders, Sharon Carstairs and Gary Doer. He spoke to Carstairs and Doer on the morning of 19 December and secured their consent for the withdrawal of the resolution. Filmon also spoke to Robert Bourassa and attempted to call Prime Minister Mulroney in Ottawa. Senator Lowell Murray returned the call just before

Filmon was to enter the legislature to make the announcement. Senator Murray attempted to persuade Filmon to reconsider, but the Manitoba premier was adamant. The decision to pull the resolution out of the legislature had been made and was final, Filmon told Senator Murray. Filmon also told Senator Murray that he was sending a letter to the prime minister, calling for a meeting of First Ministers 'on an urgent basis' to discuss constitutional reform.

Filmon was twenty-five minutes late for the afternoon sitting of the Manitoba Legislature. When he finally arrived, he told the House that he had decided to suspend the debate on the Meech Lake Accord because of Premier Bourassa's decision to invoke the notwithstanding clause. Calling Bourassa's decision a 'national tragedy,' Filmon argued that the limitation of minority rights was contrary to the spirit of Meech Lake. 'We understood Meech Lake was to have represented harmony and unity and protection of minority language rights throughout Canada,' Filmon told the legislature. 'The Quebec government's decision obviously went counter to that understanding.' Filmon indicated that he would not reintroduce the resolution into the legislature until Quebec gave some sort of assurances that the accord would not be used to trample minority rights. He refused to state whether he would insist on direct amendments to the accord, suggesting that he might be satisfied with 'interpretations or agreements' designed to protect minority rights. Filmon told a news conference that the decision to withdraw the accord from the legislature was 'without a doubt the most difficult of my political career.'[17] But he said that he was 'shocked and dismayed' at Bourassa's decision to override minority rights and that it would be pointless to proceed with Meech Lake without clarifying the real purpose of the accord.

Manitoba's opposition leaders, Sharon Carstairs and Gary Doer, praised Filmon for his decision, claiming that it would permit improvements to be made to the accord. But, in Ottawa and Quebec City, the reaction was predictably negative. Senator Lowell Murray said that Filmon's decision was 'made in the heat of the moment' and was a decision 'to be regretted.' Murray said he did not draw the link between Mr Bourassa's decision to invoke the notwithstanding clause and the abandonment of the principles of Meech Lake. In Quebec City, Gil Rémillard said it was 'deplorable' that Mr Filmon 'would establish a link between the Meech Lake Accord and bill 178.'[18] Rémillard complained that Quebec 'has no lesson to receive from other Canadian provinces, and especially not from Manitoba, on how to treat its linguistic minorities.' How unfair and unwise, Rémillard complained, for Filmon to try to hold the Meech Lake Accord hostage over this issue.

The weekend of 17–19 December 1988 represented the moment of truth for the Meech Lake Accord. The use of the notwithstanding clause by Premier Bourassa was the watershed event in the three-year struggle over the ratification of Meech Lake. After 19 December 1988, there was virtually no chance that the Meech Lake Accord would be ratified. To understand why this is so, it is necessary to return to the rationale that was used to justify the accord's creation in the first place – the necessity to remedy the 'exclusion' of Quebec in 1982. It was an attempt to respond to the 'legitimate grievances' of the province of Quebec. This story line may have had a measure of plausibility within the rest of Canada during the period in which the accord was being negotiated. But, after 19 December 1988, anyone who tried to peddle this story outside the province of Quebec was likely to be shouted down. After 19 December, it seemed to most Canadians outside of the province of Quebec that *they* were the ones with the legitimate grievances, not Quebeckers.

The use of the notwithstanding clause touched a nerve among Canadians outside of Quebec. It was as though these non-Quebeckers had been wronged personally by the ban on English signs in Quebec, even though many of them had likely never even visited the province. To understand why this sense of grievance was so strongly held it is necessary to remember that the 'signs' issue, both inside and outside Quebec, was primarily a matter of symbols. What was at stake was an important symbol of the nature of Quebec society and, by implication, of Canadian society as a whole. Was Quebec essentially a French-speaking society in which people would be expected to live and work in the French language? Or was it a bilingual society, in which the use of English in the workplace and in public institutions would be widely accepted? This was the symbolic question at stake in the dispute over signs. It is why the issue was such an emotional and politically charged one, both inside and outside of the province of Quebec.

For the next eighteen months, Robert Bourassa would maintain that the use of the notwithstanding clause was unconnected with Meech Lake. He would point out that the notwithstanding clause was established in the 1982 constitution, approved by former prime minister Pierre Trudeau. It had nothing to do with the Meech Lake Accord, Bourassa would repeat over and over. But, of course, Bourassa's attempt to separate the notwithstanding clause from the accord was totally unconvincing. Bourassa himself had publicly drawn the connection between the accord and the notwithstanding clause at his 18 December news conference. The connection was obvious and undeniable. The use of the notwithstanding clause gave meaning to the concept of the 'distinct society' of Quebec. It indicated in stark terms the vision Bourassa had of Quebec's distinctiveness. It was the distinct-society clause in action.

That is why the Meech Lake Accord had essentially no hope of being ratified after 18 December 1988. After that date, ratification would have seemed to the rest of Canada to require them to sacrifice their idea of the country. It would have required them to acquiesce implicitly in Robert Bourassa's right to ban English signs in the province of Quebec – something the vast majority of Canadians outside of Quebec was simply unprepared to do. Having glimpsed what they thought was the real meaning of distinct society, they were certain of one thing: they did not like it.

Thus the decision to invoke the notwithstanding clause damaged in an irreparable fashion the support for the accord outside of the province of Quebec. Public-opinion polls, which had traced a growing indecisiveness among Canadians about the accord in 1988, now began to pick up a hardening of the opposition. By early 1989, a plurality of Canadians were opposed to Meech, and this number would grow in the months leading up to the spring of 1990.[19] The demands for the renegotiation of the accord began to grow louder and more persistent. A consensus of sorts began to develop outside of the province of Quebec that the accord had to be renegotiated.[20] The focus of the call for 'better terms' was the distinct-society clause. There was a widespread fear that the distinct-society clause would somehow permit Quebec to limit further the rights of the anglophone minority in the province. Outside of Quebec, the consensus was that the distinct-society clause had to be amended to preclude this possibility. The call for amendments to the distinct-society clause was important, again, in symbolic rather than substantive terms. It was an attempt to reaffirm a particular vision of the country, one in which a ban on English signs in Quebec would simply not be seen as acceptable.

This way of understanding what was at stake in the debate makes it crystal clear why Robert Bourassa was in no position to offer any such amendments. If Bourassa had agreed to limit the distinct-society clause, he would have been admitting, at least implicitly, that his decision to invoke the notwithstanding clause had been illegitimate. Bourassa would never agree to such an admission. The reason was simple. It had nothing to do with 'pressure' from Quebec nationalists and everything to do with Bourassa's own identity as a Quebecker. Bourassa himself could never agree to renounce his own vision of Quebec society and his own commitment to the promotion of the French language and culture. To retreat in these circumstances would have required Bourassa to sacrifice his own identity and beliefs, and that was something which he was simply unprepared to contemplate.

The result was that Bourassa was even less likely to accept amendments to Meech Lake after Bill 178 than he had been previously. Bourassa would be even more insistent that Meech Lake be ratified in its current form. He was well aware of the fact that the prospects for ratification were fading fast, but the issue was no longer simply the success or failure of a package of constitutional amendments. What was now at stake was whose vision of Quebec society was to triumph – Robert Bourassa's or that of English Canadians intent on obtaining redress for the ban on English signs.

There are those who argue that Robert Bourassa was responsible for creating this situation through his delay in announcing a policy on signs. 'What a fearful price this country pays for its Robert Bourassas,' argued the *Globe and Mail* in an editorial following the Quebec premier's decision to override the Supreme Court. The *Globe* argued that Bourassa should have acted in 1985 to fulfil his election commitment to implement bilingual signs in the province. 'His years of dithering and frittering, dissimulation and weakness – followed by Sunday's bold decision to do the wrong thing – condemns us all to a diminished union.' But the *Globe* had the wrong culprit. The problem was not Robert Bourassa but the notwithstanding clause itself. The existence of the notwithstanding clause in the 1982 constitution was a ticking time bomb waiting to explode in the face of the country. The existence of the notwithstanding clause made it a certainty that, sooner or later, Canadians would be divided along French-English lines in a way they had never been divided before.

Remember that the ban on English signs in Quebec was not new. It had been in place since 1977, enacted as part of the Quebec Charter of the French Language by the PQ government of the day. While this legislation had met with grumbling in the rest of the country when it had been enacted, such grumbling had subsided by the early 1980s. What was new was not the signs legislation but the fact that Canada now had a charter of rights with a very peculiar feature: certain court decisions under the charter were subject to reversal by a majority vote in the legislature. This feature was peculiar because most guarantees of human rights in other countries are not subject to reversal in this fashion.

When the 'override' provision was inserted in the charter in 1982, it was justified on the grounds that it was necessary to serve as a 'safety valve' for legislatures that might be faced with rogue judges. This safety valve was necessary, so the argument went, to guard against aberrant or unacceptable judicial interpretations of the constitution. It was inserted at the insistence of certain western provinces that were sceptical of the idea of a rights charter in the first place.

What was evident was that the drafters of the charter gave little or no thought as to what the effect of such a safety valve would be within the province of Quebec. With the benefit of hindsight, it is now evident that the existence of the notwithstanding clause was a serious threat to the unity of the country. It created a situation in that it was inevitable that legislation promoting the French language in Quebec would be challenged as unconstitutional. This situation, in itself, was not necessarily fatal. What *was* fatal was the fact that, if any such challenges ever succeeded, there would be irresistible pressure to nullify the court decision through the use of the override clause. No Quebec premier can afford to be seen to be half-hearted in his or her defence of the French language in Quebec. Having provided the Quebec premier with a tool to promote the French language, you compel him or her to use it. Thus, sooner or later, the premier of Quebec would be challenged to override individual rights as a kind of badge of honour, as a demonstration of a genuine commitment to the protection of the French language in Quebec.

To illustrate the political dynamic that the notwithstanding clause creates within Quebec, compare the situation in December 1988 with the aftermath of an earlier Supreme Court decision on language of schools. Historically, the language-of-schools issue had been far more politically explosive in Quebec. It was the right of English-speaking Canadians to send their children to English schools in Quebec that had sparked the greatest debate in the late 1970s and early 1980s. The schools issue, not the language of commercial signs, was the focus of anglophone anger over Bill 101. This issue was seen as so fundamental that it was specifically addressed in the Charter of Rights in 1982. A 'bottom line' for Pierre Trudeau in the 1981 constitutional negotiations was to secure the right of English-speaking Canadians from outside Quebec to send their children to English schools in the province. The clear intent was to reverse the policy of Bill 101 on the point. Moreover, the federal government refused to permit the section of the charter guaranteeing this right to be subject to the override clause in the charter.

The result? In 1984, the Supreme Court of Canada strikes down the sections of Bill 101 restricting the right of Canadian citizens to send children to English schools in Quebec. Predictably, the Quebec government protests long and loud against the ruling. But nothing much else happens. There are no marches in the streets. There are no demonstrations at the Paul Sauvé Arena, demanding the Quebec premier restore the rights of the francophone majority. Since there is nothing the political branch of government can do about the court's ruling, it becomes a non-issue. The matter does not even feature in the 1985 Quebec election campaign. Quebeckers are concerned about the economy and about getting on with their lives, not with the pronouncements of a group of judges in Ottawa.

Now return to the political situation in December 1988. Suddenly, an issue that had seemed much less significant in the 1970s and early 1980s assumes monumental proportions. Thousands march on the Paul Sauvé Arena to demand action from the Quebec premier. His response to the court decision on the language of signs will be seen as the litmus test of whether he is committed to the promotion of the French language in Quebec. Why? Because this time, the Supreme Court does not have the last word on a language issue. This time, the Quebec government is provided with the opportunity to overrule the court's ruling. A 'safety valve' is available to be used. Therefore it *must* be used.]

The timing of the situation was certainly unfortunate. Language tensions were already running high because of the debate over the ratification of the Meech Lake Accord. But the political dynamic created by the existence of the notwithstanding clause was an accident waiting to happen. Sooner or later, a Quebec premier would be faced with overwhelming pressure to override a Supreme Court decision limiting the right of the province to promote the French language. Whenever this situation occurred, the results outside of Quebec were as predictable as those inside the province. It is one thing for a Quebec government to enact ordinary language legislation that other Canadians find objectionable. It is quite another for Quebec to override an interpretation of the constitution handed down by the Supreme Court. Supreme Court judges continue to evoke an image of impartiality, their judgments seemingly standing above the petty infighting of partisan politics. When the Court speaks, Canadians listen. A ruling by the Court that an entitlement is a constitutionally protected right transforms the nature of that entitlement. It then becomes a matter of high principle, a right entrenched in the constitution. It is not something lightly to be tampered with.]

The decision by a Quebec premier to invoke the notwithstanding clause to protect the French language was entirely predictable. But so was the reaction to the decision in the rest of the country, which would inevitably see the decision as one that challenged the very idea of Canadian citizenship. It would represent a rebuff to the idea that Canadians had equal rights across the country. There would be anger, resentment, and an attempt to reassert the values of a common Canadian citizenship. The 'English-only' resolutions in numerous municipalities in Ontario over the winter of 1989–90 were a direct manifestation of this backlash. So, too, was the 'Quebec flag' incident in the fall of 1989, in which a small group of protesters in Brockville, Ontario walked on the Quebec flag. These incidents in the rest of Canada then had a 'rebound effect' within Quebec, contributing to a sense of resentment and anger among Quebeckers. The result was a long-term and fundamental breaking of the bonds of Canadian citizenship.

I conclude that the inclusion of the notwithstanding clause in the 1982 constitution was clearly a very serious mistake. It created a political dynamic that was totally unforeseen at the time, a dynamic that was to drive a wedge between Quebec and the rest of the country. Of course, it is too late now to contemplate removing the notwithstanding clause from the constitution. Any suggestion that this should be done would be seen as an attack on the right of the Quebec government to promote the French language. The notwithstanding clause has become truly embedded in the charter in a permanent way. This situation is most unfortunate, because we have not heard the last of the notwithstanding clause. There are certain to be other court judgments down the road that will be seen as a threat to the French language in Quebec. If any of those court rulings are open to reversal through use of the notwithstanding clause, then the same scenario will play itself out. We are still suffering from the after-shock of the first such incident. How and whether Canadians will cope with the future use of the notwithstanding clause is certainly an unpleasant prospect to contemplate.

The irony is that those who originally insisted on the inclusion of the notwithstanding clause will eventually find the clause totally useless. As the Meech Lake debate illustrated, the Charter of Rights is very quickly assuming symbolic importance for Canadians outside of Quebec. It was the potential impact of the distinct-society clause on the charter that served to galvanize opposition to the accord. In this political context, it is safe to predict that the notwithstanding clause will soon fall into disuse outside of the province of Quebec. It will remain a theoretical option with no practical value. The notwithstanding clause will become the forbidden fruit of the Canadian constitution: any politician who touches or tastes it will be banished from the garden. Indeed, the notwithstanding clause may already have become a dead letter outside of Quebec. Its association in the public mind with the Quebec signs legislation may well be sufficient to render it politically untouchable. It will remain for Quebec, the sole province that refused to take part in the 1982 constitutional negotiations, to jealously guard the forbidden fruit of the Canadian constitution.

7

Canada on a Collision Course

By the spring of 1989, the Meech Lake Accord was nearly two years old. The accord was now on life support. With each passing month, its heartbeat was growing more faint and irregular. Events in Manitoba and New Brunswick in early 1989 confirmed the deteriorating prognosis for the accord. Both provinces began their long-awaited public hearings on Meech Lake early that year. Predictably, these hearings provided a forum for the growing public opposition to the accord to build to a new crescendo. Over 90 per cent of the witnesses at both sets of hearings condemned the accord and called for it to be substantially rewritten or else scrapped entirely. Even its supporters condemned the 'élitist process' that had led to its creation.

The Manitoba and New Brunswick committees retired to ponder the witnesses they had heard and to prepare their respective reports on the accord. But, given the overwhelming opposition to Meech Lake that had manifested itself at the hearings, there could be little doubt about the overall thrust and direction of their conclusions. There would be the usual platitudes about the willingness and the desire to bring Quebec 'back in' to the constitution. The committees would insist that New Brunswickers and Manitobans were willing to meet the 'legitimate demands' of the province of Quebec. What they would ask for would be better terms. Meech Lake was unacceptable in its current form. The committees would call on Robert Bourassa to demonstrate flexibility and a willingness to compromise. There would have to be amendments, they would argue, if the accord were ever to be taken off life support.

The Manitoba and New Brunswick committees refused to be rushed in their deliberations. Never mind the fact that the Meech Lake debate was about to enter its third year. Gary Filmon and Frank McKenna continued to insist that there was plenty of time to ponder the issues and search for a 'consensus.' The two committee reports were not expected until the fall of

1989. Then, armed with the committee recommendations, Filmon and McKenna would present their fellow premiers with their shopping list of changes to the accord. Viewed from the vantage-point of Winnipeg or Fredericton, the arguments in favour of these changes seemed self-evident and irresistible. Sooner or later Mulroney and Bourassa would have to wake up to the fact that Meech Lake had to be amended. Outside of Quebec, the Filmon–McKenna strategy of 'ragging the puck' seemed to be working. Surely it was only a matter of time before the defenders of Meech would be forced to recognize that 'compromise' was inevitable.

Enter Clyde Wells, the new premier of Newfoundland. In early 1989, Brian Peckford had announced his retirement after a decade as Newfoundland premier. His successor as conservative leader and premier was Tom Rideout, who called an election for 20 April 1989. Ironically, Meech Lake was not an issue in the campaign. The focus of opposition leader Clyde Wells's attack was the mismanagement of the provincial economy by Peckford's government. One of Wells's favourite objects of attack was the provincial government's disastrous effort to promote a cucumber industry on the island. The most devastating Liberal television commercial of the campaign was said to be a slow-motion depiction of a cucumber turning rotten, symbolizing the Peckford government's folly in believing that a viable cucumber industry could be created in Newfoundland.

Wells was swept into office on 20 April, winning thirty-two of the fifty-two seats in the Newfoundland House of Assembly. While Meech Lake had not been an issue in the election campaign, Wells's position on the accord had been clear and unequivocal from the very beginning. Wells believed that the accord was not in the best interests of the province of Newfoundland. He had spoken against the accord when the issue was debated in the Newfoundland Legislature in the spring of 1988. Now, he quickly reiterated his tough and principled opposition to Meech Lake. The morning after his election victory, Wells told reporters that he was opposed to Meech Lake because it conferred 'special status' on the province of Quebec. He also argued that it would make Senate reform impossible and forever relegate Newfoundland to an inferior status in the federal Parliament. Wells also objected to what he regarded as an unacceptable weakening of the powers of the federal government under the accord.

Newfoundland had already ratified the accord in July 1988. But Wells indicated that he was prepared to introduce a resolution into the House of Assembly revoking the province's support if his concerns were not addressed. Wells's threat of revocation immediately set off alarm bells in Ottawa. Senator Lowell Murray responded to Wells's talk of revoking

Meech by warning the new premier that to overturn the constitutional endorsement would be a 'very, very bad precedent indeed if a province can renege on a constitutional resolution that has already been passed by a legislature.' According to Senator Murray, such a move would pose a threat to the 'climate of co-operation and harmony needed to make a country like this work.'[1]

But despite the senator's use of the word 'reneging' to describe Wells's proposed course of action, it was clear that the Newfoundland premier was fully within his rights to revoke the province's support for Meech. Wells's plan may have been unwise and unnecessary. But the 1982 amending formula specifically provided that a province could withdraw its support for a constitutional amendment at any time prior to that amendment being ratified. There was no question that Wells had the legal and moral right to undo the policy of the previous government, just as Filmon and McKenna had the right to reverse the constitutional policy of their predecessors.

What was disturbing about Wells's plan to revoke was not that he was trying to renege on a commitment, but that a motion to revoke support for Meech appeared so definitive. The man was clearly deadly serious about his opposition to the accord. Moreover, if Wells proceeded to actually revoke Newfoundland's support for Meech, it appeared almost inconceivable that he could ever be persuaded to reverse course and support the accord at some later time. It was clear that, if Wells went through with his plan, Meech Lake would be dead in the water.

But how could Wells be persuaded to soften his opposition to Meech and shelve his plans to revoke Newfoundland's support for the accord? No one in the pro-Meech camp had any bright ideas. The major difficulty was that Wells's objections went to the very heart of the accord. He was not simply seeking minor adjustments in wording. Wells wanted the distinct-society clause totally rewritten so as to delete any reference to the 'role' of the province of Quebec to promote its distinctiveness. He wanted the amending formula changed so that Quebec would not have a veto over Senate reform. Wells objected to the limitations on the federal spending power set out in the accord. In fact, Wells wanted major changes to every clause in the accord. What he was seeking was to begin the negotiations from square one. Wells wanted the accord to be treated as an initial rough draft rather than a final agreement.

The federal government seemed somewhat at a loss as to how to deal with the Newfoundland premier. It was clear that there was absolutely no way that his concerns could be met in a manner that would be acceptable to Robert Bourassa. Wells was asking Bourassa to gut totally the Meech

Lake Accord. Lacking a game plan, the federal government resolved to sit and wait. A First Ministers' meeting had been planned for Prince Edward Island in September to discuss the impasse over the accord. But that meeting had been scheduled earlier in the year, prior to the election of Clyde Wells. The presence of Wells and his hammer-and-tong opposition to Meech caused the federal government to rethink the wisdom of the September meeting. On 5 July, the prime minister announced the cancellation of the meeting in Prince Edward Island. Mulroney declared that little progress could be made on resolving the differences on Meech Lake in the current environment. He indicated that it would be preferable to await the committee reports from Manitoba and New Brunswick before convening the First Ministers. What Mulroney did not say, but was clearly hoping, was that the passage of time might also reveal some strategy for dealing with the intransigence of Clyde Wells.

The opponents of Meech Lake continued to operate on the assumption that amendments to the accord were possible. Frank McKenna, Gary Filmon, and Clyde Wells denied that their intention was to kill Meech Lake totally. All they were seeking, they maintained, were improvements to the accord that would make it more acceptable to 'all Canadians.' What never seemed to enter into the calculation was whether Robert Bourassa was actually in a position to entertain amendments to the accord. Yet, every indication from the province of Quebec over the summer and fall of 1989 was that Bourassa was not prepared to amend the accord, directly or indirectly. In fact, while the opponents of the accord were busy hardening their demands for amendments, Bourassa was moving in precisely the opposite direction. On 9 August, Bourassa called an election for 25 September 1989, saying he needed a mandate for his position on the Meech Lake Accord. Four days later, in an interview on the TéléMedia television network, Bourassa reiterated his position that the accord had to be ratified in its existing form. He also indicated that the Quebec government had an 'alternative strategy' in the event the accord was not ratified by 23 June 1990. He did not specify, however, what these 'alternative plans' might be.

Three things were happening in the debate, all of them troubling for the long-term future of the country. First, there was a clear polarization between the pro- and anti-Meech camps. The opponents of Meech, intoxicated by the success of their campaign to discredit the accord outside of Quebec, had become more definitive and persistent in their demands for changes. The list of 'fundamental flaws' in the Meech Lake Accord was growing longer by the month. Its opponents began stating openly that the accord would die if it were not amended to take account of their concerns.

At the same time, Robert Bourassa was becoming more persistent in his claims that the accord could not be reopened. The Quebec premier had staked his political fortunes on having the accord ratified unamended. After repeating for more than two years that the accord had to be ratified 'as is,' Bourassa had little or no room for manoeuvre. For Bourassa to accept amendments to Meech at this stage would have been a fatal reversal of direction that would have totally destroyed his political credibility within the province of Quebec.

The second feature of the debate, even more dangerous than the first, was that neither side seemed to have a clear understanding of the position or intentions of the other. This tendency to misread the real intentions of the other side had been a feature of the debate since the fall of 1987 and the election of Frank McKenna. But, by the fall of 1989, there was a growing and alarming confusion about what was possible and what was at stake in the negotiations. The opponents of Meech Lake, particularly Clyde Wells and Gary Filmon, essentially scoffed at the suggestion that the accord had to be ratified 'as is' or not at all. They refused to believe that Robert Bourassa was serious in his demand that the accord was not open to amendments. They also rejected the argument that serious consequences would follow if the accord were not ratified. Any reference to the consequences of the failure of the accord was dismissed as mere rhetoric or 'sabre-rattling.' At the same time, there was an alarming tendency within Quebec to equate opposition to Meech Lake with a rejection of Quebec. The accord had attained a symbolic quality that made discussion of its merits virtually impossible. Any attempt to discuss changes to the accord was seen as an attack on Quebec's distinct character within Canada. Within Quebec, the accord had become a sort of icon or cultural artefact. To even talk of tampering with it was a form of sacrilege. The accord had become a test of the willingness of the rest of Canada to accept Quebec's cultural and linguistic distinctiveness. Only one answer – an outright 'yes' – would be acceptable. 'Maybe' was simply not good enough.

The third element of the debate was also alarming. By the fall of 1989, the rhetoric surrounding the debate was becoming more extreme and apocalyptic. Brian Mulroney referred continually to the disastrous consequences for the country that would ensue if the accord were not ratified. There was increasing reference to the 'humiliation' that Quebec had suffered in the 1981 constitutional settlement. As the rhetoric increased, so too did the prominence and attention given to extremist or fringe organizations. Groups such as the Association for the Preservation of English in Canada (APEC) had existed for many years but had tended to be marginalized by the media and the political establishment. Whenever groups such as APEC were featured in the media, they tended to be portrayed as extremists with illegitimate political views. This portrayal began to change in the fall and winter of 1989. Groups such as APEC began to receive unprecedented attention in the national media. The new story line suggested that APEC had tapped into a 'grass-roots rebellion' against the traditional or established values of Canadian politics. Jock Andrews, the author of a scurrilous but little-known attack on French Canadians entitled *Bilingual Today, French Tomorrow*, suddenly became a national media figure. Dozens of municipalities within Ontario began passing 'English only' resolutions as a protest against the alleged encroachment of French within their communities.

Within the province of Quebec, the rhetoric also was becoming extreme and volatile. One began to hear extreme labels such as 'traitor' used to describe those such as Jean Chrétien who were calling for changes to Meech Lake. There was an overwhelming preoccupation with considerations of 'honour,' political face-saving, and the 'dignity of Quebec.' The opportunity for reasoned debate and the tolerance for differences of opinion with the Quebec political community were disappearing rapidly.

What these three elements indicated was that the debate surrounding Meech Lake was beginning to spin out of control. Both sides were hardening their positions and rejecting any suggestions of compromise. There was confusion on all sides about what was politically possible. No one seemed to be able to agree on the consequences of failure. With extremist and fringe organizations attaining a new prominence and legitimacy for their views, the debate had become dominated by symbols rather than substance. In such a context, it began to seem less and less likely that there could be a satisfactory resolution of the impasse. It also began to seem that the future of the country might well be riding on the outcome.

In October 1989, the Manitoba and New Brunswick committees finally released their reports on the Meech Lake Accord. Frank McKenna and Gary Filmon had talked for months in general terms about the need for changes to the accord. But these general musings had failed to set out in specific terms what changes in the accord were necessary in order to secure the support of these two provinces. Now, with just eight months remaining before the final deadline for ratification of the accord, the anti-Meech forces had at least reduced their demands to writing.

The Manitoba task force report emphasized that its recommendations were unanimous. All three parties in the provincial legislature had supported the recommendations. The task force seemed to believe that the fact that the recommendations were unanimous somehow added to their moral or political weight. But, on closer examination, it became apparent that this unanimity had been achieved by simply adding together the objections to Meech Lake put forward by each of the three parties. By including everyone's particular objections, the task force was able to ensure that all three Manitoba parties would sign the report. But this procedure ignored the need to ensure that the amendments might be acceptable to Canadians outside of Manitoba, particularly the government and people of the province of Quebec. The Manitobans had achieved unanimity within their own province, but only at a cost of ensuring that the recommendations could never form the basis of a national consensus.

The Manitoba political leaders openly admitted that this had been the procedure utilized in writing the report. The task force, as a matter of policy, denied anyone from outside of Manitoba the right to appear. The effect of the approach on the task force's recommendations was obvious. Consider the task force recommendation on the spending-power clause in Meech Lake. The Liberals and the New Democrats wanted the spending-power clause changed in order to require provinces to meet 'national standards' in order to receive compensation under the clause. But the Progressive Conservatives were unhappy with the Liberal/New Democrat proposal. Filmon's Conservatives liked the flexibility associated with the idea of a province having to meet 'national objectives' rather than 'national standards.' The solution to the impasse between the three parties? Simply drop the clause entirely. The task force recommended that the accord should be amended by deleting the clause dealing with the federal spending power.

The three Manitoba parties could each live with this proposal. In defending the report, Gary Filmon, Sharon Carstairs, and Gary Doer suggested that remaining silent on the spending-power issue represented a 'compromise' between their different positions. But the trouble with this 'compromise' was that it made absolutely no attempt to take into account the position of Quebec. Quebec's demand to impose some kind of limitation on the federal spending power had been a key demand during the Meech Lake round. It had been a focus of discussion during the all-night Langevin meeting in June 1987, at which time certain modifications had been made in the clause to address the concerns of then-premier Howard Pawley. Now, two and a half years later, the Manitobans were coming forward and arguing that the clause had to be dropped entirely. There could be no limit of any kind, no matter how modest, on the power of the federal government to use spending to intervene in provincial jurisdiction. Robert Bourassa, who had maintained throughout the exercise that he had to receive something on each of his five 'minimum demands,' was now being told to drop one of his demands from the list. The proposal was simply breathtaking. Not only could it not form the basis of an agreement with Quebec, it also ignored the fact that other provinces such as British Columbia and Alberta had argued strenuously in favour of limits on the federal spending power.

This same disregard for the implications of the recommendations in the broader national community was evident throughout the task force report. The committee operated as a kind of collective 'adding machine,' totalling up the demands for changes from the opponents of Meech Lake and presenting them in the form of a single shopping list. In some cases, the demands contained in the report contradicted each other. Consider the task force recommendation on the distinct-society clause, one of the key targets for the opponents of Meech Lake during the Manitoba public hearings. The Manitoba report says the 'distinct society' clause should be rewritten as a 'Canada Clause,' which will refer to the 'fundamental characteristics of Canada.' The 'Canada Clause' would refer to the existence of Canada as a federal state with a 'distinct national identity,' to the existence of the aboriginal peoples and to Canada's multicultural heritage. The fourth item on the list of these fundamental characteristics would be the 'distinct society' of Quebec. But then, for good measure, the Manitobans go on to demand a separate clause that would specify that nothing in the 'Canada Clause' could affect the interpretation of the Charter of Rights.

The second demand effectively contradicted the first. The Manitobans first propose writing a 'Canada Clause' into the constitution, setting out the fundamental characteristics of Canada, but then ask for a separate clause saying that nothing that they have described in the Canada Clause can be used to interpret the Charter of Rights. The Manitobans want to write an interpretive clause into the constitution, but then say that the interpretive clause they have drafted can't be used to interpret the constitution. The whole exercise is entirely circular. It is the constitutional equivalent of digging a hole and then refilling it with dirt so as to disguise its existence. What is the point of specifying all of these 'fundamental characteristics' of Canada in the constitution, but then saying that they can't be used in interpreting the charter?

The explanation for the Manitoba recomendation on this point is, in reality, quite simple. The task force is simply proceeding on its appointed task of adding together the various recommendations for amendments that had been presented in the public hearings. Some witnesses had called for the distinct-society clause to be rewritten as a 'Canada Clause.' Others had argued that the distinct-society clause should not affect the Charter of Rights. The result? The task force decides to include *both* recommendations in its list of proposed amendments. Never mind the fact that the two recommedations effectively contradict each other. They have responded to the objections and ensured that their report will reflect the will of the people of Manitoba.

There should be nothing terribly surprising in the fact that the Manitobans were playing to their own constituency in this manner. There was no incentive for any of the three parties to attempt a true compromise in their proposals. Any attempt to present a shorter list ran the risk of alienating politicial support in Manitoba, where the coals of anti-Meech sentiment were now flaming hot. But what was truly bizarre about the Manitoba report was the fact that its authors seemed to believe that these proposals represented a basis for a national consensus. The report argued that if the proposed changes were adopted, the accord could become a 'constructive constitutional amendment.'[2] The report claimed that it had 'attempted to balance our responsibility to Manitobans with our obligations to the rest of Canada.' Liberal leader Sharon Carstairs even went on a mini-tour to Ontario and Quebec following the release of the report in order to promote the Manitoba proposals. During her Quebec visit, Carstairs was outraged by a newspaper cartoon depicting her as a member of the Ku Klux Klan. Carstairs stormed out of a meeting with the newspaper's editors after she failed to receive an apology for the cartoon. The cartoon was undoubtedly in bad taste, but it indicated the extent to which the Manitoba demands for changes to Meech Lake were regarded as totally unacceptable in other parts of the country. The Manitoba task force report was entirely insular and inward-looking. Its hard-line criticisms of the accord were entirely insensitive to the need to reach an accommodation with the province of Quebec.

The week before the Manitoba task force released its report, Clyde Wells had made public his list of objections to the accord. Wells's list of objections was set out in a ten-page open letter to the prime minister, dated 18 October 1989. Like the Manitoba task force report, Wells's 18 October letter made no attempt to put forward proposals that might form the basis of a national consensus. Indeed, Wells's letter was even more uncompromising in his rejection of Meech Lake. Wells seemed to go out of his way to find flaws with every aspect of the accord. Reading his letter, one is struck by the one-sided nature of the analysis. Wells finds absolutely nothing in the accord that is acceptable. It is almost as if the Newfoundland premier regarded himself as acting on instructions to prepare a brief against the accord. A skilful advocate, he manages in his letter to set out a critique of virtually every aspect of the accord. But one searches in vain for any sense of balance or proportion, for any evidence that Wells has sought to consider the accord's merits as well as its flaws.

On the issue of the 'distinct society' clause, for example, Wells insists that the clause must be placed in a constitutional preamble, rather than in the main body of the constitution. But he also insists that the clause must not make any reference to the 'role' of the government of Quebec to promote the distinct identity of the province. The reference to the 'role' of Quebec is objectionable, according to Wells, since it creates a 'special legislative status for one province. No federation is likely to survive for very long,' Wells writes, 'if one of its supposedly equal provinces has a legislative jurisdiction in excess of that of the other provinces.'

Wells's critique of the distinct-society clause has apocalytic and messianic overtones. Wells's letter argues that the fate of the nation hinges on the wording of a subclause in the proposed clause 2 of the Constitution Act, 1867. If the reference to the 'role' of Quebec to promote its distinct identity is entrenched, 'the end of the nation, as we know it, would not likely be far off.' There is more than a little irony here. Wells had complained bitterly whenever the prime minister had warned of dire consequences in the event that the accord were not ratified. Yet, Wells is making use of the same apocalyptic arguments in making his case that the accord ought to be rejected. Wells's argument on the point is simply the flip side of Mulroney's. He casts himself in the role of saviour, riding to rescue Canadians from the disaster that will befall them in the event that Meech Lake is entrenched.

What assessment can be made of Wells's claims about the dire consequences inherent in the wording of the 'distinct society' clause? The argument appears more than a little overblown. Are we really to believe that the fate of the country actually turns on the presence or absence of a constitutional reference to the 'role' of the government of Quebec? Wells's analysis displays a belief in textual determinism. According to Wells, the entire fortunes of a nation can rise or fall on the presence of the 'correct wording' in the constitution. This rather naïve belief in the power of constitutional language is perhaps not surprising, given that Wells had spent his career as a lawyer arguing cases in front of the courts. However, Premier Wells was rather selective in making his argument. The Newfoundland premier had neglected to mention a recent Supreme Court of Canada judgment that in effect contradicted the argument he was making in his letter.

In its December 1988 judgment on the 'signs' case, the Supreme Court of Canada had considered the very question Wells was discussing in his 18 October letter. The issue before the Court was the ability of the Quebec government to limit constitutional rights in order to promote the French language.[3] The Quebec government had argued that it had the right to pass laws to 'see the quality and influence of the French language assured.' In fact, the Quebec government had argued that this legislative purpose was so important that it justified imposing limits on rights protected under the Charter of Rights. The response of the Court? The Supreme Court agreed that it was legitimate for the Quebec government to pass laws promoting the French language in Quebec. The province of Quebec was justified in taking 'steps to assure that the "visage linguistique" of Quebec would reflect the predominance of the French language.'[4] In fact, not only was such legislation appropriate, it furthered an interest that was 'pressing and substantial' and would justify legislation that imposed limits on the rights of the anglophone minority in Quebec.

The Court does not use the language of the distinct-society clause itself. There is no reference to Quebec's 'distinct society' or to the 'role' of the government of Quebec. But the Court's description of the legislative jurisdiction of the province of Quebec perfectly matches the description set out in the distinct-society clause. The Court says that the Quebec government is justified in passing laws to protect and *to promote* the French language in Quebec. Quebec has this right, even in the absence of the distinct-society clause. If this is so, how can Clyde Wells's apocalyptic predictions be regarded as plausible?

It seems that the distinct-society clause would largely codify the existing constitutional doctrine established by the Supreme Court of Canada in the *Ford* case. At worst, the distinct-society clause would have led to a relatively modest increase in the legislative powers of Quebec. Quebec would have been able to argue that limitations on charter rights were justified by the need to promote Quebec's distinct identity. But the impact would have operated at the margins. There is simply no basis for believing Wells's prediction that it would lead to the 'end of the nation, as we know it.'

Wells's attack on the other provisions in the accord is equally one-sided and apocalyptic. In each instance, Wells uses rather colourful language to detail the devastating and 'inevitable' consequences he sees flowing from the accord. For instance, Wells claims that the restriction on the federal spending power would relegate the federal government to the 'sterile role as chief cashier.' The 'inevitable' result of this situation, Wells argues, is a 'patchwork of programs' and the steady weakening of 'our sense, however fragile, of national community.' But Wells ignores the fact that provincial programs already vary widely from one province to the next. There is already a 'patchwork of programs' in place across the country. Canada does not seem in imminent danger of collapse because of this flexibility in program standards and administration in areas of exclusive provincial jurisdiction.

Wells was no doubt sincerely motivated by an attempt to achieve an accommodation with Quebec. But the one-sided quality of his presentation made it clear that there was no possibility that his proposals could form the basis for a national consensus that would include Quebec.

At the same time as Manitoba and Newfoundland were detailing their objections to the accord, the New Brunswick Select Committee on the 1987 Constitutional Accord was tabling its report in the New Brunswick Legislature. The tone and conclusions of the New Brunswick committee were much more measured and moderate. The Select Committee had praise for many aspects of the Meech Lake Accord. The accord was described as a 'serious and commendable effort to accommodate the aspirations of Quebec.' The accord was said to reflect a 'spirit of compromise' and a desire to 'achieve a balanced and a united nation.' The New Brunswick committee endorsed the main thrust of the accord, including the distinct-society clause and the limitations on federal spending power. The committee accepted the principle that Senate reform would be subject to unanimous provincial consent.

The changes the committee proposed were limited in number and circumscribed in effect. The committee wanted a specific guarantee that women's rights were not affected by the distinct-society clause. They thought that the admission of new provinces should not require unanimous provincial consent. The committee wanted the role of the federal Parliament to promote linguistic duality to be affirmed.

What was also important was that the committee did not seek to lay down any preconditions or ultimatums. The recommendations were offered as a 'basis of discussion for improving the 1987 Constitutional Accord.' The committee did not dictate the timing of any improvements to the accord. The way was left open for Premier McKenna to endorse the accord and negotiate changes through a 'parallel accord' that might take effect after ratification.

Had Frank McKenna been the lone hold-out on Meech Lake, it might have been possible to achieve some sort of accommodation. McKenna had clearly modified his earlier opposition to Meech Lake. The changes he was now seeking were so modest that he was very close to accepting the accord in its existing form. The difficulty was that McKenna was not the lone hold-out. Standing immediately behind him were Gary Filmon and Clyde

Wells, each armed with demands for a total rewriting of the accord. The moment the federal government indicated that it was willing to negotiate with McKenna, it would be compelled to discuss the changes proposed by Filmon and Wells, which would lead to the certain unravelling of the accord. Moreover, even if the federal government could somehow separate McKenna from Filmon and Wells and negotiate a deal with McKenna alone, the ratification of the accord would be no nearer. The consent of all ten provinces was required. Reducing the number of hold-outs from three to two was constitutionally irrelevant in terms of securing the ratification of the resolution.

In the succeeding months, Frank McKenna would begin to sound more and more like a supporter of Meech Lake. By the spring of 1990, McKenna was to join the chorus of those who would be warning Canadians of the dire consequences that would follow from the rejection of the accord. While he was continuing to demand changes to the accord, his list had grown so short that it was almost inconceivable that he would reject the accord if the changes were not achieved. Faced with the prospect of ratifying the accord in its present form or rejecting it outright, there was little doubt about the choice he would make.

The problem was how to move Gary Filmon and Clyde Wells in the same direction as Frank McKenna. Neither Filmon nor Wells seemed a likely candidate to follow in McKenna's footsteps. Filmon was in a minority position in the Manitoba Legislature and had declared himself to be 'bound' by the report of the Manitoba task force. Wells was so totally opposed to Meech Lake that it was difficult to imagine how he could ever be persuaded to support the main elements of the accord. Thus, despite McKenna's conversion in the fall of 1989, the prospects for the ratification of the accord appeared as remote as ever.

The November 1989 First Ministers' conference in Ottawa was a near total disaster. On the eve of the meeting, Clyde Wells had indicated that he was going to proceed with his motion to rescind Newfoundland's support for Meech Lake. Wells's threat to rescind became the focus of the two days of meetings. There was a general consensus among the other governments at the meeting that if Wells carried through with his threat, Meech Lake was finished. Thus there was a coordinated effort to persuade Wells to postpone taking any definitive action that would spell the death of Meech Lake.

Wells eventually relented in his threat to proceed immediately with the motion to rescind. But he insisted that the supporters of Meech Lake were merely postponing the inevitable. Wells told the other First Ministers that it was a foregone conclusion that Newfoundland would eventually withdraw its support for the accord. The only issue that was in doubt was when, not if, Newfoundland would act to kill Meech Lake. At the private First Ministers' dinner at the National Gallery on the eve of the conference, Wells was warned that his intransigence over the accord was endangering the future of the country. But Wells insisted that he could never accept Meech Lake in its current form. The accord was 'fundamentally flawed' and had to be totally rewritten.

The conference did provide great television. The highlight of the public sessions was an angry twelve-minute exchange between Brian Mulroney and Clyde Wells. Wells presented his vision of the 'equality of the provinces,' arguing that Meech Lake established a Canada with a 'Class A province, a Class B province, and eight Class C provinces.' Wells challenged the view that Quebec had been wrongly excluded from the constitutional settlement in 1981. No one province has the right to hold up the constitutional development of the country, Wells maintained. Nor does any province have a right to demand 'special legislative status.' If Ontario had demanded special status in 1981, it would also have been excluded or isolated from the constitutional settlement. Wells argued that in rejecting Meech Lake he was not rejecting Quebec. He was simply rejecting the unreasonable demands being made by the province's political leadership.

Clyde Wells was echoing the arguments of former prime minister Pierre Trudeau. Trudeau was fond of making a distinction between the 'people' of Quebec and the province's political leadership. Trudeau always said he would listen to the former but not the latter in formulating his policy towards Quebec. Clyde Wells was a graduate of the Trudeauvian school of Canadian federalism. He maintained that his opposition to Meech Lake was not based on a rejection of Quebec or of its people. His objection was merely to the unreasonable demands of the province's political leaders. If only these political leaders would cease with their demands for 'special status,' it would be possible to achieve a compromise that would be acceptable to the vast majority of the people of Canada.

Brian Mulroney could not resist rising to the bait. When Wells had finished speaking, he attempted to trip the Newfoundland premier up on one aspect of his remarks. Mulroney did not take issue with Wells's main argument – that Quebec was making 'unreasonable demands.' Instead, Mulroney chose to focus on Wells's analogy between the position of Quebec and Ontario. Wells had suggested that if Ontario had made 'unreasonable demands' in 1981, it would also have been excluded from the patriation package. Mulroney challenged Wells on the point, questioning his right to exclude anyone from the constitution. Mulroney claimed that the constitution had to bind everyone together and that to exclude any province or region would undermine its basic legitimacy. 'When you said we would proceed without Ontario if Ontario had demanded something we thought was unreasonable or a special status, that is where you and I separate fundamentally in terms of a vision of Canada,' Mulroney argued. 'For me a constitution without Ontario is no constitution at all.'

It was a curious and rather tortured argument for Mulroney to make. Mulroney had engaged Wells on Wells's chosen terrain. He had effectively conceded that the issue was how to respond to the 'unreasonable demands' of a particular province. Once you define the issue in that way, you have effectively conceded the argument. Wells saw the opening and drove home his point. He reiterated his argument that no single province making 'unreasonable demands' had a right to hold up the rest of the country 'forever.' Mulroney attempted to respond again, speaking of the need for 'foresight and leadership' in building a strong and united country. But by then it was too late. Wells had carried the day. He had succeeded in forcing the others around the table to discuss the issue on his terms. Everyone was talking Wells's language – suggesting how to respond to a province making 'unreasonable demands.' Watching the television exchange, one was given the impression that Quebec was acting 'unreasonably' and that only Clyde Wells had the courage to stand up for the equality of the provinces.

Score one for Clyde Wells. Coming out of the First Ministers' conference he had clearly gained momentum in his campaign to derail Meech Lake. Wells had agreed to postpone any immediate action to rescind the accord in Newfoundland. But he had bested the prime minister on live national TV and succeeded in framing the issue on his terms. Public opposition to Meech Lake within English Canada was now overwhelming, and Wells had been appointed as champion of the cause.

The pro-Meech forces, however, were in disarray. The federal government was clearly floundering, searching in vain for a strategy to save the accord. The Meech Lake puzzle seemed insoluble. Every possible gambit still left Ottawa facing checkmate on the next move. There was not even a process in place to deal with the issue. Following the November First Ministers' Conference, there were no further First Ministers' meetings scheduled prior to the June 1990 deadline for Meech Lake. As a kind of holding action, Mulroney dispatched Senator Murray on a tour of the provinces to search for common ground. The focus of Murray's tour was apparently to be the issue of Senate reform. It was agreed that there would be a First Ministers' conference on Senate reform by 1 November 1990, if

Meech Lake were ratified. Unfortunately, there appeared to be virtually no possibility that Meech would be ratified.

Senator Murray's tour over the winter was a non-event. He met with the hold-out provinces, who rehearsed their objections to Meech Lake. Senator Murray reiterated the federal position that Meech had to be ratified before 23 June 1990 and that the concerns of the dissidents could be addressed only in a second round of negotiations. Meanwhile, the sound of the constitutional clock ticking in the background began to grow louder. There were now less than six months left in the three-year ratification period for the accord. All indications pointed to the fact that the accord would fail to be ratified by the 23 June deadline.

The debate over Quebec's place in confederation was clearly taking its toll on the country as a whole. By January 1990, with the country staring the Meech deadline in the face, the constitutional issue assumed centre stage on the public and media agenda. The debate seemed to be veering dangerously out of control. On 29 January 1990, the city of Sault Ste Marie, Ontario, declared itself to be officially 'English-only.' The city's resolution declared that the English language was the municipality's only 'official language of communication.' The city's mayor, Joe Fratesi, denied that the resolution was anti-French or that it had been passed in retaliation for Bill 178 in Quebec. Fratesi argued that the resolution had been motivated by economics, not prejudice. He claimed that the city could not afford to provide bilingual services and that local residents objected to the fact that Sault Ste Marie had been designated as a bilingual district under the provincial French Language Services Act. He claimed to have received a petition signed by more than 24,000 residents supporting the resolution. The city's priorities were hospitals and roads, not French-language services, asserted the mayor. Such was the motivation and the message of the 'English-only' resolution.

The Sault Ste Marie resolution immediately caused a storm across the country. Ontario premier David Peterson and Prime Minister Mulroney denounced the resolution as being motivated by anti-Quebec sentiment. Peterson pointed out that the provincial French Language Services Act did not even apply to municipalities. There was no obligation on the city to provide French-language services to anyone. The 'official language' of the municipality was already English. Peterson argued that the resolution passed by the city was entirely superfluous and was certain to increase language tensions across the country.

But Mayor Fratesi and the Sault Ste Marie city council were unrepentant. At the next meeting of council on 5 February, about a thousand demonstrators picketed outside the municipal offices, calling on the city to rescind the English-only resolution. But the mayor vowed that the resolution would not be withdrawn or modified. 'We're not going to back off because certain heavy-duty politicians don't like what we've done,' Fratesi proclaimed. At the same time, numerous other municipalities in Ontario began debating similar resolutions. A week later, Thunder Bay followed Sault Ste Marie's lead and declared itself to be English-only. Within a month, dozens of other municipalities had debated or passed similar resolutions. The 'English-only' movement became a magnet for the national media. The municipal resolutions were taken as evidence of a generalized rejection of the policy of official bilingualism.[5] Media accounts suggested that 'many Canadians still reject the idea that just as doctors should go to medical school and lawyers should go to law school, public servants should learn French'.[6] But the evidence for this 'trend' was largely anecdotal or else a mere extrapolation from the existence of the 'English-only' resolutions. The fact, for example, that enrolment in French-immersion classes in the province of Ontario had increased over the 1980s was rarely mentioned. Canadians were told that they were becoming more 'intolerant' and less willing to accommodate language differences.

Within Quebec, the media message was particularly damaging. Reports of the English-only resolutions were combined with television pictures of an English-rights group trampling on the Quebec flag. The flag incident, which had occurred in Brockville in September 1989, during a visit to the city by Ontario premier David Peterson, had attracted relatively little media attention at the time. These types of protests by English-rights groups were commonplace. The media traditionally ignored them on the basis that they represented the views of a marginal or fringe organization. But, in early 1990, the media took a different approach to the issue. The message that the French-language media broadcast to Quebeckers was that their language and culture were no longer welcome in the rest of the country. The 'English-only' resolutions in major Ontario cities such as Sault Ste Marie and Thunder Bay were taken as evidence that the views of groups such as APEC were not marginal at all within English Canada. Television pictures of APEC members trampling on the Quebec flag in Brockville fit perfectly with the new theme. The 'Quebec flag' incident was rebroadcast repeatedly in Quebec, the implication being that the small group of anglo protesters was somehow representative of general English-Canadian attitudes towards Quebec. The link with Meech Lake was direct and obvious. The accord was increasingly being seen as a barometer of

English Canada's attitude towards Quebec. A rejection of Meech would be taken as confirmation that the rest of Canada was unwilling to recognize or to accommodate Quebec's distinctiveness.

Quebec premier Robert Bourassa continued to maintain that he was confident that Meech would eventually be ratified. But he also began to muse openly about the consequences of the failure of the accord. During a ten-day trip to Europe in the first week of February, Bourassa raised the possibility of a new type of 'political superstructure' that might arise in the wake of the failure of Meech Lake. The Quebec premier refused to clarify his vision of what this new 'superstructure' might involve. Upon his return to Quebec City, the premier indicated that his comments had been intended to reassure European investors that Quebec would be a safe place to invest in the event that Meech Lake failed. 'If [Meech] is not ratified,' Bourassa said, 'I can guarantee that there will be a superstructure or institution or supranational institution, whatever name we could use, which could reassure the German investors or the foreign investors that Quebec and Canada are safe places to invest.'[7] Bourassa also indicated that the Quebec Liberal party was beginning to study options for Quebec in the event that Meech failed. The director-general of the Liberal party was quoted as saying that 'all options are being analysed, nothing is excluded,' including sovereignty. On 25 February, the Quebec Liberal party formally established a committee to study Quebec's options if Meech Lake was not ratified. Bourassa denied that the study group was designed to dismantle the country. But Bourassa warned that serious consequences would follow the failure of Meech since 'we haven't received a mandate to practise federalism on our knees.'

Canada was in trouble. The battle lines had been drawn and the trenches had been dug. Now, everyone seemed content to pursue the battle to the bitter end, regardless of the consequences. However, the fact was that no one would win, and everyone would lose from this confrontation. Business leaders, who had largely remained on the sidelines in this debate, finally began to speak out about the negative consequences of the failure of the accord. A group of former politicians and academics formed an organization known as the Friends of Meech Lake to lobby for ratification of the accord. But the appeals and the warnings fell on deaf ears. Clyde Wells and Gary Filmon dismissed Bourassa's musings about a new political superstructure as 'sabre-rattling.' The Quebec premier was bluffing, they suggested to English Canadians, who welcomed the reassurance. Meanwhile, Quebeckers were told by respected financial institutions such as the Toronto Dominion Bank and Merrill Lynch & Co. that an independent Quebec was viable. Plainly, no one was in a mood for compromise.

Meech Lake had become a game of constitutional chicken. English- and French-speaking Canadians were barrelling down the highway towards each other, heading for a certain collision. No one wanted to be the first to veer off to the side of the road. Everyone was too intent on keeping a foot on the accelerator, pressing the metal down to the floor, and trying to coax a little more speed out of their straining engines.

By the end of March 1990, the pressure on the federal government to 'do something' was mounting. There were barely three months left before Meech would die, and yet the federal government seemed to have no plan to save the accord. This situation was intolerable. Prime Minister Mulroney had been warning for months of the dire consequences that would follow from the failure of the accord. Yet, his government was doing absolutely nothing to save the accord and avoid those consequences.

The final week of March saw the unveiling of a long-expected federal 'strategy' to save the accord. The first move was made on 21 March in Fredericton by Frank McKenna. McKenna, although nominally one of the Meech hold-outs, was now firmly within the pro-Meech camp. The federal strategy was premised on the idea that the process of bringing McKenna formally on board for Meech might be used to isolate Filmon and Wells, the 'real' hold-outs. The pressure on Filmon and Wells to modify their opposition might then be increased, leading to a compromise acceptable to everyone. That, apparently, was the theory.

On 21 March, Frank McKenna introduced two resolutions into the New Brunswick Legislature. The first was the Meech Lake resolution itself. The second was a 'companion resolution' containing a number of 'add-ons' to the accord. The changes proposed in the companion resolution were modest, even more limited than the amendments that had been proposed by the New Brunswick legislative committee the previous October. Federal officials had met with New Brunswick officials in the weeks leading up to McKenna's announcement, seeking to pare down McKenna's list of add-ons to an absolute minimum. McKenna's demands were now incredibly modest. He wanted a guarantee that women's rights could not be overridden by the distinct-society clause. He wanted to recognize the right of the federal government to promote linguistic duality across the country as well as a recognition of linguistic duality in New Brunswick. He wanted the federal government to have the right to create new provinces without the requirement of obtaining the consent of existing provinces. McKenna wanted the Yukon and the Northwest Territories to have the right to nominate senators and Supreme Court judges.

But these proposed changes were mere tinkering. McKenna accepted the key elements of the accord: the distinct-society clause, the limitations on the federal spending power, the new procedure for nomination of Supreme Court judges. McKenna had come almost full circle from the position he had articulated on 25 August 1987 before the Special Joint Committee of the Senate and House of Commons. In August 1987, McKenna had set out a long litany of complaints about the accord. He had raised fears about the impact of the distinct-society clause on the Charter of Rights. He had objected to the requirement of unanimous provincial consent for Senate reform. He was opposed to giving the provinces the right to nominate Supreme Court judges.

Comparing McKenna's position in March 1990 with his testimony in Ottawa in August 1987, it is hard to believe that the same man was capable of advancing two positions so diametrically opposed to each other. But no one pressed McKenna for an explanation of the apparent contradiction. The New Brunswick premier had gone from the role of villain to saviour. His companion resolution was to light the path that would lead Canadians to the rescue of the accord, and of the country itself. 'It is time we spike our guns with flowers,' McKenna told Canadians. It was a little uncertain just whose guns McKenna was referring to, his own or someone else's. But the message to Canadians seemed clear enough. McKenna's companion resolution was the way out of the Meech Lake impasse.

The federal government moved quickly to appropriate ownership of McKenna's companion resolution. On the evening of 22 March, Prime Minister Mulroney went on national television to announce that he was referring McKenna's resolution to a special committee of the House of Commons. Mulroney spoke the language of moderation, of public consultation and of compromise. 'I believe that Canadians want to participate themselves in the resolution of this great national issue,' Mulroney told his television audience. He promised that the Commons committee would hold hearings across the country and that the resolution would then be brought back into the House of Commons for a final vote. The resolution was not a 'take it or leave it' proposition, Mulroney noted, suggesting that it could be modified or improved as a result of the committee hearings.

Here, within the space of two days, was a second national leader performing an about-face on national television. Brian Mulroney had maintained for two years and nine months that the Meech Lake Accord was a 'seamless web' that could not be reopened. Suddenly, he was reversing course. The purpose and effect of the companion resolution were to amend Meech Lake. In embracing the McKenna resolution, Mulroney was, in effect, agreeing to reopen the accord.

Mulroney refused to acknowledge this rather dramatic shift in his position. He maintained that McKenna's plan contemplated the ratification of Meech Lake first, followed by the enactment of a companion resolution containing amendments. But it was self-evident that the McKenna scheme contemplated amendments to the Meech Lake Accord, something that Mulroney had thus far maintained was impossible. What was also apparent was that the McKenna amendments represented a floor rather than a ceiling. The effect of the public hearings would be to raise the level of the floor. The hearings by the House of Commons committee, headed by Jean Charest, would provide a platform for the opponents of Meech Lake to demand additional changes. If Charest was to be responsive to the testimony at the hearings, he would have to recommend additional amendments to Meech Lake, beyond those contained in McKenna's resolution.

All of this led to an inevitable question: how could these amendments be sold in the province of Quebec? Bourassa would not be overly impressed by the technical argument that the McKenna resolution was a two-stage operation. It was clear enough that amendments to Meech Lake were now in the works. Was the Quebec premier prepared to accept these amendments, despite his repeated protestations that Meech Lake had to be ratified 'as is'?

Every indication coming out of Quebec City was that Bourassa was not prepared to accept amendments. The Parti Québécois had howled in protest following the introduction of the McKenna resolution, claiming that Bourassa was preparing to accept amendments to Meech Lake through the 'back door.' PQ leader Jacques Parizeau taunted Bourassa and dared him to take a position on the McKenna 'companion resolution.' Parizeau introduced a resolution into the Quebec National Assembly officially rejecting the New Brunswick amendments. The opposition leader thought he had Bourassa pinned and that his resolution would force the Quebec premier to reveal his imminent collapse in the face of pressure from the rest of the country. But Bourassa surprised Parizeau by announcing on 28 March that he was prepared to endorse the PQ resolution. The slightly amended resolution, passed overwhelmingly by the Assembly on 5 April, declared that the Quebec government 'officially rejects in the name of Quebecers, all constitutional proposals including New Brunswick's which would constitute an amendment or modification susceptible to changing the content and the scope of the Meech Lake Accord.'

Some commentators outside of Quebec professed to perceive a small measure of ambiguity in the resolution. These commentators took some comfort from the fact that the resolution did not openly and directly condemn the McKenna initiative. But this reading of the Quebec resolution seemed to be fairly strained and implausible. The operative and key feature of the Quebec resolution was that it closed the door to any proposals that had *the effect* of amending Meech Lake. It, of course, spoke directly to the McKenna device of passing a companion resolution. Because the McKenna strategy contemplated what amounted to amendments to Meech Lake, it ran directly afoul of the National Assembly's 5 April resolution. The Quebec government had reaffirmed its commitment to Meech Lake and essentially rejected the 'companion resolution' approach even before the Commons committee had begun its hearings.

In the meantime, Clyde Wells didn't seem to be finding much encouragement from the McKenna companion resolution either. On the same day that the prime minister announced his plan to refer the resolution to committee, Wells introduced his motion to rescind support for the accord in the Newfoundland House of Assembly. Wells pronounced himself dissatisfied with the modest amendments McKenna had proposed. He also objected to the continued insistence by both Brian Mulroney and Robert Bourassa that Meech Lake had to be ratified first and changed later. That just wasn't good enough for the Newfoundland premier. In his motion, he proposed that Meech Lake might be ratified only if it was approved by a referendum in Newfoundland or in all of Canada. This referendum would be called in the unlikely event that both Manitoba and New Brunswick ratified the accord and Newfoundland was left as the lone hold-out.

The opposition Progressive Conservatives tried to stall debate on Wells's motion to rescind Meech Lake. But Wells forced the issue to a vote on 6 April, and the motion was carried. Newfoundland had become the first province to rescind a constitutional resolution of a previous government. Later that same day, federal environment minister Lucien Bouchard happened to be holding a press conference with Quebec's Gil Rémillard in Quebec City. Bouchard suggested that English Canadians may well be forced to choose between Quebec and Newfoundland. He intimated that there was little doubt as to what choice the rest of the country would make.

Wells's rescinding motion could have been interpreted as the final blow to the accord. But as the Charest committee prepared to commence its nation-wide hearings, the defenders of Meech refused to write its obituary. Publicly, Brian Mulroney professed to have confidence that the committee might produce a solution to the impasse. In fact, there was little basis for this optimism. Still, the decision to hold committee hearings on the accord would serve one important and salutary function. For nearly three years, the opponents of Meech Lake had decried the unwillingness of the federal government to consider amendments. These critics had argued that, if the federal government would only demonstrate a little flexibility, a new national consensus could be formed around the accord.

Here, finally, was an opportunity to test the hypothesis of the critics. In striking the committee, Brian Mulroney was effectively opening the accord up for amendments. Now it would be possible to find out once and for all whether the accord really was a 'seamless web,' or whether amendments, were in fact, possible. If there was a possibility of a 'new compromise,' the Charest committee would surely discover it.

The Charest committee began its hearings 9 April in Ottawa. The first witness was Frank McKenna, who explained to the committee the rationale behind his companion resolution. After McKenna, the committee heard from a total of 160 witnesses in Yellowknife, Whitehorse, Vancouver, Winnipeg, St John's, and back in Ottawa. It is instructive to compare the Charest committee hearings with the hearings held by the special joint committee on Meech Lake back in the summer of 1987. In August 1987, the passage of the accord had appeared a virtual certainty. The special joint committee hearings were dominated by the anti–Meech Lake lobby, who saw the hearings as a last-gasp attempt to derail ratification. Aboriginal groups, women's organizations, child-care advocates, and multicultural groups, among others, had appeared to denounce the process and substance of Meech Lake. The only witnesses who spoke in favour of the accord in August 1987 tended to be academics and constitutional experts.

Now, by the spring of 1990, the tables had been turned. The prospects for ratification of Meech Lake had become extremely remote. With the accord on its last legs, a variety of supporters came forward to try to make a case for the accord. Business groups, which had largely remained silent in 1987, argued that Meech Lake should be ratified in order that the country could resolve the constitutional issue and get on with other matters. The Friends of Meech Lake lobby group made its case for the accord. Even three premiers – Ontario's David Peterson, Prince Edward Island's Joe Ghiz, and Nova Scotia's John Buchanan – testified in favour of the ratification of Meech Lake.

So, between 1987 and 1990, the pro-Meech constituency had recruited a number of important allies and spokespersons. Despite this important shift, the public hearings were still better suited to the purposes of the critics than to the proponents of Meech Lake. By 1990, both the process and the substance of Meech Lake had been largely discredited within English Canada. Even the defenders of Meech Lake had to concede that there were important flaws or deficiencies in the accord. In fact, the assumption underlying the creation of the Charest committee was that, in its current form, the accord was unacceptable. It was inevitable, in other words, that the focus of the hearings would be on the shortcomings in the accord and on the need to make amendments. Moreover, the Charest committee had been given explicit authority to consider amendments beyond the limited list set out by Frank McKenna. It was thus a virtual certainty that the committee would expand the list of 'add-ons' in McKenna's companion resolution. Only by adding to the list of proposed amendments would the committee be able to claim that it had been responsive to the testimony at the hearings.

That is precisely what happened in the committee's final report, tabled in the House of Commons on 17 May. As expected, the committee approved all of the amendments McKenna had proposed in his 21 March companion resolution. The committee then came up with a list of additional amendments of its own. Charest proposed the addition of an amendment specifying that the linguistic-duality/distinct-society clause did not impair the effectiveness of the Charter of Rights. Charest also wanted the companion resolution to clarify that the linguistic-duality/distinct-society clause did not grant any new legislative powers to Parliament or the provinces. With respect to Senate reform, the committee proposed a 'sunset clause' for the requirement of unanimous provincial consent. If there was no agreement on Senate reform after a period of three years, the committee recommended that some less restrictive formula with 'some form of regional approval' be substituted. The Charest committee also took up the Manitoba task force suggestion of the addition of a 'Canada Clause' that would include recognition for the aboriginal people and recognize the multicultural dimension of Canada's heritage. Charest recommended that these other fundamental elements of Canada be recognized 'in the body of the Constitution.'

The committee report was not terribly surprising. The recommendations were crafted so as to respond to the agenda of the hold-out provinces and of the critics of Meech Lake. The committee had no real choice but to end up in this position. In the process, what began as a relatively modest list of amendments proposed by Frank McKenna had grown in both number and significance. The committee's report was greeted with cautious optimism by the opponents of the accord. After three years of 'stonewalling' from the federal government, the critics of the accord finally seemed to be making real headway. It appeared that Quebec would have to back down and accept amendments to Meech Lake. Manitoba's Gary Filmon indicated that the 'companion resolution' approach recommended by the Charest committee was, in reality, an indirect way of securing amendments to the accord. 'You can virtually reverse the entire meaning and intent of something by adding something to it,' Filmon told reporters in Winnipeg.[8] Filmon indicated that he had been advised by legal experts that it was possible to 'essentially wipe out' parts of the accord through additions to it. 'That's what the report is recommending and I assume it's so that everybody who has already signed the accord can save face and preserve their honour.' Filmon indicated that the Charest Committee had done a good job of identifying Manitoba's concerns and that the report represented a 'good basis for negotiations.' But Filmon warned that Manitoba would insist that the changes proposed by Charest come into effect at the same time as Meech Lake. 'We won't pass it now and fix it later,' Filmon added.

The opponents of Meech evidently believed that they were nearing the finish line, and the wind was in their sails. Sharon Carstairs also sounded upbeat about the report, calling it a 'vindication' of Manitobans who had been demanding improvements to the accord. Newfoundland's Clyde Wells was also cautiously optimistic. 'While I can't just accept everything that's in the report,' Wells said, 'I'm encouraged by the content and general direction of it.'

Quebec and its premier, Robert Bourassa, still posed a problem. In early April, the National Assembly had already rejected the modest set of amendments proposed by Frank McKenna. Now, Quebec was confronted with a much more substantial list of proposed changes in the Charest report. Moreover, while the Charest report argued that its amendments would '*add to* and not *subtract from* the Meech Lake Accord,'[9] it was evident that this description was misleading, if not plain wrong. Certain of the committee recommendations, dealing with issues such as the creation of new provinces or Senate reform, directly contradicted Meech Lake. Describing them as 'add-ons' could not conceal the fact that what was being proposed were substantive amendments to the Meech Lake Accord. This reality was evident to Gary Filmon, Sharon Carstairs, and Clyde Wells, and it would certainly not escape the attention of Robert Bourassa.

Bourassa wasted no time in rejecting the Charest committee proposals. On the afternoon of 17 May, after being briefed on the contents of the Charest report, he made it plain the proposals were unacceptable. 'I have the feeling that English Canada does not understand Quebec and that is why they are making unacceptable demands of us,' Bourassa told an impromptu media scrum in Montreal.[10] Bourassa complained in particular about the committee's recommendation that a companion resolution should affirm that recognition of Quebec as a distinct society does not impair the effect of the Charter of Rights. 'When they propose amendments suggesting that the distinct society does not entail any new power, that's the type of amendment which waters down something that was already quite limited,' Bourassa argued. He complained that English Canada was trying to 'limit and limit again' specific powers that were necessary to protect Quebec's language and culture. Bourassa was also sceptical about the value of holding a First Ministers' conference, saying that he had nothing new to offer: 'I will repeat what I have always said, that is, that we have always respected our word . . . We never changed our minds. We always respected our word and we wish others would do the same.'

The reaction to the report elsewhere in Quebec was even more harsh. The following day, Quebec Conservative MP François Gérin resigned from the federal Conservative caucus in protest over the Charest committee recommendations. Gérin argued that the Charest committee was proposing substantive amendments to Meech Lake, something he said Brian Mulroney had promised would never happen. Gérin said it was clear that the rest of Canada was unwilling to accept Quebec's minimum conditions as reflected in the Meech Lake Accord. He said he decided to resign when he was told that, as a member of the Tory caucus, he could not freely express his objections to the report. He vowed to promote Quebec sovereignty while sitting as an independent MP in Parliament. 'Like many Quebecers, I now believe fundamentally, at the centre of my being, with my guts, my heart and my head, that the future of Quebec leads to sovereignty,' Gérin told a hushed House of Commons.[11]

The Quebec media denounced the Charest report in quick and unequivocal terms. Typical of the reaction was that of Lysiane Gagnon, a columnist for *La Presse* in Montreal, who had tended to be a voice of moderation in the debate. Her column on Saturday, 19 May, let loose a torrent of anger and frustration about the Charest committee process and the report. 'The insult is not in the recommendations considered in isolation,' Gagnon wrote. 'The insult is not in the Charest report but in the process which led to it: in the tone, the manner, in this new grocery list, in this block of demands that they've hurled in our faces to put us in our place.' Gagnon denounced what she termed the 'irresponsible stubbornness' of the three hold-out provinces, each of whom insisted that Quebec could be readmitted to the 'family' only on conditions that they would establish.

If there was any lingering doubt about the acceptability of the Charest recommendations in the province of Quebec, that doubt was removed by the words and actions of federal environment minister Lucien Bouchard. Bouchard had been in Europe when the Charest report was released. His physical absence did not impede him from immediately thrusting himself into the centre of the debate. Over the weekend of 20 May, the Parti Québécois national council had been meeting to mark the tenth anniversary of the Quebec referendum. Bouchard decided to send a telegram to the PQ meeting, commending those who fought for sovereignty-association and praising the leader of the *oui* campaign, former premier René Lévesque. 'The referendum directly concerns us all,' Bouchard wrote. 'Its commemoration is another occasion to remind everyone of the honesty, the pride and the generosity of the Yes that we all defended around René Lévesque and his team.'

Jacques Parizeau read the telegram aloud to the PQ meeting, prompting the audience to burst into applause and cheers. But the telegram immediately caused a sensation across the country. Outside of Quebec, there was universal condemnation of the fact that a federal cabinet minister had publicly praised a political movement dedicated to the destruction of the country. Opposition politicians were astonished, and questioned whether Bouchard could remain in the cabinet.

Apparently, Bouchard himself was of the same opinion. Returning to Montreal's Mirabel Airport on 20 May, Bouchard was unapologetic about the telegram, claiming that it 'speaks for itself'. On the evening of 21 May, Bouchard tendered his resignation to the prime minister. His five-page letter of resignation said that he could not accept the Charest committee report, since the recommendations would make Quebec's five conditions devoid of all meaning. His letter was a searing and venomous indictment of the 'betrayal' and 'humiliation' of Quebec by English Canada. In the letter, and at a news conference the next day, Bouchard had ominous words of warning for the rest of the country about the consequences that would follow the failure of Meech Lake. 'If you think this is a bluff, then I called my bluff. I quit the cabinet,' he told the news conference. 'Read our lips, because we mean business.'[12]

The federal government was in disarray, its Meech strategy in tatters. A haggard and tired Brian Mulroney tried to limit the damage caused by the Bouchard resignation and to prevent further defections from his caucus. The prime minister told the House of Commons that Quebec would never be isolated at the constitutional table. He denied that there was any plan afoot to weaken or to water down the Meech Lake Accord. Although one additional Tory MP from Quebec did quit the Conservative caucus, Mulroney's reassurances were sufficient to avert any further resignations. The problem for Mulroney was that his efforts to salvage Meech Lake appeared to have run up against a brick wall. The Charest committee report had responded to the concerns of the hold-out provinces but, in the process, had alienated Quebec. Bourassa and Rémillard were now saying that they would not even attend a First Ministers' meeting based on the Charest recommendations. With only a month to go before the deadline, the accord seemed doomed.

The constitution suddenly became a hot topic of interest on the financial markets. In the wake of the Bouchard resignation, the Canadian dollar tumbled a full cent against the u.s. dollar, prompting the Bank of Canada to intervene to quell the selling frenzy. On Thursday, 24 May, the Bank of Canada raised interest rates, with finance minister Michael Wilson blaming fear of political instability as the reason for the hike. Eighteen months earlier, the falling value of the dollar and high interest rates had played a key role in building support for the Canadian–u.s. Trade Agreement. Some Canadians wondered whether they were in for a repeat performance. But, with only thirty days left in the 'Meech countdown,' no one had any sense of how to deal with positions that appeared to be totally irreconcilable.

8

This Dinner Has Seven Days

During the first half of the month of May 1990, there had been little or no activity on the intergovernmental Meech front. Political leaders across the country had been awaiting the release of the Charest committee report before deciding when and how to undertake a final push to achieve a constitutional settlement. The release of the report on 17 May set off a final extended flurry of intergovernmental negotiations designed to salvage the accord. These negotiations culminated in a seven day, closed-door meeting of First Ministers that began with dinner on 3 June and continued for the next six days at the Conference Centre in Ottawa. But this 'seven-day dinner' was merely a continuation of a series of non-stop negotiations that began on 19 May and spanned a total of twenty-two days.

These twenty-two days of negotiations were to tell the fate of the Meech Lake Accord. Later, the prime minister boasted that the federal government executed a strategy that had been carefully planned and worked out in advance. Mulroney claimed that, before the Charest report was even released, he had called his advisers together and identified for them the day on which he would 'roll the dice.' But the actual way in which the negotiations were conducted between 19 May and 9 June belies the claim that Ottawa was executing a 'master plan.'

The reality was that the federal government changed its strategy midway through the process. The federal government began by attempting to craft a compromise based on the recommendations of the Charest committee. Ottawa drafted a series of 'add-ons' that sought to meet the concerns of the three hold-out provinces. The first version of these 'add-ons' was circulated to the provinces by Senator Lowell Murray, who undertook a whirlwind cross-country tour between 19 May and 22 May. A second, revised version of the federal proposals was discussed between Prime Minister Mulroney and all the premiers in a series of 'one-to-one' discussions at 24 Sussex Drive between 24 and 28 May. By 30 May, it was clear that this strategy was going nowhere. The Charest committee proposals simply could not serve as the basis of a consensus, principally because the province of Quebec was flatly opposed to the main thrust of the committee report.

On 2 June, the federal government reversed course. Abandoning the key elements of the Charest proposals, the federal government reverted to the position it had advanced prior to 22 March 1990 – ratify Meech now and fix it later. The federal government proposed that the significant flaws or omissions in Meech Lake should be addressed through a 'second round' of negotiations that would take place after 23 June 1990. This was the federal position that was tabled at the opening of the First Ministers' dinner on 3 June and that was maintained throughout the week-long meeting at the Conference Centre.

By changing horses in midstream, the federal government revealed that it had no clear idea of how to resolve the constitutional impasse. Far from executing a master plan, the federal government was desperately searching for a solution to the Meech Lake puzzle. The sudden reversal in strategy at the end of May also made it more rather than less difficult to fashion a consensus. The shift in the federal approach produced manifest confusion in some of the provincial delegations about what was being discussed and where a possible consensus might be found. The 'hold-out' provinces, who had come to Ottawa expecting to discuss amendments based on the Charest committee proposals, were taken off guard. They had expected the meeting to be conducted on their terms, not Quebec's. They thought the discussion would centre on amendments to the Meech Lake Accord.

Imagine the frustration and surprise when the First Ministers were told at dinner that Meech Lake had to be ratified without any substantial changes. This was the 'pass it now, fix it later' approach that the hold-out provinces assumed had long since been abandoned. Surely there was some mistake. Someone must have gotten his or her signals crossed. The purpose of the meeting was to put pressure on Robert Bourassa to make amendments, not to put pressure on Gary Filmon and Clyde Wells to ratify the accord. Or was it? A fundamental confusion over what was possible, over whether someone was bluffing, and over the real purpose of the negotiations stymied the efforts of the First Ministers for days. It was this confusion, more than anything else, that was responsible for the fact that the meeting dragged on for seven days. It took the better part of four days for all the parties around the table to come to terms with the real choices that had to be made. It was only then that the real negotiations could begin.

What is truly remarkable is that, after all of these false starts, the hold-out provinces were still prepared to abandon their demands that Meech Lake be amended prior to 23 June. Yet, that is precisely what happened over the final seven days of discussions in Ottawa. When they arrived in Ottawa on 3 June, Gary Filmon and Clyde Wells had stated in the clearest possible fashion that they would never agree to 'pass Meech now and fix it later.' When they left town six days later, they had put their names on an agreement that contemplated precisely such an approach. The 9 June final communiqué essentially postponed the attempt to resolve the concerns of the hold-out provinces to a second round of negotiations.

In the end, this was simply too big a bite for the dissidents to swallow. The proximate causes of the failure of Meech were, of course, the actions of Elijah Harper in Manitoba and Clyde Wells in Newfoundland. But viewed from a larger perspective, it is evident that the accord had been lost sometime well before 22 June. The opponents of the accord had been led to believe that they had won the battle to force amendments to it. As late as 2 June, Clyde Wells and Gary Filmon had assumed that the only question to be answered was how many concessions they would be able to extract from Robert Bourassa. When they got to Ottawa, they discovered that the actual choice they would be called upon to make was quite different. Filmon and Wells could either ratify the accord 'as is,' or else they could reject the accord entirely. Neither premier had the stomach or the inclination to walk away from the table and reject the accord outright. But the groundwork had simply not been laid for a final agreement that would require them to hold their noses and pass the accord 'as is.' In the end, while Clyde Wells signed the 9 June communiqué, he simply could not bring himself to go through with the dirty deed.

This chapter will tell the story of the twenty-two days of frantic negotiations to save the accord between 19 May and 9 June 1990. We will see the initial attempts to build a consensus out of the Charest committee proposals, followed by the eventual abandonment of that strategy by the federal government. Then, we will trace the working-through of the 'fall-back' federal strategy over the 'seven-day dinner' attended by the First Ministers in Ottawa. On the evening of 9 June, some people thought there was a deal to resolve the constitutional impasse. The problem was that this 'deal' asked people to do something they had vowed they would never do. It would have taken a miracle for this agreement to have settled Canada's constitutional wars and brought peace to a troubled land.

Stage One: Searching for 'Compromise'

On Saturday, 19 May 1990, Prime Minister Mulroney dispatched his constitutional 'point man,' Senator Lowell Murray, on a whirlwind tour of provincial capitals. Murray was to test the waters in the wake of the release of the Charest committee report two days earlier. He would bring with him a package of federal proposals modelled on Charest. The senator would discuss these federal proposals with the provincial premiers and determine whether there was sufficient consensus to justify holding a First Ministers' conference.

Murray and his deputy, Norman Spector, were utilizing the same process that they had employed with such success in the months leading up to the Meech Lake meeting on 30 April 1987. Keep the discussions informal and bilateral, meeting individually with the provinces. Try to narrow the areas of disagreement and broaden the areas of consensus. Call a full-scale meeting only when there was broad agreement and the likelihood of a successful outcome.

But the times and the atmosphere had changed between the spring of 1987 and the spring of 1990. In 1987, everyone had been eager to search for compromise. There had been flexibility and a willingness to make concessions on all sides. By 1990, virtually all of this flexibility had been drained out of the system. Most of the provinces had spent the intervening three years painting themselves into small corners. Compromising at this late stage in the game meant 'losing face,' something that no one was much interested in contemplating. And, most important, Murray and Spector now had a deadline hanging over their heads. In 1987, they had been able to proceed at a leisurely pace, without the necessity of settling the differences by a fixed time. In 1990, the time available to achieve a consensus could be measured in weeks, if not days.

Spector and Murray set a gruelling, almost superhuman pace in their travels over the Victoria Day weekend. On 19 May they met with Gary Filmon in Gimli, Manitoba; the next day they met with Bill Vander Zalm in Vancouver, and then jetted to St John's for a discussion with Clyde Wells; on Monday, 21 May, they saw the third hold-out, Frank McKenna, in Fredericton, and on Tuesday met with Robert Bourassa in Quebec City. In between these meetings with the key players, they also had discussions, over the telephone or face to face, with all the other premiers. The federal delegation presented each of the premiers with a document entitled 'State of Play on a Companion Resolution to the Meech Lake Accord.' The federal proposal set out the elements of a proposed companion resolution that would 'add on' to or amend the Meech Lake Accord.

. The 'State of Play' document was an attempt to utilize the 'no author' text approach that had been employed with such success in the 1981 round of constitutional negotiations. Under this approach, the federal government was cast in the role of 'holding the pen,' seeking to identify areas of possible emerging consensus. The 'no author' text was supposed to represent the distillation of where a possible consensus on the issues might be located. It did not necessarily represent the view of the federal government itself or of any other government participating in the talks. The 'no author' quality of the proposals was reflected in their title; they were styled 'State of Play on a Companion Resolution,' rather than as 'Federal Government Proposals on a Companion Resolution.' By employing this 'no author' approach, the federal government was trying to maintain some distance from the proposals in the event that they failed to meet with general agreement.

The 'State of Play' document tracked the recommendations of the Charest report. Three proposed constitutional amendments were particularly controversial. The first two dealt directly or indirectly with the distinct-society/linguistic-duality clause. On the distinct-society clause itself, the federal government proposed a clarification of the relationship between the clause and the charter. The clarification would state that the rights in the charter were not 'overridden or denied' by the distinct-society clause. There would also be a clause providing that the distinct-society clause did not 'confer any legislative power' on either the provinces or the federal Parliament. These clarifications would take the form of formal constitutional amendments, although the federal proposals did not state precisely where such amendments would be placed in the constitution. A fair assumption was that the amendments would be added to the distinct-society clause itself.

A related issue was the question of a 'Canada Clause,' a recommendation that the Charest committee had taken up from the Manitoba task force report. The federal government proposed to entrench a preamble in the constitution that would refer to a variety of 'fundamental characteristics' of Canada. These characteristics would include the rights of the aboriginal peoples, the distinct identity of Quebec, the 'cultural diversity of Canadian society,' the principle of the equality of the provinces, and a 'commitment to the well-being of all Canadians in whatever part of Canada they live.'

The third key issue was the question of Senate reform. Here, the 19 May 'State of Play' document picked up the Charest recommendation that the requirement of unanimous provincial consent for Senate reform be relaxed at some point in the future. The federal proposal was that, if unanimous agreement was not reached within three years, a new system of 'regional vetos' would kick in. Under this 'default option,' the consent of seven provinces comprising at least 50 per cent of the population would be required for Senate reform. But the seven provinces would have to include Quebec, two western provinces representing at least 50 per cent of the total western Canadian population, and two Atlantic provinces. This proposal was the so-called Mendes formula, named after its author, Professor Errol Mendes of the University of Western Ontario. The unique feature of the proposal was that it provided a veto for Quebec, but not for Ontario. The absence of a veto for Ontario was thought to make the proposed veto for Quebec more palatable to the western provinces.

As Senator Murray shopped his proposals around the provinces over the Victoria Day weekend, each of these three key elements attracted considerable criticism. The proposed 'clarification' of the relationship between the distinct-society clause and the Charter of Rights was welcomed by both Manitoba and Newfoundland, although they had some questions about the precise wording of the clause. But such a clarification was regarded as entirely unacceptable by the province of Quebec. Robert Bourassa had already publicly denounced the Charest report as 'unacceptable,' singling out the recommendation on the Charter of Rights for particular criticism. Lucien Bouchard had resigned over the weekend as Senator Murray was making his rounds of the provinces, stiffening Bourassa's resolve to reject any attempt to tamper with the distinct-society clause. Quebec did not seem to have any quarrel with the actual wording of the proposed clarification. The problem was political and symbolic. Agreeing to the federal proposal would have been regarded in Quebec as a fatal 'watering down' of the distinct-society clause. Quebec officials made it clear that they could simply not agree to a 'clarification' of the meaning of the clause at this stage in the negotiations.

No one seemed very happy with the federal proposal on the 'Canada Clause.' The clause went too far for Quebec, and not far enough for Manitoba. The Quebec position was that they would discuss a 'Canada Clause' as a second-round item, following the ratification of Meech. They were unprepared to sign on to such a clause now, even one that was included in the preamble to the constitution. Gary Filmon, however, was unhappy that the federal government was proposing to include the 'Canada Clause' in the preamble as opposed to the main body of the constitution. The Manitoba task force had explicitly demanded that the clause be included as part of the main body of the constitution, alongside the distinct-society clause. Filmon indicated that including the Canada Clause in the preamble, when the distinct-society clause was in the main body of the constitution, would create the impression that the distinct-society clause had constitutional primacy. Filmon wanted the federal proposals to reflect the approach recommended by the Manitoba task force.

The federal proposal on Senate reform was the target for attack by virtually all the provinces. Manitoba and Newfoundland said that they could never accept a situation where a single province had a veto over future Senate reform. Thus they objected to the federal proposal because it continued to grant Quebec a veto. The other western provinces took the same position they had articulated during the initial Meech Lake round in 1987: if Quebec had a veto, they also had to have one. They said they could never accept a situation where Quebec had a veto over Senate reform but they lacked the same power. Ontario was also unhappy with the federal proposal since it made a fundamental distinction between the positions of Ontario and Quebec whereby Ontario, with over 35 per cent of the total Canadian population, was denied a right of veto that was being granted to Quebec. It seemed difficult to justify a formula that granted a veto to the second-largest province while denying the same right to the largest.

After completing his four-day whirlwind tour of the provinces, Murray realized that none of his proposals on the three key issues was capable of attracting a consensus. The senator emerged from his meeting with Quebec's Robert Bourassa on Tuesday, 22 May, saying: 'I can't in good conscience, say that a First Ministers' conference called now would have a chance of success.'[1] Murray and Norman Spector decided to attempt to redraft the proposals in light of the objections they had heard during their tour of the provinces. They wanted to postpone calling a First Ministers' meeting until they had some confidence that the meeting would result in success. They proposed to the prime minister that Mulroney personally launch one more round of bilateral discussions with the premiers in an attempt to broaden the areas of consensus.

On Thursday, 24 May, the prime minister announced that he was summoning the premiers to 24 Sussex Drive for a series of one-to-one meetings. The meetings began on Thursday night with Alberta's Don Getty and continued through the weekend. Gary Filmon met with Mulroney on Saturday, 26 May; Frank McKenna and Clyde Wells arrived at 24 Sussex on Sunday; Robert Bourassa was, once again, the final premier on the cycle, meeting with Mulroney on the morning of Monday, 28 May. Each premier was permitted to bring only a single advisor to the meeting; the prime minister and the premier would meet alone upstairs at 24 Sussex and the designated provincial official would remain downstairs with Norman Spector. Another twist was the manner in which the meetings were actually conducted. The federal government had drafted a revised version of the 'State of Play' or 'no author' text for consideration by the provinces. But the 24 May version of the 'State of Play' was not discussed by the prime minister with any of the premiers. Instead, the revised federal document was handed to the provincial official downstairs by Norman Spector while the prime minister and the premier met alone upstairs. The discussion upstairs was evidently to proceed at a more general level. The point of this rather complicated set of manoeuvres was to keep some distance between the prime minister and the pieces of paper that were circulating among the provinces. Various topics and proposals were certainly under active consideration. But none of them had touched the hand of Brian Mulroney. His position on Meech was the same as it always had been: the ratification of Meech Lake was essential to the unity of the country.

The revised version of the 'State of Play on a Companion Resolution to the Meech Lake Accord' contained only one major variation from the 19 May federal proposals. On the issue of Senate reform, the federal government abandoned the idea of sustituting a less restrictive formula if agreement could not be reached after three years. The 24 May 'State of Play' document simply deleted the proposal entirely. It was back to the Meech formula of requiring unanimous provincial consent for Senate reform. The federal government had concluded that this proposal was the only one with any chance of securing unanimous consent. It was simply impossible to contemplate granting Quebec alone a veto over changes to the Senate. If Quebec had a veto, the other provinces had to have one as well. That, of course, was the lesson of the Meech round itself. A rule requiring unanimous consent was an unattractive prospect since it would make Senate reform much more difficult to achieve. Unfortunately, this formula was the only one with even a ghost of a chance of proving generally acceptable. Having flirted with alternatives, the federal government had now fallen back on the original Meech Lake formula.

While Norman Spector was handing out this revised 'State of Play' document over the weekend of 26–28 May, Newfoundland premier Clyde Wells circulated his own set of counter-proposals. The Wells proposals indicated that there was still a wide gulf separating his position from that of the federal government. On certain issues, the Newfoundland premier had modified his opposition to Meech Lake. The most important of these was the distinct-society clause, which Wells was now prepared to accept. But Wells wanted a clarification of the relationship between the distinct-society clause and the charter, along the lines of the federal proposal in the 19 May 'State of Play' document. Wells also wanted a clarification of the fact that the distinct-society clause did not extend legislative powers.

On these issues, Wells's position was now very close to the current federal proposals as reflected in the 24 May 'State of Play' document. But

Wells put forward a host of other amendments to various other aspects of the accord, amendments that went far beyond the 'State of Play' approach. Wells wanted Senate reform to be subject to the approval of only seven provinces with 50 per cent of the population if agreement was not reached within three years. Quebec would not have a veto. The Newfoundland premier wanted substantial changes to the 'spending power' provision in Meech Lake. He proposed that the right of a province to receive compensation be limited to cases where the province undertook an initiative that was 'substantially similar to' the national shared-cost program. Wells also wanted to remove the right of the provinces to nominate Supreme Court judges. Wells proposed that Supreme Court nominations should be approved by an elected Senate.[2]

The weekend of one-to-one discussions between the prime minister and the premiers did not seem to bring the various sides any closer to an agreement. Both Gary Filmon and Clyde Wells emerged from their private sessions with Mulroney to reiterate their opposition to a Quebec veto on Senate reform. Media reports of the discussions focused on the Senate reform issue, suggesting that the hold-out provinces' rejection of a Quebec veto was the major stumbling-block to an agreement.[3] But the reality was that the areas of disagreement were far broader than the Senate issue. Robert Bourassa was unwilling to contemplate any 'clarification' of the meaning of the distinct-society clause. He also continued to insist that any discussions about a 'Canada Clause' be put over to a second round of discussions, following the ratification of Meech Lake. But Newfoundland and Manitoba were insisting that the distinct-society issue and the 'Canada Clause' be included in any agreement to pass Meech. Newfoundland and Manitoba also seemed to be under the impression that Quebec was prepared to be somewhat flexible on these proposals. They believed that Quebec was basically on side for the amendments to Meech that were set out in the 24 May federal proposals. So the problem was twofold: not only were there differences in the substantive positions of the two sides, there were also misunderstandings about the real intentions of the other parties to the negotiations.

The prime minister had originally promised that he would have 'something to report' on a First Ministers' meeting by the time he concluded his individual sessions with the premiers. The expectation in Ottawa had been that the premiers would be summoned for a First Ministers' meeting beginning with a dinner on Thursday night, 31 May. But the inconclusive nature of the weekend meetings at 24 Sussex Drive caused a change in plans. On Tuesday, 29 May, the federal government announced that Senator Murray would embark on a final trip to St John's to meet with

Newfoundland premier Clyde Wells. Wells had met for four hours with the prime minister at 24 Sussex just two days earlier and so it was unclear what precise purpose would be served by the additional meeting in St John's. The federal government described the meeting with Premier Wells as an attempt to determine whether there was sufficient common ground on the issues of the distinct-society clause and Senate reform.[4] The plans for a First Ministers' meeting were put on hold pending the outcome of the meeting between Murray and Wells.

Murray and Wells met for three hours in St John's on 29 May. The senator had brought along Roger Tassé, the former deputy attorney general of Canada, to discuss the wording of the 'clarification' of the distinct-society clause. By all accounts, the discussion was constructive. Afterwards, Premier Wells suggested that Newfoundland and the federal government were close to an agreement on an amendment on the distinct-society clause. 'I would say we had an excellent discussion on the distinct society question today,' Wells said. 'We clearly have an understanding on concepts, and I don't think we should have extreme difficulty finding wording that should accommodate both of us.'[5] Wells suggested that this left Senate reform as the major stumbling-block to an agreement. The Newfoundland premier continued to reject any proposals that would grant Quebec a veto over Senate reform.

For his part, Senator Murray indicated that he thought there had been progress on the distinct-society clause. The senator told reporters that he thought there was 'almost an agreed understanding as to how the distinct society clause works.'[6] But the senator, as always, chose his words extremely carefully. While there may have been almost an 'agreed understanding,' that did not necessarily mean that there was agreement on a proposed amendment to Meech Lake. Senator Murray did not actually say that Quebec was prepared to accept a formal amendment to the clause. This was no accident, since Quebec continued to insist that it would not accept any amendments to the distinct-society clause – period. The Quebeckers had told the federal government in no uncertain terms that they were not prepared to accept any changes to the clause, even what were described as mere 'clarifications.' Clyde Wells was proceeding on an assumption that was clearly mistaken. Wells assumed that, if he could reach agreement with the federal government, this agreement would automatically be acceptable to the province of Quebec. The reality was that Quebec was continuing to insist that the 'State of Play' proposals on the distinct-society clause were unacceptable.

Wells's confusion on the point was understandable, since he was relying almost totally on the federal government for information as to Quebec's position in the negotiations. Wells apparently did not have any means of verifying for himself the actual position and intentions of the Quebec government. There were no ongoing and direct discussions between officials in Newfoundland and Quebec City. Wells formed his impressions of the real 'bottom line' of Quebec based on information he obtained from third parties. This lack of reliable intergovernmental intelligence was in part attributable to Wells's decision to hire Toronto lawyer Deborah Coyne as his senior constitutional adviser. Coyne was totally opposed to the Meech Lake Accord. She had written extensively on the accord and had been one of the founders of a broad-based coalition designed to derail its ratification. Wells had hired Coyne as his senior adviser in the fall of 1989, just before the November First Minister's Conference in Ottawa. Because of Coyne's extreme anti-Meech stance, there was little opportunity for a constructive dialogue between the Quebec and Newfoundland delegations. In fact, over the final six-month period leading up to the Meech deadline, there does not appear to have been even a single meeting between Newfoundland and Quebec officials.

Thus, over the crucial period leading up to the final meeting of First Ministers, Wells was operating under a mistaken assumption. His belief, based on discussions with the federal government but not with Quebec, was that Robert Bourassa had a good deal more flexibility than his public statements might have indicated. Had Newfoundland officials been meeting regularly and directly with Quebec officials, a much different picture would have emerged. Other provinces, such as Ontario, which had maintained close contact with Quebec officials throughout these discussions, were getting a consistent and simple message from Quebec City: any amendments to Meech Lake based on the Charest committee proposals were unacceptable. Robert Bourassa had rejected these proposals publicly. He would do so privately as well.

Returning to Ottawa from St John's, Senator Murray acknowledged that there were still substantial differences remaining between the various provincial positions. 'My evaluation is that a First Ministers' conference held today would probably fail,' Murray admitted.[7] But Senator Murray's problem was that his time had run out. There were now only a little more than three weeks left before the 23 June Meech deadline. Manitoba, which was required to hold another round of public hearings on the accord, had indicated that these hearings might take four weeks to complete. Senator Murray thus had no more time to lay the groundwork for a First Ministers' meeting.

In any event, most provinces had come to the view that any additional bilateral meetings would be pointless, and even counter-productive.

Ontario's David Peterson had told the prime minister that, if he put off a meeting of First Ministers any longer, Ontario would convene a meeting of its own in Toronto. Peterson had undertaken informal soundings of the idea of a Toronto meeting with the other premiers, and there was broad support for the idea. Peterson told the prime minister that the only way for any additional progress to be made was to bring all the First Ministers together in the same room. That way, at least everyone would obtain an accurate and first-hand understanding of the real bottom-line positions of the other parties around the table. It would then be possible to determine whether a consensus could be fashioned on the key issues in dispute.

Peterson's efforts in this regard were hampered by the 'leak' of a memo that had been prepared by officials in Ontario's Ministry of Intergovernmental Affairs. The memo set out a 'strategy' for the Ontario government to pursue in the expected meeting of First Ministers. One portion of the memo argued that the Ontario premier should attempt directly and publicly to challenge the views and arguments of Newfoundland premier Clyde Wells and Manitoba premier Gary Filmon. When the memo was leaked to the media it caused a furore, with Wells and others deploring the 'media manipulation' being planned by the Ontario government. David Peterson telephoned Clyde Wells and Gary Filmon personally to assure them that he had no prior knowledge of the existence of the memo, nor did he intend to follow its recommended strategy. While Peterson's personal intervention appeared to mollify the dissident premiers, it contributed to the growing mood of distrust and suspicion surrounding the discussions. The incident over the 'leaked memo' was just another factor making it more difficult to fashion a consensus that would include all the various players and interests.

On Thursday, 31 May, the prime minister finally made the announcement that everyone had been anticipating for at least a week. Mulroney summoned the premiers to a private dinner on Sunday, 3 June, at the Museum of Civilization in Hull, Quebec. Mulroney told the House of Commons that, if sufficient progress was made at the private dinner, the First Ministers would convene a formal constitutional conference, beginning on Monday morning. Mulroney sounded cautious in evaluating the prospects for success, noting that 'crucial differences remain' in the positions of the parties. Those differences were underlined by the reaction of the premiers to the announcement of the dinner. Quebec's Robert Bourassa warned again that he would not accept any changes to the accord. 'Already what we have on the table is a compromise on a compromise,' Bourassa said in Quebec City. 'I can't accept a compromise on a compromise on a compromise.'[8] But both Gary Filmon and Clyde Wells repeated their view that Bourassa would have to compromise if he wanted a deal since what was on the table was not satisfactory.

In convening the First Ministers, Brian Mulroney entered a new phase in his effort to secure the ratification of Meech Lake. It had been precisely two weeks since Jean Charest had tabled his report in the House of Commons. In the intervening fourteen days, Senator Murray had frantically attempted to build a consensus around the Charest recommendations. But Murray had failed. Charest went too far for Bourassa, but not far enough for Clyde Wells and Gary Filmon. Murray himself had acknowledged as much on 29 May, after his final trip to St John's. He had been forced to admit that a First Ministers' conference would probably end in failure. In fact, Robert Bourassa had made it clear to Senator Murray that he was not even prepared to attend such a conference if the discussion was to be based on the Charest recommendations. A new approach to the issue was needed. Otherwise the dinner meeting on 3 June threatened to end in a débâcle.

Stage Two: Ratify Meech and Fix It Later

As the eleven First Ministers gathered for dinner in Hull on the evening of 3 June, 1990, one remarkable fact had gone unnoticed in the growing furore over the constitution. Since the November First Ministers' conference in Ottawa, there had not been any multilateral meetings between governments on the constitution. Not only had the premiers themselves not been meeting to discuss the issues, there had not even been an opportunity for officials of all governments to sit down and explore their differences. The only discussions that had taken place had been conducted on a bilateral basis, primarily involving the federal government and individual provinces. Now, with just twenty days before the Meech deadline, the premiers were finally sitting down face to face to see whether an accommodation could be worked out.

Gary Filmon and Clyde Wells were in for a rather rude surprise that evening. They had come to Ottawa believing that they would be discussing amendments to deal with their objections to the Meech Lake Accord. Entering the meeting, Gary Filmon had defiantly predicted that 'we need change in order to proceed any further.'[9] But the discussion around the table in the museum's fifth-floor dining-room proceeded on an entirely different footing. Prime Minister Mulroney opened the meeting by warning of the serious economic and political consequences that would follow from a failure to ratify the accord. Mulroney warned that investments in Canada were no longer considered 'Triple A' but were now on a 'watch' basis because of the uncertainty over the accord. It was essential to the future of the country that the three hold-outs agree to ratify the accord, Mulroney argued.

The other pro-Meech premiers echoed Mulroney's line. Robert Bourassa indicated that he could not accept any amendments to the accord. He reiterated what he had been saying in public for months: Meech Lake was already a compromise; he was not prepared to make any further concessions. The real eye-opener was when Bourassa indicated that he was not prepared to go along with the federal proposals contained in the 'State of Play' document of 24 May. It seemed that the issue of the distinct-society clause, which Filmon and Wells had assumed was already settled as a result of Senator Murray's tour, was still unresolved. Bourassa insisted that he was not prepared to change even a comma in the distinct-society clause. Nor would he agree to entrench a 'Canada Clause' in the constitution. The Quebec premier insisted that the accord had to be ratified 'as is' first and then there could be discussions designed to deal with the concerns of the hold-out premiers.

The dinner was less of a true bargaining session than an opportunity for the premiers to state their positions formally. Filmon and Wells rejected the doomsday scenario that had been offered by the prime minister. They maintained that they required 'certainty' that their concerns would be addressed before they could agree to ratify the accord. Thus it would be necessary to have unanimous agreement on concrete amendments prior to 23 June. Otherwise the accord would die.

The problem for Filmon and Wells was that they were alone in demanding changes. They faced a united front from the pro-Meech premiers, calling on them to put aside their objections and ratify the accord. Something was wrong here. Filmon and Wells had come to Ottawa assuming that the federal government had obtained Quebec's approval for the proposed amendments set out in the 'State of Play' document of 24 May. But Bourassa had flatly rejected the proposed amendments. His message in private was identical to what he had been saying in public: Meech Lake or nothing. What made matters even worse was that Mulroney and all the other pro-Meech premiers were supporting Bourassa. Emerging from the meeting, Gary Filmon sounded somewhat pessimistic. 'We certainly haven't made much progress on dealing with many of the issues that still separate us,' Filmon told reporters. But at least there had been an agreement to continue the discussions the next morning at the Conference Centre in Ottawa. The federal government had promised to table a formal written proposal at the meeting the next day. Filmon and Wells agreed to continue meeting in private in order to see whether the federal proposal might serve as the basis for a consensus.

The prime minister and the premiers convened the next morning at 11:00 a.m. on the fifth floor of the Conference Centre in Ottawa. The premiers were alone in the room with the prime minister. Across the hall, three or four officials from each province were gathered in a large committee room. In turn, these officials were in constant communication with the remainder of the provincial delegations assembled in offices on the main floor of the building.

After an inconclusive ninety-minute session in the morning, the meeting broke for lunch. It was agreed that the First Ministers would reconvene at 4:00 p.m., at which time the prime minister would table the written federal proposal. When the long-awaited proposal finally appeared at the late-afternoon session, it reflected the approach Mulroney had articulated at the dinner the evening before.

The federal proposal was structured as a complex four-part agreement. But stripped down to its essentials, the proposal was rather straightforward. The federal government proposed that the hold-out premiers ratify the accord now in return for a promise that their concerns would be discussed later. On all the key issues, the federal government proposed some type of conference or committee to study the matter. On Senate reform, the federal government proposed to move up the timing of a First Ministers' conference on the issue from 1 November to 17 September. But Mulroney proposed no change in Meech Lake's requirement that there be unanimous consent for future Senate reform. On the issue of the 'Canada Clause,' which Manitoba had identified as a 'bottom line' demand, the prime minister proposed to strike a parliamentary committee to hold hearings over the summer. There was no reference at all to the issue of the relationship between the distinct-society clause and the Charter of Rights, a matter Clyde Wells had thought was already settled in his favour. The prime minister indicated that he had a proposal to make on this issue, but he was not prepared to put it forward yet.

The issue of the admission of new provinces had been identified as a key concern by the Charest committee. In the 24 May 'State of Play' proposals, the federal government had suggested that the creation of new provinces in the territories should require the consent of the federal Parliament only. Now, the federal government proposed only that the matter should be added to the agenda of future constitutional conferences, with a proviso that there should be a consideration of the 'possibility' that new provinces could be created without the consent of existing provinces. A separate constitutional process was to be established to consider aboriginal issues. The issue of minority-language rights was to be added to the agenda of future constitutional conferences.

One needed a timetable and a road-map to keep track of the maze of constitutional conferences and committees that would be travelling the country, debating the constitution. Anyone have a problem with Meech Lake? The solution: strike a committee or add the issue to the agenda of future First Ministers' conferences. Boiled down to its essentials, that is what the federal government was proposing.

Predictably, Gary Filmon and Clyde Wells were upset and disappointed. None of their concerns was being addressed in a tangible manner. Instead, they were being asked to ratify the accord unamended and to put over their concerns to a second round of negotiations. Gary Filmon wanted to know what had happened to the Charest committee recommendations. Wells said he wanted to see the federal proposal on the relationship between the distinct-society clause and the Charter of Rights. But the prime minister suggested that the meeting had to proceed in an orderly fashion. He wanted to begin the discussion with a consideration of the question of Senate reform. After three and a half hours, there seemed to be a huge and potentially unbridgeable gulf separating the parties around the table. There was talk that the meeting might break up in failure the next morning.

The premiers emerged one by one to face a horde of reporters gathered behind barriers outside the Conference Centre. Gary Filmon and Clyde Wells said the talks were going nowhere. Filmon said that there had been no progress made on resolving his concerns, and Clyde Wells told reporters that he was 'quite unhappy' with the federal proposal on the table. Alberta premier Don Getty said that he was not the 'slightest bit optimistic' and that the meeting the next morning could be very short. Only New Brunswick's Frank McKenna sounded a different line. McKenna said that the federal proposal that had been tabled in the afternoon was 'a very favourable response to the concerns that we raised.'[10] McKenna did not specify what it was in the federal proposal that 'met his concerns.' McKenna indicated that his only remaining question was over the timing of the federal plan. Once this question was settled, McKenna said that he would be prepared to ratify the Meech Lake Accord.

The New Brunswick premier's performance seemed somehow out of place, even contrived. All the other premiers were sounding pessimistic and fearful of failure the next morning. Filmon and Wells were saying that the federal proposal did not address any of their concerns. Against this backdrop, McKenna's half-hearted conversion to the pro-Meech camp seemed staged and unreal. It also came too late in the day to matter. Most observers had already counted him as part of the pro-Meech camp. The attention had shifted to Gary Filmon and Clyde Wells, who were regarded as the 'real' hold-outs. The New Brunswick premier's conversion to Meech Lake would once have been regarded as a major turning-point. Now, it went almost unnoticed by the national media, which were preoccupied with the general air of pessimism surrounding the talks.

The premiers had been meeting two days, but there had been no real negotiations. At the dinner on Sunday evening and during the two sessions on Monday, the prime minister and the premiers had simply stated and restated their competing positions. There had been no attempt to discuss possible compromises or ways of accommodating the differences around the table. But midway through the day on Tuesday, the atmosphere changed. For the first time, real negotiations actually commenced. Rather than merely restate fixed positions, the premiers actually began talking about possible compromises. The catalyst for this change was a proposal suggested by Prince Edward Island premier Joe Ghiz.

Ghiz tabled a proposal that he said had originated with Jack Pickersgill. It was based on the idea of creating a 'default option' in the event that unanimous agreement on a new Senate could not be achieved. Under the proposal, if Senate reform were not achieved by 1993, then the size of the Senate would be automatically expanded. Each of the four western provinces and Newfoundland would receive an additional four senators, and Prince Edward Island one new senator. The additional twenty-one senators added under the 'default option' would bring the total numbers in the Senate to 125. Ontario and Quebec would remain at twenty-four senators, Prince Edward Island would have five, and all the other provinces would have ten each. The territories would each continue to be represented by a single senator.

The main advantage of the Ghiz 'default option' idea was that it was new. Since the others hadn't thought about it in advance, no one rejected it out of hand. Instead, the premiers actually began discussing the merits of the proposal. It seemed to offer something for everyone. Bourassa got to keep his veto on future Senate reform. But the western provinces and Newfoundland, who were the strongest proponents of a 'Triple-E' Senate, got a guarantee of some additional seats in the event that a comprehensive agreement could not be negotiated. As the discussion went around the table, everyone seemed to like the idea. Even Bourassa, who up to that point had indicated that he wasn't willing to budge on anything, suggested that he might accept the proposal. It didn't tamper with anything in

Meech Lake. His veto was protected. As for Wells and Filmon, they didn't like the fact that the proposal still contemplated a requirement of unanimous consent for future comprehensive Senate reform. But they thought the 'default option' idea was at least worth considering.

The operating principle in the discussions was that nothing was agreed until everything was agreed. Only when all the elements of a package were in place would premiers finally sign off on any part of it. Still, the discussion on the Senate was encouraging. There seemed to be greater flexibility and room for creative compromise than anyone had imagined. The question was whether it would be possible to fashion similar creative solutions to the other areas of dispute.

Unfortunately, by Tuesday evening there did not appear to be any tangible progress on these other issues. The two most difficult questions involved the distinct-society clause. Clyde Wells was continuing to insist that there be an amendment that would clarify the relationship between the distinct-society clause and the Charter of Rights. Wells wanted an amendment similar to the proposals set out in the federal 'State of Play' document circulated by Senator Murray on his tour of the provinces. Wells and Filmon were also insisting on the addition of a 'Canada Clause' that would identify other fundamental characteristics of Canada, in addition to the distinct identity of Quebec. But Bourassa was unwilling to make concessions on either issue. He was adamant that there could be no clarification of the operation of the distinct-society clause. On the 'Canada Clause,' Bourassa indicated that he would be willing to discuss the issue following the ratification of Meech Lake. He would not agree to any such clause prior to 23 June.

When the prime minister and the premiers emerged from the Conference Centre around 9:00 p.m. to face the media scrum outside, most sounded upbeat and optimistic. 'My sense is that we had a good day,' Mulroney reported. But he cautioned that there had been no final agreements and that 'we have a lot of work to do tomorrow.' Clyde Wells was also cautiously optimistic, saying that 'progress is being made, but we're not there yet.' Alberta premier Don Getty spoke positively about the fact that the premiers had stopped 'stating positions and bottom lines' and that there was 'almost magic in the room.' Most suggested that there had been the outlines of a tentative deal on Senate reform hammered out over the course of the Tuesday session. Everyone was reaching for the silver lining in the cloud, emphasizing the positive and ignoring the negative.

'Tentative deal reached on Senate reform' proclaimed the banner headline in the *Globe and Mail* the next morning. The media, like the premiers themselves, were eager to accentuate the positive. By the middle of the week, the pattern of media reporting of the conference was set. The small army of reporters surrounding the Conference Centre clearly believed that some kind of 'compromise deal' was inevitable. The reporting of the meeting thus tended to highlight the 'progress' that was being made or the 'areas of consensus' that were emerging. Even on Monday evening, when the conference had been in danger of falling apart and the premiers had all sounded extremely negative about the prospects for success, the *Globe and Mail* headline read 'Ottawa tables plan to save Meech: Senate reform to be main issue when PM, premiers meet today.' The media reporting consistently downplayed the wide differences remaining in the positions around the table.

In part, this view was attributable to the fact that the major news organizations relied heavily on senior federal officials who would conduct late-night 'briefings' on the day's events. These briefings were convened by Stan Hartt, the prime minister's chief of staff, and Norman Spector, who would provide the official federal interpretation of what had happened on the fifth floor of the Conference Centre. The Hartt/Spector briefings tended to emphasize the elements of any current federal proposal that was on the table. Hartt and Spector also tended to downplay the concerns or objections of the hold-out provinces, suggesting that these differences could be 'crunched' at the appropriate time. The impression that was left was that progress was being made slowly but consistently, and that the differences were being narrowed. A major preoccupation among the media, of course, was who would be the first to report the inevitable 'compromise deal' that everyone assumed was certain to emerge at some point. As the week wore on, reports of 'tentative deals' began to circulate more frequently through the ranks of the media encamped on the sidewalk outside the Conference Centre.

Most of the provincial delegations had a somewhat different view of what was happening. By Wednesday afternoon, there seemed to have been little or no tangible progress towards reaching a settlement. The differences between Wells and Filmon, on the one hand, and Bourassa, on the other, over the distinct-society clause were as wide as ever. Even the tentative deal on the Ghiz 'default option' for Senate reform began to unravel on Wednesday. Bourassa indicated that he was having second thoughts about the merits of the idea. Bourassa's problem was that Quebec's proportion of seats in the Senate would decline under the Ghiz scheme. Whereas Quebec had 24 of 104 seats in the existing Senate, it would have only 24 of an expanded 125-seat Senate after the 'default option' kicked in in 1993. Quebec's overall weight in the Upper Chamber would be reduced, something Bourassa said would be difficult to sell in his province. Bourassa proposed that Quebec be granted additional senators as well, so that its proportion of the total Senate seats would be maintained at a constant level.

Bourassa's backtracking on the Senate proposal was exasperating to a number of his colleagues around the table. But what was evident to a number of the provincial delegations was that the talks were in a kind of holding pattern. The premiers were spending their days closeted together in a windowless room, talking 'at' each other. All of them had stated their 'bottom line' positions countless times. But, by late Wednesday, after nearly four days of talking, there did not appear to have been any progress towards reaching a solution.

A key turning-point in the week's events was a meeting convened on Wednesday evening involving members of the Newfoundland, Quebec, Manitoba, and Ontario delegations. The meeting was convened, apparently on the suggestion of Clyde Wells, to discuss the operation and meaning of the distinct-society clause. Attorney general Ian Scott and Peter Hogg attended from Ontario. Newfoundland sent Neil Finkelstein, a prominent Toronto constitutional lawyer whom Wells had retained as a legal adviser for the week. A number of Quebeckers were there, including André Tremblay, Jean Samson, and Benoît Morin.

A large part of the meeting was spent restating the positions of the parties. The previous December, Finkelstein had prepared a legal opinion for Wells, outlining how the distinct-society clause might impact on the federal-provincial division of powers and on the Charter of Rights. Finkelstein had argued that the distinct-society clause might lead the courts to expand the constitutional authority of Quebec in areas such as broadcasting regulation. He also had argued that the clause might permit Quebec to introduce more stringent limits on rights of anglophones in the province of Quebec. Finkelstein restated his arguments at the Wednesday evening meeting. Manitoba lawyer Greg Yost supported Finkelstein. Ian Scott, Peter Hogg, and Roger Tassé responded, claiming that the impact of the distinct-society clause would be minimal. André Tremblay indicated that the entire discussion was academic, since Quebec was not prepared to accept any clarifications to the distinct-society clause. Tremblay said that Newfoundland's choice was to accept the clause as written, or to reject it.

The important thing about the meeting was not so much what was said – everyone had heard the arguments before – but that, for the first time, direct contact had been established between the Newfoundland and Quebec delegations. Up until Wednesday evening, they had no face-to-face discussions. Finally, and almost by accident, the seal on the bottle had been broken. Representatives from Newfoundland were finally talking to those from Quebec.

As the meeting broke up, the Quebeckers and Finkelstein decided to talk further about the issues that had been debated at the meeting. The idea was to put aside for the moment the question of whether there ought to be a formal constitutional amendment clarifying the meaning of the distinct-society clause. It was clear that there was no chance of an agreement on that particular issue at the present time. Why not discuss a separate question? Why not discuss, in the abstract, the meaning of the distinct-society clause? Perhaps the two sides could agree on wording that might describe the operation and meaning of the clause. If that much could be agreed, then it might be possible to turn to the separate question of whether that agreed-upon wording should be placed somewhere in the constitution.

The Quebeckers and Finkelstein discussed the matter late into the evening. They exchanged wording that would describe the possible impact of the distinct-society clause. No one was committed to anything; the discussions were on the basis that any proposals offered were 'without prejudice.' After discussing the various possibilities for a few hours, they agreed to examine the numerous suggestions that had been made and continue talking the next day.

The late-night discussions between Finkelstein and the Quebec delegation appeared to shed a glimmer of real hope on the distinct-society issue. On Thursday morning, Quebec's André Tremblay told Finkelstein that he liked the wording Finkelstein had proposed on the meaning of the distinct-society clause. Finkelstein's wording suggested that the Charter of Rights would be interpreted in a manner 'consistent with' the distinct-society clause, but that the rights in the charter were not 'infringed or denied.' The proposed wording was based on the federal 'State of Play' document of 24 May.

Tremblay continued to insist that Quebec could not accept a formal amendment to the distinct-society clause, even one based on Finkelstein's wording. But Tremblay had a counter-proposal, a novel suggestion that he thought might represent a compromise. Why not set out the proposed wording in the form of a letter written by legal experts? These experts would write to the prime minister, describing the impact of the distinct-society clause in the manner set out by Finkelstein. They might then be called into the room where the First Ministers were meeting and read out the letter.

Although André Tremblay presented the idea as a compromise, it was evident that it required far greater movement from Clyde Wells than from Robert Bourassa. The opinion letter would have no official status and carry minimal legal weight. It would not represent a constitutional amendment. It would not even be a letter signed by the premiers or the prime minister, expressing their understanding of the distinct-society clause. It was simply a letter from third parties expressing their opinion on the meaning of the constitution. Opinion letters are not legally binding or authoritative. They simply set out the views of lawyers as to how the courts are likely to rule on a legal issue. The courts take into account the opinions of judges in interpreting the constitution, not the opinions of lawyers. The courts would be free to ignore entirely the opinion letter on the distinct-society clause. Asking Clyde Wells to accept an opinion letter in lieu of a constitutional amendment was tantamount to asking him to abandon his objections to the distinct-society clause entirely.

In the meantime, while Finkelstein and Tremblay were discussing the distinct-society clause, the First Ministers had been debating the other outstanding issue, the so-called Canada Clause. By lunch on Thursday, there was talk circulating around the fifth floor that there had been a tentative agreement on the Canada Clause issue. This seemed a little hard to believe. The Quebec delegation was continuing to insist that the discussion of a 'Canada Clause' be deferred to a second round of discussions following the ratification of the accord. If there was, in fact, a 'tentative deal' on the clause, this must have meant that Filmon and Wells had totally conceded the issue. But this possibility was almost mind-boggling. It also did not accord with the messages that were coming from the Manitoba and Newfoundland officials who were insisting that they still wanted an agreement on a 'Canada Clause' prior to Meech being ratified, not after.

The First Ministers broke for lunch and briefed their delegations on the morning's discussions. It seemed that Wells and Filmon were to meet downstairs with Sharon Carstairs and Gary Doer, the Manitoba opposition leaders, who were in Ottawa for the talks. But the precise purpose of the Newfoundland/Manitoba meeting was unclear. Some premiers suggested that Wells and Filmon were to present the opposition leaders with the outlines of a proposed deal on the Canada Clause issue. Wells would then report back to the First Ministers on whether the deal was acceptable.

But when the Newfoundland/Manitoba meeting began in the early afternoon, it quickly became apparent that there was no tentative deal on the Canada Clause issue. Wells began the meeting by indicating that the purpose was to consider various options for a proposed Canada Clause. No mention was made of a 'tentative deal' on the issue. The question, Wells suggested, was whether the proposed Canada Clause should be included in the main body of the constitution, or merely be set out in a preamble. The Newfoundland premier told Carstairs and Doer that they would hear from a number of legal experts on this issue, and then meet privately to settle on a common position to be presented to the other First Ministers.

The Manitoba and Newfoundland political leaders heard from Neil Finkelstein of Newfoundland, Greg Yost from Manitoba, Peter Hogg of Ontario, and Roger Tassé of the federal delegation. Each was asked to express his views on the different weight that courts would attach to a Canada Clause included in the main body of the constitution as opposed to in a preamble. The lawyers referred to various Supreme Court of Canada judgments that indicated that courts tended to attach the greatest weight to wording contained in the main body of the constitution. But the lawyers also agreed that courts would look to other materials in interpreting the constitution, including clauses in the preamble or even statements made by First Ministers.

The way in which the discussion was conducted suggested that there had not been any tentative deal on the Canada Clause issue. Wells, Filmon, Carstairs, and Doer were discussing whether to place the Canada Clause in the preamble or in the main body of the constitution. The problem was that *neither* option was acceptable to Quebec. Bourassa was not interested in the placement of the Canada Clause. He wasn't prepared to discuss the Canada Clause at all. He wanted the whole matter put over to a second round of discussions that would follow the ratification of the accord.

After about an hour, Wells, Filmon, Carstairs, and Doer dismissed the lawyers and had a private discussion. At four o'clock, they were joined briefly by Quebec premier Robert Bourassa. At six o'clock, the eleven First Ministers reconvened on the fifth floor to hear Wells's report on the meeting with Carstairs and Doer. Standing in his place, Wells's reported that Manitoba and Newfoundland had agreed that the proposed Canada Clause had to be placed in the main body of the constitution, rather than the preamble. The Newfoundland premier told the other First Ministers that this common position had been agreed upon on the basis of the best legal advice available.

Wells presented a series of other demands, in addition to the inclusion of a 'Canada Clause.' The Newfoundland premier rejected the idea of an opinion letter as a basis for clarifying the meaning of the distinct-society clause. Wells said that such an opinion letter would carry little legal weight. He needed some kind of declaration from the First Ministers themselves in order to settle his concerns on this issue. He also wanted an amendment clarifying the proposed limits on the federal spending power.

Wells's presentation caused confusion and consternation among the other First Ministers. Some of them had been under the impression that there was an agreement to refer the whole question of the Canada Clause to a parliamentary committee that would meet over the summer. Now Wells was suggesting that there had to be an immediate agreement on the Canada Clause, rather than a reference to committee. Further, Wells was insisting that the clause be included in the main body of the constitution rather than as a preamble. A heated discussion ensued, with some premiers accusing Wells and Filmon of reneging on a tentative deal that had supposedly been reached prior to the meeting with Carstairs and Doer. For their part, Wells and Filmon expressed amazement that the other premiers believed that there had been a tentative agreement. They insisted that there had never been any such agreement, maintaining that the purpose of the meeting with Carstairs and Doer was merely to settle on a common position on the issue of the Canada Clause.

Regardless of how or why the confusion had arisen, one thing was certain: after five days of meetings, the talks were back to square one. Wells and Filmon were continuing to insist that Meech had to be amended to deal with their concerns. Robert Bourassa was equally adamant that these concerns could be addressed only after Meech Lake had been ratified. Where the parties had been on Sunday night is where they remained on Thursday. The five days of talk appeared to have achieved nothing.

A major part of the problem seemed to be that Wells and Filmon had a mistaken impression about the possible shape of a final agreement on the issue. They were still working off the 24 May 'State of Play' document, which had proposed a 'Canada Clause' in the preamble to the constitution and various other amendments to the accord. Bourassa's repeated protestations that he would not agree to amendments to Meech seemed to have made little impression on the two hold-out premiers. Wells and Filmon were still debating where the Canada Clause should be placed in the constitution and were still talking about an amendment clarifying the relationship between the charter and the distinct-society clause.

The practical political reality was that Wells and Filmon were simply not going to get general agreement on amendments to the Meech Lake Accord at this meeting. The best they could hope for was an agreement to address their concerns through subsequent negotiations. The hard choice facing Wells and Filmon, and it was a very hard choice indeed, was whether or not such an agreement was good enough. If it was, then there could be a general agreement. If it wasn't, then Wells and Filmon would have to walk away from the table and assume the political responsibility for their decision. The problem was the two hold-out premiers had not yet come to grips with this hard political reality. They were still debating the type of amendments that would be made to Meech Lake. The fact that these amendments were simply not politically possible had not yet sunk in.

Bourassa and the Quebec delegation realized on Thursday night that this basic message had not been getting through. There was a growing restlessness among all the delegations on the fifth floor of the Conference Centre. A number of provincial officials began complaining that the whole exercise was going nowhere and that the five days of discussion had been a waste of time. Ontario's Ian Scott met with Gil Rémillard and urged him to make their real 'bottom line' explicit. Following Scott's urging, the Quebeckers decided that something had to be done to impose a 'reality check' on the negotiations. At 9:30 p.m., without providing advance notice to the other provinces, Bourassa's press secretary issued a one-paragraph press release, stating that the Quebec premier would refuse to participate in any further discussions 'directly or indirectly on the clause in the Meech Lake Accord recognizing Quebec as a distinct society.'

Issuing the press release was like dropping a bomb on the negotiations. When word reached the fifth floor that Bourassa had issued the release, there was mass confusion and a sense that the negotiations had reached the breaking-point. Emotions among the officials were running high. Heated arguments broke out in the hallways, with officials from different provinces blaming others for the impasse. The meeting between the First Ministers broke up, and the premiers went downstairs to face their nightly ritual before the television cameras. It was difficult to put a positive spin on the state of the negotiations. The Bourassa press release had revealed just how little progress had been made since Sunday evening.

All of the premiers tried to put the best face on the situation, stressing that the talks would continue the next morning. But a number of the premiers appeared to be clearly shaken by the evening's developments. New Brunswick's Frank McKenna said the week's discussions had been a roller-coaster and that, on Thursday, he 'almost lost [his] stomach.'[11] An emotional Don Getty said that the focus had to be on saving the country, not just the accord. 'Stop taking shots at Meech Lake, because you're hitting Canada in the heart,' Getty warned. As for Filmon and Wells, they sounded frustrated and unhappy. Wells railed against the closed-door nature of the process and the pressure he was facing to capitulate. 'We're in a room where we've been for four days, closeted, and you're under tremendous pressure, there are things being discussed ... [and] the public are not aware of it, yet we're supposed to agree to act because of these reasons that aren't being discussed publicly.' Filmon complained about the fact that the distinct-society clause was being roped off from debate. 'I'm concerned that we are being told that there are several of those issues that we can't discuss,' Filmon told reporters. Both Filmon and Wells maintained that they were not giving up the fight to secure changes to Meech. But the bold rhetoric and confident predictions of Sunday night were no longer in evidence. Wells and Filmon appeared uncertain of their footing and disturbed about the way in which the talks were developing. At the time, the Bourassa press release appeared certain to scuttle the talks. Ironically, the Quebec premier's unilateral action was a key factor in bringing the negotiations to some kind of resolution. After five days of non-stop negotiation, the biggest problem seemed to be a lack of communication and understanding among the various delegations. The Quebec premier had at least brought some clarity to the discussions. Wells and Filmon could hardly misconstrue the message. They now understood what was at stake and what the choices were. By clearing the air in this fashion, Bourassa signalled that it was time everyone got down to business and starting making some decisions.

On Friday morning, the discussion of the distinct-society clause and the Canada Clause was scheduled to resume. Robert Bourassa remained in his suite in the Château Laurier. The distinct-society clause would be debated in his absence. The empty chair at the table was a graphic message to the hold-out premiers that they should not expect any movement of any kind on these issues. There was only one person in a position to make any concessions on the distinct-society clause, and he was not even in the room.

The prime minister explained the outlines of a possible deal. Everyone would ratify Meech prior to 23 June. There would be no amendment to the distinct-society clause. Wells would have to settle for a legal opinion signed by constitutional experts. The issue of a 'Canada Clause' would be referred to a parliamentary committee, which would begin public hearings over the summer. There would be a national commission established to study the issue of Senate reform. But the Ghiz 'default option,' under which the smaller provinces would gain seats in an expanded Senate after three years, seemed to be off the table. Quebec was unwilling to accept a reduction in its proportion of the total Senate seats.

Over the course of the day, it became apparent that Wells had significantly softened his stand from the evening before. The Bourassa press release had evidently brought home to Wells the fact that his expectations had to be lowered substantially. Wells dropped his demands on the Canada Clause. He was prepared to accept the striking of a parliamentary committee to deal with the issue after the ratification of Meech. He also dropped his demand that there be a formal amendment to the distinct-society clause, clarifying its relationship to the charter. Wells said he was prepared to accept some kind of 'political declaration' on the distinct-society clause. But Wells wanted more than a letter signed by constitutional experts. He said the legal opinion had to have some official status. It had to be acknowledged by First Ministers as being a correct description of the operation of the distinct-society clause. Otherwise, Wells said, it would have no real legal weight. Wells also said that he had to have something on Senate reform.

The shift in Wells's position was nothing short of dramatic. Overnight he had moved to within striking distance of agreeing to ratify the accord without any changes. For the first time since Sunday night, the differences between Wells and Bourassa appeared bridgeable. The only two sticking-points were the status of the legal opinion on the distinct-society clause and the Senate reform issue. The question was whether a way could be found to give something to Wells on these two issues without losing the support of Bourassa.

The meeting adjourned late in the afternoon. It was agreed that the meeting would reconvene at 6:00 p.m., at which time the prime minister would table a written version of the revised federal proposal. There was a widespread sense that the six o'clock meeting would be the 'make or break' point for the whole week's discussions.

Downstairs, David Peterson gathered the Ontario delegation for a final briefing and discussion of the options. Peterson told his delegation that he thought the talks were on the verge of failure. Peterson's judgment was that the key to the whole package was now Senate reform. He informed his advisers that the Ghiz 'default option,' which would have added seats to the Senate after three years, had now been moved off the table. That meant that Wells would not even gain the additional four Senate seats that the Ghiz plan had contemplated. Peterson thought that this would be too much for the Newfoundland premier to swallow. He predicted that Wells and Filmon were probably going to walk out when they saw the latest federal proposal at six o'clock. He asked his advisers whether they had any 'crazy ideas' on the Senate reform issue that might give something to Wells without taking anything away from Bourassa.

Peterson had brought along a number of outside constitutional experts as part of the Ontario delegation. One of these experts was James MacPherson, dean of Osgoode Hall Law School in Toronto and a leading constitutional authority. MacPherson responded to Peterson's invitation by offering an idea that he described as 'off the wall.' MacPherson suggested a variation on the Ghiz 'default option' for Senate reform. Rather than expanding the Senate after three years, MacPherson suggested a redistribution of the existing seats. Under MacPherson's proposal, Ontario, New Brunswick, and Nova Scotia would each give up some seats, enabling the western provinces and Newfoundland to gain additional seats without disturbing the proportion of total seats allocated to Quebec. Quebec would retain 24 seats in the 104-seat chamber. Ontario would give up 6 seats and be left with 18. New Brunswick and Nova Scotia would each give up 2 seats, while Manitoba, Saskatchewan, Alberta, British Columbia, and Newfoundland would gain 2 seats each.

Peterson was intrigued by the idea. He thought it might just be enough to induce Wells and Filmon to sign on. It gave them a guarantee of at least an additional two Senate seats if there was no agreement after a specified time period. Such a guarantee may not have been earth-shattering but at least it was tangible and certain. Everything else on the table involved promises to study or discuss issues without any guarantee of concrete results. It was also a demonstration of good faith and of a genuine commitment to Senate reform on the part of Ontario. Peterson indicated that perhaps the greatest appeal of the idea was this symbolic quality. It was a kind of 'down-payment' indicating that Ontario was a serious buyer in the Senate-reform market. The Ontario premier asked his delegation to debate the merits of MacPherson's idea further. In the meantime, he dispatched his trusted chief of staff, Dan Gagnier, to brief the senior federal officials about the proposal. Gagnier was instructed to inform federal officials that Peterson might make the offer to sacrifice Senate seats if the talks seemed about to collapse.

The First Ministers reconvened in the fifth-floor boardroom at six o'clock to receive the latest federal proposal. As David Peterson had predicted, the federal proposal offered almost nothing to Wells and Filmon. There would be a legal opinion from constitutional experts on the meaning of the distinct-society clause. The legal opinion would be appended to the conference communiqué, but it would not be signed or even acknowledged by any of the premiers. The Canada Clause would be referred to a parliamentary committee. On Senate reform, the Ghiz 'default option' had disappeared. A new 'default option' was substituted, picking up on a suggestion that had been made by BC premier Bill Vander Zalm earlier in the week. The federal government proposed that, if there was no agreement on Senate reform after three years, all Senators would automatically become directly elected. But there would be no redistribution of Senate seats. Ontario and Quebec would each retain 24 of the 104 seats in the elected Senate. And any further reform would be subject to a requirement of unanimous provincial consent.

Wells said the proposal was unacceptable. He said that he had been forced to make concessions all week. He was at the point where none of his three major concerns about the accord was being addressed in any meaningful way. He had failed to win a clarification of the distinct-society clause. The Canada Clause issue had been shoved off to a second round of negotiations. Senate reform was still subject to a requirement of unanimous consent. Now, Wells complained, he was even being denied the additional four Senate seats he thought he had won under the Ghiz plan earlier in the week. The Newfoundland premier said the whole exercise was pointless. Gathering his papers to leave, he said he was going to hold a news conference to make his concerns and his position publicly known. Gary Filmon agreed, and said he was leaving with Wells.

The others around the table all joined in a chorus of protest and tried to persuade Wells and Filmon to stay. The prime minister asked Wells not to hold the press conference for the good of the country. Alberta premier Don Getty moved his swivel chair between Wells and the door, as if to block the Newfoundlander's exit. With the meeting about to collapse, Ontario's David Peterson decided to play his final card, the MacPherson plan to redistribute Senate seats. The Ontario premier asked Wells whether he would change his mind if Ontario, New Brunswick, and Nova Scotia agreed to give up some of their existing Senate seats. These seats could be reallocated to the four western provinces and to Newfoundland. The redistribution would not achieve parity in the Senate, but it would reduce the preponderance of Ontario in the Upper Chamber and bring Wells a little closer to his goal of provincial equality in representation.

Peterson's offer changed the atmosphere in the room. Wells sat down and agreed to resume the discussion. The offer of the additional Senate seats seemed to deal with his concerns on the Senate reform issue. On the distinct-society clause, Frank McKenna suggested the idea of reviewing the way in which the courts interpreted the distinct-society clause in order to see whether it conformed to the proposed legal opinion. Wells thought this idea was worth pursuing. The prime minister asked Roger Tassé of the federal delegation to meet with Wells and see whether a clause along these lines could be developed.

Within an hour, there seemed to be the elements of a tentative deal shaping up. The First Ministers adjourned while the officials worked on the preparation of a legal text. There were a number of loose ends that had to be settled. There had to be language drafted to reflect the Ontario plan to redistribute the Senate seats. The wording of the legal opinion on the distinct-society clause had not yet been finalized. There was also some confusion about who was to sign the legal opinion on the distinct-society clause. At one point, there were some twenty or thirty lawyers from the various delegations who had indicated an interest in signing the opinion. Roger Tassé, who was responsible for the preparation of the opinion, felt that this was too large a number. He wanted to reduce the signatories to a more manageable number.

Tassé also met with McKenna and Wells to discuss McKenna's idea of a review of the distinct-society clause. Wells proposed that the interpretation of the distinct-society clause would be reviewed after a period of ten years. If the review found that the court's interpretation had departed from the legal opinion, the clause would be amended accordingly. This commitment would be included as part of the final conference communiqué.

Tassé agreed to consider Wells's proposed language. But after reviewing the clause with the federal government's legal advisers and discussing it with the Quebec delegation, senior federal officials came to the view that it was unworkable. It contemplated a commitment to amend the constitution automatically in accordance with a two-paragraph legal opinion. The wording of the legal opinion was so vague as to make the commitment almost meaningless. At the same time, this ambiguity meant that the inevitable result would be endless wrangling over whether, in fact, the legal opinion was being adhered to by the courts. The federal officials proposed instead a more general clause requiring a review of the interpretation of the constitution as a whole on a continuing basis by First Ministers. The review would specifically refer to the Charter of Rights and would be part of the agenda of the annual constitutional conferences contemplated by the accord. Quebec agreed to the proposed review. But no one from the federal delegation had an opportunity to discuss the revised clause with Premier Wells.

The First Ministers reconvened shortly before 11:00 p.m. to review the text of the final communiqué. The section dealing with Senate reform had been modified to incorporate the Peterson proposal to redistribute seats in favour of the smaller provinces after a five-year period. But where, Premier Wells wanted to know, was the clause he had drafted dealing with the review of the distinct-society clause? Wells said he couldn't find it anywhere in the agreement. Someone had removed the clause without telling him, Wells charged. The Newfoundland premier became angry, claiming that the federal government was trying to deceive him into signing an agreement that had been altered without his knowledge or consent. He accused the prime minister of bargaining in bad faith, of manipulating him into signing a document under false pretences.

The prime minister summoned Roger Tassé to the room for an explanation. Where was the 'missing clause' that had been drafted by Premier Wells? Tassé was asked. Tassé pointed out that the clause was not missing, it had just been reworked. Tassé explained that the problem with the clause proposed by Wells was that it tried to commit governments in advance to enact constitutional amendments. Tassé indicated that this type of clause was regarded as unworkable by federal officials as well as by the Quebeckers. What was proposed instead was to require a general review of the constitution as a whole on a continuing basis. This general review would include an examination of the interpretation of the distinct-society clause. Tassé apologized for failing to inform Wells of the change. He explained that he had been finalizing the legal opinion at a meeting one floor below and had simply been unable to brief the Newfoundland premier prior to the arrival of the text.

Wells didn't want to listen to any explanations or accept any apologies. The 'missing clause' was the final straw. His voice rising, Wells vented his frustration and anger at the whole process. He complained that he had spent the past six days locked up in a room with people who were telling him he was trying to ruin the country. No one would debate the substance of his concerns. He was simply told that he had to cave in to the unreasonable demands of a single province because it was necessary for the good of the country. Wells said he would have no part of it. He was finished with the closed-door negotiations. He refused to sign anything.

The meeting broke up in disarray. Before he returned to his hotel for the night, Wells summoned his legal adviser, Neil Finkelstein, into the First Ministers' boardroom. Prime Minister Mulroney was at the head of the table, flanked by Norman Spector, Stan Hartt, Roger Tassé, and Paul Tellier, the clerk of the privy council. All the other premiers had left. Wells introduced Finkelstein to the prime minister. He told Mulroney that Finkelstein would discuss the issue of the 'missing clause' with federal officials and with Quebec. Wells said he was going back to his hotel and he didn't want to be disturbed before morning.

When Wells left, the prime minister told Finkelstein that they were very close to a final agreement and that it was essential that the trouble over the wording of the final communiqué be resolved. He urged Finkelstein as well as his own advisers to come up with a creative solution to the problem. After a few minutes of general discussion, Mulroney left the room and three members of the Quebec delegation filed in. André Tremblay, Jean Samson, and Benoît Morin were the three Quebeckers who had been designated to negotiate with Newfoundland and Ottawa over the issue.

The meeting lasted four hours. Finkelstein and the federal officials attempted to persuade the Quebeckers to accept some type of review of the distinct-society clause. What Wells wanted was an assurance that the legal opinion on the distinct-society clause had some standing or weight. But the Quebeckers took a hard line. They said they would not accept any wording in the final communiqué that suggested that they were 'bound' by the legal opinion. They were prepared to have the legal opinion appended to the conference communiqué, but they would not countenance any statement suggesting that they were obliged to amend the constitution to conform with the opinion.

By four o'clock in the morning, all the possible options had been explored. The only wording that was acceptable to the Quebeckers was general language stating that there would be an annual review of the constitution 'with a view to making any appropriate amendments.' But the Quebeckers were not prepared to define what an 'appropriate amendment' might be. That determination would have to be left to annual discussions between the First Ministers. Quebec was not prepared to tie its hands in advance. Finkelstein, who had not discussed this wording with Wells, told the Quebeckers and the federal officials that he would take it back to the premier in the morning and see whether it met his concerns.

The next morning, Wells's anger had subsided somewhat. But the premier told the federal officials he didn't want to discuss the contents of the agreement. He said he was not going to sign the agreement, so it didn't matter what was in it. He would take the agreement back to Newfoundland and put it to a referendum or a free vote in the Newfoundland Assembly. But he wasn't going to commit himself to anything.

The prime minister and the other premiers tried to get Wells to change his mind. Mulroney had apologized for the 'missing clause' in front of the television cameras when he had arrived at the Conference Centre. Upstairs, Mulroney went over the matter again, trying to explain that the whole misunderstanding was the result of an error by federal officials. Wells and Roger Tassé had a private meeting, with Tassé assuring the Newfoundland premier that there had never been any intent to mislead anyone. Wells and Tassé had known each other for many years, from the days when Tassé had been the deputy minister of justice and Wells had been a lawyer retained by the department. That personal connection no doubt bolstered Tassé's credibility with Wells. By the end of the morning, Wells seemed convinced that the incident over the missing clause had been the result of inadvertence rather than bad faith. But Wells still refused to discuss the agreement. As far as Wells was concerned, the negotiations were over.

Wells and Filmon had lunch in Wells's room in the Château Laurier. When the Newfoundland premier returned to the Conference Centre in the afternoon, he seemed to have softened his resistance somewhat. Wells looked at the wording that had been worked out overnight on the 'missing clause.' He also went over the wording of the legal opinion on the distinct-society clause that was to be signed by the constitutional experts. Wells had some suggestions about the wording of the legal opinion. He wanted a clause added to the opinion saying that the distinct-society clause did not derogate from legislative powers. The proposed change was discussed with federal officials and with Quebec, who both agreed to amend the legal opinion in the manner suggested by Wells. Wells also said that he would not commit himself to support the ratification of the accord in Newfoundland. The most he would do would be to take the agreement back to his cabinet and caucus colleagues in St John's and ask them to make their own determination. The wording of the final communiqué was modified so as to delete any reference to Wells's seeking approval of the Meech Lake Accord. The final version promised only that Meech Lake would be submitted for 'appropriate legislative or public consideration and [there would be] every possible effort to achieve decision prior to June 23, 1990.'

While these last-minute wording changes were being made to accommodate Wells, the Manitoba delegation indicated that it had some problems of its own with the legal opinion on the distinct-society clause. The Manitoba legal advisers were concerned that the wording of the legal opinion actually increased Quebec's powers, rather than limited them. They said that the legal opinion would have to be substantially rewritten to accommodate their concerns. There was a series of hastily convened meetings between the Manitoba delegation and officials from Newfoundland and the federal government. Eventually, it was agreed that the Manitoba concerns could be resolved through a relatively minor change in the wording of the legal opinion. The change was taken to Quebec for its consideration. After some discussion, the word came back that Quebec would accept the changes proposed by Manitoba.

In the midst of these discussions with Manitoba and Newfoundland, some unexpected problems cropped up between Quebec and New Brunswick. The final communiqué contained an amendment affirming the role of New Brunswick to 'preserve and promote the equality of status and equal rights and privileges of the province's two official linguistic communities.' This amendment was to apply to New Brunswick only, and would be passed by the federal Parliament and the New Brunswick Legislature. No other province would be involved in the amendment. On Saturday afternoon, the Quebec delegation said it had a problem with the use of the word 'promote' in the proposed amendment. Quebec said that the proposed amendment tracked the wording of its distinct-society clause too closely. Quebec wanted the reference to 'promote' deleted.

This request infuriated the New Brunswickers. They complained that they had made concessions throughout the course of the week, to the point where the final communiqué bore almost no resemblance to their original companion resolution. Frank McKenna threatened to walk out if he were forced to delete 'promote' from the New Brunswick amendment. A number of other delegations supported New Brunswick, calling on the Quebeckers to drop their objections. The amendment did not even involve the Quebec National Assembly. It was a bilateral agreement between the federal government and New Brunswick. After a few hours of debate and negotiation, the Quebeckers relented and agreed to let the proposed amendment stand.

By early evening, all the final wrinkles had been ironed out. Filmon and Wells would sign the final communiqué. It would commit them to making their best efforts to 'achieve decision' on the Meech Lake Accord prior to 23 June. It would also commit all governments to a companion resolution enacting a series of 'add-ons' to the accord. But the main thrust of the agreement was to establish a series of committees or conferences that would discuss the constitution on a virtual non-stop basis. The constitutional agenda was mind-boggling. There would be a national commission on Senate reform to develop concrete recommendations for an elected Senate with effective powers. The national commission would hold public hearings and report to the First Ministers' conference that would be held before the end of the year. There would be a separate series of constitutional conferences on aboriginal constitutional issues. The first such conference would be held within one year, and then every three years thereafter, on a permanent basis. A special committee of the House of Commons would be established to deal with the issue of a 'Canada Clause.' The committee would begin public hearings by 16 July 1990 and would report in time for the First Ministers' Constitutional Conference in 1990. Of course, these various conferences and committees were additional to the annual First Ministers' conferences on both the constitution and the economy required under the Meech Lake Accord itself.

The eleven First Ministers signed off on the final draft of the communiqué at eight o'clock. A little over two hours later, they assembled downstairs in front of the television cameras for the official signing ceremony. Someone remarked that the meeting had lasted a week and yet the conference had not even officially opened. The public session would be both an opening and a closing ceremony.

Prime Minister Mulroney tried to put the best possible face on the agreement. The document that First Ministers had signed was 'fair and honourable,' Mulroney said.[12] Those who had expressed concerns about the Meech Lake Accord 'will have assurances that [those concerns] will be addressed.' The agreement would permit Canadians to 'keep faith with the Fathers of Confederation' and 'preserve for our children a united and promising land.' The prime minister treated the ratification of the Meech Lake Accord as a foregone conclusion. 'With the passage of the Meech Lake Accord,' Mulroney said, 'Quebec has achieved the requisite security for its cultural and linguistic distinctiveness.' Note the use of the past tense to describe an event that had not yet occurred. But Mulroney was also realistic about the wounds that had been opened in the Meech Lake debate. The prime minister noted that the debate over Meech Lake had been 'bitter at times' and that it had 'opened wounds in the national psyche that will not quickly close over.' He spoke of the need to rebuild the 'sense of tolerance and common interest and common purpose that lie at the root of our success as a nation.'

Mulroney spoke of Meech Lake as though its ratification were assured. But when Clyde Wells took the floor, it quickly became apparent that ratification was anything but certain. Wells's address was emotional and heartfelt. It was the first opportunity for the Newfoundland premier to explain publicly what had happened over the course of the week. Wells complained about the process, describing it as a 'whirlpool or a vortex that you can't get out of, going round and round despite the urge that everybody has to go and tell the people of Canada what we feel.' Wells said he had been faced with a grave difficulty, 'the most difficult decision I have ever had to make in my life and I hope I never have to face those circumstances again.' Wells's 'grave difficulty' was that he was being asked to approve a constitutional amendment that he felt was wrong for the country and for his province. He was being 'pressured' to accept it on the basis that failure to do so would cause irreparable harm to the country. 'I don't want any responsibility,' Wells said, 'for doing irreparable harm to any part of this nation.'

Wells's solution to the dilemma was to avoid making a decision one way or the other. He would take the document back to the cabinet and caucus in St John's and 'ask them to make a decision as to whether we would seek legislative approval on the basis of a free vote ... or whether we would hold a referendum in the province.' Wells said he did not share the opinion that the failure to ratify the accord would cause irreparable harm to the country. But, he added, 'I am only one opinion and when I see all of this talent and conviction arrayed around me, I have grave doubts that my conviction is correct. I cannot but have grave doubts.' Wells sought to step aside, to let others make the arguments and the final decision. He still did not think the Meech Lake Accord was right for Canada, but he would not seek to cause his province to reject it. He invited the other First Ministers to come to his province and make a case for the accord, since 'the future of Canada may indeed be at stake.'

Clyde Wells, a man of strong and virtually unshakable convictions, was clearly unsettled by the week's events. The harsh political reality surrounding the Meech Lake Accord had come crashing down around the Newfoundland premier. Over the months leading up to the final meeting, Wells had been treating the accord as a matter for lawyers and for technical legal argument. But, over the course of the week in Ottawa, he had been told that these legal arguments didn't matter. The accord was a symbol. Its ratification was important for symbolic and political reasons. To amend the accord was to destroy its symbolic value. Therefore such amendments could not be considered. What Wells had been told over and over was what he simply could not accept. A debate conducted on these terms seemed to Wells to be irrational. It offended common sense and all the values that Wells had cherished throughout his public life. His answer was to try to remove himself from the process, to let someone else take the responsibility for deciding the fate of the nation.

However, Wells couldn't avoid responsibility for making the decision. He had assumed precisely that responsibility when he had deliberately set out to make an issue of the Meech Lake Accord. When Wells became premier, Meech Lake had already been ratified in Newfoundland. Wells could plausibly have taken the view that the issue had been dealt with by a previous government and that, while he didn't like the accord, he was not going to make an issue of it. But Wells didn't take that path. Now, it was too late to hold a referendum. Wells would have to put the issue to a vote in the Newfoundland Assembly. His party controlled a majority in the Assembly. He would have to take a stand on the issue and the fate of the Meech Lake Accord would in all probability turn on his decision.

It was clear from Wells's remarks at the closing ceremony that he had not changed his mind on the merits of the accord. Had he been forced finally to declare himself on the question, it was plain enough what his decision would have been. That is why the agreement signed at the Conference Centre that spring evening was an illusion. There was no agreement. Wells simply could not bring himself to ratify the Meech Lake Accord. He had campaigned for too long against it. The hole he had dug for himself was so deep that he could not summon the will to pull himself out of it now. His arguments against the accord had been repeated so often and with such conviction that it was unthinkable to admit that these arguments were wrong or, even worse, merely irrelevant. Meech Lake would not be ratified in Newfoundland because Clyde Wells simply could not bring himself to vote for it.

In this sense, there is nothing surprising in the fact that Meech Lake was not ratified in Newfoundland or Manitoba by 23 June 1990. What is surprising, and more than a little disturbing, is that the legislatures in those two provinces were not even given the opportunity to vote on the acceptance of the agreement that had been worked out in Ottawa. This outcome was the product of the decisions and actions of two individuals, Elijah Harper in Manitoba and Clyde Wells in Newfoundland. In Manitoba, the government had to obtain unanimous consent in order to provide for an expedited process of public hearings and debate on the accord and the agreement signed on 9 June. All three party leaders supported the agreement that had been negotiated and the proposal to provide for expedited hearings and debate. Yet, because the procedural change required unanimous consent, the negative vote of a single member was able to block the motion to refer the issue to a committee for public hearings. No public hearings were ever held on the agreement reached on 9 June, nor was there a vote on the accord in the Manitoba Legislature.

In Newfoundland, there was no similar procedural obstacle to overcome. It would have been possible to hold a vote on the accord on 22 June. However, Newfoundland premier Clyde Wells used his majority in the Assembly to adjourn the House on that afternoon without a vote being taken. Wells's justification for this decision was that he was being subjected to 'manipulation' by Senator Lowell Murray. The manipulation in question was a television appearance by Senator Murray early in the afternoon of 22 June. The senator had indicated that the federal government would ask the Supreme Court of Canada whether the 23 June deadline for the accord could be extended. However, Senator Murray also indicated that the federal government would seek the extension in the deadline only if Newfoundland voted to ratify the accord first. In effect, a precondition for extending the deadline was a positive vote for the accord in Newfoundland.

Premier Wells rose in the House of Assembly to denounce Murray's proposal as 'the final manipulation.' Wells argued that the federal government was seeking to pressure Newfoundland to vote in favour of the accord, even though the majority of the Assembly was opposed to it. He announced that the House would be adjourned without a vote being taken.

There is no doubt that the federal proposal had the effect of increasing the pressure on the government of Newfoundland to hold a vote and to ratify the Meech Lake Accord. But it should also be said that the 22 June television appearance of Senator Murray seemed to be more an act of desperation than an element of some well-developed strategy of manipulation. The federal government had maintained consistently for three years that the 23 June deadline was fixed and unalterable. The Charest committee had concurred in this conclusion in its report in the middle of May. For the federal government to suddenly reverse course on the day before the deadline was evidence that the wheels were coming off the train in Ottawa.

Regardless of the desperation displayed by Senator Murray, there is simply no adequate explanation or justification for the decision by Premier Wells to prevent a vote from being taken in the Newfoundland House of Assembly. There had been a full and thorough debate in Newfoundland in the week leading up to the deadline. Three provincial premiers and the prime minister of Canada had travelled to Newfoundland to address the Assembly personally. Nearly every member of the Assembly had spoken on the issue, many of them in eloquent and emotional terms. The premier had indicated that the vote on the accord would be a free vote, with members permitted to vote according to their conscience rather than according to party lines. Yet, after all this debate and argument, the premier deprived the members of the Assembly of the opportunity to do the one thing that really mattered – vote aye or nay on the accord itself.

In his public statements, the premier indicated that one of his main reasons for adjourning the House was that a vote would have resulted in a rejection of the accord. Wells indicated that since this negative result would have caused 'harm and resentment' in the province of Quebec, it was better to prevent a vote from taking place. But this argument is entirely unconvincing. First, there would be just as much 'harm and resentment' from a decision to adjourn as from a negative vote since, in both cases, the result would be to kill the Meech Lake Accord. Second, Premier Wells is here attempting to rely on an argument which he had consistently denounced over the preceding months, namely, the view that a negative vote on Meech Lake implied any rejection of Quebec. Now, when it was convenient, he was resorting to precisely this argument in order to justify his decision to prevent a vote from occurring in Newfoundland.

Wells's decision to prevent a vote being taken in Newfoundland was an affront to the principle of responsible government. The central organizing principle of responsible government is the idea that the members of the legislature are accountable to the people who elect them. But the principle of responsibility can work only if legislators are required to choose publicly between competing public policies. The legislature is not simply a debating society. It is a place where political choices are demanded of those who hold public office. In the words of the old political maxim, 'to govern is to choose.' By requiring legislators to make these political choices, we make it possible for the principle of responsible government to have meaning. Conversely, when we deny legislators the opportunity to choose, we not only diminish their role, we diminish the legitimacy of the democratic institutions upon which the functioning of responsible government depends. And so Meech Lake died, not because it was rejected by elected representatives, but rather because those elected representatives were denied the opportunity to vote on the matter.

Wells's decision to prevent his legislature from voting on the accord escaped criticism because the focus of attention during this period was elsewhere – on the prime minister. Just days after the signing of the 9 June agreement, the *Globe and Mail* published an interview with Mulroney in which he had uttered his infamous 'roll of the dice' line. This phrase has already been enshrined as one of the best-known and most-ridiculed quotations in the history of Canadian politics. What was truly mind-boggling about this interview was its timing. The accord had not yet been ratified in Newfoundland and Manitoba, and a vote in favour was by no means a foregone conclusion. Mulroney's 'roll of the dice' description of the week-long meeting only fuelled the image of the prime minister as a master of manipulation. It gave Wells and Filmon an excuse to allow the accord to die without ever being put to a vote. In this sense, it represented the final and definitive nail in the coffin of the Meech Lake Accord.

One remaining question is whether these events could somehow have turned out differently. Was there an alternative strategy that, had it been pursued, might have led to the ratification of the accord? The answer is, probably not. By the spring of 1990, the accord was massively unpopular outside of the province of Quebec. The strategy of insisting that the accord be ratified unamended was not working, and it was not going to work. The only other alternative was to reverse course and reopen the accord for amendments. This would play to the agenda of the hold-out provinces and might succeed in bringing them on side. The risk was that Bourassa would balk and refuse to go along with the amendments, which, of course, is precisely what happened. The federal government agreed to reopen the accord for amendments and established the Charest committee. The Charest committee recommendations were sufficient to bring Gary Filmon and Clyde Wells on side. But Quebec was not prepared to accept amendments to the accord. This had been its position since June 1987, and this remained its position in June 1990.

By the time the First Ministers arrived in Ottawa for dinner on 2 June, it had become evident that the amendment package based on the Charest report could not form the basis for a consensus. The problem for Mulroney was that if he continued to push for those amendments, he risked isolating Bourassa at the final meeting. So, Mulroney reversed course again, abandoning the Charest committee and reverting to the original strategy of pushing for the ratification of the accord without amendments.

It is truly remarkable just how close this final gambit came to succeeding. Over the course of a single week, Gary Filmon and Clyde Wells abandoned their objections to the accord one by one in return for promises of future considerations. It is even possible to imagine that, had the mix-up over the 'missing clause' been avoided on the Friday night, Wells might have been prepared to ratify the accord. But this is merely the final 'what if' in an endless series of speculations and missed chances. All that mattered in the end was that Meech was not ratified. The country would now get to find out whether those predictions of dire consequences that Clyde Wells had found so unpleasant to contemplate would turn out to be true.

9

Why Did Meech Lake Fail?

When Canadian political leaders began negotiations aimed at securing Quebec's willing acceptance of the constitution, most commentators agreed that the time was ripe for a successful outcome. By the summer of 1986, all the elements necessary for a resolution of Quebec's historic claims for a renewed federalism seemed to have fallen in place: a federalist government had been elected in Quebec on the basis of five relatively modest 'conditions'; the nationalist fires in Quebec had cooled following the referendum and constitutional debates of the early 1980s; the government in Ottawa was committed to securing the signature of the Quebec government on the constitution; and the premiers of the other nine provinces had all agreed to put aside their own concerns and focus exclusively on a 'Quebec round' as a priority matter.

Yet, despite these positive indications, the negotiations ended in stalemate, and the country was left more divided and embittered than it had been in many years. Understanding what went wrong and how, if at all, it might be fixed becomes a matter of some urgency. For, if we were unable to resolve the 'Quebec question' in the relatively tranquil atmosphere of 1986, what prospects are there for finding a solution in the much more threatening political climate of 1991?

In the wake of the failure of Meech, there has been a kind of conventional wisdom developing as to why the accord failed. This 'wisdom' has become so universally accepted as to be regarded as virtually self-evident. Its central thesis is that Meech Lake failed because of the 'bungling' of the country's politicians. This political 'bungling' is said to involve two distinct components. First, the process was flawed. The accord was negotiated in private, without any input from the public. Then, governments refused to consider any changes to the agreement which they had negotiated behind closed doors. According to this line of argument, the undemocratic and élitist nature of the Meech process was one of the keys to understanding its demise.

A second critique of Meech focuses on the substance of the accord itself. Here, the complaint is that the accord was not a 'true compromise.' Instead of requiring concessions from Robert Bourassa and the other premiers, the prime minister simply gave the provinces everything they demanded, and more. According to this interpretation, the accord's flaw was that it was an entirely one-sided bargain. Brian Mulroney cast himself as the 'head waiter for the provinces,' meeting each provincial demand and demanding nothing in return for the federal government.

The clear implication of this line of the argument is that the solution is simply to change the country's political leaders. Since Meech Lake failed because of the shortcomings of the existing crop of politicians, all that is necessary is to recruit a new generation of leaders committed to avoiding the mistakes of the past. But in this chapter, I will suggest that this conventional understanding of the failure of Meech Lake is overly simplistic and therefore misleading. Meech Lake did not fail because of political bungling. The causes of the failure are much more fundamental and, therefore, much more difficult to overcome. Whether and how Canadians might extricate themselves from our current predicament is not yet clear. But, if anything is certain, it is the fact that a mere change in political leadership will not offer any ready solution to our current impasse.

In this chapter I will explain why neither of the existing explanations for the failure of Meech is entirely persuasive. I will first suggest that Meech Lake did, in fact, represent a 'true compromise' between competing interests. Drawing on my account of the Meech negotiations, I will argue that everyone, including Robert Bourassa, made substantial and important concessions during the negotiations. In fact, the agreement that was signed on 3 June 1987 represented a balanced set of trade-offs that would not have resulted in any substantial departure from our existing constitutional traditions and practices.

What of the Meech process? What role did the closed-door character of the Meech negotiations play in the downfall of the accord? The answer to this question must necessarily be more speculative and impressionistic. But, in general terms, I will suggest that there has been a tendency to overemphasize the degree to which the Meech process contributed to the demise of the accord. On the one hand, there can be little doubt that the 'process critique' was widely referred to by the opponents of the accord as an important reason for rejecting it. At the same time, it should be remembered that the arguments based on the process were always framed as second-order or derivative arguments. The undemocratic character of the process was typically invoked in aid of other, more fundamental objections about the substance of the accord itself. Relatively few critics seemed to be arguing that the undemocratic nature of the process was, *in itself*, a reason for rejecting Meech. Those who objected to the process proceeded from the basis that the substance of the accord itself was fundamentally flawed. The 'process critique' was a kind of rallying cry for those who objected to Meech for other reasons. In short, if we are to come to a satisfactory explanation for the failure of Meech, we will have to look behind the process critique and identify the more fundamental concerns that gave rise to this critique in the first place.

If neither of these conventional explanations for the failure of Meech is entirely convincing, how can we account for the downfall of the accord? The alternative explanation I will offer will proceed from the assumption that the Meech debate was primarily symbolic. The substance of the accord was certainly not unimportant. But, of far greater significance were the symbolic qualities the accord came to assume over the three-year debate over its ratification.

The fact that the accord had an entirely different symbolic quality in different parts of the country was problematic. Within the province of Quebec, the accord came to be seen as a symbol of belonging, acceptance, and political legitimacy. These symbolic qualities were based on the accord's recognition of Quebec as a 'distinct society.' That recognition was important not for any 'new powers' that the clause implied, but for its acknowledgement of Quebec's difference within the Canadian federation. The province of Quebec had developed a kind of *de facto* special status within the Canadian federation over a number of decades. This *de facto* special status had evolved in a piecemeal and incremental fashion through a variety of administrative agreements that had granted Quebec a particular or distinct role in a whole variety of fields, including pensions, the tax system, and immigration. But this distinct status had never been formally or explicitly acknowledged in the constitution. The importance of Meech Lake within Quebec was precisely that it proposed to entrench formal constitutional recognition of Quebec's character as a distinct society. It was what Charles Taylor has aptly described as a 'declaration of intent,' in which Canada would recognize that Quebec's distinct identity was a central part of our purpose as a federation.[1]

Outside of Quebec, the symbolic attributes of the accord were entirely negative. As in Quebec, the symbolic images of the accord in the rest of the country were derived from the distinct-society clause. But, unlike in Quebec, the distinct-society clause was regarded with suspicion in the rest of the country because it came to be associated with the idea of granting special powers or privileges to the province of Quebec. In one sense, the resistance to this recognition might be regarded as anomalous. There were a variety of provisions in the existing constitution that singled out Quebec for particular mention or differential treatment.[2] Moreover, Quebec had succeeded in carving out for itself a kind of *de facto* special status without attracting much adverse comment from the rest of the country. Given these existing arrangements, what was the problem with formally recognizing that Quebec was a distinct society within Canada? The answer seemed to lie in the fact that formal constitutional recognition raised symbolic and political considerations that informal arrangements did not. Despite the *de facto* special status that Quebec had achieved, there had never been any generalized recognition of Quebec's particular status in the constitution. What became clear during the Meech debate was that any such generalized recognition would encounter stiff and sustained resistance from the rest of the country. In part, this resistance can be explained on the basis of the inherent ambiguity associated with the idea of recognizing Quebec's 'distinct identity.' Such ambiguity meant that opponents of the clause could plausibly read into it all kinds of 'horribles' that were said to be 'inevitable' if the accord were accepted. But, at a more fundamental level, it was clear that formal recognition of Quebec's distinct identity seemed to provoke a kind of 'identity crisis' for Canadians outside of Quebec. The recognition of Quebec's distinctness seemed to challenge in some very fundamental way Canadians' conception of the nature of their country. If we are to come to an understanding of the resistance to the distinct-society clause, and, indeed, of the failure of Meech Lake itself, it will be through exploring these very profound symbolic questions which the debate engendered. In the process, we might also stumble across some insights as to the future prospects and possibilities for constitutional reform in this country.

Was Meech Lake a True Compromise?

As chapter 4 has indicated, an intensive, ten-month round of negotiations led up to the meeting of First Ministers at Meech Lake on 30 April 1987. When those negotiations began in mid-1986, Quebec put forward a number of concrete proposals on each of the 'five conditions' that had been identified by Gil Rémillard in May 1986. These original Quebec proposals were significantly modified and narrowed down over the subsequent months of negotiations. Robert Bourassa was required to make important concessions on each of his 'five conditions' in return for the agreement at

Meech Lake. Then, an additional series of concessions was made by all the governments around the table during the all-night Langevin meeting on 2–3 June 1987. The result was that the final text of the accord, as signed by First Ministers on 3 June 1987, represented a quite modest and limited series of constitutional proposals. Contrary to the claims of the critics, the package of amendments would not have produced 'massive decentralization' or led to the eventual break-up of the country. The Charter of Rights would have continued to apply in all parts of the country in much the same manner as it had previously. In short, the Meech Lake Accord represented a 'true compromise' between competing provincial and federal interests rather than an abdication of federal power in favour of Quebec, in particular, or the provinces, in general.

Chapters 4 and 5 set out in some detail the various concessions and compromises that led up to the negotiation of the accord, and I will not reproduce that analysis here. Instead, I want to focus on three particular provisions in the accord that tended to attract the greatest public attention and controversy. It is fair to say that these particular aspects of the accord were what people had in mind when they alleged that the agreement was a 'sell-out' to the provinces. The three provisions I am referring to are the distinct-society clause, the spending-power clause, and the amending formula for Senate reform.

Distinct society/lingustic duality. How was the distinct-society clause a compromise? The answer lies in the fact that this very label – 'distinct society' clause – was highly misleading. The clause was not merely a recognition of the distinct identity of Quebec. It also gave explicit constitutional status to the English minority in Quebec. The Quebec government agreed to a constitutional stipulation that the English-speaking minority in that province represented a 'fundamental characteristic' of Canada. The significance of this concession ought not to be overlooked or underestimated. Since the mid-1970s, the Quebec government had sought to give pride of place to the French language within the province. French was made the official language of communication within the province, and the Quebec government rebuffed all attempts to reinstate official bilingualism at the provincial level.[3]

Against this background, the willingness of the Quebec government to recognize the existence of the English minority as a 'fundamental characteristic' of the country represented an important departure. It must be remembered that the clause referring to the English-speaking minority was not intended to apply in areas of federal jurisdiction only. It would be utilized by the courts to interpret the whole constitution, including the exercise of provincial powers under section 92 of the Constitution Act, 1867. Thus the Quebec government, in the exercise of its own powers, would have to act in a manner that recognized the 'fundamental' nature of the English-speaking minority within the province of Quebec.

On this basis, it is certainly plausible to argue that the distinct-society/linguistic-duality clause, far from extending Quebec's powers, might actually have been interpreted by the courts in precisely the opposite fashion. On the basis of the distinct-society/linguistic-duality clause, it would be possible for the English-speaking minority in Quebec to argue that legislation limiting its rights was unconstitutional. Certainly this was the fear expressed by the Quebec government at the Langevin meeting of 2–3 June 1987. During that meeting, Quebec premier Robert Bourassa revealed that his legal advice was that Quebec might well *lose* rather than *gain* powers under the clause. It was for this reason that Bourassa was willing to accept a so-called non-derogation clause as part of the final agreement. This 'non-derogation' clause stated that no province would lose power as a result of the distinct-society clause. But, in return for this 'safeguard,' Bourassa had to agree that the powers of the Parliament and Government of Canada were not prejudiced by the distinct-society provision.[4] Thus the overall effect of adding this non-derogation clause was to further limit the ambit and possible effect of the distinct-society clause itself. Bourassa had entered the negotiations seeking to obtain greater authority and legitimacy for the promotion of the French language in Quebec. By the end of the process he was reduced to a defensive posture, attempting to ensure that he had not actually lost any of his existing powers by signing the accord.

Remember also that, at the June 1987 Langevin meeting, Robert Bourassa had attempted to add a reference to the predominantly 'French character' of Quebec society. Bourassa wanted to specify that the reference to Quebec's 'distinct identity' was intended to refer to the French-speaking majority in the province. Bourassa was afraid that the existing version of the clause might lead the courts to declare that the English minority was included as part of Quebec's 'distinct identity.' This interpretation was likely, since the English-speaking minority within Quebec was specifically referred to as a 'fundamental characteristic' of Canada. Thus, in acting to promote the distinct character of Quebec, the provincial government would have had to take into account the presence and rights of the English minority. Bourassa wanted the clause clarified so as to rule out this possibility. He wanted to link the reference to Quebec's distinct character to its French-speaking population. But Bourassa failed in this effort. He was not permitted to backtrack on the compromise that had been agreed to at Meech Lake.

Critics of the distinct-society clause tended to focus their attention on another part of the clause that referred to the 'role' of the legislature and government of Quebec. This provision affirmed Quebec's role to 'preserve and promote' its distinct identity. Elsewhere in the clause, it was stated that the role of Parliament and the provinces was merely to 'preserve' (but not promote) linguistic duality.[5] Critics of the distinct-society clause were particularly troubled by the differences in the way in which these two 'roles' were described. Pierre Trudeau was among the first to focus public attention on this particular aspect of the clause, but his criticism was quickly picked up by New Brunswick's Frank McKenna and, later, by Newfoundland's Clyde Wells. They objected to the fact that Quebec alone was recognized as having the role of 'promoting' its distinct character. These critics argued that there should also be a recognition of a role for other governments to 'promote' linguistic duality.

There can be no doubt that including a reference to a role for governments in 'promoting' (as opposed to merely preserving) linguistic duality would have strengthened the position of linguistic minorities in Canada. Within the province of Quebec, for example, it would have led to the clear implication that the English and the French languages were on an equal footing. Conversely, the failure to include such a reference represented a clear concession in favour of the primacy of the French language in the province of Quebec. The implication was that it was appropriate for the government of Quebec to take active measures to promote the use of the French language within the province. At the same time, there was no obligation on the part of the government to take any such active measures in relation to the English language or even to treat the English language as having the same status and rights as the French language.

This, in essence, was the compromise agreed to at Meech Lake. Bourassa and the Quebec government agreed to grant constitutional status and recognition to the English language in Quebec, but Bourassa was not asked to accord *equal* status to the English language. There was a clear implication that it was permissible and appropriate for the Quebec government to accord primacy to the French language within the province. In this sense, the distinct-society/linguistic-duality clause represented a compromise for everyone, including those who might have wanted to see equality of status between the English and the French languages in the province of Quebec.

To negotiate is to compromise. No one should expect to obtain everything he or she might want out of an agreement. The relevant question is whether the particular concessions involved in the distinct-society/linguistic-duality clause were of such a magnitude as to be unacceptable. I believe that the answer to this question will become clear if we pause for a moment to consider Quebec's *existing* powers under the constitution. Quite apart from the provisions in Meech Lake, it is apparent that the Quebec government *already* possesses the right to promote the French language within the province of Quebec. Moreover, Quebec is under no obligation to accord equality of status to the English and French languages within the province. Such is apparent from the Supreme Court of Canada's judgment in the 'language of signs' case, *Ford v. A.G. Quebec*. As we saw in chapter 7, this case affirmed the important principle that the promotion of the 'French character' of Quebec society was an important constitutional principle under our existing constitution. This is not to suggest that the Quebec government need pay no attention whatever to the status and rights of the English language in the province. But the Supreme Court of Canada made it clear that Quebec need not accord equality of status to the two languages. The Court even conceded that it was open to the Quebec government to impose limits on rights that were guaranteed to the English-speaking minority under the Charter of Rights.

In the context of the language of commercial signs, the Supreme Court decided that the Quebec government could require that the French language be displayed in a position of 'marked predominance.' There were, of course, limits to this prodominance. In essence, the Court said that the province could prefer French as long as it did not ban English. The Court struck a compromise between the interests of the French-speaking majority and the English-speaking minority. What is striking is that the Supreme Court's compromise is precisely that agreed to in the accord. Meech Lake permits primacy for the French language, while at the same time affirming the fundamental character of the English minority in the province of Quebec. Meech Lake is a more general statement of the very principle applied by the Supreme Court of Canada in the *Ford* case.

Viewed in this light, the distinct-society/linguistic-duality clause merely codified the existing constitutional position. Far from representing a radical or revolutionary break with Canadian tradition or practice, it was a continuation of the status quo. It was an honourable and fair compromise between the legitimate desire of the Quebec government to promote the French language and the obligation of that government to respect the rights of the English-speaking minority.

The spending-power provision. The Meech Lake Accord proposed to impose limits on the ability of the federal government to spend money in areas of exclusive provincial jurisdiction.[6] Critics of this provision argued that it amounted to a significant constraint on the ability of the federal government to mount 'social programs.' It was alleged that Meech Lake would reduce the federal government to a 'sterile role as chief cashier.' A particular focus of criticism was the fact that Meech Lake referred to the right of the federal government to set 'objectives' in areas of exclusive provincial jurisdiction. The critics argued that the federal government should have the right to set program 'standards,' rather than merely objectives, in shared-cost programs with the provinces.

As with that of the distinct-society clause, the problem with this critique was that it failed to pay attention to the existing constitutional position. The federal government did, at one time, seek to set 'standards' for shared-cost programs involving the provinces. But, in 1977, the federal government abandoned this approach in favour of offering more or less unconditional block grants to the provinces.[8] In 1984, the federal government did seek to attach some conditions to the transfer of money for health care by requiring that provinces not permit doctors to 'extra bill' or to charge user fees. But there was no attempt to regulate the 'standards' of the various provincial programs. In fact, the greatest concern of the federal government over the past decade has been how to extricate itself from shared-cost programs involving the provinces. The greatest difficulty with these programs from the federal point of view is that the central government is placed in the position of raising the tax dollars, without receiving any of the political credit for actually delivering the programs. Thus the federal government has been systematically attempting to extricate itself from these costly and politically unpopular commitments. The provinces, in contrast, have been resisting these attempts by the federal government to withdraw from these funding commitments, arguing that they are placed in the position of continuing a service that the public has come to expect without receiving the necessary funding to maintain the program.[9]

The major compromise contained in the Meech Lake Accord on this issue is the very narrow focus of the limitation on federal power that is contemplated. The accord did not seek to limit in a general way the federal government's ability to spend money in areas of exclusive provincial jurisdiction. The only limitation involved new shared-cost programs. All other forms of federal spending in areas of exclusive provincial jurisdiction were left completely untouched. Thus direct transfer payments to individuals or institutions, tax credits, and other forms of tax expenditures would have been subject to no limitation whatsoever. Nor would any existing shared-cost program.

It is important to remember that the Quebec government had entered the negotiations, attempting to impose limits on all forms of federal spending in areas of provincial jurisdiction. The original Quebec proposal in the fall of 1986 was to establish a sweeping and all-encompassing limit on the ability of the federal government to spend in areas of provincial responsibility.[10] But this approach was rejected by the federal government as well as by a number of other provinces. At the end of the negotiations, the only limit imposed was on the ability of the federal government to initiate a *new* shared-cost program. All existing shared-cost programs as well as new direct federal spending were left untouched. Given the trend of federal policy over the past decade and, in particular, its attempt to extricate itself from costly involvements with the provinces, it is apparent that the limitation contemplated by Meech Lake was very modest indeed.

It is also important to note that there were important compromises involved in the way in which the limitation on federal spending was actually drafted. These compromises were made by both sides. The federal government had to concede an important measure of provincial autonomy in the design of shared-cost programs by agreeing that the provinces, rather than the federal government, would establish the program 'standards.' At the same time, the provinces had to recognize the right of the federal government to set the 'objectives' of the program. Moreover, the federal government was not obliged to seek the consent of the provinces before offering the program, nor did it necessarily have to offer the program to all provinces. These important decisions could be made by the federal government itself, free of any constitutional constraints.

In short, the limitations on federal spending contemplated by the Meech Lake Accord were narrowly circumscribed and carefully balanced. They did not affect existing arrangements and were consistent with the long-term trend of federal policy in this field. The major criticism of the spending-power clause – that the federal government should have the right to set program 'standards' – seems to reflect a profound antipathy to any kind of provincial variation or autonomy in program design. It is worth recalling that the accord dealt only with areas of exclusive provincial jurisdiction under the constitution. If the idea of 'provincial jurisdiction' means anything, it must mean that the provinces should have a significant measure of discretion in the design and administration of programs within their authority. Those who reject the recognition of this principle are, in the end, hostile to the federal principle itself. In this sense, it was the critics of the spending-power clause, rather than its defenders, who were seeking a major change in the status quo of Canadian federalism. The proposal to require the provinces to meet 'standards' set by Ottawa would have increased dramatically the degree of national control over provincial priorities. There is no basis in principle for such massive centralization in the determination of spending priorities, nor any evidence that the Canadian people as a whole desire or support it.[11]

The amending formula for Senate reform. When the accord was originally negotiated, the provisions dealing with Senate reform received relatively limited attention. But, by the end of the process, the interest in achieving comprehensive Senate reform had grown very considerably, particularly in western Canada. This meant that the accord's requirement of unanimous provincial consent for future senate reform came to represent an important target of criticism. In fact, going in to the week-long meeting of First Ministers in early June 1990, the amending formula for Senate reform was said to be one of the major stumbling-blocks to the ratification of Meech Lake. The Charest committee had recommended that the requirement of unanimity for future Senate reform should be modified in favour of a system of 'regional vetoes.' Manitoba premier Gary Filmon and Newfoundland premier Clyde Wells had both categorically rejected granting a veto to any single province over future Senate reform.

Given the quite categorical nature of the statements by Filmon and Wells on this issue, it is rather remarkable that the agreement signed by all First Ministers on 9 June 1990 maintains the requirement of unanimous provincial consent. This outcome indicates that it was certainly no accident that the Meech Lake Accord established a requirement of unanimous provincial consent in the first place. The events of June 1990 in effect confirm that Meech Lake contained the only possible solution to two competing and potentially contradictory interests. The first interest was Quebec's demand for a veto over future constitutional amendments that had the potential to alter its status or rights within the federation. The second competing interest was the demand by the other provinces that the principle of the equality of the provinces had to be maintained. These two competing interests came to a head on the issue of the amending formula, with Quebec seeking to protect itself through a veto over changes to federal institutions such as the Senate and the Supreme Court. The position of the other provinces was that anything given to Quebec had to be given to them. The only possible way out of potential deadlock on this issue was to meet Quebec's demand for a veto by simultaneously granting a veto to all provinces.

There is no point in pretending that this new decision-rule was somehow unimportant or trivial. Imposing a requirement of unanimous consent meant that it would be extremely difficult to achieve meaningful Senate reform. The answer to the objection is simply that this formula represented the only possible way of squaring the circle between the demands of Quebec and of the other provinces. The remaining provinces were simply unwilling to grant a veto for Quebec alone, without obtaining a similar right for themselves. Conversely, one of Quebec's minimal conditions was to restore the 'historic veto' which Robert Bourassa claimed the Parti Québécois had lost in 1981. There was thus an inexorable kind of 'political logic' to the requirement of unanimous consent on Senate reform. Gary Filmon and Clyde Wells attempted to resist the implications of this logic until the very end of the process. But, in the end, even they were forced into the position of recognizing that a concession on this issue was necessary if there was to be any kind of negotiated agreement involving all the provinces.

What the analysis thus far has sought to demonstrate is that Meech Lake represented a genuine compromise between competing interests. No one came away from the table with everything he wanted. At the same time, everyone came away with something of what he wanted. As for the flaws in the agreement – such as the requirement of unanimous consent for Senate reform – these were simply unavoidable. The point is simply that the prevailing view that Meech Lake failed to achieve a genuine or 'true' compromise is not supported by close analysis of the agreement itself.

What of the other major criticism of the accord, the process by which it was negotiated? Critics of the accord continually pointed to the closed-door character of the negotiations as a reason for rejecting Meech. Nor can it be denied that the process critique struck a chord with the Canadian public, with significant numbers of Canadians indicating support for a more open constitutional process.[12] But it is doubtful that the process alone, no matter how flawed, can provide a very convincing explanation of the failure of Meech Lake.

The first point to remember is that closed-door negotiations over the constitution are nothing new. In fact, all of the major components of the Canadian constitution, from the British North America Act in 1867 to the Charter of Rights in 1982, were the product of a closed-door process. In November 1981, for example, the basic trade-offs that produced an agreement between the federal government and nine provinces were agreed to during all-night meetings involving senior ministers and civil servants. Nor could it be claimed that these trade-offs were somehow mandated or authorized by the public discussions that had preceded the final negotiations. One of the key trade-offs in November 1981 was the inclusion of a notwithstanding clause in the Charter of Rights, permitting governments to override certain provisions in the charter. This override provision was a very significant weakening of the protections contained in the charter. More important, it ran directly contrary to the sentiments of the Canadian public, as expressed during the public hearings that had been held on the constitution in early 1981. These public hearings had indicated strong support for strengthening rather than weakening the guarantees of individual and group rights contained in the charter. The constitutional deal struck by the federal government and the provinces in November 1981 essentially ignored these sentiments in favour of protecting the legislative authority of governments.

It can also be stated that the closed-door nature of all previous negotiations on the constitution has not been an accident. Nor is it attributable to bad faith or arrogance on the part of political leaders. Rather, the preference for privacy in constitutional discussions is a reflection of a dynamic that inheres in all political negotiations. Whenever political leaders are called upon to negotiate an agreement involving significant concessions or trade-offs, they will seek to meet in private. The reason is quite simple and straightforward. The making of concessions involves the taking of risks. It requires flexibility on the part of the parties to the negotiation and a willingness to consider the position of the opposing party. This type of flexibility and risk-taking is unlikely to occur in a public setting, where the media are preoccupied with identifying 'winners and losers.' Instead, the public phase of any set of negotiations tends to involve the restatement of existing positions or demands. It is only when the parties move into a private setting that the real negotiations, involving the making of concessions, can actually begin. Thus, one survey of the international experience in constitutional bargaining found that 'the final bargaining and striking of compromise appears to require meetings among small groups, in private and informal settings. The role of late night meetings in restaurants, kitchens and chateaux in the Spanish, Canadian and Belgian instances was striking.'[13]

It can be stated quite categorically that these general principles apply with particular vigour in the case of negotiations between Quebec and the rest of Canada. The issues are highly emotional and symbolic.[14] They invoke considerations of political prestige and political face-saving. The necessity of protecting the 'honour' and the dignity of the various parties was and remains a paramount consideration throughout the process. It is quite evident, in other words, that there would have been no agreement between Quebec and the other provinces if there had not been an opportunity to conduct negotiations in private. The 'behind closed doors' nature of the negotiations was an essential precondition to their success.

It can also be stated with confidence that these same considerations will apply to any future round of negotiations. It has been widely reported that the era of 'executive federalism,' in which First Ministers meet behind closed doors to 'cut a constitutional deal,' is now over. But this obituary, while widely reported and believed, is founded on little more than good intentions. It must be remembered that the amending formula continues to require resolutions of the provincial legislatures for a constitutional amendment. Given the executive control over the legislature within our system of responsible government, First Ministers will continue to play a central role in any future constitutional negotiations. And if and when First Ministers do meet to discuss the constitution, they will have to conduct some of their meetings in private if they hope to reach agreement.

As to the claim that Canadians have changed and are no longer willing to tolerate closed-door negotiations involving politicians, the evidence for this proposition is far from clear. Canadians may not turn out to be as hostile to the idea of 'closed door' negotiations as is sometimes currently assumed. It is arguable that the issue of what is negotiated will still be far more important than how it is negotiated. If we look back to the immediate reaction to the Meech Lake negotiations, for example, there was very little questioning of the process. The initial reports of the agreement at Meech Lake emphasized the 'historic character' of the breakthrough.[15] The only discussion of the process centred on the differences in the negotiating styles of Brian Mulroney and former prime minister Pierre Trudeau. It was reported that Mulroney's skills as a negotiator and conciliator had made the unanimous agreement possible.[16] Mulroney's more flexible attitude was contrasted with the approach of Trudeau, who was reported to have adopted a more confrontational and rigid style in constitutional negotiations. The departure of the 'icy, aloof Trudeau and his rigid views' and the arrival of the more conciliatory Mulroney 'who had never been committed to any specific constitutional ideology' was described as being the key to the success of the meeting.[17] No one was even questioning the fact that the meetings had been held in private. It was simply assumed that constitutional negotiations would unfold in this manner.

That is not to deny that, by the end of the three-year debate over the ratification of Meech, the 'process critique' had assumed a central importance in the debate. Nor do I suggest that any future round of negotiations will be able to be conducted in the same manner as the Meech negotiations. There will obviously have to be significantly greater opportunities for public debate and discussion prior to any meeting involving First Ministers.[18] For the present, I simply wish to make the limited point that the flaws in the Meech process cannot provide us with a sufficient explanation for the failure of the accord. There were obviously other forces at work here, forces related to either the substance or the symbolism associated with Meech Lake. The key to understanding the fate of the accord lies in an exploration of the precise character of these 'other forces.'

The Failure of Meech: A Reassessment

If none of these factors constitutes an adequate explanation for the failure of Meech Lake, the question arises: what, then, accounts for the failure of Meech? If, as I have argued, Meech represented a limited set of compromises that would not have fundamentally altered the status quo, how can we explain the degree of opposition and emotions that the agreement aroused?

The answer to this question must obviously begin with the distinct-society clause. Why is this 'obvious'? Simply because the reference to Quebec as a 'distinct society' consistently aroused the greatest suspicion and opposition to the accord outside of the province of Quebec. Virtually every sampling of public opinion during the three-year Meech debate confirmed this observation. Such was the case even at the very beginning of the process, in the days immediately following the negotiation of the agreement. During these early days, there was general support for the agreement, with a majority of Canadians indicating that they were in favour of the accord that had been negotiated. But when asked specifically about the recognition of Quebec as a distinct society, a plurality of respondents indicated that they were opposed to this provision.[19] This finding is significant, given the initial euphoria and positive media reporting that surrounded the accord during this initial period. As the media reporting turned more critical, the support for the accord, in general, and the distinct-society clause, in particular, began to fall. Whatever initial support there was for the distinct-society clause outside of Quebec essentially evaporated following the decision of Premier Bourassa to invoke the notwithstanding clause in December 1988.[20] The notwithstanding clause was not a part of the accord itself. But, as we saw in chapter 6, the decision to reinstitute the 'French only' requirement for commercial signs through Bill 178 became inextricably linked in the public mind with the distinct-society clause.

There seems little doubt, then, that the distinct-society clause was the focus of the anger and suspicion that mounted against the accord outside of Quebec. Every sampling of Canadian opinion that is publicly available is consistent with this conclusion. The more difficult question is why the distinct-society clause assumed this central importance.

A large part of the explanation must certainly be attributed to the decision of Robert Bourassa to invoke the notwithstanding clause in Bill 178. The 'French-only' signs requirement of Bill 178 came to symbolize the 'true meaning' of the recognition of Quebec as a distinct society. Quebec's distinct identity came to be linked with the idea of limiting or suppressing the rights of the English-speaking minority in the province of Quebec. It really did not seem to matter how many times it was explained that the notwithstanding clause had been inserted in the constitution in 1982 and had no formal connection with Meech Lake. The debate came to be dominated by symbols and by perceptions. Even as knowledgeable an observer as Clyde Wells consistently drew a connection between the use of the notwithstanding clause and the recognition of Quebec's distinct-ness.[21] The precise nature of the connection was never clearly identified. According to Premier Wells, granting Quebec the special recognition it sought would 'be used to enact laws further restricting Quebec's linguistic minority, similar to Quebec's recently passed Bill 178.' How this might result from the distinct-society/linguistic-duality clause was rarely stated with any precision. Certainly the fact that the clause specifically recog-nized the English-speaking minority in Quebec as a fundamental charac-teristic of the country did not seem to be widely appreciated. Over time, the use of the notwithstanding clause and the recognition of Quebec as a distinct society seemed to become almost interchangeable in the public mind outside of Quebec. No amount of argument or explanation could shake this connection once it had been made.

A variety of other factors, in addition to Quebec's Bill 178, contributed to the unpopularity of the distinct-society clause outside of Quebec. One of these factors was the attitude among Canadians outside of Quebec towards the 'exclusion' of Quebec from the 1982 constitution. In essence, Canadians outside of Quebec rejected the idea that Quebec had been 'excluded.' Instead, the refusal of Quebec to sign the 1982 constitution was attributed to the presence of a separatist government in Quebec City, a government that was seen as being unwilling to accept any federalist compromise. These attitudes were captured precisely by former prime minister Pierre Trudeau in his *Toronto Star/La Presse* polemic at the end of May 1987. Trudeau argued that the nationalists in Quebec had tried to 'blackmail' the rest of the country during the 1981 constitutional negotia-tions, but that 'Canada had refused to pay.' René Lévesque had 'lost his gamble' and he and the separatists 'should simply have been sent packing and been told to stop having tantrums like spoiled adolescents.'[22] The problem, according to Trudeau, was that the country's current political leaders lacked courage. Instead of sending the nationalists packing, they had flaunted their 'political stupidity and their ignorance of the demographic data regarding nationalism' by rushing to the rescue of the unhappy losers.[23]

These sorts of attitudes towards the events of 1982 meant that it would be extremely difficult to justify any 'concessions' specifically directed at Quebec. Any such concessions would be vulnerable to attack outside of Quebec as an unnecessary and unjustified 'appeasement' of Quebec nationalists. This political reality was well understood by Canadian political leaders as they were poised to commence the Meech Lake negotiations in the summer of 1986. For this reason, among others, the operating principle throughout the negotiations was that anything given to Quebec would be given to all provinces on similar terms. This operating principle could be applied in a relatively straightforward manner to four of the five 'conditions' announced by Robert Bourassa at the beginning of the negotiations.[24] But it could not be applied to the distinct-society clause, which, by its very nature, was specific to the province of Quebec.

There was obviously no difficulty in justifying this constitutional recognition to Quebeckers. But how could the recognition of Quebec as a distinct society be justified outside of Quebec? The most obvious way was to claim that it was necessary in order to obtain the consent of the Quebec government to the 1982 constitution. But, in trying to make this argument, you immediately ran into a major problem. Canadians outside of Quebec did not really accept the premise of the negotiations – that Quebec had a legitimate grievance requiring some form of redress. As far as the rest of the country was concerned, Quebec was already 'in' the constitution. Thus to attempt to justify the distinct-society clause on the basis that it was necessary in order to obtain the consent of Quebec to the Canadian constitution seemed totally unconvincing. Canadians were being asked to pay a price for something they saw no need to purchase. Quebec was already bound by the constitution regardless of the willingness or unwillingness of the provincial government to sign the document.

So, right from the very beginning, the distinct-society clause was vulnerable to the criticism that it was unjustified and unnecessary. The problem was compounded by the extremely general language utilized in the clause. Quebec was described as a 'distinct society.' The English-speaking minority in Quebec was described as a 'fundamental characteristic of Canada.' The Quebec government was recognized as having the 'role' of 'preserving and promoting' its distinct identity. But what, precisely, did these terms mean? Did the clause confer any new powers on the government of Quebec? How would the clause affect the interpretation of the Charter of Rights? The clause did not provide any explicit answer to these questions. The reality was that the answers to these and other questions would necessarily await the interpretation of the Supreme Court of Canada. It was impossible to predict with certainty how the clause would be applied on a case-by-case basis by the Court. The Supreme Court would be called upon to balance and weigh the competing values recognized in the distinct-society/linguistic-duality clause. The Court would strike a balance between these competing values and then apply that formula to the facts of particular cases. It was possible to identity the considerations the Court would have to take into account in reaching its decision. But it was impossible to know precisely how or where the Court would strike the balance.

Of course, the defenders of the accord could never admit this fact. Any admission that the distinct-society clause contained general language that was subject to judicial interpretation would have been taken as conclusive evidence of the fundamental flaws in the agreement. So, the defenders of the accord were placed in the unenviable position of having to deny what was, in fact, quite obvious and undeniable the fact that the distinct-society clause used general language that would be applied by the courts to the facts of particular cases in a manner that could not be conclusively determined in advance.

But was this use of general language evidence of poor drafting technique, as the critics of the distinct-society clause maintained? In reality, the use of general language is an inherent feature of the art of constitution-making. Constitutions do not generally resemble the Income Tax Act.[25] The point of a constitution is to set down the basic, fundamental principles that are to govern the making of laws in a society. Because these principles are fundamental and are meant to apply across a broad range of possible circumstances, they must necessarily be expressed in broad language. The task of applying that general language to the facts of particular cases is the responsibility of the courts.[26] This process of interpretation is inherently 'political' in the sense that it inevitably involves the exercise of significant discretion on the part of the judiciary. For example, the Charter of Rights entrenches general rights such as 'liberty,' 'security of the person,' and 'equality' and states that these rights can be limited only in circumstances that are 'demonstrably justified in a free and democratic society.'[27] It was impossible to predict in advance how these general concepts would be applied in particular cases. The precise contours and meaning of these rights, as with all constitutional provisions, must await the pronouncements of the Supreme Court of Canada.

So the distinct-society/linguistic-duality clause employed general language because such generality is inherent in the process of drafting a constitution. That is not to suggest that there was no attempt to place some boundaries around its possible scope and application. The clause was described as 'interpretive,' a clause that would affect the scope of existing constitutional powers rather than create new powers. The recognition of Quebec's distinct identity was balanced by an explicit reference to the fundamental nature of the English minority in Quebec. The clause was said not to detract from the powers of the Parliament of Canada. But the reality was that the precise working out of the meaning of the clause would ultimately be left in the hands of the Supreme Court of Canada. This was the honest answer to the complaint that the distinct-society clause was ambiguous. Difficulties arose in that this answer, if ever publicly given, would have instantly sealed the fate of the accord.

All of these various factors help to explain why the distinct-society clause became the 'hot button' for opposition to the accord. But these factors, while important, are ultimately only part of the story. They fail to capture the essence of why the distinct-society clause was regarded as so threatening to Canadians outside of Quebec.

In order to develop a more complete picture of the debate over the distinct-society clause, it is necessary to consider what might be termed the 'purely symbolic' messages it contained. Purely symbolic considerations are often brushed over as unimportant. Popular accounts of politics typically emphasize 'bread and butter' issues such as shifts in economic and political power. But what these accounts overlook is the fundamental importance of purely symbolic considerations in many political contexts.[28] Symbolic considerations are important because they define who we are as a people. They give priority or social recognition to certain values, customs, or ways of life, while downplaying others. Moreover, considerable political energy is devoted to competing for the recognition, status, and honour that symbolic goods generate. In fact, many of the political debates that have preoccupied Canadians over the past two decades, including debates over bilingualism, multiculturalism, and the status of the English language in the province of Quebec, can be profitably viewed as a struggle over social honour and recognition.[29]

What is most striking about the debate over the distinct-society clause is the degree to which it employed the language of honour, dignity, and social recognition. This way of characterizing the distinct-society clause was common to both its defenders and its critics. We have already observed how considerations of honour and dignity dominated the debate over Meech Lake in Quebec.[30] From the very beginning, the object of the exercise was described in terms of restoring Quebec to the constitutional family with 'honour and enthusiasm.' The distinct-society clause was important within Quebec precisely because of the social recognition it conveyed. What should not be overlooked is that the same language of honour and dignity was employed by those who were opposed to the accord. Alan Cairns, in his brilliant analysis of the 'discourse' surrounding Meech Lake, has emphasized the degree to which the language used in the debate was dominated by considerations of constitutional status and social recognition.[31] Cairns offers numerous examples of what he describes as an 'admittedly inchoate but not formless style of constitutional discourse.'[32] The language is highly emotional and 'haunted by comparison, driven by the ubiquitous fear that one has lost, or might lose, constitutional ground relative to some other group' (p. 122). Thus, to cite only a few of the many examples that Cairns offers, the Inuit denounced the accord for giving prominence to French- and English-speaking Canadians, arguing that this is 'offensive and insulting to the fact that we [Inuit] are not being recognized as being contributing members to this country.'[33] Georges Erasmus of the Assembly of First Nations rejected the distinct-society clause because it 'strengthens the myth that the French and English peoples are the foundations of Canada. It neglects the original inhabitants and distorts history ... If anyone is more distinct, surely it is the peoples of the First Nations.'[34] Multicultural Canadians were opposed to the accord because 'not all the people of this country have been dealt the same constitutional card, nor have they been equally credited with being a dignified and contributing part of this country.'[35]

As Cairns emphasizes, the grievances that were expressed by these so-called Charter Canadians were not narrowly instrumental. Recognition of constitutional status was being sought for its own sake, rather than for what tangible benefits might be expected to flow from it. These Charter Canadians, including aboriginals, women, and multicultural organizations, led the first wave of attack against the distinct-society clause, beginning in the summer of 1987. Then, in early 1989, a second front was opened in the symbolic battle against the clause with the election of Newfoundland premier Clyde Wells. Wells had a whole host of objections to the Meech Lake Accord. But his central concern was with the implications of the distinct-society clause for the principle of the equality of the provinces. Wells objected to the clause because he believed it created a 'special legislative status' for the province of Quebec. According to Wells, Canada could remain united only if it was made up of ten provinces 'equal in their status and rights as provinces' in the federation.[36] He saw in the recognition of Quebec as a distinct society a covert attempt to create a Class A province, a Class B province, and eight Class 'C' provinces.

Wells's objections were not framed in the emotional and highly rhetorical language employed by aboriginal or women's groups. Nevertheless, there was a broad similarity in the underlying nature of the concerns expressed. The recognition of Quebec as a distinct society was a frontal attack on Wells's idea of Canada. It undermined the basic principles Wells associated with being a Canadian. The covert message in the distinct-society clause was that Quebeckers were placing the interests of their province first, ahead of the interests of the country as a whole. What was required, according to Wells, was to reverse this equation. 'I say to my friends in Quebec,' Wells told a national television audience on 9 June 1990, 'I believe it is the responsibility of all of the citizens of Quebec to put Canada first, and recognize that, like all of the other provinces, Quebec is second.'[37] Wells's attack on the distinct-society clause, and his injunction to 'put Canada first,' resonated with Canadians outside of Quebec, who were suspicious of any suggestion that Quebec was being granted 'special legislative status.' Clyde Wells became their champion, precisely because he was seen as the defender of a particular vision of the country and of Canadian citizenship.

I believe that these symbolic messages associated with the distinct-society clause provide the most powerful explanation of its massive unpopularity outside of Quebec. The Meech Lake debate illustrated in very dramatic fashion the extent to which constitutional politics is a politics dominated by symbolism. The accord generated such fierce opposition outside of Quebec because it was seen as an attempt to change the delicate balance in the 'symbolic order' of Canada. It was regarded as an attempt to confer privileged status on French- and English-speaking Canadians or on the province of Quebec. As such, it was regarded as a frontal attack on the social identity and recognition associated with a whole variety of other constitutionally recognized groups. It was also regarded as a threat to the vision of Canada as a federation comprised of ten provinces with equal status as members.

The Meech debate demonstrated that constitutional change is extremely difficult and hazardous to achieve precisely because of these symbolic dimensions. Changes in the symbolic order will be vigorously resisted. The point can be illustrated by comparing the distinct-society clause with an existing constitutional provision – the notwithstanding clause. Remember that the existing constitution contains a notwithstanding clause permitting governments to override certain rights with impunity. One might have expected that the 'Charter Canadians' identified by Cairns might have been far more concerned about the notwithstanding clause than about the distinct-society clause. The distinct-society clause was a mere interpretive provision. It did not confer any blanket right on the Quebec government to ignore the charter. But, in the debate over Meech Lake, the distinct-society clause, not the notwithstanding clause, attracted the most anger and opposition. How can we account for this apparently anomalous evaluation of the relative impact of these two provisions? The answer seems to be simply that the notwithstanding clause was already contained in the constitution. No matter how pernicious, it was part of what was 'given.' The distinct-society clause represented an attempt to alter the symbolic balance of the constitution. Thus, that distinct-society clause became the inevitable focus of anger, frustration, and opposition. What the Meech debate illustrates is the fact that very significant flaws in the existing constitution will be overlooked or tolerated. But the moment anyone attempts to change the existing constitutional order, you can expect trouble.

This analysis of the Meech Lake debate may be regarded as leading to an entirely depressing prognosis for the future of the country. Certainly, it illustrates the extent to which constitutional change is fraught with difficulty. Quebec sought recognition of its distinct identity in the constitution because of the symbolic message this recognition conveyed. But the rest of the country resisted this recognition precisely because they were wary of the symbolic dimensions of the provision. Yet this way of understanding the Meech debate – as a symbolic struggle – points to opportunities as well as obstacles. It helps us to come to terms with what really is at stake in the current debate over our constitutional future. Agreeing on what the debate is really about is a start, albeit a small one, on the road towards finding a way out of our current impasse.

10

The Way Ahead

Commentators on the Canadian constitution have quoted virtually *ad nauseam* Michael Kirby's paraphrase of Machiavelli's dictum about the difficulties confronting the political leader who seeks to remake a country's constitution. Kirby, in his now famous memorandum written just before the First Ministers' conference in September 1980, had attributed to Machiavelli the observation that 'there is nothing more difficult to arrange, more doubtful of success, and more dangerous to carry through than initiating changes in a state's constitution.'[1] Yet the frequency of the references to Machiavelli's observation about constitution-making has done nothing to diminish its applicability to the Canadian case. Over the past decade, there were two sustained efforts to amend fundamentally the Canadian constitution. One ended in apparent success, the other in outright failure. What both episodes made plain, however, was the extremely risky and difficult character of any attempt to rewrite the constitution. If there was ever any doubt about the matter, it is now self-evident that constitution-making in Canada is an exercise in which the odds are heavily stacked against success and where defeat can almost always be snatched from the jaws of victory.[2]

Yet Canadians seem apparently undeterred by these risks and obstacles. The constitutional status quo is said to be totally unacceptable to a large majority of Canadians. The pressure for fundamental constitutional change is commonly thought to be building to a crescendo that political leaders will simply be unable to ignore or deny. Nor is the pressure for change limited to the province of Quebec. Across the country, there is said to be growing frustration with the perceived insensitivity of representative government and a desire for new forms of 'direct democracy' that permit voters to make political choices directly.[3] Politicians, bureaucrats, the media, and academics are coming under criticism for having ignored for too long the 'inherent shortcomings in a system of government that a great many Canadians feel does not listen or adequately respond to their concerns.'[4] Some fear that the increasingly urgent calls for meaningful reform will be resisted by the 'upholders of the status quo'; others suggest that reality dictates that demands for change 'cannot be ignored.'[5] Fundamental reform of our political institutions is now thought to be front and centre on the public agenda.

Whether these predictions of impending constitutional reform will come to pass is by no means as self-evident as some newspaper editorials might have us believe. Certainly the experience of the past decade on the constitutional front does cause one to pause before accepting any predictions about its inevitability. Moreover, the international experience with constitutional change over the past thirty years suggests that fundamental constitutional reform is extremely rare. Internationally, the only instances of genuine 'reconstitutions' have been in cases where established interests have been shattered by revolution, external threat, or defeat in war or similar disruption.[6] No such precipitating event is present in the Canadian case. It is also worth remarking on the curious fact that the same opinion polls that record unprecedented anger and frustration among ordinary Canadians also report that a large majority believe that governments should 'leave the [constitutional] issue alone for a while.'[7] There are evidently some mixed feelings about the desirability of returning to the constitutional bargaining table. What cannot be denied, however, is the high degree of dissatisfaction, frustration, and cynicism dominating the contemporary public mood in Canada. These are very powerful sentiments indeed, and it is impossible to predict with any certainty the precise direction in which they will lead us.

What can be done, however, is to begin to make an assessment of the viability of the various proposals for fundamental change that are emerging on the constitutional landscape in early 1991. Foremost among these proposals, of course, are the reports of the Allaire committee of the Quebec Liberal party and of the Bélanger-Campeau commission of the Quebec National Assembly. While there are a variety of other constitutional reports from other provinces or at the federal level, these two reports from Quebec represent the 'base camp' for all future assaults on the constitutional mountain. In the wake of the failure of the Meech Lake Accord, Quebec society turned inward in an attempt to formulate a new constitutional position to present to the rest of the country. The first step in that process has now been completed. Whether it will be possible to achieve an accommodation between Quebec and the rest of the country has not yet been finally determined. But what is already apparent is the fact that the debate threatens to be stymied by misconceptions and miscalculations on all sides. Unless these misconceptions are dispelled in relatively short order, the prospects for a negotiated solution to the current constitutional crisis appear to be virtually non-existent.

This chapter will examine the various proposals for fundamental constitutional change on the table in the light of some very hard and unpleasant political realities that simply cannot be avoided in the wake of the failure of Meech Lake. The main effect of these political realities, I will argue, is to limit dramatically the range of available options. While the range of theoretical possibilities is virtually limitless, the practical political possibilities are fairly limited and can be identified in relatively precise terms. Of course, being able to identify the real as opposed to the theoretical options does not diminish the difficulty of choosing between them. This difficulty is compounded by the confusion that currently prevails regarding an acceptable and workable process for resolving these concerns. The task ahead is daunting, the time available to deal with it is short, and the procedure to be employed is contested. Canadians may have many shortcomings, but minimizing their political problems is certainly not one of them.

The Current Political Context

As during the Meech Lake debate, the current political context is dominated by the wide divergence between political attitudes within Quebec and in the rest of the country. Within the province of Quebec, the existing federal regime is said to be 'bankrupt.'[8] The rejection of the Meech Lake Accord is said to have damaged the federalist cause in Quebec beyond repair. There is now thought to be a consensus on the need for a fundamental restructuring of the relationship between Quebec and the rest of the country. The Allaire committee[9] has proposed a radical restructuring of Canadian federalism that would leave the central government with only the most vestigial powers and jurisdiction. The Bélanger-Campeau report has proposed a referendum on Quebec sovereignty by October 1992.

It is widely recognized that there will be very profound resistance within the rest of the country to any constitutional changes designed to meet Quebec's demands. But it is also widely believed that this apparent intransigence in the rest of the country can be overcome through some form of 'shock therapy.' According to this way of thinking, what is needed is to demonstrate to the rest of the country that Quebec is deadly serious in its demands for increased political and economic powers. A variety of proposals have been put forward to achieve this result. Some suggest that the Quebec government should set a deadline for the negotiations with the rest of the country, after which time the Quebec people will be asked through a referendum to support sovereignty. Another proposal is to hold a referendum before any negotiations with the rest of the country, so as to give added political authority to the position of the Quebec government during the negotiations. Both scenarios assume that the rest of the country can be forced into negotiations on terms defined by Quebec through the application of pressure and ultimatums.

It would seem that this approach is more likely to have precisely the opposite result, stiffening the resolve in the rest of Canada to resist any ultimatum issued by Quebec. Outside of Quebec there seems to be relatively little willingness to deal with the emerging Quebec agenda. The overwhelming majority of Canadians outside of Quebec believe that the failure of the Meech Lake Accord was a good thing for Canada, or else that it will make no difference to the future of the country. There is overwhelming opposition in the rest of Canada to the idea of granting significant new and 'special' powers to the province of Quebec, even if this refusal means that Quebec might leave the country.[10] Canadians outside of Quebec are firmly committed to the principle of the equality of the provinces. Moreover, a majority of Canadians outside of the province of Quebec apparently believe that, if Quebec leaves, the rest of the country would be better off, or else would be no worse off.[11] In any event, by the end of 1990, only 38 per cent of Canadians outside of Quebec believed that it was likely that Quebec would separate in the 1990s. A clear majority continued to believe that Quebec would remain within Canada.[12]

These quite contradictory attitudes inside and outside Quebec on the nation's prospects are very disturbing. There is clearly no agreement on the causes of the current impasse or on the likely course of future events. Quebeckers are proceeding on the basis of one set of assumptions about the real intentions and interests of the rest of the country. The rest of Canada appears to be operating on the basis of entirely different calculations about its own 'real' interests and the 'real' interests of Quebec. Such a situation is tailor-made for miscalculations and bungled negotiations in which everyone comes out a loser. Within such an atmosphere, there is likely to be considerable energy devoted to issuing threats and ultimatums, combined with an interest in 'calling the bluff' of the other party. Issuing threats or ultimatums promotes a 'win-lose' situation in which the finding of compromise solutions becomes extremely difficult. Threats and ultimatums also come with a price attached – the author of such declarations may be required to make good on them, regardless of whether this outcome serves the interests of either side in the dispute.

The divergence in the attitudes within Quebec and the rest of the country is merely the first element in the current political context that bears emphasis. There are a number of other factors at play, each of them tending to reduce the prospects for any kind of negotiated solution to the current impasse. The first of these factors is what I would describe as general confusion about an acceptable process for constitutional change. The amending formula continues to require the participation of governments, in the form of resolutions passed by provincial legislatures and the Parliament of Canada. But there appears to be widespread suspicion of any negotiations conducted 'behind closed doors' involving First Ministers. The problem, as was pointed out in chapter 9, is that a ban on private negotiations is, in effect, a ban on the negotiation process itself. There are legions of critics but few conductors. The list of critics clamouring to point out the flaws in the existing process for constitutional amendment grows longer by the month. But there are relatively few constructive proposals for a new process that works within the existing framework of the constitution and that might stand a fair chance of actually producing a negotiated settlement.[13]

A related process problem is that the government of Quebec has asserted that it will negotiate only with the government of Canada. However, the current amending formula gives the government of Canada very limited authority to negotiate constitutional changes with the government of Quebec alone.[14] For most important constitutional amendments, the participation and agreement of the other provinces is required. But if Quebec refuses to negotiate directly with those other provinces, the prospects for reaching a negotiated settlement appear to be virtually nonexistent. If Quebec remains intransigent, the federal government will likely be forced to undertake some form of bilateral negotiations. Such negotiations would involve the federal government meeting separately with Quebec and with the other provinces in the hope of reaching a solution acceptable to everyone. But the prospects for achieving success under this approach are extremely limited. This conclusion is based on the experience during the final months of the Meech process in early 1990. In the period leading up to the final deadline in June 1990, there were extensive bilateral negotiations between the federal government and individual provinces. But these negotiations essentially went nowhere. It was only in early June, when all eleven governments sat down in the same room together, that the process of narrowing differences began in earnest. Some similar kind of multilateral negotiations will be even more necessary in the current round of discussions, given the wide differences that are likely to emerge.

The third, and perhaps most important, complication is the all-encom passing and uncontrolled agenda that is likely to emerge in any future constitutional negotiations. One of the key reasons why the Meech Lake round resulted in a negotiated agreement was that the agenda was limited in advance. But limiting the agenda in advance no longer appears possible. Instead, there is an insistence that any future negotiations must be comprehensive and resolve all constitutional claims and grievances simultaneously. There is near unanimity in the rest of the country that the Quebec agenda cannot be dealt with in isolation. At a minimum, there will have to be some satisfaction of demands by the aboriginal people for self-government, as well as some kind of meaningful Senate reform. But experience indicates that the agenda tends to expand as constitutional negotiations proceed. This happened in 1981, as an increasing number of groups and interests sought some form of constitutional recognition. The same process occurred in the 1987–90 period, with the list of constitutional grievances expanding the longer the debate continued. We can expect the same process to unfold in any future constitutional negotiations. It is safe to predict that the list of those advancing constitutional claims will be even longer this time around. The problem will be compounded by the fact that all of these groups and interests will demand satisfaction at the same time. Each group or constituency will seek to assert veto power over the proceedings, maintaining that no single concern can be resolved until all concerns have been resolved. Nor is there likely to be much willingness to accept compromise or second-best solutions. Instead, the negotiations will have to contend with groups and interests on all sides demanding that their particular agenda or concerns must be fully addressed immediately. One does not need a crystal ball to forecast how negotiations conducted on this basis are likely to turn out. The historical record, both in Canada and elsewhere, indicates that comprehensive constitutional change is extremely difficult to bring about. The most likely outcome of a comprehensive attempt to rewrite the constitution is a failure to reach an agreement.

Confronted with these very formidable obstacles, it would be easy to simply throw up one's hands and conclude that the enterprise is not worth undertaking in the first place. Ironically, I believe that the best possible result would be for Canadians to arrive at a conclusion precisely along these lines. Rather than proceeding back down the constitutional path, a path that is fraught with risks and obstacles, there is considerable attraction to setting the constitutional issue aside and attempting to deal in a more practical and pragmatic fashion with the many challenges facing Canada. Amending a country's constitution is an extremely cumbersome and dubious way of trying to resolve current political, economic, and social problems. A focus on formal constitutional amendment also ignores the extent to which it is possible to achieve very significant change without such amendment. Over the past 125 years, there have been massive shifts in the relative power of the federal and provincial governments, most of them having been achieved without any formal constitutional amendments. Instead, this rebalancing in federal and provincial roles has been achieved through a complex mix of quasi-constitutional agreements and administrative arrangements, without any amendment of the formal constitution.

Many of the aspirations for greater provincial autonomy that one currently hears across the country could be accommodated in this way. Consider, as an example, the recent report of the Allaire committee in Quebec. The committee proposed 'exclusive jurisdiction' for the province of Quebec in twenty-two areas. But close examination of this list indicates that the province already has complete or partial jurisdiction in all but one of the areas that are identified. This suggests that the Allaire committee's demand for greater autonomy could be met, at least partially, through agreements negotiated with the federal government, rather than through a formal constitutional amendment.

This approach appears to be rendered problematic by current political perception. It is now widely argued that the time for constitutional 'tinkering' is past. There are widespread calls for fundamental amendment of the constitution. The failure of the Meech Lake Accord has set in motion a chain of forces and events that all lead to the door of formal constitutional change. All indications are that Canada will be unable to avoid another round of negotiations over formal amendments to the constitution. In this context, it may be somewhat beside the point to argue that formal constitutional change is unnecessary. Nor is it helpful to focus only on the obstacles that will stand in the way of securing a comprehensive amendment to the constitution. If Canadians cannot or will not avoid another debate on the constitution, it is important to try to identify ways of maximizing the chances of bringing the proceedings to a successful resolution.

One way of achieving this result is to identify proposals or processes for change that are certain dead ends. In the current debate, the theoretical possibilities or options for change are virtually limitless. But there is a world of difference between theoretical possibility and political attainability. I will suggest, in fact, that the range of real as opposed to theoretical possibilities is extremely limited. Our past experience with constitutional amendment over the past twenty-five years demonstrates that the window of practical opportunity left open to us in 1991 is very narrow indeed. This focus on hard political realities and on the constrained nature of the available options is not particularly pleasant. But one of the greatest dangers that we confront is the tendency to promote illusions about what is possible or workable in the current situation. Nurturing these illusions is dangerous because it increases the likelihood of miscalculation and misperception dominating the discussions. The stakes are too high and the prospects too uncertain to permit illusions and miscalculations to dictate the outcome.

This process of eliminating what are essentially 'false options' will not necessarily lead us to a solution to the current impasse. What it will do is to identify the general area where such a solution might be found. The larger question is whether Canadians have the will to search for, and in some sense to create, such a solution. The answer to this question depends on Canadians themselves. In such an exercise, no outcome is predetermined, and nothing is inevitable. If there is one comforting feature to the current situation, it is that the future of Canada will not be determined by the impersonal march of history, but instead will be written by the people of this country themselves.

Narrowing the Options

Since the failure of the Meech Lake Accord, commentators and experts on the Canadian constitution have outlined an impressive array of possible options for change.[15] In general terms, the options identified tend to fall into three broad categories or 'families.' The first family of options is some form of 'renewed federalism.' There are a whole variety of ways in which federalism might be reconfigured. What all of these federalist solutions have in common, however, is the continued existence of a national parliament that is directly elected, comprising representatives from all parts of the country.[16] A second group of options involves a confederal system. The common feature of all confederal systems is that there is no directly elected national parliament with powers to tax and regulate. There would be some kind of political 'superstructure' linking a sovereign Quebec with the rest of Canada, but this superstructure would not consist of directly elected representatives with the right to tax and regulate the citizens of Canada directly. An example of a confederal system is the proposal for 'sovereignty-association' advanced by the Parti Québécois in its 1979 White Paper. Under this proposal, Quebec and Canada were to negotiate certain common institutions. But these common institutions did not include a national parliament with power to legislate in both Quebec and Canada. The members of the 'community institutions' were to remain politically responsible to either the Parliament of Quebec or the Parliament of Canada. A third category of possible options involves outright independence for Quebec. Here there are no 'supranational' and permanent political institutions linking Quebec and the rest of Canada. The relationship between Quebec and Canada is no different from that between Quebec and any other independent country.

Aside from these general categories of options, commentators on the constitution have made a key distinction between negotiated solutions and unilateral solutions. Negotiated solutions are those achieved without a break in legal continuity. They are based on the existing procedures for constitutional change, as set out in Part V of the Constitution Act, 1982. Unilateral solutions, by contrast, assume a break in legal continuity. They involve an attempt by one of the parties to unilaterally 'jump outside' of the existing rules or procedures for constitutional change. They seek to effect change without reference to the existing formal legal rules governing such change.

This is a basic mapping of possible goals and the means available to achieve them. Considered in the abstract, there appears to be a mind-boggling series of possible options for the future of Canadian federalism. But the length of the possible menu of options is deceptive. The reality is that there are relatively few options or groups of options that are desirable or attainable.

The matter can be simplified quite dramatically by pointing out that any of the so-called confederal options, including 'sovereignty-association' between Quebec and Canada, are essentially non-starters. A number of considerations point towards this conclusion. The first such consideration is that any of these confederal options cannot be achieved within the current rules governing constitutional change. They require a break in legal continuity, in the form of a unilateral declaration on the part of the province of Quebec.

The basis for this proposition is relatively simple. In order for sovereignty-association to be negotiated, it is necessary to have two parties at the table. The first is Quebec, the second is the 'rest of Canada.' The basic problem is that the 'rest of Canada' does not exist. It only comes into existence the moment that Quebec declares its political independence. Until that happens, there is no political or legal entity known as the 'rest of Canada.' There is only 'Canada,' which consists of ten provinces and a federal government representing the people who reside in those ten provinces. Thus some form of unilateral declaration of independence by Quebec is a necessary precondition before negotiations over 'sovereignty-association' can even begin.

The reader might be prepared to concede this point, but want to know why this necessarily precludes negotiations on sovereignty-association *following* a unilateral declaration from Quebec. The reasoning here is somewhat more involved, but the conclusion is equally unambiguous. There are two basic reasons why sovereignty-association could not be negotiated after a unilateral declaration by Quebec. First, there will be no political support for any such negotiations, and thus they are unlikely to be even seriously pursued. Second, even if such negotiations were to be undertaken, they are certain to end in failure because of disagreements over the relative weight to be given to the province of Quebec in the new common institutions.

A review of the history of secession movements around the world over the past century and a half indicates that the circumstances and the scenarios associated with such movements are infinitely varied. There is, however, at least one constant factor that is observable in all such situations. This constant factor is the extreme difficulty in maintaining or rebuilding political ties following a unilateral declaration of independence. Once the situation has deteriorated to the point where one of the parties has actually declared its independence from the other, a decisive corner has been turned. At this point the only realistic avenue for containing the process of disintegration is the use of force. The idea of the parties sitting down at the negotiation table and amicably agreeing to rebuild a new political structure is essentially unheard of.[17]

The reasons are fairly obvious. If one of the units within a state believes it necessary to declare unilaterally its independence, the situation has obviously deteriorated to the point where there is a profound impasse in the positions that are being put forward. Moreover, the resort to a unilateral declaration of independence is unlikely to improve the political atmosphere. Instead, the resort to a unilateral declaration is likely to engender more bitterness and anger and reduce even further the likelihood of flexibility and bargaining compromise. In effect, any unilateral declaration by Quebec will probably preclude any serious negotiations over a new form of political association. There will simply not be the will on either side to pursue seriously this option. The focus of attention will shift to problems associated with disentanglement, rather than to ways to preserve some form of confederal association.

Suppose, however, that I am wrong in this conclusion. Assume that, contrary to all reasonable expectations, there is some attempt to re-create a confederal union between Quebec and Canada. Even if such an attempt is made, the negotiations will be unable to succeed. The basic problem confronting any such negotiations would be the status of Quebec within the new arrangement. The question is simply whether Quebec would have a veto over decisions taken by the central institutions? Quebec would certainly demand such protection, at least with respect to certain issues that might affect its 'fundamental interests.' Indeed, for Quebec to sacrifice a veto would represent a net loss over its *de facto* status within the current federal arrangements. But the rest of Canada would be unlikely to grant any such veto power, since it would produce the risk of deadlock and paralysis. The rest of the country would insist that decisions of the common institutions be subject to majority rule, with no veto granted to one of the parties to the arrangement.

An interesting parallel can be drawn with the Meech Lake negotiations over the amending formula. Quebec demanded a veto over any future constitutional amendments. The only way to grant a veto to Quebec was to grant a similar veto to all the other provinces. There was absolutely no willingness to grant a veto to Quebec alone. Yet the 'Meech solution' – granting a veto to everyone – cannot provide a successful resolution in negotiations designed to create new political institutions involving Quebec and Canada. The basic problem is that a system in which everyone had a veto would be a recipe for endless political deadlock. No decisions could ever be taken that threatened the interests of one of the constituent members of the association. Political institutions cannot function effectively on a day-to-day basis under a decision-rule requiring unanimous consent.

Any negotiations designed to establish a confederal union between Quebec and Canada would founder over this basic problem. Quebec would demand a veto over at least some of the decisions of the common institutions. But the rest of the country would be unwilling to grant any such veto right, given the unworkable nature of such a decision-rule. The foregoing analysis suggests that sovereignty-association, or indeed any kind of confederal arrangement between Quebec and the rest of Canada, is unacceptable.[18] Thus the 'second family' of possible options identified earlier is essentially eliminated from the map. What is interesting about this conclusion is that there appears to be a great deal of support within Quebec for some kind of confederal arrangement with the rest of Canada. Even the Allaire committee, which proposes to negotiate a new federal arrangement with Canada, assumes that the 'fall-back' position would be sovereignty for Quebec with confederal links with the rest of the country.[19] If the analysis I have presented is correct, any such arrangement is a political and legal impossibility.[20]

Thus the range of options is reduced to just two realistic possibilities. The first is some form of renewed federalism, achieved through negotiations based on the existing rules governing constitutional change. The second is complete independence for Quebec, without any formal political ties with the rest of the country, achieved through a unilateral declaration by the province of Quebec.

Let us turn our attention first to the latter option – outright political independence for the province of Quebec. It is evident, first of all, that the current rules for constitutional change make no provision for such a unilateral declaration of independence. Nor, in any event, could any Canadian political leader be seen to be negotiating the dismemberment of the country. But these constraints do not mean that Quebec would be unable to achieve legal independence from the rest of Canada. They simply mean that such independence could not be achieved under the existing legal regime. Independence for Quebec, in effect, requires the province to 'jump outside' of the existing rules for constitutional amendment through a unilateral declaration of independence. But, if Quebec does decide to take this fateful step, the fact that the declaration is not authorized by the existing constitutional rules will not prove decisive. The ultimate determinant of the validity of such a unilateral declaration will simply be whether it is effective or not. If the Quebec government can establish its independence in a *de facto* sense, it is only a matter of time before the courts recognize its legal validity.[21]

So, we can proceed on the basis that Quebec does have the option of 'jumping outside' the existing rules for constitutional change through some kind of unilateral declaration. The more interesting and important question is what the effects of such a declaration would be on Quebec as well as the rest of the country. The question is of particular interest because of the apparently widespread belief that Quebec independence might be achieved at a relatively low cost to average Canadians. We have already noted the fact that a majority of Canadians outside of Quebec believe that they would be no worse off, or even better off, if Quebec were to separate. Within Quebec, any discussion of the political and economic costs associated with a declaration of independence is regarded as 'fearmongering.' There is a general tendency to paint a fairly rosy picture of the costs and the consequences associated with Quebec independence. What are we to make of these optimistic predictions about the likely effects of Quebec's secession?

These optimistic predictions appear to vastly underestimate the instability and the very heavy costs that will certainly be associated with any unilateral attempt by Quebec to leave Canada. While any attempt to quantify the precise nature or extent of these costs is mere guesswork, it can safely be assumed that they will be massive, on a scale that has not been appreciated. It should also be remembered that these costs will be imposed on all Canadians in all regions of the country, not only within Quebec.

To the extent that the costs of Quebec secession have been discussed at all, the focus of attention has tended to be on highly visible questions such as the division of the national debt. Other commentators have noted that, if Quebec is required to launch its own currency, there will be a period of economic uncertainty that will be costly both in Quebec and in the rest of the country. These costs, while significant, are merely illustrations of a more general problem. We might term this the problem of dislocation. The modern Canadian state is all-pervasive, affecting the lives of all Canadians in direct or indirect ways on a daily basis. The activity of the state depends upon and, in turn, creates an intricate web of interlocking legal relationships, obligations, and dependencies. This web of legal relations and dependencies is like a vast cocoon encasing the existing structure of the state and insulating it from change. The moment you try to alter the structure of the state, you affect millions of people whose lives and expectations are premised on the continuation of the existing order of things. Those premises and those expectations are suddenly rendered obsolete.

Consider the vast scale of the possible dislocations that would be associated with the secession of Quebec. One out of every eight members of the Canadian labour force is employed directly by government. If the net is cast wider to include those employed by such organizations as hospitals, school boards, and universities, which are financed through government transfers, the figure rises to almost one in four members of the labour force either directly or indirectly on the public payroll.[22] Millions more are dependent on payments under one or more social programs for either all or a significant part of their income. It is estimated that about 15 per cent of all personal income in Canada is accounted for by such transfer payments.[23] Overall government expenditure in Canada totals over 45 per cent of the gross national product.

If Quebec is to leave Canada and form an independent state, then many of these existing legal relationships and obligations are going to have to change. Overnight, Canada will lose 25 per cent of its existing population. The complex web of legal relationships, obligations, and dependencies that have grown up around the existing Canadian state will have to be reevaluated. In many cases, there will have to be new arrangements and relationships constructed to replace those that are no longer viable. This type of change will produce dislocations across the country on a scale that has been largely unappreciated. To put the matter at its most basic, an employee whose life was organized on the basis that he or she was regularly to receive a cheque from the government will suddenly find that the cheque is no longer arriving. In turn, the lives of other family members and banks and local businesses who all depend, directly or indirectly, on the continuation of that stream of income will be affected.

It is impossible to estimate in advance the precise extent of the dislocations that would be produced by the secession of Quebec. The most that can be said with confidence is that political sovereignty for Quebec will mean that a significant part of the existing web of legal obligations, relationships, and dependencies that surround and encase the existing structure of government will no longer make sense. A new set of relationships will have to be devised to replace those that have become obsolete. But the process of redefining these relationships will produce very significant disruption and dislocation for millions of Canadians.

These dislocations are merely the direct and immediate impacts associated with a radical change in the nature of government. A wide variety of 'second-order' effects will be produced by the uncertainty associated with any attempt by Quebec to establish its sovereignty. There is likely to be a significant period of legal and political uncertainty as various contending governments and interests attempt to assert the primacy of their preferred legal regime. There will be uncertainties surrounding responsibility for economic and monetary policy, both inside and outside of Quebec. Quebec will likely be forced to launch its own currency and establish its credibility and viability in the international capital market. This uncertainty, in turn, will drive down the value of the Canadian dollar while causing interest rates to rise dramatically. Business and investor confidence will be eroded during this transition period, with associated declines in investment and economic activity generally. The net effect is likely to be a significant reduction in the average standard of living in Quebec as well as the rest of Canada, at least during the transition period.

While coping with these generalized disruptions and uncertainties, both Quebec and Canada will have certain political challenges to confront. For Quebec, the main challenge will be to establish the political legitimacy of the new regime. The extent of this challenge should not be underestimated. Even if the vast majority of Quebeckers support the declaration of sovereignty, there will be hundreds of thousands, and perhaps millions, of Quebeckers who will contest the validity of the declaration. While many of these can be expected to simply leave the province, there will presumably be significant numbers of residents, numbering in the tens of thousands, who will remain. These residents will refuse to accept the legitimacy of the new regime. This challenge to political legitimacy may be reflected in largely passive responses, such as individual non-compliance or attempted evasion of the orders of the regime. But the challenge could also take the form of more active forms of direct political action, such as demonstrations or organized non-compliance to government policy. It is also possible that organized economic interests may seek to utilize their economic power to challenge the legitimacy of the new Quebec state or to force a change in its policies.

The main point is that any new state of Quebec will face a very significant internal challenge to its basic legitimacy. Thus many of the new state's orders will be defied or its laws broken, while a significant proportion of its time and energy will have to be devoted to the securing of compliance. That is not to suggest that the Quebec government will lack the will or the ability to respond to the challenge. But it can be expected that the new Quebec state will have to resort to coercive measures – the use of force – if it is to establish its legitimacy. How much force will have to be used, and what political ramifications this action will entail, are difficult questions to answer in advance. At a minimum, however, it would appear that the situation will be very volatile, with a high potential for civil disorder.

The rest of the country would have different political problems to confront but arguably they are just as serious as those facing Quebec. The assumption in the rest of the country appears to be that things will carry on pretty much as they have in the past if Quebec were to leave. The situation will be analogous to that facing the Canadian Football League when the Montreal Alouettes franchise collapsed a few years ago. The league schedule was rewritten to reflect the loss of a team, but things carried on pretty much as before. The Grey Cup game continued to take place, as always, on the last Sunday in November. The assumption seems to be that the secession of Quebec will pose no greater problem to the rest of the country than the collapse of the Alouettes did to the CFL.

But this view simply fails to recognize the very significant potential for further unravelling of the Canadian state in the wake of Quebec secession. The first point to remember is that the moment Quebec leaves, the existing constitution becomes a dead letter outside of as well as inside Quebec. The existing constitution is premised on the existence of ten provinces and a national parliament elected by voters across the country. This constitution ceases to exist the moment one of the provinces ceases to be a part of the federation. There is no 'fall-back' position that clicks in automatically. The juridical entity known as 'Canada' disappears with the secession of Quebec. A new constitution must be created, literally from the ground up, to replace the old regime.

It might be argued that the task of building a new country out of the remaining nine provinces will be a relatively straightforward matter. Certainly there will be very strong political sentiment in favour of rebuilding that new 'Canada.' This sentiment will be reinforced by the realization that some form of reconstructed Canada is the only viable alternative to eventual absorption by the United States. But despite the undeniable strength of such sentiment, the task of creating a new Canada out of the ashes of the old will be anything but straightforward.

The fundamental problem facing Canada would be the economic and political dominance of the province of Ontario. Ontario already looms large within the existing federation; its size and impact on the decisions of the central government are the source of considerable resentment elsewhere. The exit of Quebec would only exacerbate the problems associated with the imbalance between the relative positions of Ontario and the other provinces. In a federation of the remaining nine provinces, Ontario would possess approximately half of the population and generate over 50 per cent of the economic activity. Moreover, the historical trends indicate that this imbalance will increase rather than decrease over time. The issue is whether stable and credible political institutions can be created in the face of such significant imbalances. The design of the central institutions of government would be bedevilled by the problem of how to deal with the preponderance of one of the units to the federation. Ontario, of course, would resist attempts to deviate from the basic democratic principle that political institutions should be responsible to the voters who elect them. The remaining provinces would seek to provide some kind of regional accountability in the decision-making process of the central government. It will be very difficult to create stable political institutions in the face of these competing political pressures.

These difficulties are not necessarily insurmountable. In the extremely fluid and volatile political environment that is likely to prevail, nothing should be ruled out in advance. But the idea that the rest of Canada would simply carry on as before in the absence of Quebec fails to take into account the very significant difficulties that will face the rest of the country. Moreover, the negotiations over the new federation would be dominated by the provincial governments, which would each assert a veto over the shape of the new political system. Even if these negotiations 'succeeded,' the most likely result is an extremely decentralized federation with limited powers for the federal government and a weakened commitment to interregional transfers. It is difficult to see what the concrete, practical advantages of such a form of government would be to certain parts of the new federation.

This analysis leads towards a more general conclusion about the viability and desirability of outright Quebec independence. There is no question that an independent Quebec would be 'viable' and that independence could be achieved through some form of unilateral declaration. But the costs associated with any such unilateral declaration are likely to be massive and largely unanticipated. These costs are not limited to any single region of the country, but will fall on the shoulders of Canadians in all provinces. History also teaches that a break in legal continuity sets in motion a chain of events that no one can control and that will lead in totally unpredictable directions. We are likely to end up with a much different political and economic situation from that we were promised in advance.

If confederal solutions are politically unattainable, and outright independence for Quebec is politically undesirable, we are left with some form of rebalanced federalism as the only other possible option. What assessment can we make of this final set of options for Canada's future?

Let me offer the following generalizations about the likely prospects and possibilities for achieving a federalist resolution to the current impasse.

1. *There is virtually no prospect of achieving a comprehensive constitutional amendment prior to the end of 1992. As such, the focus of discussion should be on the possibilities of achieving incremental, as opposed to comprehensive change.*

I have already indicated the factors militating against the possibility of achieving a comprehensive settlement of all outstanding constitutional claims. As the experience in Canada and elsewhere over recent decades makes evident, the chances of a negotiated agreement that would simultaneously settle all existing constitutional 'grievances' are minimal. Banting and Simeon's conclusion on this point bears emphasis: 'The more the amendment process is dominated by incumbent actors, and the closer the decision-rules lie to unanimity, the less will amendment be a device for fundamental change or the enshrining of new norms and values.'[24] Some have claimed that the experience in Philadelphia in 1787 or Charlottetown in 1864 could serve as a model for a constitutional convention designed to fundamentally rewrite the rules of the existing Canadian constitution. But the United States in 1787 and British North America in 1864 were radically different societies from the Canada of 1991. Those earlier societies were characterized by a low degree of complexity and political mobilization. The intervention of government in the economy was very rudimentary, which meant that interdependence between state and society was much less developed. This level of intervention promoted a situation in which élites could comprehensively design a new political order with little external opposition. But the political context of the eighteenth and nineteenth centuries is a far cry from the situation prevailing in Canada today. The dimensions of contemporary politics, with its complex web of interdependencies between state and society, severely limit the prospects for a repeat performance of the experience at Philadelphia or Charlottetown.[25] If there is to be a negotiated solution that maintains a federal framework, then it will necessarily be a solution that tries to move away from a comprehensive approach to the problem and seeks to achieve incremental solutions.

2. *There is no need to rewrite fundamentally the division of powers between the federal and provincial governments. The existing division of powers is flexible and is characterized by functional concurrency rather than watertight compartments. Rather than attempting to solve all problems through rewriting the constitution, we should reinstitute the boundary between constitutional politics and ordinary politics.*

The wording of the Constitution Act, 1867, speaks in terms of 'exclusive' areas of jurisdiction. The federal government is assigned exclusive jurisdiction over a specified range of subjects, while the provinces are assigned exclusive jurisdiction over a different list of subjects. The presence of these two lists of 'exclusive' powers promotes the impression that the division of powers is a series of 'watertight compartments.' In fact, precisely the opposite is the case. Judicial interpretation of the constitution has followed a flexible approach, permitting extensive overlap between the responsibilities of the federal and provincial governments. In virtually any important area of current government activity, both the federal and provincial governments operate in the field. Thus, as Peter Meekison has pointed out in a recent paper, important fields such as energy, consumer protection, the environment, and economic development are subject to regulation by both the federal and provincial governments.[26] Another example of the extensive concurrency that currently exists is illustrated by the proposals of the Allaire committee. The committee announced with considerable fanfare in January 1991 that a list of twenty-two 'exclusive' powers should be granted to the Quebec government. Since Quebec already exercises jurisdiction in twenty-one of these areas, the real change proposed by Allaire is to eliminate the role of the federal government in these areas of jurisdiction, rather than to increase the jurisdiction of Quebec.

Adding to the confusion on these issues is a breaking down of the distinction between ordinary politics and constitutional politics. Issues that can and should be dealt with through the normal political process are being thrust onto the constitutional agenda. The result is an increase in the demands and the pressure for a total rewriting of the constitution, in general, and of the division of powers, in particular. Consider the way in which the debate over the size of the federal deficit has recently been transformed into a constitutional issue. The Allaire report refers repeatedly to the size of the federal deficit as an illustration of the need for a fundamental reallocation of powers between the federal and provincial governments. Allaire argues that the size of the debt makes it imperative that the central government's powers be reduced dramatically and that constitutional limits be imposed on its powers to tax and spend. But the federal deficit did not arise because of anything in the constitution. Indeed, a comparative analysis would reveal that the trend towards large government deficits is an international phenomenon, not limited to Canada.[27] Thus it is misleading to attempt to pin responsibility for the deficit on the constitution. Moreover, it is naïve to believe that an amendment to the constitution could solve the problem. Indeed, legislators in the United States have found that attempting to control government deficits through quasi-constitutional limits simply shifts the problem into a different forum, without resolving it.

We need to restore some balance and perspective to our discussion of the constitution in this country. Few of Canada's problems are constitutional; even fewer of the solutions are to be found through rewriting the terms of the constitution. We have a workable and a working constitution that permits us to resolve most of our political problems through the normal processes of democratic decision making. If we lack the political will to confront and resolve some of these problems, we are only fooling ourselves if we attempt to pin the blame for that failure on the terms of the constitution.

3. *Instead of attempting to rewrite the division of powers, the goal should be to increase the flexibility and adaptability of the current scheme of constitutional responsibilities.*

As I have indicated earlier, it is possible to achieve very fundamental changes in the constitution without resort to formal constitutional amendments. There are a variety of mechanisms in the existing constitution that permit informal, non-constitutional adjustments to be made in the balance of power between the federal government and the provinces. These informal adjustments can nevertheless result in a significant shift of authority from one level of government to the other. Examples of these types of adjustments include constitutional conventions, ordinary legislation, and agreements between the federal and provincial governments.[28] These mechanisms have been employed, particularly over the past thirty years, to achieve a significant decentralization of power to the provinces without any formal amendment to the constitution.

There are, however, limits on the degree of flexibility that is present in the current system. One important limit is the fact that governments cannot directly delegate powers to each other. Another is that there is a limited number of fields in which jurisdiction is explicitly concurrent. It would be useful to expand the range of mechanisms that increase the flexibility in the division of powers. As Peter Meekison has argued, these mechanisms treat all the provinces equally in formal terms, while allowing for considerable variation in the *de facto* authority of individual provinces.[29] They also permit incremental change and the ability to make adjustments to suit changing political realities. Meekison identifies a total of seven mechanisms, some of which already exist in the constitution, that would promote this flexibility without conferring 'special status' on any particular province. This is a pragmatic, step-by-step approach to reconstituting the federation.

4. *To the extent that formal constitutional change is unavoidable, it should focus on proposals that treat Quebec in terms similar to those applied to other provinces. It should also address the aspirations of all regions of the country, rather than those of Quebec alone.*

The failure of the Meech Lake Accord has profoundly destabilized political support for Canadian federalism within the province of Quebec. It is evident that the only possible form of 'renewed federalism' that would be acceptable to the Quebec population is one that involves enhancements to Quebec's constitutional authority. However, public opinion in the rest of the country continues to run strongly in favour of the principle of the equality of the provinces. Sentiment on this point has, if anything, hardened in the aftermath of the failure of Meech Lake. Canadians outside of the province of Quebec have consistently indicated their opposition to any arrangement that would provide 'special' powers for the province of Quebec alone.[30]

This leads us an important conclusion. Any form of renewed federalism involving significant 'asymmetry' between the province of Quebec and the other provinces *in terms of the formal constitution* has absolutely no prospect of success. To put this another way, the only possible *federalist* resolution of Quebec's claims is through changes that place Quebec on the same footing as the other provinces.

A second important conclusion is that any type of renewed federalism, if it is to be credible, must be *seen* to be balanced. One of the basic problems with the Meech Lake Accord was that Ottawa was seen as giving up everything and receiving nothing in return. Thus a wholesale or massive decentralization of powers from Ottawa to the provinces will simply not wash. Any new arrangements will be credible only if they involve a rebalancing or realignment of roles between Ottawa and the provinces. The implication is that, if the provinces gain additional powers in some areas, the federal government must gain additional powers of its own in certain others. The 'rebalancing' cannot operate as a one-way street. The new federal structure must be seen to be a balanced redefinition of the roles of the federal and provincial governments.

What might such a 'rebalanced' federalism look like? In general terms, one base principle might be that provincial and local governments (including aboriginal governments) should have primary responsibility for most social- and cultural-policy issues. The reasoning behind this principle is that provincial and local governments are in the best position to give effect to the preferences of their citizens on these issues. Thus the provincial and local government role in health-care policy, educational policy, language policy, telecommunications, and social-welfare policy would be enhanced. This enhanced role for provincial and local governments need not necessarily involve constitutional amendments. Changes to legislation, to the structure of federal agencies, or to federal-provincial agreements might accomplish the same objectives in a much more direct and flexible manner. But presemably certain constitutional amendments could be included as part of a package of measures designed to increase provincial autonomy in defined areas.

A second base principle of a rebalanced federalism would be that the federal government should have an important and even a strengthened role in policy areas that implicate national interests. The most obvious examples of such policy areas are economic and environmental policy. These policies, unlike social and cultural policy, require national coordination and direction. The actions and policies of one region or province in the economic sphere have inevitable consequences for the rest of the country. Trade, investment, and monetary policy are most effectively managed at a national rather than a local level. Provincial attempts to restrict the free flow of trade between regions diminish overall economic welfare and require some form of national oversight. As for the environment, it is now commonplace that activity that harms the environment has a national, even an international, dimension and impact.

These two base principles suggest that the federal government should be prepared to consider enhancing the responsibility of the provincial and local governments, including governments established by the aboriginal peoples of Canada, for social and cultural policy. That does not necessarily imply a devolution of power from Ottawa to the provinces. Another possibility is joint decision making in which provincial input is provided for within national institutions. The provinces and local governments should be prepared to recognize the need for national institutions and national decision making in the framing of economic and environmental policy. One benefit of this approach is that the efforts of both levels of government in a given policy area might be coordinated, thereby reducing duplication or overlap in the administration of government programs.

5. *All outstanding constitutional issues need not be resolved at the same time or through a single process. It might be possible to establish individualized processes to deal with particular issues, such as Senate reform and aboriginal self-government.*

It is evident that the current round of constitutional discussions cannot focus on Quebec issues alone. A wide variety of other constitutional matters will have to be dealt with at the same time as any attempt to resolve Quebec's demands. But that does not mean that all these issues have to be dealt with through a single process. One of the virtues of the agreement between First Ministers signed on 9 June 1990 was that it attempted to disaggregate the various constitutional issues and reconfigure them into a more manageable form. There were a series of separate 'tracks' established to deal with the issues of aboriginal self-government, Senate reform, the creation of new provinces, and minority rights. The process and timing for these various tracks were quite varied. The advantage of this approach is that it 'delinks' constitutional issues from each other and demonstrates that progress can be achieved in incremental fashion.

6. *The government of Canada cannot be held hostage to the timetable or the demands of a single province. It should develop a set of proposals for a 'rebalanced' federalism according to its own timetable and present those proposals to the people of Canada.*

With the release of the Bélanger-Campeau commission report, the province of Quebec has attempted to establish an eighteen-month deadline for future talks on the constitution. If a 'new deal' is not reached within that time frame, Quebec will hold a referendum on sovereignty. But this approach of setting deadlines and delivering ultimatums will simply not work. This is the road we have already travelled during the three-year Meech debate. It did not work then, and it will not work now. Given the heightened tensions and bitterness following the failure of Meech, the effect of this strategy will be to lead Quebec out of Canada.

The only approach to this issue that stands a fair chance of succeeding is one that avoids artificial deadlines or the drawing of lines in the sand.

I will have more to say about the future process of constitutional reform in the next section of this chapter. For the moment, I would simply note that whatever proposals are eventually developed by the government of Canada will have to be put to the people of Canada directly in the form of a national referendum. Referenda are divisive and highly risky. They should be invoked only as a measure of last resort. But it now seems fairly clear that the province of Quebec will be voting on a referendum on sovereignty sometime in 1992. Faced with this threat to its very existence, the government of Canada simply cannot afford to sit on the sidelines. It will have to put its proposals for a rebalanced federalism to the people directly, on its own terms and according to its own timetable. The government of Canada should, of course, seek the cooperation of the government of Quebec as well as the other provinces in establishing the manner in which this consultation with the people ought to be undertaken. But the national government cannot allow itself to be held hostage to the terms or to the timetable of any single province. The people of Quebec and of Canada as a whole must be given the opportunity to make a clear choice between the real alternatives that are available to them.

Towards a Credible Constitutional Process

One of the greatest challenges in the wake of the failure of Meech Lake will be to devise a new process for negotiating amendments to the constitution. This new process will have to satisfy two quite distinct objectives. The first is that it must be credible. The decisions that are made and the compromises that are proposed must be seen to be politically legitimate within the wider Canadian community. The second objective is that the process must be workable. It must be a process that stands a reasonable prospect of actually achieving a negotiated solution to the various demands put on the table.

One suggestion that has been widely discussed is some form of constitutional convention. While the exact nature of this procedure is not entirely clear, it seems to involve bringing together individuals and groups from across the country, charged with the task of rewriting the country's constitution. Delegates to the convention might include representatives from various governments. But the idea appears to be to remove consciously the responsibility for rewriting the constitution from the hands of government and put it into the hands of 'the people.' The delegates to the constitutional convention would not be representatives of government, but rather would represent the various interests within the community as a whole. These representatives would then attempt to negotiate some new constitutional arrangements that would meet with general approval.

The problem with this approach is that it satisfies the first objective identified above but not the second. There seems little likelihood that any broad-based constitutional convention could actually lead to the ratification of a constitutional amendment. One reason is that such a constitutional convention makes sense only if what is contemplated is a total rewriting of the constitution. I have already indicated my pessimism about the prospects for achieving this type of comprehensive constitutional change.[31]

But a second problem attends the idea of convening a constitutional convention. The premise behind the idea is that it is necessary to remove the primary responsibility for constitutional negotiations from the hands of government and elected members of legislatures. I believe this is precisely the wrong approach. In my view, any workable process for constitutional renewal will have to recognize a key and central role for governments and members of legislatures. There are two reasons for this conclusion. The first is the entirely practical but unavoidable observation that the current amending formula requires the participation and consent of the federal and provincial legislatures. Given the fact that a change to the amending formula requires unanimous provincial consent, we can assume that the existing formula will continue to govern any future process. Thus it seems impractical to assign the responsibility for the negotiation of a constitutional amendment to some non-governmental and non-legislative body. There would be no guarantee that the proposals adopted by the constitutional convention would prove acceptable to all the provincial legislatures.

There is a second objection to the idea of a constitutional convention that is perhaps more fundamental. This second objection relates to the relative advantage enjoyed by governments and legislatures in the achievement of compromise solutions to complex political problems. It must be recognized in advance that any resolution of the current impasse will be extremely difficult precisely because it will require compromises and concessions from all Canadians. No one can expect to obtain everything he or she wants from the exercise, and everyone will be called upon to make important sacrifices in the interests of the country as a whole. Nor should we naïvely assume that such compromises will be quietly accepted by everyone who is affected by them. There will no doubt be various groups or interests who will reject the necessity of having to compromise *their* particular agenda or preferred solution.

The art of compromise is inherent in the business of government and legislatures. Governments and legislatures are driven to compromise because they must simultaneously attempt to give effect to the interests of all members of the political community. It is impossible to satisfy everyone's interests at the same time. Thus the only way for lawmakers to maintain broad-based support is to seek to achieve and implement political compromises. It is important to recognize that governments and legislatures are the only institutions that stand in this particular position and assume this particular responsibility. Corporations, trade unions, or various interest groups represent particular interests within the community. Government and legislatures alone are responsible to the community as a whole. These bodies *by definition* are committed to finding compromise solutions that meet the needs of the community as a whole.

Political compromise is not yet a lost art, but it threatens to become a disreputable one. Politicians are subject to constant criticism precisely because they put forward 'second-best' solutions to complex problems. The political process is often denounced because it is designed to 'make deals' rather than defend principles. But Canada in 1991 has no lack of those prepared to defend their constitutional principles. What it sorely needs is political leadership with the capacity and the courage to force a compromise between these competing principles. I believe that this objective will be best served if governments are recognized as continuing to have a special responsibility in the constitutional reform process. Governments are in the best position to be able to propose and to implement the significant compromises that the current constitutional impasse demands of all Canadians.

That does not mean that major renovations should not be undertaken to the process of constitutional reform. Quite clearly, there is an overwhelming desire and need for greater popular participation in the constitutional reform process. The question is how to achieve this greater participation and yet preserve a special and distinctive role for governments and legislatures.

Peter Russell, in his important work on this question, has offered a number of interesting suggestions as to how this compromise might be achieved.[32] First, Russell makes an important distinction between three separate stages of the constitutional reform process. The first stage involves public discussions; the second stage involves negotiations; the third stage involves ratification. Russell proposes that the second stage of the process should involve negotiations between delegations from the various provincial legislatures. The delegations would include representation from the governments as well as the opposition parties from each legislature. While Russell describes this procedure as involving a 'constituent assembly,' he also makes it clear that each provincial delegation would vote as a single unit. Russell also argues that there must be an opportunity for private negotiations, although a good part of the proceedings could be open to the public.

There is already some precedent for the type of approach Russell is proposing. At the meeting of First Ministers in June 1990, the Manitoba delegation included the two opposition leaders from that province, Sharon Carstairs and Gary Doer. Carstairs and Doer were included primarily because of the minority position of Gary Filmon's Conservative government. The opposition leaders were intimately involved in the negotiations leading to the final agreement signed on 9 June. In fact, some modifications were made in the final agreement in order to secure their support.

Russell's proposal would build on this experience by generalizing it to all the provinces as well as the federal government. Each delegation would include representation from all the parties in the provincial legislature. One advantage to this approach is that it provides for a greater representation of interests and constituencies without compromising the effectiveness of the process. A second advantage is that it seems to offer a solution to the problems posed by the three-year time period for ratification of constitutional amendments. As the Meech process demonstrated, the length of this time period meant that governments were likely to change during the ratification phase. Given the ordinary dynamic of parliamentary government, it is likely that a successor government might well reject or seek to modify a constitutional amendment that had been accepted by its predecessor. But this difficulty can be essentially eliminated if the opposition leaders are included in the negotiations in the first place, thereby ensuring that any negotiated agreement will be written in a way that is acceptable to both the government and the opposition in each legislature. A change in government will thus not represent the threat to ratification that was evident during the Meech process.

While there are advantages to Professor Russell's proposal, it seems to me that the chances of a positive outcome would be increased if the federal-provincial meeting were preceded by national hearings by a parliamentary committee. The fact remains that national parliamentary hearings have consistently been the best vehicle for building national consensus on constitutional issues. In 1972 a parliamentary committee produced a comprehensive series of recommendations for amendment to the constitution that reflected an all-party consensus. The parliamentary hearings on the proposed Charter of Rights in early 1981 helped to fashion an all-party as well as a national consensus in favour of the patriation package.

And the Charest committee put forward a credible and thoughtful set of proposals designed to resolve the impasse over the Meech Lake Accord in the spring of 1990.

A parliamentary committee would have representation from all parties and from all regions in the country. Appointed in the fall of 1991, it would be in a position to consider the recommendations of the various provincial commissions that have been appointed as well as the report from the Spicer Commission. Its mandate would be to develop a concrete and practical package of proposals that would reflect the interests of the country as a whole. This package of proposals could then be referred to a gathering of federal and provincial delegations along the lines proposed by Professor Russell.

If Meech Lake has taught us anything, it is the importance of building on our history rather than ignoring it. If history is to be our guide, the chances for fashioning some sort of compromise acceptable to all parts of the country are maximized through resort to a parliamentary committee. The other alternatives are untested and are unlikely to achieve any sort of compromise that is generally acceptable. Only a parliamentary committee can credibly and realistically fashion a set of proposals that could then be placed before the governments and the people of Canada for their consideration.

What of the third phase of the amending process, the ratification phase? The first question that arises is whether there should be an opportunity to propose amendments during the ratification phase. This was one of the most hotly contested issues during the Meech Lake negotiations. Governments were denounced for their unwillingness to consider amendments to the agreement after it had been negotiated. There was profound resentment arising from the fact that the agreement was presented as a package on a 'take it or leave it' basis.

As the analysis of this book indicates, there were in fact very sound reasons for this policy. There were two basic problems with opening the agreement to amendments after it had been signed. The first is that the agreement that was negotiated represented a fragile series of compromises and trade-offs. A subsequent attempt by one of the parties to reopen the agreement and ask for better terms would have effectively terminated the process.[33] Such is likely to be the case in any future agreement that involves trade-offs and concessions from all the parties.

The second problem with permitting amendments during the ratification phase relates to the lack of coordination between the various provincial legislatures. Each individual legislature would be in the position of drafting its own set of amendments without having any way of determining whether those amendments were acceptable elsewhere because each legislature is a self-contained and autonomous unit. There is no institution or mechanism for integrating the deliberations of individual legislatures with each other. Thus there would be no way of making the trade-offs that would be required in order to accommodate the concerns of each legislature simultaneously. Instead, the agreement would simply unravel as each legislature went off in its own separate direction, proposing amendments that met only the concerns of its particular constituency.

These factors combine to point towards an important conclusion about how the debate during the ratification phase ought to be structured. During the third and final phase of the reform process – the ratification phase – no amendments to any agreement that has been negotiated should be permitted. The only question for consideration during the ratification period should be whether the agreement should be accepted or rejected as a package.

This approach is not as novel as it might at first appear. There is ample precedent for this type of approach to the ratification of agreements. When international treaties are ratified by individual countries, for example, it is typically on the basis that the treaty must be considered as a package. There is normally no scope for individual countries to propose amendments at the ratification stage, particularly when the treaty involves a number of parties and there have been significant trade-offs involved in the negotiations. In fact, in the U.S. context there is explicit provision for the Senate to invoke a 'fast-track' procedure for the ratification of international treaties. Under the fast-track procedure, the treaty must be voted on as a package, without any opportunity for proposing amendments. My suggestion is that we should import this 'fast-track' procedure into the ratification phase of Canada's constitutional amendment formula. Any agreement that is negotiated must be considered and voted upon as a single package.

This bring me to my final suggestion for reforming the constitutional amendment process. Thus far, I have argued for ways in which the process must be structured so that it is workable. But this is merely one of the two important values I earlier identified as being important to the design of a future process. The other value is that of democratic legitimacy. Any future constitutional settlement must be seen to be the result of a democratic process that is endorsed by the people of Canada themselves. Unless this paramount consideration is kept firmly in mind, the whole exercise will be futile and counter-productive. In my view, there is really only one way to ensure that this democratic imperative is seen to be satisfied: it is to place any proposals for a rebalanced federalism before the people of Canada for ratification in the form of a national referendum.

Such an exercise is obviously fraught with risks. There is no guarantee that such a referendum would succeed. A negative answer would almost certainly increase the centrifugal forces that threaten to dismember the country. But the answer to this concern is that we are already confronting a perilous situation that threatens the life of the nation. The province of Quebec will be voting on a referendum on sovereignty in 1992. The bridge has already been crossed and there is no turning back.

A referendum is risky but it is also cleansing. It will provide us with the opportunity for a fresh start. If we endorse a vision of a new Canadian nationality, we will turn the page of history and provide the basis for moving forward into the twenty-first century. However, we might discover that there is no longer a basis for any such national renewal. If that is really the case, then it is better that we find out now rather than a few years from now. And at least there will be the satisfaction of knowing that this choice has been made by the people of the country themselves.

Canadians rarely give themselves the credit they deserve. Spread across a vast land, we have succeeded against all odds in building a set of free and democratic political institutions that have permitted us to flourish as a people. Now we are confronted by the greatest challenge we have yet encountered to our integrity as a nation. Perhaps the best and only place to find the answer to that challenge is in the hearts and minds of the ordinary men and women who have built this country and who must live with the consequences of the answer that is given.

Constitutional Chronology 1985–90

1985

3 March	Quebec Liberal party sets out five conditions for accepting 1982 constitution
17 May	Parti Québécois government of Quebec announces twenty-two conditions for accepting 1982 constitution
20 June	René Lévesque announces his retirement
26 June	Liberals, under David Peterson, form new government in Ontario
5 September	Macdonald Commission report recommends seeking Quebec's approval of 1982 constitution
2 December	Liberals, under Robert Bourassa, win Quebec election
13 December	Bourassa and Mulroney meet; agree to begin negotiations designed to secure Quebec's acceptance of 1982 Constitution Act

1986

6 March	Quebec ceases practice of automatically exempting all laws from the Charter of Rights
9 May	Gil Rémillard defines new government's conditions for accepting constitution
4 July	Mulroney appoints Senator Lowell Murray to conduct talks with provinces based on Quebec conditions
7 July	David Peterson states that Quebec demands for veto and for limits on federal spending will prove to be sticking-points in negotiations
21 July	Mulroney writes to premiers, proposing talks on Quebec proposals
12 August	Premiers issue Edmonton Declaration, identifying Quebec proposals as top constitutional priority

24 September	Lowell Murray and Gil Rémillard meet to discuss Quebec proposals
2 November	Federal Liberals in Quebec agree on a constitutional preamble recognizing the 'distinct character' of Quebec as the 'principal, but not exclusive source of the French language and culture in Canada'
20–21 November	First Ministers' conference in Vancouver reviews progress and authorizes continued discussions on Quebec's proposals

1987

5 March	First full federal-provincial officials' meeting on Quebec proposals
15 March	Federal NDP agrees to recognize Quebec's 'unique status' and its right to self-determination in a constitutional preamble
17 March	Mulroney invites premiers to Meech Lake for private meeting
26–27 March	Final required First Ministers' conference on aboriginal issues ends in failure
10 April	Mulroney writes premiers, setting out general federal approach at Meech Lake meeting and identifying the principal outstanding issues
15 April	Senator Murray writes premiers with specific federal proposals to be tabled at Meech Lake meeting
30 April	Agreement on principles achieved at Meech Lake
11 May	Meech Lake Accord is debated in House of Commons; all three major parties support the agreement
12 May	Quebec National Assembly begins public hearings on Meech Lake Accord
20 May	Federal-provincial officials meet in Ottawa to discuss draft legal text of agreement
27 May	Trudeau attacks Meech Lake in media
29–30 May	Second meeting of federal-provincial officials fails to achieve agreement on final legal text; issues in dispute are referred to First Ministers for 2 June meeting
2–3 June	Nineteen-hour meeting of First Ministers at Langevin Block produces agreement on legal text for an amendment
18 June	Gallup poll finds that 56 per cent of Canadians think the accord is a 'good thing for Canada,' 16 per cent think it not a good thing, and 28 per cent have no opinion

23 June	Quebec National Assembly ratifies the accord
4 August	Joint Senate–House of Commons Committee begins hearings on accord
28 August	Premiers' conference agrees not to reopen the accord
21 September	Senate-Commons committee recommends accord be ratified by Parliament
23 September	Saskatchewan ratifies the accord
13 October	Liberals, led by Frank McKenna, win New Brunswick election
14 October	McKenna calls election win 'broad mandate' to change or reject Meech Lake; promises public hearings
26 October	House of Commons ratifies the accord by vote of 242 to 16
7 December	Alberta ratifies the accord
18 December	Manitoba premier Howard Pawley, objecting to federal government decision to sign trade agreement with United States, announces that he will not ratify Meech agreement until after free-trade debate concludes; states that final vote on accord may not be held until sometime in 1989

1988

8 March	Manitoba government defeated in legislature; Howard Pawley resigns as premier and election is called for 26 April
17 March	New Brunswick premier Frank McKenna sets six conditions for ratifying Meech accord; meets with Premier Bourassa
30 March	Gary Doer selected as new leader of Manitoba NDP
18 April	Senate proposes amendments to accord
25 April	Saskatchewan approves bill overriding francophone rights
26 April	Conservatives, under Gary Filmon, win minority government in Manitoba elections; premier-elect Filmon states that he is in no hurry to ratify the accord, while opposition leader Sharon Carstairs announces 'Meech is dead'
28 April	Gallup poll finds support for accord has slipped to 28 per cent, with 25 per cent opposed and 47 per cent undecided
13 May	Prince Edward Island ratifies the accord
25 May	Nova Scotia ratifies the accord
22 June	Alberta introduces a bill limiting francophone rights House of Commons rejects Senate changes, ratifies the accord a second time by vote of 200 to 7
29 June	Ontario and British Columbia ratify the accord

7 July	Newfoundland ratifies the accord
21 July	Manitoba Speech from the Throne announces that Meech resolution will be presented for debate during upcoming legislative sitting
29 September	New Brunswick begins public hearings on the accord
1 October	Federal election called for 21 November; New Brunswick hearings on the accord suspended until 1989
21 November	Tories win federal election
15 December	Supreme Court strikes down Quebec sign law
16 December	Manitoba government introduces Meech Lake resolution, supported by the government
18 December	Bourassa announces that he will override the Supreme Court's decision
19 December	Filmon withdraws Meech resolution from Manitoba Legislature

1989

27 February	Meeting of the prime minister and nine premiers fails to resolve impasse over the accord
20 April	Liberals, under Clyde Wells, win Newfoundland election; Wells vows to rescind province's support for the accord
2 May	Manitoba public hearings on Meech Lake conclude; the overwhelming majority of participants oppose the accord
25 May	Newfoundland Speech from the Throne pledges to rescind support for the accord if changes are not made
22 June	Gallup poll finds 30 per cent support the Accord, 31 per cent oppose it, and 40 per cent are undecided
25 September	Bourassa re-elected with majority government in Quebec
16 October	Stan Waters wins election for vacant Senate seat in Alberta
18 October	Clyde Wells writes open letter to prime minister, specifying objections to the accord; states that Newfoundland will rescind support for the accord if these concerns are not addressed adequately
23 October	Manitoba task force tables report on Meech Lake; states that amendments must be made prior to the accord being ratified
24 October	New Brunswick legislative committee tables report on Meech Lake, recommending improvements to the accord
9 November	First Ministers' conference in Ottawa fails to resolve impasse over the accord; Wells agrees not to introduce rescinding motion immediately

1990

19 January	William Vander Zalm makes proposals designed to break the impasse over Meech; proposals would involve proclaiming part of the accord immediately and enacting a clause recognizing the distinct character of all ten provinces and territories
21 March	Frank McKenna introduces companion resolution into New Brunswick Legislature
22 March	Brian Mulroney announces that McKenna's resolution will be referred to Commons committee headed by Jean Charest
5 April	Quebec National Assembly passes resolution stating that Meech must be ratified unchanged
6 April	Newfoundland rescinds support for the accord
17 May	Charest committee recommends companion resolution involving amendments to the accord
19–22 May	Tour of provincial capitals by Senator Lowell Murray to test reaction to the Charest report
22 May	Federal environment minister Lucien Bouchard resigns in protest over Charest report
25 May	Clyde Wells writes open letter to Prime Minister Mulroney with specific amendments designed to address Newfoundland concerns
25–28 May	Prime Minister Mulroney meets with premiers individually at 24 Sussex in attempt to achieve consensus on federal proposals for a companion resolution
29 May	Senator Murray meets with Clyde Wells in St John's
3 June	First Ministers gather for dinner in Hull
4–9 June	First Ministers meet behind closed doors for six days in effort to resolve impasse
9 June	First Ministers all sign final communiqué committing them to seek a final decision on Meech prior to 23 June
15 June	New Brunswick ratifies the accord
22 June	Newfoundland and Manitoba legislatures adjourn without voting on the Meech Lake Accord

The Meech Lake Communiqué, 30 April 1987

At their meeting today at Meech Lake, the Prime Minister and the ten Premiers agreed to ask officials to transform into a constitutional text the agreement in principle found in the attached document.

First Ministers also agreed to hold a constitutional conference within weeks to approve a formal text intended to allow Quebec to resume its place as a full participant in Canada's constitutional development.

Quebec's Distinct Society

1) The Constitution of Canada shall be interpreted in a manner consistent with

   a) the recognition that the existence of French-speaking Canada, centred in but not limited to Quebec, and English-speaking Canada, concentrated outside Quebec but also present in Quebec, constitutes a fundamental characteristic of Canada; and

   b) the recognition that Quebec constitutes within Canada a distinct society.

2) Parliament and the provincial legislatures, in the exercise of their respective powers, are committed to preserving the fundamental characteristic of Canada referred to in paragraph (1)(a).

3) The role of the legislature and Government of Quebec to preserve and promote the distinct identity of Quebec referred to in paragraph (1)(b) is affirmed.

Immigration

– Provide under the Constitution that the Government of Canada shall negotiate an immigration agreement appropriate to the needs and circumstances of a province that so requests and that, once concluded, the agreement may be entrenched at the request of the province;

– such agreements must recognize the federal government's power to set national standards and objectives relating to immigration, such as the ability to determine general categories of immigrants, to establish overall levels of immigration and prescribe categories of inadmissible persons;

– under the foregoing provisions, conclude in the first instance an agreement with Quebec that would:

- incorporate the principles of the Cullen-Couture Agreement on the selection abroad and in Canada of independent immigrants, visitors for medical treatment, students and temporary workers, and on the selection of refugees abroad and economic criteria for family reunification and assisted relatives;
- guarantee that Quebec will receive a number of immigrants, including refugees, within the annual total established by the federal government for all of Canada proportionate to its share of the population of Canada, with the right to exceed that figure by 5% for demographic reasons; and
- provide an undertaking by Canada to withdraw services (except citizenship services) for the reception and integration (including linguistic and cultural) of all foreign nations wishing to settle in Quebec where services are to be provided by Quebec, with such withdrawal to be accompanied by reasonable compensation;

– nothing in the foregoing should be construed as preventing the negotiation of similar agreements with other provinces.

Supreme Court of Canada

– Entrench the Supreme Court and the requirement that at least three of the nine justices appointed be from the civil bar;

– provide that, where there is a vacancy on the Supreme Court, the federal government shall appoint a person from a list of candidates proposed by the provinces and who is acceptable to the federal government.

Spending Power

– Stipulate that Canada must provide reasonable compensation to any province that does not participate in a future national shared-cost program in an area of exclusive provincial jurisdiction if that province undertakes its own initiative on programs compatible with national objectives.

Amending Formula

– Maintain the current general amending formula set out in section 38, which requires that consent of Parliament and at least two-thirds of the provinces representing at least fifty percent of the population;

– guarantee reasonable compensation in all cases where a province opts out of an amendment transferring provincial jurisdiction to Parliament;

– because opting out of constitutional amendments to matters set out in section 42 of the Constitution Act, 1982 is not possible, require the consent of Parliament and all the provinces for such amendments.

Second Round

– Require that a First Ministers' Conference on the Constitution be held not less that once per year and that the first be held within twelve months of a proclamation of this amendment but not later than the end of 1988;

– entrench in the Constitution the following items on the agenda:

1) Senate reform including:
    – the functions and role of the Senate
    – the powers of the Senate
    – the method of selection of Senators
    – the distribution of Senate seats

2) fisheries roles and responsibilities; and

3) other agreed upon matters

– entrench in the Constitution the annual First Ministers' Conference on the Economy now held under the terms of the February 1985 Memorandum of Agreement;

– until constitutional amendments regarding the Senate are accomplished the federal government shall appoint persons from lists of candidates provided by provinces where vacancies occur and who are acceptable to the federal government.

The 1987 Constitutional Accord

Following is the text of the Constitutional Accord approved by the Prime Minister and all provincial Premiers on June 3, 1987, which provided the basis for submitting a resolution to Parliament and the provincial legislatures, seeking approval to the *Constitution Amendment, 1987.*

WHEREAS first ministers, assembled in Ottawa, have arrived at a unanimous accord on constitutional amendments that would bring about the full and active participation of Quebec in Canada's constitutional evolution, would recognize the principle of equality of all the provinces, would provide new arrangements to foster greater harmony and cooperation between the Government of Canada and the governments of the provinces and would require that annual first ministers' conferences on the state of the Canadian economy and such other matters as may be appropriate be convened and that annual consitutional conferences composed of first ministers be convened commencing not later than December 31, 1988;

AND WHEREAS first ministers have also reached unanimous agreement on certain additional commitments in relation to some of those amendments;

NOW THEREFORE the Prime Minister of Canada and the first ministers of the provinces commit themselves and the governments they represent to the following:

1. The Prime Minister of Canada will lay or cause to be laid before the Senate and House of Commons, and the first ministers of the provinces will lay or cause to be laid before their legislative assemblies, as soon as possible, a resolution, in the form appended hereto, to authorize a proclamation to be issued by the Governor General under the Great Seal of Canada to amend the Constitution of Canada.

2. The Government of Canada will, as soon as possible, conclude an agreement with the Government of Quebec that would

(a) incorporate the principles of the Cullen-Canada agreement on the selection abroad and in Canada of independent immigrants, visitors for medical treatment, students and temporary workers, and on the selection of refugees abroad and economic criteria for family reunification and assisted relatives,

(b) guarantee that Quebec will receive a number of immigrants, including refugees, within the annual total established by the federal government for all of Canada proportionate to its share of the population of Canada, with the right to exceed that figure by five per cent for demographic reasons, and

(c) provide an undertaking by Canada to withdraw services (except citizenship services) for the reception and integration (including linguistic and cultural) of all foreign nationals wishing to settle in Quebec where services are to be provided by Quebec, with such withdrawal to be accompanied by reasonable compensation.

and the Government of Canada and the Government of Quebec will take the necessary steps to give the agreement the force of law under the proposed amendment relating to such agreements.

3. Nothing in this Accord should be construed as preventing the negotiation of similar agreements with other provinces relating to immigration and the temporary admission of aliens.

4. Until the proposed amendment relating to appointments to the Senate comes into force, any person summoned to fill a vacancy in the Senate shall be chosen from among persons whose names have been submitted by the government of the province to which the vacancy relates and must be acceptable to the Queen's Privy Council for Canada.

Motion for a Resolution to Authorize an Amendment to the Constitution of Canada

WHEREAS the *Constitution Act, 1982* came into force on April 17, 1982, following an agreement between Canada and all provinces except Quebec;

AND WHEREAS the Government of Quebec has established a set of five proposals for constitutional change and has stated that amendments to give effect to those proposals would enable Quebec to resume a full role in the constitutional councils of Canada;

AND WHEREAS the amendment proposed in the schedule hereto sets out the basis on which Quebec's five constitutional proposals may be met;

AND WHEREAS the amendment proposed in the schedule hereto also recognizes the principle of the equality of all the provinces, provides new arrangements to foster greater harmony and cooperation between the Government of Canada and the governments of the provinces and requires that conferences be convened to consider important constitutional, economic and other issues;

AND WHEREAS certain portions of the amendment proposed in the schedule hereto relate to matters referred to in section 41 of the *Constitution Act, 1982*;

AND WHEREAS section 41 of the *Constitution Act, 1982* provides that an amendment to the Constitution of Canada may be made by proclamation issued by the Governor General under the Great Seal of Canada where so authorized by resolutions to the Senate and the House of Commons and of the legislative assembly of each province;

NOW THEREFORE the (Senate) (House of Commons) (legislative assembly) resolves that an amendment to the Constitution of Canada be authorized to be made by proclamation issued by Her Excellency the Governor General under the Great Seal of Canada in accordance with the schedule hereto.

Schedule

Constitution Amendment, 1987
Constitution Act, 1867

1. The *Constitution Act, 1867* is amended by adding thereto, immediately after section 1 thereof, the following section:

2.(1) The Constitution of Canada shall be interpreted in a manner consistent with — Interpretation

  (a) the recognition that the existence of French-speaking Canadians, centred in Quebec but also present elsewhere in Canada, and English-speaking Canadians, concentrated outside Quebec, constitutes a fundamental characteristic of Canada; and

  (b) the recognition that Quebec constitutes within Canada a distinct society.

(2) The role of the Parliament of Canada and the provincial legislatures to preserve the fundamental characteristic of Canada referred to in paragraph (1)(a) is affirmed. — Role of Parliament and legislatures

(3) The role of the legislature and Government of Quebec to preserve and promote the distinct identity of Quebec referred to in paragraph (1)(b) is affirmed. — Role of legislature and Government of Quebec

(4) Nothing in this section derogates from the powers, rights or privileges of Parliament or the Government of Canada, or of the legislatures or governments of the provinces, including any powers, rights or privileges relating to language. — Rights of legislatures and governments preserved

2. The said Act is further amended by adding thereto, immediately after section 24 thereof, the following section:

25.(1) Where a vacancy occurs in the Senate, the government of the province to which the vacancy relates may, in relation to that vacancy, submit to the Queen's Privy Council for Canada the names of persons who may be summoned to the Senate. — Names to be submitted

(2) Until an amendment to the Constitution of Canada is made in relation to the Senate pursuant to section 41 of the *Constitution Act, 1982*, the person summoned to fill a vacancy in the Senate shall be chosen from among persons whose names have been submitted under subsection (1) by the government of the province to which the vacancy relates and must be acceptable to the Queen's Privy Council for Canada. Choice of Senators from names submitted

3. The said Act is further amended by adding thereto, immediately after section 94 thereof, the following heading and sections:

Agreements on Immigration and Aliens

95A. The Government of Canada shall, at the request of the government of any province, negotiate with the government of that province for the purpose of concluding an agreement relating to immigration or the temporary admission of aliens into that province that is appropriate to the needs and circumstances to that province. Commitment to negotiate

95B.(1) Any agreement concluded between Canada and a province in relation to immigration or the temporary admission of aliens into that province has the force of law from the time it is declared to do so in accordance with subsection 95C(1) and shall from that time have effect not withstanding class 25 of section 91 or section 95. Agreements

(2) An agreement that has the force of law under subsection (1) shall have effect only so long and so far as it is not repugnant to any provision of an Act of the Parliament of Canada that sets national standards and objectives relating to immigration or aliens, including any provision that establishes general classes of immigrants or relates to levels of immigration for Canada or that prescribes classes of individuals who are inadmissable into Canada. Limitation

(3) The *Canadian Charter of Rights and Freedoms* applies in respect of any agreement that has the force of law under subsection (1) and in respect of anything done by the Parliament or Government of Canada, or the legislature or government of a province, pursuant to any such agreement. Application of Charter

95C.(1) A declaration that an agreement referred to in subsection 95B(1) has the force of law may be made by proclamation issued by the Governor General under the Great Seal of Canada only where so authorized by resolutions of the Senate and House of Commons and of the legislative assembly of the province that is a party to the agreement. Proclamation relating to agreements

(2) An amendment to an agreement referred to in subsection 95B(1) may be made by proclamation issued by the Governor General under the Great Seal of Canada only where so authorized

(a) by resolutions of the Senate and House of Commons and of the legislative assembly of the province that is a party to the agreement; or

(b) in such other manner as is set out in the agreement.

Amendment of agreements

95D. Sections 46 to 48 of the *Constitution Act, 1982* apply, with such modifications as the circumstances require, in respect of any declaration made pursuant to subsection 95C(1), any amendment to an agreement made pursuant to subsection 95C(2) or any amendment made pursuant to section 95E.

Application of sections 46 to 48 of Constitution Act, 1982.

95E. An amendment to sections 95A to 95D or this section may be made in accordance with the procedure set out in subsection 38(1) of the *Constitution Act, 1982*, but only if the amendment is authorized by resolutions of the legislative assemblies of all the provinces that are, at the time of the amendment, parties to an agreement that has the force of law under subsection 95B(1).

Amendments to section 95A to 95D or this section

4. The said Act is further amended by adding thereto, immediately preceding section 96 thereof, the following heading:

General

5. The said Act is further amended by adding thereto, immediately preceding section 101 thereof, the following heading:

Courts Established by the Parliament of Canada

6. The said Act is further amended by adding thereto, immediately after section 101 thereof, the following heading and sections:

Supreme Court of Canada

101A.(1) The court existing under the name of the Supreme Court of Canada is hereby continued as the general court of appeal for Canada, and as an additional court for the better administration of the laws of Canada, and shall continue to be a superior court of record.

Supreme Court continued

(2) The Supreme Court of Canada shall consist of a chief justice to be called the Chief Justice of Canada and eight other judges, who shall be appointed by the Governor General in Council by letters patent under the Great Seal.

Constitution of court

101B.(1) Any person may be appointed a judge of the Supreme Who may be Court of Canada who, after having been admitted to be bar of any appointed province or territory, has, for a total of at least ten years, been a judge judges of any court in Canada or a member of the bar of any province or territory.

(2) At least three judges of the Supreme Court of Canada shall be Three judges appointed from among persons who, after having been admitted to from Quebec the bar of Quebec, have, for a total of at least ten years, been judges of any court of Quebec or of any court established by the Parliament of Canada, or members of the bar of Quebec.

101C.(1) Where a vacancy occurs in the Supreme Court of Canada, Names may the government of each province may, in relation to that vacancy, be submitted submit to the Minister of Justice of Canada the names of any of the persons who have been admitted to the bar of that province and are qualified under section 101B for appointment to that court.

(2) Where an appointment is made to the Supreme Court of Appointment Canada, the Governor General in Council shall, except where the from names Chief Justice is appointed from among members of the Court, ap- submitted point a person whose name has been submitted under subsection (1) and who is acceptable to the Queen's Privy Council for Canada.

(3) Where an appointment is made in accordance with subsection Appointment (2) of any of the three judges necessary to meet the requirement set from Quebec out in subsection 101B(2), the Governor General in Council shall appoint a person whose name has been submitted by the Government of Quebec.

(4) Where an appointment is made in accordance with subsection Appointment (2) otherwise than as required under subsection (3), the Governor from other General in Council shall appoint a person whose name has been provinces submitted by the government of a province other than Quebec.

101D. Sections 99 and 100 apply in respect of the judges of the Tenure, salaries Supreme Court of Canada. etc., of judges

101E.(1) Sections 101A to 101D shall not be construed as abrogating Relationship to or derogating from the powers of the Parliament of Canada to make section 101 laws under section 101 except to the extent that such laws are inconsistent with those sections.

(2) For greater certainty, section 101A shall not be construed as References to abrogating or derogating from the powers of the Parliament of the Supreme Canada to make laws relating to the reference of questions of law or Court of Canada fact, or any other matters, to the Supreme Court of Canada.

7. The said Act is further amended by adding thereto, immediately after section 106 thereof, the following section:

106A.(1) The Government of Canada shall provide reasonable compensation to the government of a province that chooses not to participate in a national shared-cost program that is established by the Government of Canada after the coming into force of this section in an area of exclusive provincial jurisdiction, if the province carries on a program or initiative that is compatible under the national objectives. <small>Shared-cost program</small>

(2) Nothing in this section extends the legislative powers of the Parliament of Canada or of the legislatures of the provinces. <small>Legislative power not extended</small>

8. The said Act is further amended by adding thereto the following heading and sections:

XII – CONFERENCES ON THE ECONOMY AND
OTHER MATTERS

148. A conference composed of the Prime Minister of Canada and the first ministers of the provinces shall be convened by the Prime Minister of Canada at least once each year to discuss the state of the Canadian economy and such other matters as may be appropriate. <small>Conferences on the economy and other matters</small>

XIII – REFERENCES

149. A reference to this Act shall be deemed to include a reference to any amendments thereto. <small>Reference includes amendments</small>

Constitution Act, 1982

9. Sections 40 to 42 of the Constitution Act, 1982 are repealed and the following substituted therefor:

40. Where an amendment is made under subsection 38(1) that transfers legislative powers from provincial legislatures to Parliament, Canada shall provide reasonable compensation to any province to which the amendment does not apply. <small>Compensation</small>

41. An amendment to the Constitution of Canada in relation to the following matters may be made by proclamation issued by the Governor General under the Great Seal of Canada only where authorized by resolutions of the Senate and House of Commons and of the legislative assembly of each province: <small>Amendment by unanimous consent</small>

(a) the office of the Queen, the Governor General and the Lieutenant Governor of a province;

(b) the powers of the Senate and the method of selecting Senators;

(c) the number of members by which a province is entitled to be represented in the Senate and the residence qualifications of Senators;

(d) the right of a province to a number of members in the House of Commons not less than the number of Senators by which the province was entitled to be represented on April 17, 1982;

(e) the principle of proportionate representation of the provinces in the House of Commons prescribed by the Constitution of Canada;

(f) subject to section 43, the use of the English or the French language;

(g) the Supreme Court of Canada;

(h) the extension of existing provinces into the territories;

(i) notwithstanding any other law or practice, the establishment of new provinces; and

(j) an amendment to this Part.

10. Section 44 of the said Act is repealed and the following substituted therefor;

44. Subject to section 41, Parliament may exclusively make laws amending the Constitution of Canada in relation to the executive government of Canada or the Senate and House of Commons. *Amendments by Parliament*

11. Subsection 46(1) of the said Act is repealed and the following substituted therefor:

46.(1) The procedures for amendment under sections 38, 41 and 43 may be initiated either by the Senate or the House of Commons or by the legislative assembly of a province. *Initiation of amendment procedures*

12. Subsection 47(1) of the said Act is repealed and the following substituted therefor:

47.(1) An amendment to the Constitution of Canada made by proclamation under section 38, 41 or 43 may be made without a resolution of the Senate authorizing the issue of the proclamation if, within one hundred and eighty days after the adoption by the House of Commons of a resolution authorizing its issue, the Senate has not adopted such a resolution and if, at any time after the expiration of that period, the House of Commons again adopts the resolution. *Amendments without Senate resolution*

13. Part VI of the said Act is repealed and the following substituted therefor:

PART VI

CONSTITUTIONAL CONFERENCES

50.(1) A constitutional conference composed of the Prime Minister Constitutional
of Canada and the first ministers of the provinces shall be convened conference
by the Prime Minister of Canada at least once each year, commencing
in 1988.

(2) The conferences convened under subsection (1) shall have Agenda
included on their agenda the following matters:

(a) Senate reform, including the role and functions of the Senate,
its powers, the method of selecting Senators and representation in
the Senate;

(b) roles and responsibilities in relation to fisheries; and

(c) such other matters as are agreed upon.

14. Subsection 52(2) of the said Act is amended by striking out the word
'and' at the end of paragraph (b) thereof, by adding the word 'and' at
the end of paragraph (c) thereof and by adding thereto the following
paragraph:

(d) any other amendment to the Constitution of Canada.

15. Section 61 of the said Act is repealed and the following substituted
therefor:

61. A reference to the *Constitution Act 1982*, or a reference to the References
Constitution Acts 1867 to 1982, shall be deemed to include a reference
to any amendments thereto.

General

16. Nothing in section 2 of the *Constitution Act, 1867* affects section 25
or 27 of the *Canadian Charter of Rights and Freedoms*, section 35 of the
Constitution Act, 1982 or class 24 of section 91 of the *Constitution Act,
1867*.

CITATION

17. This amendment may be cited as the *Constitution Amendment, 1987.* Citation

1990 Constitutional Agreement

(Final Communiqué, First Ministers' Meeting
on the Constitution, 9 June 1990)

WHEREAS on April 30, 1987, the Prime Minister of Canada and the Premiers reached agreement in principle on means to bring about the full and active participation of Quebec in Canada's constitutional evolution;

AND WHEREAS on June 3, 1987, all first ministers signed the 1987 Constitutional Accord and committed themselves to introducing as soon as possible the *Constitutional Amendment, 1987* in Parliament and the provincial legislative assemblies;

AND WHEREAS the *Constitution Amendment, 1987* has been authorized by Parliament and the legislative assemblies of Quebec, Saskatchewan, Alberta, Prince Edward Island, Nova Scotia, Ontario and British Columbia:

1. THE MEECH LAKE ACCORD

The Premiers of New Brunswick, Manitoba and Newfoundland undertake to submit the *Constitution Amendment, 1987* for appropriate legislative or public consideration and to use every possible effort to achieve decision prior to June 23, 1990.

2. SENATE REFORM

After proclamation, the federal government and the provinces will constitute a commission with equal representation for each province and an appropriate number of territorial and federal representatives to conduct hearings and to report to Parliament and the legislative assemblies of the provinces and territories, prior to the First Ministers' Conference on the Senate to be held by the end of 1990 in British Columbia, on specific proposals for Senate reform that will give effect to the following objectives:
– The Senate should be elected.

- The Senate should provide for more equitable representation of the less populous provinces and territories.
- The Senate should have effective powers to ensure the interests of residents of the less populous provinces and territories figure more prominently in national decision-making, reflect Canadian duality and strengthen the Government of Canada's capacity to govern on behalf of all citizens, while preserving the principle of the responsibility of the Government to the House of Commons.

Following proclamation of the Meech Lake Accord, the Prime Minister and all Premiers agree to seek adoption of an amendment on comprehensive Senate reform consistent with these objectives by July 1, 1995.

The Prime Minister undertakes to report semi-annually to the House of Commons on progress achieved towards comprehensive Senate reform.

The Prime Minister and all Premiers, reaffirming the commitment made in the Edmonton Declaration and the provisions to be entrenched under the *Constitution Amendment, 1987*, undertook that Senate reform will be the key constitutional priority until comprehensive reform is achieved.

If, by July 1, 1995, comprehensive Senate reform has not been achieved according to the objectives set out above under section 41 of the *Constitution Act, 1982*, as amended by the *Constitution Amendment, 1987*, the number of Senators by which a province is entitled to be represented in the Senate will be amended so that, of the total of one hundred and four Senators, the representation of Ontario will be eighteen Senators, the representation of Nova Scotia, New Brunswick, British Columbia, Alberta, Saskatchewan, Manitoba and Newfoundland will be eight Senators each, and the representation of all other provinces and the territories will remain unchanged. In the case of any province whose representation declined, no new appointments would be made until that province's representation had by attrition declined below its new maximum. In the event of such a redistribution of Senate seats, Newfoundland would be entitled to another Member of Parliament in the House of Commons under section 51A of the *Constitution Act, 1867*.

3. FURTHER CONSTITUTIONAL AMENDMENTS

(1) *Charter – Sex Equality Rights*
- Add section 28 of the *Canadian Charter of Rights and Freedoms* to section 16 of the *Constitution Amendment, 1987*.

(2) *Role of Territories*
- In appointments to the Senate and the Supreme Court of Canada.
- In discussions on items on the agenda of annual constitutional and economic conferences where, in the view of the Prime Minister, matters to be discussed directly affect them.

(3) *Language Issues*
- Add to the agenda of constitutional conferences matters that are of interest to English-speaking and French-speaking linguistic minorities.
- Require resolutions of the House of Commons, the Senate and the legislative assembly of New Brunswick to amend that province's *Act Recognizing the Equality of the Two Official Linguistic Communities in New Brunswick* (Bill 88).

(4) *Aboriginal Constitutional Issues*
- First Ministers' constitutional conferences to be held once every three years, the first to be held within one year of proclamation; representatives of aboriginal peoples and the territorial governments to be invited by the Prime Minister to participate in the discussion of matters of interest to the aboriginal peoples of Canada.

The Prime Minister of Canada will lay or cause to be laid before the Senate and House of Commons, and the Premiers will lay or cause to be laid before their legislative assemblies, a resolution, in the form appended hereto, and will seek to authorize a proclamation to be issued by the Governor General under the Great Seal of Canada to amend the Constitution of Canada as soon as possible after proclamation of the *Constitutional Amendment, 1987.*

4. AGENDA FOR FUTURE CONSTITUTIONAL DISCUSSIONS

(1) *Creation of New Provinces in the Territories*
The Prime Minister and all Premiers agreed future constitutional conferences should address available options for provincehood, including the possibility that, at the request of the Yukon and Northwest Territories to become provinces, only a resolution of the House of Commons and Senate be required.

2. *Constitutional Recognitions*
The Prime Minister and Premiers took note of repeated attempts by First Ministers over the past twenty years to draft a statement of constitutional recognitions. All such attempts were unsuccessful.

The Prime Minister and Premiers reviewed drafts submitted by the federal government and Manitoba, Saskatchewan, Ontario and British Columbia, and agreed to refer immediately the drafts to an all-party Special Committee of the House of Commons. Public hearings would begin across Canada on July 16, 1990 and a report on the substance and placement of the clause – in a manner consistent with the Constitution of Canada – would be prepared for considera-tion by First Ministers at their Conference in 1990.

(3) *Constitutional Reviews*
The Prime Minister and all Premiers agreed jointly to review, at the constitutional conference required by section 49 of the *Constitution Act, 1982*, the entire process of amending the Constitution, including the three-year time limit under section

39(2) of that Act and the question of mandatory public hearings prior to adopting any measure related to a constitutional amendment, including revocation of a constitutional resolution.

Pursuant to section 50 of the *Constitution Act, 1982*, as proposed in the *Constitution Amendment, 1987*, the Prime Minister and the Premiers also committed to a continuing review of the operation of the Constitution of Canada, including the *Canadian Charter of Rights and Freedoms*, with a view to making any appropriate constitutional amendments.

5. SECTION 2: CONSTITUTIONAL AMENDMENT, 1987

The Prime Minister and Premiers took note of public discussion of the distinct society clause since its inclusion in the Meech Lake Accord. A number of Canada's most distinguished constitutional authorities met to exchange views on the legal impact of the clause. The Prime Minister and Premiers reviewed their advice and other material.

The Prime Minister, in his capacity as chairman of the Conference, received from the above-noted constitutional authorities a legal opinion which is appended to the final Conference communiqué.

6. NEW BRUNSWICK AMENDMENT

– Add a clause that within New Brunswick, the English linguistic community and the French linguistic community have equality of status and equal rights and privileges.
– Affirm an additional role of the legislature and government of New Brunswick: to preserve and promote the equality of status and equal rights and privileges of the province's two official linguistic communities.

The Prime Minister of Canada will lay or cause to be laid before the Senate and House of Commons, and the Premier of New Brunswick will lay or cause to be laid before the legislative assembly of New Brunswick, a resolution, in the form appended hereto, and will seek to authorize a proclamation to be issued by the Governor General under the Great Seal of Canada to amend the Constitution of Canada as soon as possible after proclamation of the *Constitution Amendment, 1987*.

Signed at Ottawa,
June 9, 1990

Fait à Ottawa
le 9 juin 1990

Canada

Ontario

Québec

Nova Scotia
Nouvelle-Écosse

New Brunswick
Nouveau-Brunswick

Manitoba*

* Subject to the public
hearing process

* Sous réserve du processus
d'audiences publiques

British Columbia
Colombia-Britannique

Prince Edward Island
Île-du-Prince-Édouard

Saskatchewan

Alberta

Newfoundland*
Terre-Neuve

* The Premier of Newfoundland endorses
now the undertaking in Part I of this
document and further undertakes to
endorse fully this agreement if the
Constitutional Amendment, 1987 is given
legislative or public approval following
the consultation provided for in Part I.

* Le premier ministre de Terre-Neuve
endosse maintenant l'engagement
figurant dans la Partie I de présent
document et s'engage en outre à
endosser la totalité de la présente
entente si la *Modification constitutionnelle
de 1987* reçoit une approbation
législative ou publique à Terre-Neuve
suite aux consultations prévues à la
Partie I.

Motion for a Resolution to authorize an amendment
to the Constitution of Canada

The (Senate) (House of Commons) (legislative assembly) resolves that an amendment to the Constitution of Canada be authorized to be made by proclamation issued by His Excellency the Governor General under the Great Seal of Canada in accordance with the schedule hereto, but only after the *Constitution Amendment, 1987* comes into force.

Schedule

Constitution Amendment

Part I
Constitution Act, 1867

1. Section 25 of the *Constitution Act, 1867*, as enacted by section 2 of the *Constitution Amendment, 1987*, is amended by adding thereto, immediately after the word 'province' wherever it occurs therein, the words 'or territory.'

2.(1) Subsection 101C(1) of the said Act, as enacted by section 6 of the *Constitution Amendment, 1987*, is amended by adding thereto, immediately after the word 'province' wherever it occurs therein, the words 'or territory.'

(2) Subsection 101C(4) of the said Act, as enacted by section 6 of the *Constitution Amendment, 1987*, is amended by adding thereto, immediately after the word 'province' where it occurs therein, the words 'or territory.'

3. Section 148 of the said Act, as enacted by section 8 of the *Constitution Amendment, 1987*, is renumbered as subsection 148(1) and is further amended by adding thereto the following subsection:

'(2) The Prime Minister of Canada shall invite elected representatives of the governments of the Yukon Territory and the Northwest Territories to participate in the discussion on any item on the agenda of a conference convened under subsection (1) that, in the opinion of the Prime Minister, directly affects the Yukon Territory and the Northwest Territories.' *Participation of Territories*

Constitution Act, 1982

4. Section 43 of the *Constitution Act, 1982* is renumbered as subsection 43(1) and is further amended by adding thereto the following subsection:

'(2) An amendment to the Act of the Legislature of New Brunswick entitled *An Act Recognizing the Equality of the Two Official Linguistic Communities in New Brunswick*, chapter 0–1.1 of the Acts of New Brunswick, 1981, may be made by proclamation issued by the Governor General under the Great Seal of Canada only where so authorized by resolutions of the Senate and House of Commons and of the Legislative Assembly of New Brunswick.' Amendment to New Brunswick Act

5.(1) Subsection 50(2) of the said Act, as enacted by section 13 of the *Constitution Amendment, 1987*, is amended by adding thereto, immediately after paragraph (a) thereof, the following paragraph:

'(a.1) matters of interest to English-speaking and French-speaking linguistic minorities';

(2) Section 50 of the said Act, as enacted by section 13 of the *Constitution Amendment, 1987*, is further amended by adding thereto the following subsection:

'(3) The Prime Minister of Canada shall invite elected representatives of the governments of the Yukon Territory and the Northwest Territories to participate in the discussions on any item on the agenda of a conference convened under subsection (1) that, in the opinion of the Prime Minister, directly affects the Yukon Territory and the Northwest Territories.' Participation of the Territories

6. The said Act is further amended by adding thereto, immediately after section 50 thereof, as enacted by section 13 of the *Constitution Amendment, 1987*, the following section:

'51.(1) A constitutional conference composed of the Prime Minister of Canada and the first ministers of the provinces shall be convened by the Prime Minister of Canada within one year after this Part comes into force and at least once every third calendar year after the first such conference is convened. Constitutional conference

(2) Each conference convened under subsection (1) shall have included in its agenda matters of interest to the aboriginal peoples of Canada, and the Prime Minister of Canada shall invite representatives of those peoples to participate in the discussions on those matters. Participation of aboriginal peoples

(3) The Prime Minister of Canada shall invite elected representatives of the governments of the Yukon Territory and the Northwest Participation of Territories

Territories to participate in the discussions on any item on the agenda of a conference convened under subsection (1) that, in the opinion of the Prime Minister, directly affects the Yukon Territory and the Northwest Territories.

(4) Nothing in this section shall be construed so as to derogate from section 35.' *Non-derogation*

Constitution Amendment, 1987

7. Section 16 of the *Constitution Amendment, 1987* is amended by adding thereto, immediately after the reference to section 27 where it occurs therein, the following: 'or 28.'

Part II
Constitution Act, 1867

8. All that portion of section 22 of the *Constitution Act, 1867* following item 4 and preceding the last paragraph thereof is repealed and the following substituted therefor:

'which Four Divisions shall, subject to the provisions of this Act, be represented in the Senate as follows: Ontario by *eighteen* Senators; Quebec by twenty-four Senators; the Maritime Provinces and Prince Edward Island by *twenty* Senators, *eight* thereof representing Nova Scotia, *eight* thereof representing New Brunswick, and four thereof representing Prince Edward Island; the Western Provinces by *thirty-two* Senators, *eight* thereof representing Manitoba, *eight* thereof representing British Columbia, *eight* thereof representing Saskatchewan, and *eight* thereof representing Alberta; Newfoundland shall be entitled to be represented in the Senate by *eight* members; the Yukon Territory and the Northwest Territories shall be entitled to be represented in the Senate by one member each.'

9. Section 27 of the said Act is repealed and the following substituted therefor:

'27. In case of such addition being at any time made, the Governor General shall not summon any person to the Senate, except on a further like direction by the Queen on the like recommendation, to *Reduction of Senate to normal number*

represent one of the Four Divisions until such Division is represented by *the number of Senators provided for by section 22* and no more.'

10. Notwithstanding section 22 of the *Constitution Act, 1867*, any province that is represented in the Senate on the coming into force of this *Transitional provision*

Part by more Senators than are provided for under that section may continue to be so represented, but no additional persons may be summoned to the Senate to represent that province until the number of Senators representing that province falls below the number set out in section 22, and thereafter, subject to section 26, the number representing that province shall not exceed that number.

11.(1) This Part shall not come into force if an amendment in relation to the Senate that is consistent with the objectives set out in the *1990 Constitution Agreement* signed at Ottawa on June 9, 1990 is made before July 1, 1995.

(2) If an amendment described in subsection (1) is not made before July 1, 1995, this Part shall come into force on that date.

CITATION

12. This amendment may be cited as the *Constitution Amendment, (year of Citation proclamation)*.

A Note on Sources

This book is based on my observations and recollections of the Meech Lake process from July 1986 until June 1990. From July 1986 until March 1989 I was senior policy adviser to the Honourable Ian Scott, attorney general of Ontario. From March 1989 until September 1990, I was senior policy adviser to the Honourable David Peterson, the premier of Ontario.

Since the book does not focus on my own role in the events I describe, I believe it important to set out here in a more precise way the nature of my participation in the Meech Lake process.

I attended the meeting held on 20 October 1986 between Ian Scott and Gil Rémillard, and my account of that meeting is based on notes taken at the time. I also attended the meeting held on 4 December 1986 between Ian Scott and Senator Lowell Murray in Senator Murray's office in Ottawa.

I attended the meeting between Ian Scott and Gil Rémillard on 27 April 1987 in Quebec City that is described in chapter 4. I also attended the dinner meeting on 27 April 1987 between Lowell Murray, Norman Spector, and Ian Scott held at Rideau Gate in Ottawa. During this dinner meeting the overall progress in the negotiations was reviewed and the federal strategy for the meeting on 30 April was discussed at some length.

I attended the meeting held at Meech Lake on 30 April 1987. As my account in chapter 4 indicates, the provincial advisers were restricted to the first floor of Willson House for the duration of the meeting. Thus my primary source of information regarding that meeting is Premier David Peterson. However, my reconstruction of that meeting is also based on numerous conversations with officials from other governments held at the time or shortly thereafter. Of particular significance were the meetings held in May 1987 in which federal and provincial officials attempted to transform the agreement in principle of 30 April into a formal legal text. At those meetings, officials discussed the manner in which the agreement of 30 April had been negotiated. My account of the Meech Lake meeting has also benefited from interviews with Norman Spector in the fall of 1990.

I attended the meetings of officials that took place in Ottawa on 20 May and 29 May 1987. I also attended the nineteen-hour meeting of First Ministers held on 2–3 June 1987. Again, my account of that meeting is based primarily on discussions held during the meeting or shortly thereafter with David Peterson. However, I also held very extensive discussions with officials from other provinces both during the meeting itself and in the weeks immediately following it. I was one of the Ontario officials assigned the task of attempting to negotiate some kind of accommodation with the province of Quebec during the Langevin meeting itself. I was also one of the Ontario officials invited into the meeting of First Ministers at approximately 3:00 a.m. on 3 June 1987 to discuss the impact of the distinct-society clause on the Charter of Rights. Finally, my account of the Langevin meeting has benefited from interviews with Norman Spector, Roger Tassé, and Peter Hogg held in late 1990 and early 1991.

With respect to the meeting of First Ministers in June 1990, throughout that week I was in a large committee room immediately adjacent to the meeting room of the First Ministers. Officials from all provinces were located in the same room. First Ministers would emerge periodically from the meeting to brief their respective teams of officials. This information tended to circulate throughout the committee room on a fairly continuous basis. By the end of the week, the divisions between the various delegations in the room had blurred, and most provinces traded information back and forth quite freely. Thus my account of that week's events is based on briefings provided by David Peterson to the Ontario delegation, as well as on numerous conversations with officials from all other provinces and the federal government held over the course of the week.

Notes

Foreword

1 In Ronald L. Watts and Douglas M. Brown, eds., *Options for a New Canada* (Toronto: University of Toronto Press 1991), 53–76.

Preface

1 See *A Deal Undone: The Making and Breaking of the Meech Lake Accord* (Vancouver: Douglas & McIntyre 1990), 4.

Chapter 1

1 For an excellent summary and discussion of the criticisms of the Meech Lake process, see Andrew Cohen, *A Deal Undone: The Making and Breaking of the Meech Lake Accord* (Vancouver: Douglas and McIntyre 1990), 270–7.
2 Pierre Trudeau, 'Say Goodbye to the Dream of One Canada,' *Toronto Star*, 27 May 1987, A1, A12.

Chapter 2

1 As reported in the *Globe and Mail*, Toronto, 16 April 1982, p. 10.
2 Quoted in R. Sheppard and M. Valpy, *The National Deal: The Fight for a Canadian Constitution* (Toronto: Fleet Books 1982), 317–18.
3 See *A.G. Quebec* v. *A.G. Can.* [Quebec Veto case] [1982] 2 SCR 793. The Supreme Court confirmed that the constitution had full legal force in the province of Quebec and that the decision to patriate the constitution did not violate any of the 'conventions' or unwritten rules of the constitution. The Court's analysis on 'conventions' is not particularly persuasive, given its reasoning in the Patriation Appeal in September 1981. In the Patriation

Appeal, the Court had relied on precedents in which the objection of Quebec alone had blocked a constitutional amendment.

4 See 'Say Goodbye to the Dream of One Canada,' in R. Gibbins, ed., *Meech Lake and Canada: Perspectives from the West* (Edmonton: Academic Print and Pub. 1988), 65–71. For similar arguments, see B. Schwartz, *Fathoming Meech Lake* (Winnipeg: Legal Research Institute of the University of Manitoba 1987), 205–12, and George Radwanski, 'Meech Lake Accord said dangerous, unnecessary to the unity of our nation,' *Toronto Star*, 25 August 1987.

5 Trudeau, in 'Say Goodbye to the Dream . . .,' 69.

6 Ibid., 70.

7 For a handy summary of the positions taken by the Quebec government in the constitutional debates of the 1960s and 1970s, see 'Constitutional Reform and the Traditional Claims of Quebec: Main Points,' Federal-Provincial Conference of First Ministers on the Constitution, Document 800-10/034, Ottawa, 5–6 February 1979.

8 See Lowell Murray, 'Trudeau one who bungled,' *Globe and Mail*, Toronto, 30 May 1987, p. 1. This article by Senator Murray sets out the extent to which the terms of the Meech Lake Accord had been proposed by previous federal governments led by Pierre Trudeau.

9 Speech by Trudeau at Paul Sauvé Arena, 16 May 1980, quoted in Sheppard and Valpy, *The National Deal*, 33.

10 See Trudeau, 'Say Goodbye to the Dream . . .,' 71: 'with the assurance of a creative equilibrium between the provinces and the federal government, the federation was set to last a thousand years.'

11 See Royal Commission on the Economic Union and Development Prospects for Canada, *Summary of Conclusions and Recommendations* (Ottawa: Minister of Supply and Services Canada 1985), 53–4.

12 'Quebec's turn on the Constitution' [editorial], *Toronto Star*, 9 August 1986, B2.

13 See Trudeau, 'Say Goodbye to the Dream . . .,' 70.

14 See 'Federal Statements in the Quebec Constitutional Issue,' Office of the Prime Minister, Ottawa, 1987 ['Annex,' 1, for reproduction of extracts from speech of 6 August 1984].

15 For a copy of the text of the speech, see Peter Leslie, *Rebuilding the Relationship: Quebec and Its Confederation Partners* (Report of a Conference, Mont Gabriel, Quebec, 9–11 May 1986) (Kingston: Institute of Intergovernmental Relations, Queen's University 1987).

16 For a discussion, see Michael Stein, *Canadian Constitutional Renewal 1968– 1981: A Case Study in Integrative Bargaining* (Kingston: Institute of Intergovernmental Relations, Queen's University 1989).

17 For a discussion of the importance of symbolic questions in Canadian politics and society, see Raymond Breton, 'The Production and Allocation of Symbolic Resources: An Analysis of the Linguistic and Ethnocultural Fields in Canada,' *Canadian Review of Sociology and Anthropology* 21–2 (1984): 123–43.

18 See Alan Cairns, 'Political Science, Ethnicity and the Canadian Constitution,' in D. Shugarman and R. Whitaker, eds., *Federalism and Political Community: Essays in Honour of Donald Smiley* (Toronto: Broadview Press 1989), 121.

19 Subsequent commentators suggested that the package should be separated into two groups, with those amendments requiring the consent of only seven provinces treated separately. There was never any discussion of this possibility in 1987. The assumption was that it was important to get all provinces to agree to the reintegration of Quebec and that anything less than unanimity would be a failure. This imperative was more political than legal.

20 See *A.G. Man.* v. *A.G. Can.* (*sub nom* Ref. re Amendment of the Constitution of Canada, Nos. 1, 2, 3) 125 DLR (3d) 1.

21 There was some debate over whether this three-year time limit was required under the constitution or whether it was simply a 'political' requirement. For an argument that the Meech Lake Accord was not subject to any time limit, see G. Robertson, *A House Divided: Meech Lake, Senate Reform and the Canadian Union* (Halifax: Institute for Research on Public Policy 1989).

22 The agreement was signed on 5 November 1981; the Canada Act was enacted by the U.K. Parliament on 25 March 1982 and given Royal Assent on 29 March 1982. Of course, it should be noted that in 1981 only the federal Houses and the British Parliament had to ratify the constitutional resolution; this was obviously the primary reason for the much speedier ratification in 1981.

23 For example, it was proposed that there should be an explicit statement that the 'national objectives' would be defined by the Parliament of Canada rather than by the provinces. This proposal was unacceptable to Quebec, which was willing only to include a reference to the program being 'established by the Parliament of Canada.'

24 See Trudeau, 'Say Goodbye to the Dream ...,' 71.

Chapter 3

1 At the March 1987 First Ministers' conference, up to six provinces were prepared to accept a constitutional amendment entrenching the principle of aboriginal self-government. But most of these provinces were prepared to support the amendment only on the condition that the precise parameters of the right to self-government would be specified through further negotiations. This approach was unacceptable to the four aboriginal organizations

participating in the talks. It should also be noted that section 35 was amended to clarify the meaning of treaty rights and of the section's impact on sexual equality, without the participation of the province of Quebec, in 1984.

2 See Robert McKenzie, 'PQ tables shopping list for Constitution deal,' *Toronto Star*, 18 May 1985, A4.

3 See Graham Fraser, 'PQ wants sweeping changes in new constitutional stand,' *Globe and Mail*, Toronto, 18 May 1985, A1.

4 This was the headline in an editorial in the *Toronto Star*, 22 May 1985, A18.

5 'More separatist mischief,' *Toronto Star*, 22 May 1985, A18.

6 See 'How it is distinct,' *Globe and Mail*, 23 May 1985, A6.

7 Parti liberal du Québec, 'Les Conditions d'acceptation de la nouvelle constitution,' in *Mastering Our Future* (Quebec Liberal Party Policy Platform, 1985), 49.

8 See *Mastering Our Future*, 56–7.

9 'New adviser favors freedom for Quebec,' *Globe and Mail*, 26 July 1985, A5

10 'Bourassa hoping for deal on the Constitution,' *Toronto Star*, 13 December 1985, A5.

11 I do not believe that the 'strategy' I describe was ever actually formulated in precisely the manner I set out in the text. Indeed, it may be that the elements of the strategy remained largely implicit rather than explicit. My account is an attempt to reconstruct the federal approach based on a variety of informal conversations over an extended period of time with a number of federal and provincial officials who were involved in the process. It also draws heavily on a published analysis of the process by Senator Lowell Murray. See L. Murray, 'The Process of Constitutional Change in Canada: The Lessons of Meech Lake,' *Choices* (Institute for Research on Public Policy Newsletter), February 1988.

12 For an extended discussion of these various factors, see chapter 2, 'The Inheritance of 1982.'

13 It would be common for the federal rolling text to indicate areas of controversy by the use of square brackets. But even the choice of where and when to place the brackets was itself a contested matter.

14 See R. Presthus, *Elite Accommodation in Canadian Politics* (Toronto: Macmillan 1973).

15 See R. Gunther, 'Constitutional Change in Contemporary Spain,' in K. Banting and R. Simeon, eds., *Redesigning the State: The Politics of Constitutional Change* (Toronto: University of Toronto Press 1985), 42; M. Covell, 'Possibly Necessary But Not Necessarily Possible: Revision of the Constitution in Belgium,' in Banting and Simeon, eds., *Redesigning the State*, 71.

16 'Quebec ends exemption from Charter,' *Globe and Mail*, 7 March 1986, A4.

17 See Jeffrey Simpson, 'To include Quebec,' *Globe and Mail*, 18 April 1986, A6.
18 For a summary and report of the discussions, see Peter Leslie, *Rebuilding the Relationship: Quebec and Its Confederation Partners* (Report of a Conference, Mont Gabriel, Quebec, 9–11 May 1986) (Kingston: Institute of Intergovernmental Relations, Queen's University 1987).
19 'Premiers weighing Quebec demands on accord,' *Toronto Star*, 7 July 1986, A3.
20 Under the existing formula, the consent of seven provinces totalling 50 per cent of the population was required.
21 See Andrew Cohen, *A Deal Undone: The Making and Breaking of the Meech Lake Accord* (Vancouver: Douglas & McIntyre 1990), 271.

Chapter 4

1 Quebec proposed to enact the following amendment: 'Section 1: Any interpretation of the Constitution must be consistent with the recognition of the fundamental duality of the Canadian federation and the specific character of Quebec as a distinct society and the main homeland of Quebec francophones. Quebec is vested with a special responsibility to protect and promote its specific character and that duality.'
2 Federal officials later confirmed that Quebec had given consideration to advancing this more radical approach. However, the federal officials claimed that the Quebec proposal had been modified after meetings between Ottawa and Quebec in which the unworkability of the idea had been stressed by the federal government.
3 The current general amending formula requires the support of seven provinces with 50 per cent of the total Canadian population, in addition to the federal Senate and House of Commons. Under Bourassa's proposal, as set out in the fall of 1986, the right to 'opt out' would also have been abolished.
4 Quebec proposed the following constitutional amendment on the spending power issue:
Section 36A is added to the Constitution Act, 1982, as follows:
36A.(1) The government of a province shall receive fair financial or fiscal compensation from the government of Canada in respect of any program of expenditures offered to all the provinces within the fields of their legislative authority which is to be funded jointly by the government of Canada and the provincial governments, if it decides not to participate in the program. The government of Canada shall not of its own initiative modify such a program while it is being carried out.
(2) Any other program of expenditures of the government of Canada in relation to matters coming within the classes of subjects under the legislative authority of a province must be carried out under the terms of an

agreement with the province. The government of Canada shall not of its own initiative modify the terms of such an agreement.

(3) Programs existing on January 1, 1988 are not subject to subsection 1. Parliament, after consultation with the provinces, shall appropriate the public revenue for the funding of the renewal of such a program. Nevertheless, such renewal or any decrease in the financial contribution of the federal government entails the obligation to renegotiate its existing terms and criteria with all the governments. Neither the government of Canada nor Parliament may modify such terms and criteria of its own initiative.

5 On immigration, Quebec proposed the following:

The Constitution Act, 1867 is amended by inserting, after section 95, the following heading and sections:

Quebec Powers in Immigration

95A. The legislature of Quebec has the power to make laws in relation to (a) the determination of the number of immigrants that Quebec deems it appropriate to receive; (b) the selection of all aliens wishing to settle in or to stay in Quebec.

Such laws prevail over any federal law inconsistent therewith.

95B. The legislature of Quebec may exclusively make laws in relation to services with respect to the reception, integration and training of permanent residents or persons who are becoming permanent residents.

6 The Quebec proposal on the Supreme Court of Canada was as follows:

The Constitution Act 1867 is modified by inserting, after section 101, the following section:

101A. The Court now existing under the name of the Supreme Court of Canada is hereby continued under that name, as a general court of appeal for Canada, and as an additional court for the better administration of the laws of Canada, and shall continue to be a court of record.

The Supreme Court shall consist of a chief justice to be called the Chief Justice of Canada, and eight puisne judges, who shall be appointed by the Governor General by letters patent under the Great Seal. The Chief Justice of Canada shall be appointed for one term of seven years or until the age of retirement, whichever occurs first, and shall be appointed alternately from among the judges appointed under the third paragraph and the other judges of the Supreme Court.

At least three of the judges shall be appointed from among the judges or the barristers or advocates of Quebec.

The judges appointed under the third paragraph shall be appointed by the Governor in Council following an agreement between the Prime Minister of Canada and the Prime Minister of Quebec.

Failing agreement, a college shall be formed consisting of the Attorney General of Canada, the Attorney General of Quebec and the Chief Justice of Quebec, who shall preside. The college shall make its recommendation to the Governor in Council, and he shall appoint the person so recommended.

7 The current amending formula restricts the right to receive compensation to amendments affecting 'education or other cultural matters.'

8 Under section 42 of the Constitution Act, 1982, such amendments require the consent of seven provinces with 50 per cent of the population (plus the federal houses). No opting out is permitted.

9 'Getty opposed to formal talks on Constitution,' *Globe and Mail*, Toronto, 12 March 1987, A4.

10 *Mastering Our Future* (Quebec Liberal Party Policy Platform, 1985), 44.

11 Patricia Poirier and Matthew Fisher, 'PM invites 10 premiers to discuss Quebec constitutional proposals,' *Globe and Mail*, 18 March 1987, A3.

12 Poirier and Fisher, 'PM invites 10 premiers,' A3.

13 The passage in Murray's letter on the issue was as follows:

It appears that there would be a consensus among governments to recognize in the Constitution the distinctive nature of Quebec society as the principal though not exclusive centre of French-speaking Canadians, and that a fundamental characteristic of the Canadian federation is the existence of French-speaking Canada, centred in but not limited to Quebec, and English-speaking Canada, concentrated in the rest of the country but also present in Quebec.

It should be possible to describe factually the Canadian and Quebec sociological reality, and to ensure that any interpretation clause not alter the present distribution of powers between the federal and provincial governments.

The federal government supports the consensus which seems to have formed as to the recognition of Quebec's distinct society and of the existence of Canada's two major language communities. The federal government would also agree to a constitutional stipulation that the Quebec National Assembly has a responsibility to preserve and promote the former characteristic, and that Parliament and the provincial legislatures have a responsibility to preserve and promote the latter characteristic; and to a requirement that constitutional interpretation take the foregoing provisions into account, without derogating from the legislative powers or the rights of Canada or the provinces.

14 See Joel Ruimy, 'Legal weight offered for Quebec special status,' *Toronto Star*, 24 April 1987, A1; 'Veto for Quebec, Ontario limited, Government says,' *Globe and Mail*, 24 April 1987, A10.

15 See 'Bourassa confident about talks,' *Globe and Mail*, 27 April 1987, A1; 'Ottawa needs Quebec on side in trade talks, Bourassa says,' *Toronto Star*, 27 April 1987, A1; Graham Fraser, 'Premiers want Quebec to sign Constitution, PM says,' *Globe and Mail*, 28 April 1987, A5.
16 See Graham Fraser, 'Pledge to Quebec on the line,' *Globe and Mail*, 25 April 1987, D2.
17 See 'Opposition leaders back PM in bid to woo Quebec at talks,' *Toronto Star*, 30 April 1987, A1.
18 See Matthew Fisher, 'Quebec to receive priority at meeting, Getty warned,' *Globe and Mail*, 27 April 1987, A3.
19 Ibid.
20 As quoted in Joel Ruimy, 'How styles made the difference,' *Toronto Star*, 9 May 1987, B1.
21 As quoted in Graham Fraser, 'Getting Quebec to sign,' *Globe and Mail*, 2 May 1987, D1.

Chapter 5

1 See Joel Ruimy, 'How styles made the difference,' *Toronto Star*, 9 May 1987, B1.
2 See 'Pact needs rewording, Pawley says,' *Globe and Mail*, Toronto, 6 May 1987, A3.
3 Rémillard's remarks were reported in Robert MacKenzie, 'Quebec may seek to bolster powers in Constitution deal, minister says,' *Toronto Star*, 9 May 1987, A8. See also R. MacKenzie, 'Will Bourassa pull plug on Meech Lake pact?' *Toronto Star*, 12 May 1987, A18.
4 See Robert MacKenzie, 'Quebec seeks new power for opting out,' *Toronto Star*, 16 May 1987, A1.
5 See Denise Harrington, 'Scott says compensation limited to same area,' *Toronto Star*, 20 May 1987, A9.
6 Quoted in R. MacKenzie, 'Quebec may block quick constitutional accord,' *Toronto Star*, 24 May 1987, A1.
7 'Premier not perturbed about wording problem,' *Globe and Mail*, 25 May 1987, A4.
8 See R. MacKenzie, 'Bourassa at odds with Pawley on wording of Constitution deal,' *Toronto Star*, 26 May 1987, A1.
9 See ibid.
10 See Andrew Cohen, 'New jitters threaten Meech Lake deal,' *Financial Post*, 25 May 1987, 2.
11 See Derek Ferguson, 'Manitoba to seek changes in clause on spending power, Pawley declares,' *Toronto Star*, 28 May 1987, A21.
12 See Stanley Oziewicz, 'Peterson promises hearings before province ratifies deal,' *Globe and Mail*, 28 May 1987, A5.

13 See R. MacKenzie, 'Bourassa pledges to push for deal,' *Toronto Star*, 1 June 1987, A9. See also Graham Fraser, 'Quebec raises new question about accord,' *Globe and Mail*, 1 June 1987, A1.
14 See 'Meech Lake accord gains general support, poll shows,' *Toronto Star*, 1 June 1987, A1.
15 See Graham Fraser, Stanley Oziewicz, and Christopher Waddell, 'First Ministers stalled in drafting accord,' *Globe and Mail*, 3 June 1987, A1.
16 See ibid.
17 See Joe O'Donnell, 'It's a deal,' *Toronto Star*, 3 June 1987, A1.
18 See Denise Harrington, 'Canadians will have a say in the deal, Peterson says,' *Toronto Star*, 3 June 1987, A1, A8.

Chapter 6

1 See R. MacKenzie, 'Ontario could still threaten deal's adoption, Ryan says,' *Toronto Star*, 6 June 1987, A15.
2 See the Gallup poll released on 18 June 1987, which found that 56 per cent of those polled favoured the accord, 16 per cent were opposed, and 28 per cent had no opinion. See 'Most Canadians give OK to constitutional pact,' *The Gallup Report* (Gallup Canada, Inc., 18 June 1987).
3 See Joel Ruimy, 'Meech hearings: High drama,' *Toronto Star*, 9 August 1987, B1.
4 See Joel Ruimy, 'Women's groups differ on effect of Meech Accord,' *Toronto Star*, 1 September 1987, A2.
5 Ross Howard, 'Panel approves Meech Lake pact without changes,' *Globe and Mail*, Toronto, 22 September 1987, A5.
6 See Alan Story, 'McKenna calls win "broad mandate" to change or reject Meech Lake,' *Toronto Star*, 15 October 1987, A8.
7 See 'Irate Pawley "rethinking" support for Meech pact,' *Toronto Star*, 19 December 1987, A1. See also Daniel Drolet, 'Meech opponents cheer Pawley's new stance,' *Ottawa Citizen*, 19 December 1987, A3.
8 See 'Irate Pawley "rethinking" support for Meech pact.'
9 See Susan Delacourt, 'Eight months bring big changes to pals from Meech Lake hearing,' *Globe and Mail*, 30 April 1988, A5.
10 See David Hatter, 'Manitoba election opens new cracks in Meech Lake Accord,' *Financial Post*, 30 April 1988, 1.
11 See David Vienneau, 'Only 28% now support the constitutional accord latest Gallup poll says,' *Toronto Star*, 28 April 1988, A2.
12 See, for example, Robert McKenzie, 'Quebec lobbying provinces to end N.B.'s Meech delay,' *Toronto Star*, 23 March 1988, A14.
13 See Robert McKenzie, 'Amend Meech or its no deal McKenna informs Bourassa,' *Toronto Star*, 18 March 1988, A10.

14 See *Toronto Star*, 17 December 1988, A8; *Globe and Mail*, 17 December 1988, 1.
15 See Edison Stewart, 'Quebecers jam rally to condemn "sellout,"' *Toronto Star*, 18 December 1988, A1, A3; Patricia Poirier, 'Thousands turn out in Montreal for rally in support of Bill 101,' *Globe and Mail*, 19 December 1988, 1.
16 See Benoît Aubin, 'New Quebec policy to require French on outside signs,' *Globe and Mail*, 19 December 1988, 1.
17 As quoted in Geoffrey York and Benoît Aubin, 'Manitoba Premier ends Meech debate: Quebec language move "national tragedy", Filmon says,' *Globe and Mail*, 20 December 1988, A1.
18 See 'Manitoba Premier ends Meech debate,' *Globe and Mail*, 20 December 1988, 1.
19 For a review of the evolution of Canadian public opinion to the accord, see *Focus Canada Report, 1990–1* (Toronto: Environics Research, Spring 1990), 73–6.
20 See *Focus Canada Report, 1990–1*, p. 75 (noting that only 13 per cent of all Canadians, including Quebeckers, would carry through with the accord, 17 per cent would cancel it, and 42 per cent would seek to renegotiate it. Quebeckers were significantly more likely to believe that the accord should be ratified than renegotiated. Thus the numbers of those outside of Quebec who wanted to renegotiate the accord were, in fact, significantly higher than 42 per cent).

Chapter 7

1 As quoted in Hugh Winsor, 'Newfoundland Liberals' win raises alarms in Ottawa,' *Globe and Mail*, 22 April 1989, A2.
2 See *Report of the Manitoba Task Force on Meech Lake*, 'Summary of Recommendations,' 23 October 1989, 80.
3 See *Ford v. Quebec (A.G.)* [1988] 2 SCR 712.
4 See *Ford v. Quebec* [1988] 2 SCR 712 at p. 778.
5 See, for example, Graham Fraser, 'Politicians grope awkwardly to respond to municipalities' English-only resolutions,' *Globe and Mail*, 9 February 1990, A11.
6 Ibid.
7 See Rhéal Séguin, 'Bourassa raises spectre of new federalism,' *Globe and Mail*, 9 February 1990, A11.
8 See Geoffrey York and Robert Matas, 'Manitoba leaders praise report but say it fails to resolve key issues,' *Globe and Mail*, 18 May 1990, A11.
9 See *Report of the Special Committee to Study the Proposed Companion Resolution to the Meech Lake Accord* (The Honourable Jean Charest, MP, Chairman) May 1990, 5.

10 See Patricia Poirier and Rhéal Séguin, '"Unacceptable demands" being made, Bourassa says,' *Globe and Mail*, 18 May 1990, A1.
11 See Graham Fraser, 'Quebec Tory MP quits caucus, declares belief in sovereignty,' *Globe and Mail*, 19 May 1990, A5.
12 See Alan Freeman, 'Bouchard quits, warning "we mean business,"' *Globe and Mail*, 23 May 1990, 1.

Chapter 8

1 As quoted in Susan Delacourt and Rhéal Séguin, 'PM faces scramble to save Meech: First ministers' conference unlikely to work, Murray says,' *Globe and Mail*, Toronto, 23 May 1990, 2.
2 For a full text of the Wells proposals, see 'Possible "add-ons" to meet the concerns of Newfoundland and Labrador with the Meech Lake Accord,' 24 May 1990 (on file with Osgoode Hall Law School Library, York University).
3 See, for example, Susan Delacourt, 'Senate reform key to deal on Meech,' *Globe and Mail*, 28 May 1990, 1.
4 See Susan Delacourt and Graham Fraser, 'Murray taking Meech shuttle to St. John's: PM's emissary to discuss position of Wells,' *Globe and Mail*, 29 May 1990, 1.
5 As quoted in Susan Delacourt, 'Harmony close on key clause of Meech accord, Wells says,' *Globe and Mail*, 30 May 1990, 1.
6 Ibid.
7 See ibid., 1.
8 See Susan Delacourt, 'PM, premiers head for Meech talks,' *Globe and Mail*, 1 June 1990, 1.
9 See Susan Delacourt, Allan Freeman, and Graham Fraser, 'PM, premiers to keep talking on Meech Lake,' *Globe and Mail*, 4 June 1990, 1.
10 See Susan Delacourt, Alan Freeman, and Graham Fraser, 'Ottawa tables plan to save Meech: Senate reform to be main issue when PM, premiers meet today,' *Globe and Mail*, 6 June 1990, 1.
11 As quoted in Susan Delacourt, Graham Fraser, Richard Mackie, and Hugh Winsor, 'Bourassa won't discuss distinct society,' *Globe and Mail*, 8 June 1990, 2.
12 For a partial text of the remarks of Brian Mulroney and Clyde Wells, see *Globe and Mail*, 11 June 1990, A13.

Chapter 9

1 See, for example, Charles Taylor, 'Shared and Divergent Values,' in Ronald L. Watts and Douglas M. Brown, eds., *Options for a New Canada* (Toronto:

University of Toronto Press 1991), 53–76; Guy Laforest, 'Quebec beyond the Federal Regime of 1867–1982: From Distinct Society to National Community,' in Watts and Brown, eds., *Options for a New Canada*, 103–22.

2 See sections 22, 94, 133, of the Constitution Act, 1867.

3 Of course, section 133 of the Constitution Act, 1867 mandated official bilingualism in the courts and the legislature, and this requirement could not be unilaterally altered by the province of Quebec.

4 See section 2(4) of the accord, which provided: 'Nothing in this section derogates from the powers, rights or privileges of Parliament or the Government of Canada, or of the legislatures or governments of the provinces, including any powers, rights or privileges relating to language.'

5 See sections 2(2) and 2(3) of the accord, which provided: '2(2). The role of the Parliament of Canada and the provincial legislatures to preserve the fundamental characteristic of Canada referred to in paragraph 1(a) is affirmed. 2(3). The role of the legislature and Government of Quebec to preserve and promote the distinct identity of Quebec referred to in paragraph 1(b) is affirmed.'

6 See section 106A, which provided: '106A(1) The Government of Canada shall provide reasonable compensation to the government of a province that chooses not to participate in a national shared-cost program that is established by the Government of Canada after the coming into force of this section in an area of exclusive provincial jurisdiction, if the province carries on a program or initiative that is compatible with the national objectives. (2) Nothing in this section extends the legislative powers of the Parliament of Canada or of the legislatures of the provinces.'

7 See letter from the Honourable Clyde Wells, Premier of Newfoundland and Labrador, to the Right Honourable Brian Mulroney, Prime Minister of Canada, 18 October 1989, 6.

8 See the Federal/Provincial Fiscal Arrangements Act. For a discussion, see David Perry, 'The Federal Provincial Fiscal Arrangement Introduced in 1977,' *Canadian Tax Journal*, 25 (1977): 429.

9 See, for example, the current dispute involving the federal government's attempt to 'cap' its contributions to the Canada Assistance Plan, announced in the spring 1990 federal budget. The federal attempt to impose a cap on its contribution provoked litigation from the province of British Columbia, which obtained a declaration that the federal government could not unilaterally alter its obligations under the program. This issue is currently before the Supreme Court of Canada at the time of this writing (February 1991).

10 See the discussion of these negotiations in chapter 3.

11 See, for example, 'A Shaken Nation Bares Its Anger,' *Maclean's*, 7 January

1991, 34 (reporting the results of an opinion poll conducted by Decima, indicating that the most popular political option for Canada's future is a federal system giving all the provinces much more power).

12 See the Decima poll referred to in note 11, which found that 46 per cent of respondents indicated that they would be more likely to support a constitutional proposal that was introduced after a process 'involving extensive consultation and public input,' 33, question 14.

13 K. Banting and R. Simeon, 'Introduction: The Politics of Constitutional Change,' in Banting and Simeon, eds., *Redesigning the State: The Politics of Constitutional Change* (Toronto: University of Toronto Press 1985), 20.

14 See the discussion of these factors in chapter 2.

15 See, for example, Carol Goar, 'Constitution: Last piece in place,' *Toronto Star*, 2 May 1987, B1.

16 See Joel Ruimy, 'How styles made the difference,' *Toronto Star*, 9 May 1987, B1.

17 See ibid.

18 See chapter 10 for a more detailed discussion of a future process that might be employed.

19 See 'Meech Lake accord gains general support, poll shows,' *Toronto Star*, 1 June 1987, A1 (finding majority support for the accord as a whole, but opinion on the distinct-society clause was split almost evenly); see also 'Most Canadians Give OK to Constitutional Pact (Gallup Canada Inc. 18 June 1987) (finding that 56 per cent of respondents support the accord, with 16 per cent opposed; however, only 38 per cent support the recognition of Quebec as a distinct society, while 40 per cent were opposed).

20 For a summary of data on public opinion on Meech Lake, see Michael Adams and Mary Jane Lennon, 'The Public's View of the Canadian Federation,' in R.L. Watts and D.M. Brown, eds., *Canada: The State of the Federation 1990* (Kingston: Institute of Intergovernmental Relations 1990), 97–108.

21 See the letter from Clyde Wells to the prime minister of Canada, 18 October 1989, 3.

22 See Trudeau, 'Say Goodbye to the Dream of One Canada,' in R. Gibbins, ed., *Meech Lake: Perspectives from the West* (Edmonton: Academic Print and Pub. 1988), 69–70.

23 Trudeau, 'Say Goodbye,' 70.

24 Note, however, the fact that Quebec's demands on the Supreme Court included a constitutional entrenchment of its right to three of the nine judges on the court. This entrenched a right already legally protected in the Supreme Court Act. Nevertheless, the issue was one of the most hotly debated during the Meech Lake meeting, illustrating the high degree of sensitivity to any attempt to single out Quebec for 'special treatment.'

25 The obvious exception is section 92A of the Constitution Act 1982, which

seeks to set out, by way of a 'schedule,' a detailed definition of certain terms. But section 92A is the exception; most constitutional provisions are of the general type I describe.

26 For an elaboration and justification of this theory of constitutional interpretation, see R. Dworkin, *Taking Rights Seriously* (London: Duckworth 1977), 131–49, and 'The Forum of Principle,' in *A Matter of Principle* (Cambridge: Harvard University Press 1985), 48–57.

27 See the Charter of Rights, sections 7, 15, and 1.

28 See R. Breton, 'The Production and Allocation of Symbolic Resources: An Analysis of the Linguistic and Ethnocultural Fields in Canada,' *Canadian Review of Sociology and Anthropology* 21 (1984): 123.

29 See ibid., 132.

30 See, for example, the discussion in chapter 2 on the role of honour and dignity in the debate.

31 See Alan Cairns, 'Political Science, Ethnicity and the Canadian Constitution,' in David Shugarman and Reg Whitaker, eds., *Federalism and Political Community: Essays in Honour of Donald Smiley* (Peterborough: Broadview Press 1989), 120–6.

32 Ibid., 126.

33 See testimony of Z. Nungak before the Special Joint Committee of the Senate and House of Commons on the 1987 Constitutional Accord, 5 August 1987, cited in Cairns, 'Political Science Ethnicity, and the Canadian Constitution.'

34 See testimony of G. Erasmus before the Special Joint Committee, 19 August 1987, cited by Cairns, 123.

35 Sergio Marchi, *House of Commons Debates*, 6 October 1987, quoted in Cairns, 124.

36 See letter from the Honourable Clyde Wells to the Prime Minister of Canada, 18 October 1989, 2.

37 See remarks of Premier Clyde Wells at the closing ceremonies of the First Ministers' meeting, 9 June 1990, reprinted in the *Globe and Mail*, 11 June 1990, A13.

Chapter 10

1 As quoted in R. Sheppard and M. Valpy, *The National Deal: The Fight for a Canadian Constitution* (Toronto: Fleet Books 1982), 55.

2 This conclusion is by no means limited to the Canadian case. A recent study of comparative constitutional change concluded as follows: 'While examples of demands for constitutional change abound, examples of actual change are scarce. Clearly it is easier to get a constitutional claim on the agenda than it is to win. The predominant pattern is of frustrated demands, not wholesale

renewal.' See K. Banting and R. Simeon, 'Introduction: The Politics of Constitutional Change,' in Banting and Simeon, eds., *Redesigning the State: The Politics of Constitutional Change* (Toronto: University of Toronto Press 1985), 25.

3 See, generally, 'A Shaken Nation Bares Its Anger,' *Maclean's*, 8 January 1991 (reporting on Maclean's/Decima poll that is said to demonstrate that 'Canadians as a whole are suffering a massive loss of confidence in politicians and in the political system itself' [p. 2]).

4 See 'The pressures to reform Canada's political system' (editorial), *Globe and Mail*, Toronto, 8 November 1990, A20.

5 Ibid.

6 See Banting and Simeon, 'The Politics of Constitutional Change,' 25.

7 See *Maclean's*, 8 January 1991, 33, question 13 (reporting that 70 per cent of respondents believe that governments should leave the constitutional issue alone, while only 28 per cent think this is the right time to return to the issue).

8 See Guy Laforest, 'Quebec beyond the Federal Regime of 1867–1982: From Distinct Society to National Community,' in Ronald L. Watts and Douglas M. Brown, *Options for a New Canada* (Toronto: University of Toronto Press 1991), 103–22.

9 See *A Quebec Free to Choose* (Constitutional Committee of the Quebec Liberal Party, 29 January 1991).

10 See the Maclean's/Decima poll, *Maclean's*, 7 January 1991, 34. See also the findings of the Gallup poll reporting that a majority of Canadians outside of Quebec believe that Canada should refuse to grant Quebec new powers, even if this means that Quebec might leave. See *Globe and Mail*, 26 January 1991, A1.

11 See Environics Research, *Focus Canada Report, 1990–1* (Toronto, Spring 1990), question 82.

12 See *Maclean's*, 7 January 1991, chart entitled 'Constitutional Differences,' 19.

13 A notable exception in this regard is the admirable work of Professor Peter Russell of the University of Toronto, who has put forward a number of practical suggestions for reforming the process of constitutional amendment. See Russell, 'Towards a New Constitutional Process,' in Watts and Brown, eds., *Options for a New Canada*, 141–56. I will have more to say about Professor Russell's proposals later in this chapter.

14 The current procedure for bilateral amendments is section 43 of the Constitution Act, 1982, which permits amendments 'in relation to any provision that applies to one or more, but not all, provinces.'

15 The best analysis to date of these various options can be found in Watts and Brown, eds., *Options for a New Canada*.

16 In this sense, the proposals of the Allaire committee, published on 29 January 1991, are to be considered 'federalist,' even though they envisage a radical decentralization of powers and jurisdictions.

17 For a survey of the historical experience with secession in a wide variety of contexts, see L.C. Buchheit, *Secession: The Legitimacy of Self-Determination* (New Haven: Yale University Press 1978), 138–215. See also Greg Craven, 'Secession and Quebec,' manuscript, November 1990.

18 The reader might ask about the possibility of a multi-member confederacy, involving Quebec and a number of other 'sovereign' provinces. But this type of arrangement would almost certainly prove unworkable. Once again the basic problem would be the demand by Quebec for a veto over decisions taken by the central institutions. If this demand is met by granting a similar veto to the other members of the confederacy (which seems the only realistic possibility), then the system will be subject to endless deadlock. But, if the central institutions are subject to the principle of majority rule, with no vetoes for the individual members, then Quebec's interests will be insufficiently protected.

19 See *A Quebec Free to Choose* (Report of the Constitutional Committee of the Quebec Liberal Party, 28 January 1991), 49.

20 I share Peter Leslie's conclusion that any of the 'confederal' options are 'fantastic,' which Leslie defines as 'eccentric, quaint, or grotesque in design or conception.' See Leslie, 'Options for the Future of Canada: The Good, the Bad and the Fantastic,' in Watts and Brown, eds., *Options for a New Canada*, 123–40.

21 See *Madzimbamuto* v. *Lardner-Burke*, [1969] 1 AC 645, in which the Privy Council held that 'the essential condition to determine whether a constitution has been annulled is the efficacy of the change' (p. 725).

22 See S. Brooks, *Public Policy in Canada: An Introduction* (Toronto: McClelland and Stewart 1989), 13.

23 See ibid., 14.

24 See Banting and Simeon, 'The Politics of Constitutional Change,' 25.

25 For an elaboration of this theme, see G. Lehmbruch, 'Constitution-making in Young and Aging Federal Systems,' in Banting and Simeon, *Redesigning the State*, 30–41.

26 See Peter Meekison, 'Distributions of Functions and Jurisdiction: A Political Scientist's Analysis,' in Watts and Brown, eds., *Options for a New Canada*, 259–84.

27 See, for example, I. Bakker, 'The Size and Scope of Government: Robin Hood Sent Packing?' in M. Whittington and G. Williams, *Canadian Politics in the 1990's*, 3d ed. (Scarborough: Nelson Canada 1990), 421–43.

28 For a discussion of these mechanisms and the broad scope for change that they permit, see Peter Leslie, 'Options for the Future of Canada.'

29 See Meekison, 'Distributions of Functions and Jurisdictions.'
30 See, for example, *Maclean's*, 7 January 1991, which found that 74 per cent of those polled outside of Quebec indicated that they would be opposed to granting Quebec 'special powers that would allow it to make more decisions on its own.' When asked to choose among six possible constitutional options, a federal system giving Quebec special powers was the least popular option among Canadians outside of Quebec.
31 Obviously a constitutional convention makes sense if one is attempting a comprehensive revision of the constitution. While I have my doubts about a comprehensive approach, I will not repeat those arguments here. For purposes of the present discussion I am assuming that a decision has been made to undertake a comprehensive revision to the constitution. The discussion that follows discusses further complications that flow specifically from the idea of convening a constitutional convention.
32 See P. Russell, 'Towards a New Constitutional Process,' in Watts and Brown, eds., *Options for a New Canada*, 141–56.
33 It is interesting that many critics of Meech Lake tried to rely on the fragile character of the accord as a reason for rejecting it. According to this line of argument, the accord was flawed precisely because any changes in it would cause it to fall apart. But this argument seems to have the matter precisely backwards. The fragility of the agreement was, in fact, evidence of the fact that it had been the product of bargaining compromise: everyone had given up something in order to achieve the agreement. Having already extracted concessions from everyone, you simply could not ask them to return to the table and offer more. This was true not only of Robert Bourassa, but was equally the case with any of the other premiers or the prime minister. Certainly David Peterson or Don Getty was not prepared to return to the bargaining table to make further concessions in favour of Robert Bourassa. Had Bourassa demanded further concessions, he would have been greeted with a polite 'no' and told that the agreement that had been negotiated was as good as he was going to get. There had been extensive negotiations over a ten-month period, with concessions being made by all parties around the table. Having engaged in that process and achieved a unanimous agreement in June 1987, there was simply no possibility that one or another of the parties could return to the table and ask to reopen the negotiations. Any attempt to do so would effectively signal the end of the agreement.

Index

aboriginal issues, 20, 22, 27, 38, 40, 67, 79, 83, 95, 116, 119, 125, 129, 141, 146, 157, 177, 192, 202, 213, 231, 257–8, 265, 280–1

Alberta, 31, 48, 59, 64, 81, 82, 88, 89, 91, 154, 225

Allaire committee, 261–2, 266, 270, 277–8

amending formula, 56–60 passim, 67, 68, 71, 74–8 passim, 85, 87, 89, 90–1, 92, 96, 99–100, 108, 172, 248, 270

Andrews, Jock, 175

Association for the Preservation of English in Canada, 174–5, 186

Bélanger-Campeau commission, 261–2, 281

Bill 101, 123, 155–6, 159, 167

Bill 178, 12, 163, 166, 185, 252–3

Blakeney, Allan, 38

BNA Act, 243, 249, 277

Bouchard, Lucien, 191, 195–6

Bourassa, Robert, 42, 46–7, 49, 54–6, 60–3, 72–4, 109, 111, 114–15, 201, 204, 241, 249; Charest committee, 194–5, 197, 203, 210; decision to use notwithstanding clause, 4, 81, 187; failure of the accord, 12, 156, 159–66, 253; distinct-society clause, 118, 122–3, 125, 127–31, 224, 243; federal spending powers, 90, 96–7, 102, 105, 108, 177; five conditions, 21–2, 24–5, 58–62; Langevin Block meeting (1987), 120, 132–3, 137–8; Meech Lake meeting (1987), 86, 88, 99–100; Ottawa meeting (1990), 214–17, 219–20, 237; refusal to amend the accord, 147–9, 153–5, 170–4, 199–200, 206, 208–9, 210–11, 222

British Columbia, 59, 73, 78, 92–3, 153–4, 225

Broadbent, Edward, 81, 101, 158

Buchanan, John, 48, 59, 93, 96, 120, 131, 192

Cairns, Alan, 257

Canada clause, 177–8, 193, 202–3, 206, 211–12, 215, 219–21, 223, 225–6, 231

Carstairs, Sharon, 151, 155, 158, 162, 176, 194, 219–21, 285

CF–18 contracts, 64, 150

Charest, Jean, 190

Charest committee, 191–7, 198–202, 208, 210, 212–13, 235–7, 248, 286

Charter of Rights and Freedoms, x, 30, 43, 54–6, 70, 110, 161, 169, 177,

242, 245, 249, 250, 285; distinct–
society clause, 118, 124, 126, 143,
180, 189, 193–5, 203, 212, 215, 217–
18, 255; 'signs' case, 123, 155, 166–
7, 245; supporters of, 26, 257, 259
Chrétien, Jean, 39, 102, 175
Ciacca, John, 160
Clark, Joe, 50, 89
Cohen, Andrew, 62
Conservatives, 3, 41, 42, 64
Constitution Act (1982), 6, 8–9, 17,
36, 38, 42, 43, 44, 46, 76, 83, 123,
144, 166, 169, 249–50, 268;
exclusion of Quebec, 9, 12, 14–26,
36, 55, 84, 99, 111, 113, 164, 183,
253–4; provisions for amending, 6,
8–9, 10, 16, 28–9, 30, 31–3, 35–6,
44, 50, 76, 144, 264, 283
cost-sharing programs. See federal
spending powers
Coyne, Deborah, 208

Devine, Grant, 48, 59, 88, 131
Dion, Leon, 103–4, 123
distinct-society clause, 5–6, 20, 44, 72,
74, 75–6, 78, 84, 86, 93–4, 103–4,
116–18, 138, 142, 149–50, 154, 165,
169, 174, 177–8, 188–9, 193–4,
202–3, 206, 211, 240–6, 252–9;
Langevin Block meeting (1987),
120–32, 141, 156, 162; Mont
Gabriel, 56–7, 66–7; Ottawa
meeting (1990), 215–24, 226–7,
229, 231; Trudeau commentary,
110–12, 114; Wells concerns, 172,
179–81, 205, 207, 212–13
Doer, Gary, 151, 158–9, 162, 176, 219–
21, 285

Eberts, Mary, 141–2

Edmonton Declaration, 60–2, 65, 73,
82, 89
Eldridge, James, 157
equality of the provinces, 26, 27, 45,
48, 52, 68, 71, 78, 79, 84, 183, 202,
248, 257, 263, 279
Erasmus, Georges, 83–4, 257
executive federalism, 6

federal spending powers, 34, 56, 57,
59, 68–9, 72, 75, 76, 78, 89, 102,
104–7, 108–9, 114–15, 117, 120–1,
146, 153–4, 176–7, 180, 189, 206,
220, 242, 246–7; Langevin Block
meeting (1987), 122, 126–7, 130;
Meech Lake meeting (1987), 92,
96–7; opting out, 85, 87
Filmon, Garry, 151–2, 155–9, 162–3,
170–6, 181–2, 187–8, 193–4, 199–
201, 203–4, 206, 209–11, 213–16,
219, 221–3, 225–6, 230–1, 236–7,
248–9, 285
Finkelstein, Neil, 217–20, 228–9
fisheries, 61, 87, 95–6, 146
Forsey, Sen. Eugene, 100
Fratesi, Joseph, 185–6
Free-Trade Agreement, 3, 6–7, 64, 88,
145, 147, 149–50, 197
French, Richard, 160
French Language Services Act, 185
Friends of Meech Lake, 187, 192

Gagnier, Dan, 225
Gagnon, Lysiane, 195
Garneau, Raymond, 74
Gérin, François, 195
Getty, Donald, 48, 49, 61, 79, 81, 82,
88, 89, 91, 94–5, 96, 120, 122, 131,
204, 213, 215, 222, 226
Ghiz, Joe, 48, 131, 192, 214, 216, 223–6

Harper, Elijah, 33, 200, 234
Hartt, Stan, 216, 228
Hatfield, Richard, 48, 61, 93, 96, 131, 139
Hogg, Peter, 47, 127–9, 217, 220
Horsman, Jim, 89

Iacobucci, Frank, 127–9, 142
immigration, 43, 44, 56, 57, 69–70, 71, 78, 79, 85, 86–7, 93, 108, 112, 240; Cullen-Couture Agreement, 70, 78, 85, 87, 93

Jewett, Pauline, 143
Johnson, Pierre Marc, 46, 67, 102, 117–18, 138
Johnston, Donald, 74

Kirby, Michael, 260

Langevin Block meeting (1987), 11, 34, 115, 120, 127, 132–5, 137–9, 141, 148, 152, 154, 156, 162, 176, 242–3
Laporte, Pierre, 39
Laskin, John, 141
Leitch, Don, 157
Lennie, Oryssia, 92, 121
Lévesque, René, 14, 15, 18, 21, 30, 39, 41, 42, 43, 46, 47, 74, 196, 253
Liberals, 4, 42, 43, 73–5, 84, 143
Lincoln, Clifford, 160

Macdonald Commission, 22
McGilp, Ian, 47
McKenna, Frank, 139, 146–9, 151, 153–5, 170–5, 181–2, 188–94, 201, 213, 222, 227, 231, 244
McKenzie, Francine, 142
MacPherson, James, 224–6
McCrae, James, 157

Manitoba, 3, 11, 33, 34, 64, 65, 72, 76, 83, 88, 90, 106–7, 116–18, 133, 138, 149–51, 153–4, 158, 163, 170, 173, 176, 178, 181, 191, 203–4, 206, 212, 217, 219, 225, 230, 234, 236, 285
Marx, Herbert, 46, 160
Mazankowski, Don, 89
Meech Lake Accord, 5, 9–10, 12, 85–7, 102–3, 105, 108–9, 120–1, 127, 131–2, 135–6, 137–44, 151–4, 161–8, 199–200, 201, 205, 208, 210, 215, 221–4, 242, 245–9, 251–2, 255–7, 270; deadline, 3–4, 12, 32, 33, 155, 184–5, 197, 200, 208, 210–11, 215, 223, 230–1, 234–5, 264; failure of, 170, 186–7, 235–7, 239–40, 261–3, 266–7, 279, 280, 282, 286; process, 7–8, 17, 134, 140, 143–4, 149, 192, 238–40, 251–2, 264; proposed amendment of, 166, 125, 147–50, 154–7, 171–4, 188–96, 213; Trudeau criticism, 7–9, 11, 109–14; see also amending formula; distinct-society clause; federal spending powers; immigration; Senate, reform of; Supreme Court, reform of
Meech Lake meeting (1987), 10–11, 34, 80, 81, 82, 83, 84–5, 87–8, 89, 91, 92, 97, 98, 101, 119, 127, 133–4, 135, 176, 201, 241
Meekison, Peter, 277, 279
Mendes, Errol, 203
Mont Gabriel conference, 22, 55, 56, 57, 58, 59, 65, 67, 68, 73
Morin, Benoît, 217, 228
Morin, Claude, 39
Mulroney, Brian, 46, 52–3, 58, 64–5, 77, 101, 133, 135–6, 162, 173–4, 179, 183–4, 185, 188, 196, 204–6, 251; Charest committee, 198, 200–1;

Langevin Block meeting, 114, 128, 131–2; Meech Lake meeting (1987), 80–5, 94, 99–100; Ottawa meeting (1990), 209–12, 215, 226, 228–9, 232; refusal to change the accord, 149–50, 155, 171, 190–1, 237; 'roll of the dice' interview, 236; Sept-Iles speech, 24, 41–2, 45, 50; Trudeau criticism, 2, 109, 111, 123, 239; willingness to amend the accord, 189, 192
multiculturalism, 20, 27, 67, 110–11, 125, 129, 141, 177, 192, 257
Murray, Sen. Lowell, 49–51, 72, 75–7, 78, 89–90, 100, 112–13, 137, 162–3, 171–3, 184–5, 206–8, 211, 234–5; 15 April letter of proposals, 84–8, 92–6, 105, 109; Charest committee, 198, 201, 203–4, 210; recommendation not to amend the accord, 140, 142–3, 145

New Brunswick, 145–6, 153–4, 170, 173, 181, 191, 225–6, 230–1
New Democrats, 81–2, 143
Newfoundland, 3, 72, 76, 88, 90, 153, 171, 181, 191, 203–4, 206, 208, 214, 217–19, 225–6, 228–30, 234–6
Northwest Territories, 188
notwithstanding clause, 40, 54, 70, 123–4, 156–7, 159–61, 163–9, 250, 252–3, 258–9
Nova Scotia, 83, 88, 153, 225–6

Ontario, 11, 47, 88, 133, 145, 149, 153, 175, 178, 183, 204, 208, 209, 219, 275; amending formula, 68, 90, 94; federal spending powers, 34, 42; proposals to amend the accord, 106, 116–17, 126; Senate reform, 214, 225–6

Ottawa Conference (1981), 38, 44
Ottawa Conference (1989), 182
Ottawa Conference (1990), 100, 198, 200, 209–10, 212, 233, 281, 285
Ouellet, André, 140

Parizeau, Jacques, 42, 159, 190, 196
Parti Québécois, 21, 39, 42, 43, 44, 67, 79, 117, 138, 160, 190, 196, 249, 267
patriation round, 31, 32
Pawley, Howard, 48, 59, 64, 96, 97, 102, 109, 112, 114, 120, 122, 125–7, 131–3, 150–1, 158, 176
Peckford, Brian, 48, 59, 62, 95–6, 97, 120–1, 131, 171
Penner, Roland, 75
Peterson, David, 11, 47, 49, 59, 60, 64, 72, 88, 89, 91–2, 94, 100, 112, 119–22, 125–33, 139, 145, 156, 185–6, 192, 209, 224–6
Pickersgill, Jack, 214
Posen, Gary, 48
Pratte, Yves, 123
Prince Edward Island, 149, 153, 214
property rights, 61, 87
provinces, creation of, 10, 142–3, 188, 281

Quebec, 14–15, 31, 39, 52, 75, 77, 79, 82, 88, 92–3, 102, 106, 135, 153, 178, 183, 186–7, 190, 208, 260, 277, 279, 281, 282, 288; amending formula, 68, 71, 100, 203–4, 206; distinct-society clause, 107, 117, 126, 207, 217–18, 230–1, 240–5, 255–9; failure of the accord, 4, 262–74; federal spending powers, 34, 42, 69, 90, 176, 247; five conditions of, 9, 10, 24, 25–6, 29, 45, 56, 57, 59, 60, 61, 66, 73, 80, 83, 85, 89, 94, 105, 177, 195–6, 238, 241, 254;

independence of, 271–6; notwith-standing clause, 163–4, 167, 169, 250, 252–4; Senate reform, 48, 89, 214, 216, 225, 249; sovereignty-association, 268–70

Quebec Liberal party, 21, 42, 44, 45, 66, 67, 68, 76, 90, 156, 159, 187, 261

Quebec round, 10, 12, 17–18, 23–4, 25, 26, 27–8, 52, 61, 65, 238

Reagan, Ronald, 149
Reform party, 82
Rémillard, Gil, 45, 54, 61, 63, 69–71, 75–7, 89–90, 103–7, 117, 135, 157, 163, 191, 197, 222, 241; Langevin Block meeting (1987), 120, 126; Meech Lake meeting (1987), 100; Mont Gabriel conference, 55–9, 65–8, 73, 100

Rheame, Gilles, 120
Rideout, Thomas, 171
Rivest, Jean-Claude, 59
Rockefeller, David, 120
Romanow, Roy, 38
Rose, Jacques, 39
Russell, Peter, 284–6
Ryan, Claude, 15, 20

Samson, Jean, 126, 128, 217, 228
Saskatchewan, 31, 38–9, 225
Scott, Ian, 47, 66–7, 69, 71, 75, 76, 77, 89–90, 104–6, 126, 128–30, 135, 217, 222

Sept-Iles speech, 24, 41, 45, 50
Senate, reform of, 19, 22, 48, 61, 64, 77, 82, 87, 88, 89, 91, 94–5, 96, 153–4, 171–2, 181, 184, 189, 193–4, 202–6, 212–17, 223–7, 231, 242, 248–9, 265, 281

Simpson, Jeffrey, 88
Spector, Norman, 50, 51, 72, 77–9, 80,

89, 90, 92, 108, 121, 142, 201, 204–5, 216, 228

Stevenson, Don, 47
Supreme Court of Canada, 17–18, 29–30, 32, 39–40, 123–4, 155–7, 159, 166–8, 179–80, 234, 245, 255–6; reform of, 19, 43, 44, 56, 57, 69–71, 77, 78, 82, 85, 86, 87, 92–3, 95, 108, 111, 142, 146, 188–9, 206, 248

Tassé, Roger, 39, 127–9, 207, 217, 220, 226–9
Taylor, Charles, x, 240
Tellier, Paul, 228
Tremblay, André, 59, 126, 128, 217–19, 228
Trudeau, Pierre, 22, 27, 30, 41, 46, 52, 74, 102, 123, 164, 183, 244, 251; criticism of the accord, 8, 11, 109–16, 119–22, 124–5, 134, 142, 253–4; legitimacy of 1982 constitution, 14–16, 18–19, 21, 23; patriation round, 20, 30, 52
Turner, John, 41, 73, 74, 101
two founding nations vision, 5, 27, 66, 67

Vancouver conference (1986), 63, 72–3
Vander Zalm, William, 48, 49, 61, 92–3, 95, 96, 122, 131, 201, 225
veto. See amending formula
Volpe, Joseph, 119

Wells, Clyde, 100, 171–4, 178–84, 187–8, 191, 194, 199–201, 205–17, 219–34, 236–7, 244, 248–9, 253, 257, 258
Wilhelmy, Diane, 59
Willson House, 86, 92, 98, 99
Wilson, Michael, 197

women's rights, 141–3, 146, 157, 181,
    188, 192, 257–8

Yukon, 188
Yost, Greg, 217, 220